The Complete Buyer's Guide To The Best

Outdoor & Recreation Equipment

by Kevin Jeffrey

ISBN 0-935701-80-X

Avalon House

BOOKS BUILDING COMMUNITY

9 780935 701807

51495 >

Foghorn Press, Inc./Avalon House Publishing

Foghorn Press
555 DeHaro Street #220
The Boiler Room
San Francisco, CA 94107
(415) 241-9550

Credits
Managing Editor—Ann-Marie Brown
Illustrations—Jeff Camish
Copy Editing—Samantha Trautman and Howard Rabinowitz
Cover Photo—Michael Lewis Photography

Cover photo shot on location at REI in Berkeley, California

Library of Congress Cataloging-in-Publication Data

Jeffrey, Kevin, 1954-

The complete buyer's guide to the best outdoor & recreation equipment/Kevin Jeffrey
p. cm.
Includes bibliographical references and index.
ISBN 0-935701-80-X: $14.95
1. Outdoor recreation—equipment and supplies. 2. Travel—equipment and supplies. I. Title. II. Title: Complete buyer's guide to the best outdoor and recreation equipment.
GV191.76.J44   1993
796.5—dc20   92-21178 CIP

The Complete Buyer's Guide To The Best

Outdoor & Recreation Equipment

by Kevin Jeffrey

Avalon House

Foghorn Press

BOOKS BUILDING COMMUNITY

ACKNOWLEDGEMENTS

I would like to thank everyone who helped make this project possible, including all of the equipment manufacturers and suppliers who gave me their time, their expertise or samples of their products for field testing. In particular, I would like to thank Scott Curtis and Mark Sandone of Eastern Mountain Sports, Jim Rowinski and Fred Robie of L.L. Bean, Jeff Roush and Chris Doyle of REI, and Patrick Leahey. I would also like to thank Jeff Camish, Chuck Steacy and Nicole Jones.

NOTE TO READERS

Please note that while I have tried to be as accurate as possible in my descriptions of outdoor and recreation equipment products, the outdoor/recreation market changes rapidly. New products are constantly being developed, and other products are made obsolete. Prices change frequently. Always check with your outdoor retailer for the latest information on available outdoor and recreation products before you buy.

Contents

I ntroduction

This book is an activity and equipment planning guide for would-be adventurers, those willing to place themselves beyond the pale of modern existence, beyond the protective cocoon of normal routine. Consumed with desire, outdoor enthusiasts dream of adventures, whether they are challenging trips to exciting destinations or simple afternoon getaways. Given the opportunity, the dream flirts with reality, assuming both form and substance. An itinerary is conceived, then developed and finalized. Somewhere amid the myriad practical details comes the tantalizing prospect of selecting what outdoor activities to pursue, what necessary gear to acquire.

For the initiated, an inventory of existing equipment is taken. Decisions are made about what is appropriate for this particular trip, what needs mending or should really be replaced. Tents are pitched in the backyard and the cookstove is tried out. Sleeping bags are aired and bicycle parts assessed. Children try on last year's hiking boots, only to find them too small—again. Memories of past trips come flooding back as gear sprawls across the living room floor. The realization hits that somehow you've developed a bond with these inanimate objects, a kinship forged by dependency, by shared challenges and experiences.

For the novice these memories are eagerly anticipated, something to strive for, making the quest for proper equipment that much more intriguing. This book is about equipment and activity planning, yet in a deeper sense it is about making choices that help create good memories, ones that will last a lifetime.

The Complete Buyer's Guide to the Best Outdoor & Recreation Equipment was written with this in mind. My intention is to provide an up-to-date resource that reviews and recommends currently available gear for the major outdoor activities of lightweight camping, car and van travel, hiking, backpacking, bicycling, canoeing and kayaking. The more you know about the equipment on the market, the more likely it is you'll make the right decisions when outfitting.

Instead of attempting to place an exact price on each piece of gear, prices that would almost certainly be out of date soon after publication, I've listed a general price range for each category of gear in U.S. dollars. Remember that outdoor and recreation gear changes rapidly. If you find that a particular make or model described in this book has been discontinued, ask your outdoor retailer for a list of other models currently available from that manufacturer. Chances are the company offers a similar piece of gear under a new name.

For most of us, a visit to an outdoor equipment store is like a child's visit to a toy store—there is a great temptation to go on a spending spree. But capturing the essence of adventure doesn't require expensive new gear, just appropriate gear. Those on a fixed budget may find they are trading inessential pizazz for time and experience at their chosen destination. Even worse, they may discover after purchasing all that great new equipment that they can't afford the trip.

I consider the experience the primary goal, and therefore look for reasonably affordable equipment that allows my family and me to achieve that goal in relative safety and comfort. Comfort can be especially important when you are new to a sport or activity. If you choose gear that makes the learning phase of a sport much easier, you are more likely to have fun and continue pursuing it.

Equally important is assessing how vital the latest hi-tech equipment really is for you. The nature of active travel, for instance, puts little emphasis on speed and high-output performance. Because the experience itself is most important, the equipment doesn't have to be the fastest or lightest, the most advanced or top-of-the-line. When purchasing equipment, I try to balance my family's needs with the desire to take advantage of some of the nice features incorporated into today's outdoor gear.

Most of us are pleasantly overwhelmed when we walk into an outdoor equipment store—the merchandise all looks so good. That's partly due to the nature of the merchandise. Products made for outdoor activities are typically well designed and fabricated, embodying quality of form and function. Combining art with engineering is a concept the Europeans have long been familiar with, and a philosophy that most manufacturers of outdoor equipment have taken to heart. Not only can you easily envision yourself using these products in remote wilderness areas or exotic destinations, the products themselves are simply nice to look at and handle. Wanting to own some of them is only natural.

Most of us, however, are also subject to the restraints of a budget when it comes to outfitting, so it's important to keep a healthy perspective on new purchases. There are certain pitfalls which are best avoided. One common bugaboo is the subconscious delusion that the best equipment will somehow guarantee the best experience, when in fact the gear you use is only one facet of a successful trip. Ultimately, the success of any trip will depend largely on your ability to make it work. Many of the world's most renowned adventurers lived in an era when outdoor equipment was nothing more than a combination of ingenuity and making do with what one already had.

Another pitfall to avoid is using the purchase of new, high-quality equipment as a motivation to go ahead and do an activity, even though existing or lesser-quality gear would have performed just as well. How many people have purchased a brand new pack because they want to resume their hiking travels, or a new bicycle with more features because they'd really like to start biking again?

Try to keep in mind that adventure equipment should be appropriate to the person, the place and the activity. It doesn't have to be state-of-the-art, or shiny and new—just appropriate. If appropriate for your needs means purchasing the latest model piece of gear, that's fine. Fantastic advances have been achieved lately in making outdoor equipment smaller, lighter, safer, and more comfortable or efficient. After researching what is available, we've often purchased the high-end item because it made the most sense for us. The higher priced, higher quality items can frequently pay for themselves in the long run.

On the other hand, if appropriate for you means making do with less expensive gear, or gear you already own, that's fine, too. Outdoor travel isn't a fashion show and no one will care that your equipment has unknown brands or looks a little worn. As long as it performs as it should, and allows you to be comfortable and safe while adventuring, you've made the right choice. It's worth remembering that the money you don't spend on equipment can help buy more time at your destination. And isn't it the experience, in the end, that we're all really after?

Use of this Book

The chapters in this book are organized by activity. Each major activity begins with a brief description of the activity and a comprehensive list of appropriate types of equipment. Individual items are then reviewed. Most are discussed in detail according to the following format:

Review of Generic Types. Here you'll get a chance to see what basic types of products are being produced for each item on your list, regardless of the fluctuations in individual makes or models. It's helpful to have a clear idea of what is possible before narrowing your focus to a particular product.

Features and Options. This section reviews all of the things to look for when selecting a piece of gear, including all of those ancillary items that make it more versatile.

Construction and Operation. This covers the nuts and bolts of what an item is typically made of, how it's put together, and how to operate it. Familiarizing yourself with the general construction and operation of each generic type of product helps you select appropriate gear for your needs. These needs may change depending on where and how you adventure.

Author's Recommendations. In this section I give advice, along with recommendations of gear that works, is reasonably priced and readily available. While not attempting to list *every* piece of gear on the market, I do provide a comprehensive sampling of appropriate adventure equipment. Equipment is compared, a typical price range is targeted for each recommended item, and equipment performance is reviewed. For instance, if the category is "stoves," I compare facts such as *size and weight, ease of use,* and *fuel consumption.* For "tents," I use criteria such as *ease of set-up, weight and length, weather-tightness,* and *wind resistance.*

Maintenance and Repair. You'll keep your equipment in top shape if you follow a few simple maintenance guidelines. I explain these, along with suggested spare parts and methods of field repair.

Innovative Products. Every so often, truly outstanding products or manufacturing techniques are conceived. When a manufacturer puts one of those ideas into practice, I salute them for their efforts by highlighting their product. Products might be selected for their design, performance, or other criteria such as recognized environmental achievement.

Book Content

Part I—Personal Gear, deals with gear that would be useful for any type of adventure.

Part II—Lightweight Camping, discusses the gear for camping when weight must be kept to a minimum. The term "lightweight" is meant to differentiate the type of camping done when you are traveling under your own steam from that done with a car or van. The gear described here would be appropriate for any type of backpacking, including hiking, ski touring, mountaineering, and general travel.

Part III—Car and Van Travel, covers the camping equipment choices available when load-carrying ability and space are more abundant. In some regions of the world, where the distances to be covered are large, car or van travel might be the best option. With this mode of travel you have the opportunity to upgrade elements such as tent size and sleeping gear, cooking and provisioning arrangements, lighting and specialty tools.

Part IV—Backpacking, reviews all the various types of packs, load carriers, backpacking boots, gaiters, overboots, and hiking sticks designed specifically for adventurers carrying their gear on their back. Personal travel and lightweight camping gear that could be used in a variety of activities is covered in Parts I and II.

Part V—Bicycling, embraces the broad category of cycling. This includes everything from mountain biking to long-distance touring. Mountain, cross and touring bicycles are reviewed, along with all of the accessories available to make your cycling trip a success.

Part VI—Canoeing and Kayaking, deals with adventuring by canoe or kayak on rivers, lakes and coastal areas. Traveling and exploring by small boat can be an exciting way to adventure. Basic how-to information supplements a review of all the related gear for these activities.

I hope you'll find this book an easy-to-use resource, helpful in selecting the right gear for your trips. While it's not possible to feature every item on the market, I have tried to highlight the best, most practical equipment available. If you feel I've omitted an important piece of gear, please let me know so I can include it in the next edition. Write to me at Foghorn Press, 555 DeHaro Street, Suite 220—The Boiler Room, San Francisco, CA 94107.

Best wishes for successful adventures,

Kevin Jeffrey

I PERSONAL GEAR

While it could be argued that the best way to travel in the outdoors is with the least amount of gear, I feel the most successful trips are the ones you enjoy—which is often directly related to how well equipped you are to supply your needs away from home. In many ways, outdoor adventuring is an extension of your every day life. You will be establishing a home wherever you are. The personal gear you bring along allows a basic level of comfort and safety to prevail as you experience the joys and challenges of being in the outdoors.

There are several important precepts to keep in mind when selecting what personal gear, and how much of it, to bring on any trip. The first is to come up with a list of items to help you establish a familiar routine—things that provide for the vital necessities of life, as well as a few niceties to help make your time adventuring more fun. This list will vary according to your personal requirements and whether you are traveling alone or as a group, independently or with an outfitter. The longer or more ambitious the trip, the more important establishing a familiar routine will be. There's usually enough to cope with when traveling in the outdoors without making everything a novel experience. Your personal gear helps to recreate a home away from home.

Another helpful hint for selecting personal gear is to include items on your list that are probably going to be hard to find away from home. This includes medicines and a well-stocked first aid kit, as well as certain foods like peanut butter, unusual spices, favorite tea bags, natural brands of toothpaste and soaps, and your regular brands of dental floss and sunscreen. Of course, what you can pack depends on what mode of travel you are using—those on a week-long backpacking trip won't be able to carry the same amount of personal items as those traveling by car or van. I also recommend packing a pillowcase, cup, bowl, spoon, and even a cloth napkin for everyone. With a few simple items you can create a home anywhere. Being prepared for the unexpected and having some of your favorite personal items with you are nice ways to ease into a new place or situation.

Once you complete your list and have a good idea of what gear you'd like to carry, take the opposite approach and try to find ways to reduce the size and weight of your load to a comfortable level, something that can be easily packed and carried. Be ruthless. Take a second look at all items. Do everything you can to eliminate excess weight and bulk while keeping the list of necessary items intact. The more adept you are at trimming down, the easier it will be to stay mobile, and mobility is all-important when you travel in the outdoors.

Try to choose clothing that gives you warmth without bulk. Use personal gear that doubles for two or more purposes. When traveling in a group, you'll find it's easy to share certain items instead of bringing one for each member. Determine what gear works for the whole group and distribute the load. Different people have different needs. Figure out your own set of requirements, then do your best to supply those needs with lightweight gear. Remember, when you travel it's best to pack so your gear is compact, efficient, weather-tight, and unbreakable.

A battle you'll wage when outfitting for any trip is trying to be prepared and well equipped, yet comfortable and mobile at the same time. You may need to be flexible with your equipment budget in order to escape this apparent paradox. Replacing some existing gear with newer, lightweight gear may make all the difference. In most instances outdoor travel gear is priced according to size and weight, which typically relates to cost of manufacture. What you are paying extra money for in many cases is getting the same or better performance in a smaller, lighter package.

Spend time planning and preparing the equipment you'll need before leaving home, but, above all, remember to have fun. Adventure travel offers the opportunity to experience, if only briefly, a nomadic lifestyle, the unbridled freedom of being able to go when and where you choose, knowing your home is always with you.

C lothing

- Fibers and Fabrics
- The Art of Layering
- Under Layer Clothing
- Middle Layer Clothing
- Outer Layer Clothing
- Footwear, Hats, Gloves

The first thing to organize for any trip is what clothing to take. You won't have much room for variety when traveling light, so what you bring should be considered with care. All of your clothes should have certain characteristics that make it easier for you to be on the road. Clothing for the active traveler should be:

Durable. This is of primary importance. Only bring clothes that can stand up to the conditions you'll encounter. Bring along a sewing kit just in case, but try to start out with well-made clothing that can withstand repeated wear.

Comfortable. Don't underestimate this consideration. The success of adventures is based to a certain extent on your personal comfort level, which is in turn influenced by your clothing and how comfortable it is.

Suitable for the Climate. Many adventures cross multiple climate zones, with hiking in high mountains a good example. In one day you could start out in sunny, warm conditions in the foothills, hike through a forested temperate zone mid-morning, and end up at an alpine picnic spot by noon. Climate changes drastically with elevation, as it does with geography. Try to have something for each situation. Having clothes that can be worn in layers is an excellent way to achieve this (see the following section on layering).

Lightweight and Easily Packed. This ties in with the concept of reducing your load. Find clothes that are durable, yet able to pack down to the smallest size or give maximum comfort for the least amount of weight. Every ounce and cubic inch is important when packing for a trip.

Able to Cover All Situations. When you work out your layers of clothing, try to have something for all occasions. When one change of clothing gets wet or dirty, have something in reserve. Also, try to bring clothes that serve equally well hiking a trail or strolling through town at the end of the day. Have something for those special, unexpected occasions. You'll find there can be more to adventure travel than just outdoor activities, so choose clothing that allows you to feel comfortable in a variety of situations.

FIBERS AND FABRICS

Before heading out to the store, take some time to get familiar with the types of fabrics currently available. Fabrics consist of one or more types of fibers, either natural or synthetic. These fibers are woven in a variety of configurations, each having its own characteristics and recommended use. Fabric descriptions apply not only to clothes, but also to packs, tents, sleeping bags, and other gear. Some commonly used terms to describe fabrics are listed below.

• *Denier* is a term that's often used to describe a yarn or fabric for outdoor gear. It refers to a unit of fineness for the individual filaments of yarn. The smaller the denier, the finer the filaments of a fabric. The denier of some synthetic microfiber fabrics such as Polartec™ Series 100M is very small. These fabrics are useful in creating wind and water-resistant garments. The larger the denier, the less fine the filaments. Some abrasion-resistant nylon gear is made from high-denier fabrics such as Cordura® nylon.

• The *weave* of a fabric refers to the configuration of the individual strands of the woven fabric. *Warp* refers to the vertical strands and *woof* to the horizontal strands. Some fabrics are tightly woven for wind and water resistance, others loosely woven for greater air movement.

• *Thermal* fabrics have the ability to inhibit air movement and trap body heat efficiently. They are typically used in middle layer clothing.

• *Hydrophobic*, or moisture-repelling, is the term given to polypropylene and many polyester fabrics that rapidly wick moisture away.

• *Hydrophilic*, or moisture-attracting, refers to fabrics like cotton that absorb moisture readily.

• *Wickable* is a word used to describe hydrophobic fibers and fabrics capable of drawing moisture away from your skin and transporting it to either the next layer of clothing or the outside air. Wickable fabrics are typically used in under layer clothing.

• *Breathable* fabrics allow air to move freely. Cotton is a great example of a breathable natural fabric. Hydrofil® nylon is an example of a breathable synthetic fabric.

• *Push/Pull* fabrics use raised hydrophobic fibers in the under layer next to the skin and hydrophilic fibers near the outer surface. Body moisture is then pushed and pulled simultaneously toward the outside air. Duofold's Microclimate Moisture Escape Fleece® (a combination of Coolmax® and cotton) and Terramar's Transport™ (polyester and Hydrofil® fibers combined) are good examples of this type of fabric.

• *Windproof and Breathable* describes a fabric that has been constructed so it allows body perspiration to pass through, while inhibiting air movement from the outside. These types of fabrics are used in outer layer clothing for active sports.

• *Waterproof/Breathable* fabrics allow body perspiration in the form of vapor to exit without allowing water molecules from the outside to enter. They are also highly resistant to wind and are used in rainwear and outer layer clothing for active sports.

Natural Fibers

Cotton. Cotton is soft, cool, and comfortable, so it feels great next to your skin. It is also highly absorbent, making it the fiber of choice for hot climates. Cotton is found in many under, middle, and outer layer garments. It is not able to effectively wick moisture away from your body, and is therefore a poor choice as an under layer garment for really active sports in cold climates. *Combed peeler* cotton refers to yarns where the short and immature fibers have been removed, then the yarn is combed for parallelization. This process leaves a more even, stronger, higher quality yarn. Cotton yarns are woven together to produce various fabrics such as cotton terry, flannel, chamois, twill, ripstop and canvas. Cotton yarns are also often blended with synthetic yarns to provide added strength, stretch, or other desired characteristics.

Innovation - Environment-Friendly Cotton Fabrics

We all know how comfortable cotton clothing is, and that cotton is a natural fiber as opposed to a synthetic one. But did you know that most cotton is grown using heavy doses of chemicals and pesticides, and that most cotton clothing is processed using toxic chemicals, bleaches and dyes? Now there are some exciting new cotton fibers and fabrics that are good for the environment. *Organic Cotton* is grown without the use of chemical fertilizers and pesticides. To become certified as organic, cotton farms must be free of toxic chemicals for at least three years.

Seventh Generation's Organic Cotton

GreenCotton is a new type of cotton fabric that uses no toxic dyes or bleaches during processing, and energy and water consumption during manufacture are reduced. *Organic GreenCotton* clothing is made from Organic Cotton that is manufactured using no toxic chemicals. *Foxfibre®* is a new type of cotton fiber that grows brown in color, eliminating the need for potentially polluting dyes.

Of course, you'll pay a bit more for clothing made from these fibers and fabrics, but the price should decrease as more farmers and clothing manufacturers take this natural approach. Seventh Generation now offers a complete catalog of environment-friendly cotton clothing made from Organic Cotton, GreenCotton, and Foxfibre®. Many of their products are listed in the following pages of the clothing section, including underwear, socks, shirts of all types, and sweaters. Ecosport is another company committed to environmentally-sound cotton clothing. Their products range from comfortable pants and shirts to sweats and cardigans. Patagonia is also helping to support environment-friendly fabrics with their *Jumbo Pique* shirt made of Organic GreenCotton. The shirt itself is nice, but the way it is made is outstanding. Congratulations to Seventh Generation, Ecosport, Patagonia, and all manufacturers and suppliers with this type of forward thinking.

Wool. Wool is a soft nonabrasive fiber made from the fleece of sheep. It is a natural insulator and, even though it absorbs moisture, it seldom feels damp or clammy. Wool is used primarily in socks, sweaters, hats and gloves. Wool fibers are used to produce yarn. Garments are made from yarn that is either untreated, or raw, with the lanolin still intact, or treated with the lanolin removed. *100% ragg wool* refers to three-ply yarn, traditionally of natural undyed wool. *Worsted yarn* has uniform lengths of yarn that are twisted tightly together to form smooth, firm, compact fibers. These yarns generally wear longer and pill less than spun yarns. *Wool blend* refers to wool yarns blended with synthetic yarns to provide extra strength or stretch.

Silk. Silk is a natural heat retainer. It is also known for its luxurious softness, durability and high strength. Silk fibers have the smallest filament diameter found in nature. A good example of silk used for activewear under layers is Terramar's Thermasilk®.

Synthetic Fibers

Synthetic fibers are man-made, primarily from petrochemicals. The current trend in synthetics is toward finer (smaller denier), more comfortable fibers for use in a variety of activewear.

Nylon. Nylon is by far the most widely used synthetic fiber for active clothing and gear. You'll see many different generic types of nylon on garment and equipment labels. Some of the most common are:

• *Packcloth.* A high-denier nylon fabric used on packs and other rugged travel and outdoor gear where superior abrasion resistance is needed. Cordura® nylon is a good example of this type of cloth.

• *Ripstop.* A nylon fabric with a high tensile strength due to reinforcing fibers woven every quarter-inch in the cloth.

• *Taffeta.* Probably the most common type of nylon on the market, taffeta is used widely in tents, sleeping bags and clothing. It is relatively supple and soft, yet rugged enough to stand up to moderate abuse. It is often coated to make it waterproof.

• *Spandex.* A fiber with elasticity that doesn't readily sag or bag. It is typically used as a blend with other fibers to give extra stretch and support. Lycra® spandex is a common example of this type of fiber.

There are also some new types of nylon fabrics on the market, ones with completely different characteristics from the traditional nylon fabrics. Two of the most popular are described below.

• *Supplex®.* This is a relatively new type of nylon from Dupont. It is strong, yet cottony-soft due to the use of finer, more numerous fibers. It is now used on many garments, both as the sole fabric or as an inner lining to less soft fabrics, as well as on other types of outdoor gear. Microsupplex® uses microdenier nylon fibers that allow for tighter, more densely woven fabrics for greater wind and water resistance.

• *Hydrofil®.* This type of nylon fabric from Allied Fibers is strong and durable like other nylons, yet has the ability to breathe similar to cotton. Look for clothing made solely of Hydrofil® for warm weather activities, or Hydrofil® with an additional wicking under layer for cool weather sports.

Polyester. Although it used to be horribly out of fashion, new types of polyester fibers, along with numerous new applications, have combined to make this the second most popular fiber now used in active clothing and gear. The new generation of polyester fibers are used to produce wickable under layers, fleece middle layers, and waterproof/breathable outer layers.

• *Wickable* under layers are increasingly popular for high activity in cold conditions. Body moisture is rapidly transported from the skin toward the outside with polyester fabrics such as Bergelene® (EMS), Capilene® (Patagonia), M.T.S.® (REI), and Coolmax®. Products such as Thermax® and Thermastat® keep you warm as well as dry.

• *Synthetic fleece* has become increasingly popular as a middle layer of warmth. It is warm, rugged, water resistant, and light-weight. Most of the fleece materials on the market are made by Malden Mills under their Polartec™ label. Look for the various versions of their fleece, such as Polartec™ Series 100, 200, 300 (fabric weight increases with numbers), Series 1000 Windproof and Series 2000S multi-layer, windproof stretch fabric, as well as other brand names such as Pinnacle Fleece® (EMS) or Synchilla® (Patagonia).

• *Microfibers* of polyester, relatively speaking the new kids on the block, hold great promise for outdoor clothing. Microfibers, such as the Polartec™ Series 100M used in lightweight clothing for active sports, give chamois-like comfort and the ability to dry quickly. Microfibers such as Trevira® are used to create waterproof/breath-able fabrics for outer shells. Polyester microfibers are also used in many new insulating fill materials, such as Thinsulate™, Primaloft™, and Thinsulate™ Lite Loft to give warmth and water resistance to insulated outdoor gear.

Polypropylene. Polypropylene has been used as a wicking fiber in activewear under layers for a long time. It is functional, relatively inexpensive, and the currently available fabrics provide more comfort than wool or even polypropylene clothing of a few years ago.

Acrylic. Another long-standing synthetic fiber in the clothing industry, acrylic is typically used in sweaters and socks for its combination of strength and softness.

Waterproof/Breathable Membranes

Synthetic materials are also used to create very thin, waterproof/breathable membranes that are incorporated into outer shells for clothing, footwear, sleeping bags, and tents. The most well known of these high performance membranes is Gore-Tex®. Other brand names to look for include Sympatex®, Pertex®, Todd-Tex® (Bibler Tents), and System III® (EMS).

Waterproof/Breathable Coatings

Microporous waterproof coatings applied to tightly woven nylon fabrics are also commonly used to create waterproof/breathable fabrics. Brand names to look for include H2No® (Patagonia), Omni-Tech® (Columbia), Helly-Tech® (Helly-Hansen), Elements® (REI), HP Waterproof/Breathable® (Sierra Designs) and Ultrex® (Sportif, Cannondale).

Nonporous Coatings

Most of the moderately priced raingear on the market relies on nonporous coatings of PVC, urethane, or Hypalon® rubber to ensure waterproof characteristics. Nylon fabrics treated with these coatings do not breathe, but they offer good quality at a reasonable price.

*Note: Thermastat, Thermax, Coolmax, Lycra, Supplex, Microsupplex, and Cordura are trade names of Dupont; Hydrofil, Caprolan, and Captiva are trade names of Allied Fibers; ESP, BTU, and Trevira are trade names of Hoechst Celanese; Thinsulate and Lite Loft are trade names of 3M; Polartec is a trade name of Malden Mills; Synchilla is a trade name of Patagonia; Elements is a trade name of REI; System III and Pinnacle Fleece are trade names of EMS; Gore-Tex is a trade name of W.L. Gore and Assoc.; Thermasilk is a trade name of Terramar; and Primaloft is a trade name of Albany International.

THE ART OF LAYERING

The Benefits

Wearing layers of clothing is recommended for two reasons. The first is greater comfort, the second is more flexibility when packing space and weight are limited. The concept is simple. There are typically three layers of clothing you might wear—under, middle, and outer—each with a specific purpose.

Comfort. The under layer provides comfort next to your skin and some degree of warmth. When pursuing active sports in cold climates the under layer should be made of a material able to wick (or physically transport) moisture away from your body. The middle layer is there strictly for warmth. This layer should be able to trap as much body heat as possible, and be able to breathe without retaining much moisture so water vapor can continue on to the outside of your clothing. The outer layer provides protection from the wind and rain. For ultimate comfort, it should be windproof and waterproof as well as breathable, allowing moisture to migrate to the outside air. In extreme cold it can also provide additional warmth by incorporating layers of insulating material. Gore-Tex® and Sympatex® are widely recognized fabrics used for meeting the criteria of being both waterproof and breathable. There are many outer garments made of this and other types of breathable fabrics, including hats, jackets, pants, gloves, even parts of socks, shoes and boots. Although these items really perform, they also tend to be quite pricey. If waterproof/breathable outerwear doesn't fit into your budget, find other clothes able to give you the most for your money.

Flexibility. Weather conditions and body heat (related to your level of activity) can change often and rapidly during your adventures. Cool days when the sun plays hide and seek can drive you crazy. First you're hot, then you're cold, then you're hot again. There are those mild days when it rains intermittently—you don't want to get wet, but a waterproof outer layer can be stifling, especially if you're active. On a bicycle or ski tour, hills can play cruel tricks—uphill you want to strip down, downhill you want to zip up, and so on. What's needed are layers of clothing that come on and off easily and work in a multitude of conditions.

Other Clothing Concerns

While on the topic of choosing clothing, I mentioned previously that adventuring is not a fashion show. There's no need to fret over styles and brand names. Outdoor and recreation clothing can be relatively expensive. Before heading out to the stores, check your own closets to see if you have appropriate items. You might also check with secondhand stores. They often have a good selection of high quality, almost new clothing at minimal cost. If you don't find something appropriate, simply succumb to the pleasure of shopping at any convenient outdoor retail store or through one of the many catalog suppliers. Most of them have occasional sales on clothing, when prices are substantially marked down. Another hint is to buy at the end of the season—shorts in August and skiwear in March—for even greater savings.

UNDER LAYER CLOTHING

I know what you're thinking, "Is he really going to tell me what kind of underwear to pack?" While it is, indeed, a personal decision, I do have a few suggestions as to how much to pack, along with some alternative types of underwear and socks designed to keep you more comfortable during very active sports.

Shorts and Briefs

If you have the room and carrying capacity when on an outdoor trip, it makes sense to pack seven pairs of underwear per person, one to wear and six to carry. This way you only have to find laundry facilities once a week. Even though they don't weigh much, you'll want to reduce this number if weight is critical when doing some serious backpacking or bicycling. Then you can cut down the number and do more frequent hand laundries. I often take just a few pairs for short-term hiking or touring and leave the others at a base somewhere. Hand-washing underwear is easy and can be done almost anywhere.

Style is up to you, but material can make a big difference when exercising heavily. Inexpensive all-cotton jockey or boxer-style briefs for men and boys, or bikini briefs for women and girls, are comfortable and will be fine for most needs. For strenuous activity accompanied by heavy perspiration, you'll probably want to include a few pairs that are made from synthetic materials that help wick moisture away from the body. They will keep you more comfortable and also weigh less than all-cotton makes (moisture-related comfort is more of a factor for adults than young children who don't perspire as much). Lightweight cotton is still the material of choice in the tropics. Expect to pay anywhere from $6 to $20 for high-performance synthetic briefs. Some of the better synthetic brands available are listed below.

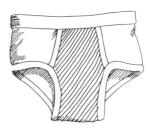

Duofold's Thermax Windbrief

Author's Recommendations - Activewear Briefs

Brand	Model	Sizes	Material
Campmor	Terry Brief	m	polypropylene/nylon
Duofold	Thermax Brief	m	Thermax
Duofold*	Thermax Windbrief	m	Thermax with wind panel
Early Winter	Padded Undershorts	m, f	cotton, Lycra, polypro, chamois
EMS	Bergelene Brief	m, f	Polartec 100
Gilda Marx	Intimates Brief, Thong	f	synthetic, Breathables® liner
Hind	Sport Systems Brief	f	polypropylene, nylon, hi-cut
Hind	Windbrief	m	polyester, Lycra
Helly-Hansen*	Lifa Prolite Windbrief	m	polypropylene
Jogbra	Power Liner (long)	f	cotton/polyester/Lycra
Max	Hipster	m	Coolmax
Max	Sportbrief	m	Coolmax
Patagonia	Underwear Brief	m, f	Capilene
Patagonia*	Windbrief	m	Capilene
Saucony	Coolmax Hi-Cut Brief	m, f	Coolmax
Speedo	Sport Brief	m	nylon/cotton crotch
Terramar	Tech Brief	m	polyester, Hydrofil, Lycra

*These models have a wind-resistant front panel for guys who want that ultimate protection.

T-shirts and Undershirts

As with briefs, if you plan on pursuing active sports on your travels, consider purchasing one or two T-shirts that keep you cool and dry by wicking moisture away from your body. These come in mesh (fishnet) or solid styles and are made from synthetic fibers. Expect to pay between $13 and $30 for high-performance T-shirts. They are more expensive, but, if you can afford it, they're worth the cost in terms of comfort. A few of my favorite T-shirts are listed below.

Author's Recommendations - Active Wear T-shirts

Brand	Model	Sizes	Material
Columbia	Tidewater Button-down T	f	cotton jersey
Duofold	Coolmax T-shirt	m	Coolmax
Duofold	Thermax T-shirt	m	Thermax
Ecosport	T , V-Neck T, Tank	m, f, youth	organic cotton
Moonstone	Micro Denier T	m, f	polyester fleece
Patagonia	Lightweight T-shirt	m, f	Capilene
Patagonia	Silk-weight T-shirt	m, f	Capilene
REI	Short Sleeve Crew neck	m, f	M.T.S. polyester
Russel Athl.	Intera T-shirt	m	polyester
Seventh Gen.	Camisole	f	GreenCotton

Bras and Support Tops

For those women who want or need to wear a bra, Jogbra offers a few good models for active sports. The *Action-Tech* and the *Passion T-Top* are lightweight, comfortable support tops styled so they can be worn alone as half-shirts. Users assure me that wearing this type of top gives them a close approximation to that amazing feeling of being shirtless. Keep in mind that these garments might not be culturally acceptable in some parts of the world. If you travel abroad, check out what the

Action-tech Bra

local women are wearing and dress accordingly. The *Coolsport* bra has molded cups and is made of an airy, stretch mesh fabric for firmer support and greater comfort. The *Sportshape* has adjustable straps and back closure, double layered cotton "baseball cups" for extra support, and ventilating mesh panels. When purchasing this bra, make certain to size it correctly to eliminate slipping shoulder straps during strenuous activity. These high-tech bras run from $17 to $32.

Author's Recommendations - Active Wear Bras and Support Tops

Brand	Model	Sizes	Material
Gilda Marx	Classic Sportbra	B, C, D	synthetic, Breathables® liner
Jogbra	Action-tech	A, B, C	cotton/Coolmax/Lycra
Jogbra	Coolsport	A, B, C	Coolmax/ outer mesh
Jogbra	Sportshape	C, D, DD	cotton/ synthetic
Jogbra	Mesh Bra	A, B, C	Coolmax, Lycra
Patagonia	Stretch Sports Bra	AB, CD	Capilene
Hind	Passion T-Top	S, M, L	cotton, nylon, Lycra
Terramar	Sport Bra	S, M, L	polyester, Hydrofil, Lycra

Leggings, Tights and Long Underwear

Long underwear tops come in several models, including crew neck, turtleneck, mock turtleneck (a lower cut), and zippered turtleneck. Leggings, longjohns, and long underwear bottoms all amount to the same thing. Since leggings and long underwear are intended for use as the first layer of clothing in cool to cold climates, they should be able to keep you warm and dry. Tights can be either an under layer or a middle layer pant. All-cotton or cotton/synthetic blends are comfortable for general wear or light to moderate activity. Inexpensive colored cotton leggings, suitable for adults and children, are fine for light to medium exercising in cool climates. We've used them during many hiking and bicycle trips as something to pull on under a pair of shorts when the weather turns cool.

Synthetic blends are more appropriate for very active sports. When exercising heavily the synthetic materials do a much better job of wicking moisture away from your body, eliminating that clammy feeling you can get with natural fibers against your skin. Although more expensive, wickable fabrics tend to be more comfortable and durable in these situations. Currently available polyester fabrics, with their rapid wicking action and comfort, are recommended.

Innovation - Duofold's *Vent·A·Layer Clothing*

Duofold recently released their *Vent•A•Layer* clothing system for active sports, a new layering system that promises to be very popular. The inner layer consists of one of three different weights of underwear pants and shirts made with Dupont's Thermastat® fabric. This fabric is highly wickable and warm, but the really innovative part comes in the form of Coolmax® venting panels where a person needs them the most—at the armpits and upper thighs. Duofold research shows that this underwear significantly reduces fluid loss and helps to stabilize body temperature more rapidly, keeping it lower during active workouts. The middle thermal layer and outer shell also have similar venting panels perfectly aligned to promote the transfer of body moisture to the outdoors.

It makes sense to have an underlayer that is versatile. Select tops that can be worn on their own and bottoms that can be worn under shorts in moderate weather. Recommended models of currently available leggings and long underwear are listed below. The After the Stork children's clothing costs $6 to $13, the other under layer clothing costs from $10 up to $50.

Author's Recommendations - Leggings, Tights and Long Underwear

Brand	Model	Sizes	Material
After the Stork	Thermal Shirts, Pants	child	cotton
After the Stork	Long John Pants (leggings)	child	cotton
After the Stork	Longsleeve Tee	child	cotton
Campmor	Lightweight Shirts, Pants	m, f, ch	polypropylene
Cannondale	Zip T & Crew Neck Innertops	m, f	Intera (synthetic)
Cannondale	A.T.W. Mountain Tight II	m, f	Cordura, Lycra
Cherry Tree	Cotton Fleece Leggings	child	cotton, Lycra
Cherry Tree	Long Underwear Shirts, Pants	child	Polartec
Duofold	Long Underwear Shirts, Pants	m, f	cotton, wool, nylon
Duofold	Vent•A•Layer Shirts, Pants	m, f	Thermast't, Coolm'x, Lycra
Ecosport	Cotton Leggings	m, f	organic cotton
EMS	Light, Med., H'w't Shirts, P'ts	m, f	Bergelene polyester
Hind	Stirrupless Sportight	m	nylon, Lycra
L.L. Bean	Expedition-weight Shirts, P'ts	m	polypropylene
L.L. Bean	Mock Turtlenecks	m, f	cotton, cotton/synthetic
L.L. Bean	SportSeries 3 Shirts, Pants**	m, f, ch	polyester
Helly-Hansen	Lifa Athletic Shirts, Pants	m, f	polypro
Helly-Hansen	Lifa Prolite Shirts, Pants	m, f	polypro
Helly-Hansen	Lifa Arctic Shirts, Pants	m, f	polypro, wool
Moonstone	Micro Denier Bottoms	m, f	polyester fleece
Patagonia*	Light, Med., Expd. Weight	m, f, ch	Capilene polyester
Performance	RageGear Tights, Shorts	m, f	cotton, Lycra
REI*	Light, Med., Expd. Weight	m,f	M.T.S. polyester
REI	Silk Underwear Shirts, Pants	m, f	silk
Schnaubelt	Polypro/Lycra Tights	m, f	polypropylene/Lycra
Seventh Gen.	GreenCotton Leggings	f	GreenCotton
Super Brynje	Mesh Underwear Shirts, P'ts	m, f	mesh polypro
Terramar	Filament Silk Shirts, Pants	m, f, ch	silk
Terramar	Silk Lycra Shirts, Pants	m, f	silk, Lycra
Terramar	Transport Shirts, Pants	m, f	polyester, Hydrofil
The North Face	Expd. Underwear Shirts, P'ts	m, f	microfleece
Wickers	Mediumweight Shirts, Pants	m	polypropylene

These long sleeve shirts come in both crew neck or zippered turtleneck versions.
** Available in lightweight, midweight, and expedition weight fabrics

Socks

Socks are the under layer for your feet. They provide comfort and warmth, and protect your feet from the ill effects of being confined in shoes and boots. Socks also protect your footgear by absorbing perspiration and reducing friction (the ultimate cause of blisters) between a sweaty foot and shoe material. They come in various lengths. Ankle or "running" socks are comfortable for warm weather sports such as walking, hiking or biking when worn with low cut shoes. "Cross" socks go a little higher up the leg for use with a wider variety of shoes. Medium height socks come about halfway up your calf and are recommended for cooler weather and when wearing higher cut shoes and boots. Just roll this sock down a few turns in warmer weather. Knee socks go over the knee or to the top of your calf and are worn with knickers or leiderhosen (European style), or for a bit of extra warmth with shorts or tights.

Review of Generic Types - Socks

Sock material varies according to expected weather conditions and type of activity you plan.

Lightweight "Liner" Socks made from polypropylene or silk are available as an under layer to wick moisture away from your foot. They are typically worn under wool socks.

"Ragg" Wool Socks are the traditional choice for hikers. They are typically made from 100% wool or an 85% wool/15% nylon blend. They can be worn over liners or on their own. The wool provides comfort by absorbing perspiration and reducing friction; the nylon gives it strength and the ability to stretch while retaining its shape. Lightweight versions of this sock are available for lightweight hiking boots, heavyweight for heavier boots and cold climates. Cotton is substituted for wool in socks for less active sports.

"Poly-Wool" Socks, typically made from a combination of polypropylene or polyester, wool, and nylon, simulate the effects of liner socks with midweight socks over them. Cotton is substituted for wool for less active sports. These are recommended for general outdoor wear and in warm weather when two layers would be too hot. A few models substitute acrylic for most of the wool, and weave in spandex for added stretch, bringing the total number of fabrics in one sock to five!

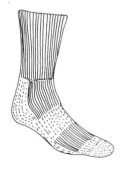

Fox River's Wick-dry Euro

"Oversocks" are made from Gore-Tex® and designed to keep your feet dry in wet conditions. They are worn over a pair of regular socks like a bootie. Even if your boots become soaked, your socks and feet remain relatively dry and comfortable.

Author's Recommendations - Socks

Plan on packing three to four pairs of socks when taking outdoor trips. As with other "adventure" clothing, you can usually get by with what you have in your drawer at home, but make sure to bring socks that are in good condition. If you are after performance and comfort, and need to replace those socks with all the holes anyway, try some of the models listed below. These good quality socks for recreation and outdoor sports cost $4 to $11.

Author's Recommendations - Socks

Brand	Model	Length	Sizes	Material
After the Stork	Crew Socks	med	child	cotton, spandex
Fox River	Raggler	med	m, f	cotton, wool, spandex
Fox River	Backpacker	med	m, f	wool, nylon
Fox River	Wick-dry Gr'd Cany'n	med	m, f	acrylic, cotton, stretch nylon
Fox River	Wick-dry Euro	med	m, f	polyester, cotton, st'tch nylon
Fox River	Wick-dry Explorer	med	m, f	acrylic, wool, stretch nylon
L.L. Bean	Trailblazer Wander	med	m, f	acrylic, wool, polyest., nylon
L.L. Bean	Boot Socks	m'd, l'g	m, f	Hollofil, wool, nylon
L.L. Bean	Sock Liner	med	m, f	polypropylene
Patagonia	Alpine	med	child	wool, Hydrofil, nylon
REI	Rugged Ragg	med	m, f	wool, nylon, spandex
REI	Gore-tex Oversocks	med	m, f	Gore-Tex; stretch top panels
Seventh Gen.	Crew Socks	med	m, f	Foxfibre, Gr'Cotton, or wool
Terramar	Unisex Socks	med	m, f	polyester, Hydrofil
Thor-Lo	Light Hiker	med	m,f	acrylic, wool, nylon, spandex
Thor-Lo	Hiking, padded	med	m, f	acrylic, nylon
Thor-Lo	Trekking, padded	med	m, f	acryl., w'l, nyl'n, p'est'r, sp'x
Wigwam	Thermax Under	med	m, f	Thermax, nylon
Wigwam	Expedition Ragg	med	m, f	wool, nylon
Wigwam	Stretch Hiker Ragg	med	m, f, ch	wool, nylon, spandex
Wigwam	Coolmax Cross Tr'n'r	low	m, f	Coolmax, cotton, nylon
Wigwam	Pathway	med	m, f, ch	acrylic, wool, Hollofil, nylon

MIDDLE LAYER CLOTHING

This is the layer you rely on to keep you warm. Since most of your time is spent without outer garments, it is also the most visible layer. Included in what is considered as middle layer clothing are short and long sleeve shirts, shorts and long pants, and sweaters and vests.

Shirts

Shirts come in a variety of styles. Select ones that best suit how, where, and for how long you plan to travel. For hot climates, take several short sleeve shirts that are loose and comfortable, preferably made of 100% cotton. A lightweight long sleeve shirt or two may be needed for daytime sun protection or cool nights. If you anticipate cold temperatures, bring along a mid-to-heavyweight long sleeve shirt. Try to think about how you might use layers to stay comfortable. Select garments that work well together, combinations such as an undershirt or T-shirt, longsleeve shirt, and sweater, vest, or jacket. I'll not attempt to list all of the shirts available for outdoor wear, but rather mention a few that are particularly functional for active wearers.

Button-down Shirts

At the risk of unseemly formality, I recommend having a button-down shirt or two (short or long sleeve, depending on climate) in your clothes inventory when doing light outdoor traveling. This type of shirt works well under a sweater or vest, and the buttons allow you to open up and cool off. Besides, there will be times when you'll want to "clean up your act" on the road, and the classic buttondown shirt gives an air of respectability. Try to select lightweight short sleeve shirts made of cotton, and long sleeve shirts of cotton or cotton flannel. Shirts should also be loose and comfortable so as not to restrict mobility. Some of my favorite buttondowns are listed below. Expect to pay $18 to $32 for these good quality shirts.

Seventh Generation's
GreenCotton Twill

Author's Recommendations - Lightweight Button-down Shirts

Brand	Model	Length	Size	Material
Columbia	Backlash Shirt	short	m, f	cotton
EMS	Twill Shirt	short, long	m, f	cotton
Helly-Hansen	Canteen Shirt	short	m, f	cotton
L.L. Bean	Cool Weave Shirt	short, long	m, f	cotton
L.L. Bean	Lightweight Tropic Shirt	short	m, f	cotton
L.L. Bean	Summer Cotton Shirt	short	f	cotton
Patagonia	Micromesh Shirt	short	child	cotton

Patagonia	Cotton Shirt	short	m, f, child	cotton
REI	Traveler Shirt	short	m	cotton
REI	Cool Tank Tops	sleeveless	f	cotton
Royal Robbins	Camp Shirt	short, long	f	cotton
Royal Robbins	Weathered Twill	short	m	cotton
Royal Robbins	Trail Shirt	short	m	cotton
Seventh Gen.	GreenCotton Twill	long	m,f	GreenCotton
Sportif	Cotton Shirts	short, long	m	cotton
Woolrich	S.S. Harbour Shirt	short	m	cotton

Author's Recommendations - Mid-to-Heavyweight Button-down Shirts

Brand	Model	Length	Sizes	Material
Columbia	Mackenzie Shirt	long	m	cotton
Columbia	Wilderness Shirt	long	m	cotton
EMS	Flannel	long	m, f	cotton
EMS	Chamois	long	m	cotton
L.L. Bean	Chamois, reg./lightweight	long	m, f	cotton
L.L. Bean	Scotch Plaid Shirt	long	m, f	cotton
Patagonia	Flannel Shirt	long	m, f	cotton
Patagonia	Canvas Shirt	long	m, f	cotton
REI	Peregrine /Wood River	long	m/f	cotton twill
REI	Classic Chamois Shirt	long	m, f	cotton
Royal Robbins	Travel Shirt*	long	m	cotton
Royal Robbins	Weathered Work Shirt	long	m	cotton
Woolrich	Chamois Shirt	long	m, f	cotton

* This shirt has hidden pockets for passport and money.

Pullover Shirts

Pullovers include the following: shirts with no collar and a crew neck; "polo" or "rugby" styles with full collar and button-down V-neck; "river" or "Henley" shirts with no collar and a button-down V-neck; and mock or true turtleneck shirts. River shirts typically have no collar, are very comfortable, and, along with some other pullovers, can be crosses between underwear and shirts. They come in short and long sleeve versions. We usually pack

Duofold's Henley Shirt

one of these long sleeve shirts to wear alone for cool weather sports or as an under layer in cold weather. Pullovers with cotton collars are comfortable and easily worn under a middle layer. Although they are good for warm weather if large and loose, the collar can be a nuisance when it's really hot. For warm weather traveling, look for a short sleeve version made of lightweight cotton with either a small stand-up collar or no collar at all. Some recommended pullovers currently on the market are listed below. After the Stork kids clothing costs $8 to $14, the others cost in the range of $14 to $32.

Author's Recommendations - Pullover Shirts

Brand	Model	Length	Sizes	Material
After the Stork	Colorful Shirt Turtleneck	sh't, l'g	child	cotton
After the Stork	Henley Front Tee*	long	child	cotton
Cannondale	A.T.W. Jersey	long	m, f	Cordura, Lycra
Cherry Tree	Mock Turtleneck	long	child	cotton
Columbia	Cutthroat Henley*	short	m, f	cotton
Columbia	Tidewater Shirt*	short	f	cotton
Duofold	Henley Shirt*	long	m	cotton
Duofold	Original Button Front*	long	m,f	cotton, wool, nylon
Ecosport	Henley* & Long Sleeve T	long	m, f	organic cotton
Ecosport	Mock Turtle	long	m, f	organic cotton
EMS	Backpacker Polo	short	m,f	cotton
EMS	Adirondack Henley	long	m,f	cotton
Gramicci	Prescott Stripe Shirt	long	child	cotton
L.L. Bean	River Driver's Shirt	long	m, f	cotton, wool, nylon
L.L. Bean	Turtlenecks	long	m, f	cotton or cot/polyest.
Moonstone	Micro Denier Ts	long	m, f	polyest. fleece
Patagonia	Jumbo Pique Crew	long	m, f	cotton
Patagonia	Knit Shirt	long	child	cotton, spandex
REI	M.T.S. Underwear**	long	child	polyester
REI	Turtleneck	long	m,f,c	cotton, spandex
Sequel	Solar Shirt	sh't, l'g	m, f	Coolmax, m'sh fabric
Seventh Gen.	Polo Shirt	sh't, l'g	m, f	GreenCot'n & Foxf're
Seventh Gen.	Turtleneck, Mock Turtle	long	m, f	GreenCotton
Terramar	Zip Turtleneck	long	m, f	polyester, Hydrofil
Terramar	Crew Top	long	m, f	polyester, Hydrofil

* River shirt. ** This soft, warm child's undershirt can be worn alone as a pullover.

Pants

One or two pairs of shorts for warm weather and one pair of long pants for cool weather are usually sufficient on a trip. A good combination is to have a pair of trail shorts for walking, hiking, or wearing around town, and a pair of lightweight shorts for more active sports and occasional swimming. For cool weather one pair of long pants is sufficient for general wear, while a combination of shorts and leggings or tights serves well for active sports.

Alternatively, pack a second pair of pants made from lightweight Supplex® nylon. These don't weigh much and are quite comfortable due to the softness of Supplex®. For colder climates you may want a wickable under layer, fleece middle layer, and rain/wind pants as an outer layer. Relatively new to the market are the two-in-one pants, which are actually shorts with zip-off legs. These are great when you only have room for one pair of pants. This is especially true for day outings, when the weather is uncertain and you don't want the extra weight of long pants or the hassle of changing into leggings.

Shorts

Traditional corduroy, cotton canvas and cotton/synthetic blend hiking or trail shorts have recently given ground in the polls to the loose-fitting, lightweight models now available. Constructed along the same lines as running shorts, with nylon liners and synthetic/cotton blend outer shells, these shorts are rugged and suitable for active sports or general wear. They are loose and comfortable, give great freedom of move-ment, but are shy on padding, a definite consideration when straddling a bicycle or lugging a backpack. Their quick-drying feature is nice for watersports, those wet times on the trail, or when you need your laundry to dry in a hurry. It also allows these type of shorts to serve easily as a swimming suit should you happen upon a good bathing spot. Cotton and cotton canvas trail shorts are still popular since they are comfortable, durable, and are equally at home on an expedition, visiting a museum, or relaxing at a cafe. You'll find that good quality shorts cost $20 to $40.

Woolrich's Ridge Shorts

Sportif's Watersports Shorts

Author's Recommendations - Shorts For Active Travel

Brand	Model/Description	Sizes	Material
Columbia	Whidbey Shorts, baggy fit, front pleats	m, f	nylon
Cherry Tree	Hiking Shorts, 6 pockets, durable	child	cotton twill
EMS	Boundary Cloth Shorts	m, f	cotton, polyester
Gramicci	Street Shorts, elastic waist, rear p'cket	m, f, ch	cotton
L.L. Bean	Sport Shorts	m, f	nylon, poly'st'r, cot.
L.L. Bean	Canvas Workshorts, 7 pockets	m, f	cotton canvas
Patagonia	Stand Up Shorts	m, f, ch	cotton
Patagonia	Baggies, elastic waist, mesh brief	m, f, ch	cotton/Supplex

REI	Explorer Shorts, 6 pockets	m	cotton canvas
REI	Super Shorts, elastic w'st, side p'ck'ts	m, f, ch	Supplex, nylon
REI	Clear Creek, el'st'c w'st, many pockets	child	Supplex
Royal Robbins	Billy Goat Shorts, elastic band, pleats	m, f	cotton canvas
Royal Robbins	Bluewater Shorts	m	cotton canvas
Royal Robbins	Basic Twill Shorts	f	cotton twill
Sierra Designs	Pick-A-Pocket Shorts, quick drying	m, f, ch	nylon
Sportif	"Twill" and "Ultralite Tropical" Stretch	m, f, ch	poly'st., cot., sp'd'x
Sportif	Canvas Stretch Shorts, elastic band	m	cotton, spandex
Sportif	Watersports Shorts	m, f	Supplex
Woolrich	Ridge Shorts, elastic waist, 6 pockets	m	cotton ripstop
Woolrich	Quarry Cotton Twill Shorts	f	cotton twill

Innovation - *Polar Shorts* from Sequel

Shorts can be easily worn over leggings, tights, or long underwear bottoms for cool weather active sports, yet shorts that allow good freedom of movement often don't give you much protection from the wet or cold. Sequel solved this problem with their *Polar Shorts*. They not only look great and keep you from overheating in cool weather, they also have a waterproof seat, some insulation in just the right places, and handwarmer pockets that protect you from the elements. *Polar Shorts* cost around $42 and come with an integral belt system that keeps them in place when shouldering a backpack.

Long Pants

The best long pants for travel and outdoor sports are those that are loose and comfortable, yet rugged enough to stand up to repeated hard use. They should also not show dirt and be easily laundered. On many trips you'll only have one pair of long pants with you, so they should be durable. Loose-fitting, mediumweight, straight-leg corduroy pants are fine for general wear while traveling. Good quality cotton canvas pants are more comfortable and allow greater freedom of movement. Children are partial to cotton pants and lightweight overalls with reinforced knees. All pack easily and launder well. If a

Early Winter's Crag Banger Pants

second pair of long pants is needed, bring something made of lightweight material such as Supplex®. Active travelers can also pack one pair of long pants and a lightweight pair of leggings that can be worn alone, under shorts for cool-weather active sports, and under long pants during colder weather. This combination is very popular with children.

If you're tempted to bring jeans, keep in mind that they tend to be hot, heavy, bulky, difficult to hand wash, take forever to dry, and really restrict your movement. Other than that they're fine. If you can't imagine life on the road without your favorite pair of jeans, by all means bring them; just pack along a loose, lightweight second pair for cool weather active sports. If you can, leave the bulkier clothing at your base camp to trim down your load for a serious hike or bike tour.

Kids can easily get by with an inexpensive combination of sweatpants and leggings. Sweatpants are good for all activities, although for extended travels you may want to consider exchanging them for pants made of cotton twill or cotton canvas with reinforced knees. They're more durable, better looking, and can always be worn over leggings if the weather turns cold.

I highly recommend the models listed below. The kids pants cost $14 to $26, the fleece pants $30 to $65, and the others $20 to $50.

Author's Recommendations - Long Pants

Brand	Model	Sizes	Material
After the Stork	Sweatpant	child	cotton
After the Stork	Canvas Pant	child	cotton canvas
Cherry Tree	Leggings, for active sports	child	cotton, Lycra
Cherry Tree	Hiking Pant, 6 pockets, durable	child	cotton twill
Columbia	Whidbey Pant	m, f child	nylon
Early Winter	Crag Banger Pant	m	cotton twill
EMS	Woodsman Twill	m	cotton twill
EMS	Ridge Twill	f	cotton twill
Gramicci	Climbing Pant, dual-layer knees	child	cotton canvas
L.L. Bean	Canvas Workpant	m, f	cotton canvas
L.L. Bean	Sweatpant	child	cotton/polyest.
Patagonia	Climbing Pant II, double layered	child	cotton canvas
Patagonia	Bombachas, pleats, cuff buttons	m, f	cotton twill
Patagonia	Canvas Pant, angled front pock'ts	m	cotton canvas
REI	Explorer Pant, 5 pockets	m	cotton canvas
REI	Kid's Supplex, lightweight pant	child	Supplex
Royal Robbins	Billy Goat Pant, elas. w'st, durable	m, f	cotton canvas
Royal Robbins	Sill Pant, reinforced seat and knees	m	cotton canvas
Royal Robbins	Camping Jean, relaxed fit	f	denim
Sequel	Solar Shants, p'nt/sh't, zip-off legs	m, f	cotton rip-stop
Sierra Designs	Quick-Dry Cargo Pant, calf zipp'rs	m, f	nylon
Sportif	2-in-1 Cargo p'nt/sh't, zip-off legs	m	cotton
Sportif	Hiking/Sport Cargo, elastic waist	m	Supplex

Author's Recommendations - Synthetic Fleece Pants

Brand	Model	Sizes	Material
Adventure 16	Polartec Pant	m, f	Polartec fleece
Campmor	Polartec 200 Pant, velour-like	m, f	Polartec fleece
Campmor	Polartec 300 Pant, reinforced	m, f	Polartec fleece
Cherry Tree	Polar Pant	child	Polartec fleece
Moonstone	Moonlite Tights and Pant	m, f	polyester fleece
NxNE	Multi-Trainer Pant	m, f	Polartec 100
NxNE	Full Zip Pant	m, f	Polartec 200
NxNE	Grand Manan Pant	m, f	Polartec 300
Sierra Designs	Fuzz Lite Pant	m, f	Polartec 200
Sierra Designs	Micro Fuzz Pant	m, f	microfiber fleece

Sweaters

Sweaters are great for pulling on when the temperatures dip, or as a middle layer under a waterproof shell. One should be sufficient for most outdoor trips. Be careful in selection; sweaters tend to be bulky and space is at a premium on the road. Try to find sweaters that provide maximum warmth in the smallest package. Sweater materials can be wool, wool/synthetic blends, or all synthetic. Currently, the most popular middle layer for all-around comfort and packability is a synthetic "fleece" (or "pile") sweater or light jacket. Polartec™ fibers are probably the most well known and most functional. Some of their advantages are high warmth-to-weight ratio, breathability, insulation even when wet, very little moisture

NxNE's Paramo Fleece Pullover

absorption, and rapid drying. Synthetic fleece sweaters are so comfortable that most models come with a high zippered collar (simulating a turtleneck) for added warmth in cold weather. Other synthetics such as polypropylene are also used—less expensive, but a bit less comfortable and effective.

Innovation - Malden Mills' Polartec™ Series 1000

A recent innovation from Malden Mills is Polartec™ Series 1000, a double-faced, velour-like fabric featuring an inner barrier that is completely windproof, yet highly breathable. This fabric is also water resistant and quick drying. Now you can get all the benefits of a warm middle layer, plus the added bonus of wind protection, in one garment. Use middle layers of this fabric in combination with a lightweight outer shell for rain protection.

Raw wool sweaters, those made with untreated wool, are notoriously warm and shed water well, but they do tend to take up a lot of space. Despite its bulk, my wife brings her Icelandic sweater on all cold weather travels. Irish and Norwegian "fishermen's" sweaters have the same capabilities to cope with wind, rain and extreme temperatures. Cotton sweaters look and feel nice, but they don't provide much warmth for their size and weight. If you want a cotton middle layer, a chamois shirt might make more sense. The exception is cotton or cotton/synthetic hooded sweatshirts for children. They are inexpensive, warm and durable, and the hood can't be forgotten or lost. Those made of cotton/synthetic blends are readily available at department and outdoor stores; the all-cotton versions are available through Patagonia, Ecosport, and mail order houses such as After the Stork. Some recommended sweaters are listed below. Kids sweatshirts cost around $17 to $20, while sweaters vary widely in price from just under $30 to just over $75.

Author's Recommendations - Sweaters and Sweater-Jackets

Brand	Model	Sizes	Material
After the Stork	Hooded Sweatshirt	child	cotton fleece
Campmor	Alpine Fleece Pullover	m	polypropylene
Campmor	Polartec Pullover, Cardigan	m,f	Polartec
Cannondale	A.T.W. Jersey/Jacket	m, f	stretch synthetic, Supplex
Cherry Tree	Polar Pullover	child	Polartec 300, spandex
Cherry Tree	Hooded Fleece Sweatshirt	child	Polartec 200
Columbia	Helvetia Fleece	m, f, child	MTR fleece
Duofold	Polar Fleece Jacket	m, f	Polartec Series 1000
Ecosport	Hooded Sweatshirt	m, f	organic cotton
EMS	Ragg Wool	m, f	Ragg wool
EMS	Greenland	m, f	untreated wool
EMS	Pinnacle Fleece	m, f	synthetic fleece
Helly-Hansen	Propile Pullover, Jacket	m, f	Propile
L.L. Bean	Hooded Sweatshirt	child	cotton, polyest.
L.L. Bean	Polartec Lite Pullover	m,f, child	Polartec
L.L. Bean	Polartec Pullover, Jacket	m, f	Polartec, nylon
L.L. Bean	Norwegian Fisherman	m, f	unscoured wool, rayon
NxNE	Paramo Fleece Pullover	m, f	Polartec fleece

Moonstone	Moonlite Zip T and Cardigan	m, f	polyester fleece
Patagonia	Sweatshirt	child	cotton
Patagonia	Baby Synchilla Cardigan	infant	Synchilla pile, nylon
Patagonia	Synchilla Jacket, Snap-T	m, f, child	Synchilla pile, nylon
REI	Polartec Pullover, Cardigan	m,f	Polartec, Supplex
REI	Polarcat and Polarcub Jacket	child	Polartec, Lycra
Sequel	Kennebec Pullover	m, f	Polartec
Sequel	Piedra Pullover	m, f	Polartec
Sierra Designs	Gust Buster Sweater-Jacket	m, f	Polartec Series 1000
Sierra Designs	Micro Fuzz Pullover	m, f	microfiber fleece
Woolrich	Tropo Polartec Pullover	m,f	Polartec, Supplex

Vests

Vests are a good alternative to a jacket when you want some additional mobility for your arms. They preserve warmth where it's needed most, over the midsection of your body. They are lightweight and can be worn over a first or middle layer. Vests can be made of a single layer of wool or synthetic "fleece"

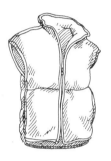 

NxNE's Carrabassett   Climb High's Down

material, or can be constructed of a water-resistant outer shell with an inner fill of down or synthetic fibers. The former are great under a shell, while the latter can provide sufficient protection on their own. I find them invaluable in cold weather, for active sports, or just staying warm at the campsite. If there's not a knitter in your family, try one of the good quality vests listed below. The child's vest from After the Stork cost about $10, the others cost $30 to $60.

Author's Recommendations - Vests

Brand	Model	Sizes	Material
After the Stork	Thermal Vest	child	cotton
Campmor	Polartec Vest	m,f	Polartec
Cherry Tree	Polar Vest	child	Polartec
Climb High	Down Vest	m	goose down
EMS	Pinnacle Fleece Vest	m, f	Pinnacle fleece
EMS	Down Lite Vest	m, f	goose down
L.L. Bean	Polartec Vest	m, f	Polartec
L.L. Bean	Whittaker Down Vest	m, f	goose down

Moonstone	Moonlite Vest	m, f	polyester fleece
Moonstone	XCR Windstopper Vest	m, f	polyester fleece, Supplex
NxNE	Carrabassett Vest	m, f	Polartec 200
REI	Polartec Vest (full zipper)	m,f	Polartec
REI	Polarcat Print Vest	child	Polartec
REI	Classic Down Vest	m,f	goose down
Sequel	Vestal	m, f	Polartec, spandex
Sierra Designs	Fuzz Lite Vest	m, f	Polartec 200

OUTER LAYER CLOTHING

No matter where you choose to travel, you'll invariably want some type of outer layer protection from the elements. Even in the tropics lightweight outer jackets are useful for the frequent afternoon showers and the occasional deluge. The most sensible approach to trip-related clothes layering is to use under and middle layers for warmth, saving the outer layer almost exclusively as the line of defense against wind and rain. Single-purpose jackets and pants good for wind protection or warmth, yet offering little protection from wet weather, don't make much sense for active travel. You rarely have room in your pack for multiple sets of outerwear. Therefore, in this section I'll only concentrate on those jacket/pants combinations intended for use as an all-purpose outer layer. This includes wind/water resistant or waterproof gear for light, moderate and extreme conditions.

Review of Generic Types - Outerwear Shells

Outer shell tops come in several different types, including jackets, parkas, anoraks and ponchos.

Jackets. A generic term for outerwear tops, this also refers to garments with a shorter length that have full collars and fully-zippered and/or buttoned fronts.

Parkas. This term commonly refers to jackets with a bit longer length, integral or detachable hoods, which are made to be more wind and water resistant. The terms jacket and parka are often interchangeable in the industry.

Anoraks. These are jackets made to slip over your head. They come with partial front zippers and/or snaps, hoods, and are longer in length. These features mean greater rain protection, although anoraks are not as versatile as fully-zippered jackets.

Ponchos. Ponchos are almost like anoraks without defined sleeves. Made to be pulled over the head, the material is simply cut to drape over your arms and provide maximum freedom of movement. They come in medium and long styles and some are cut to fit over a loaded backpack.

Backpacker Poncho

Outer shell pants typically have elastic waistbands and a drawstring. They may also have snaps or a zippered section at the bottom of the legs for greater comfort and ease of getting them on and off without removing your shoes. Some models come with a bibbed front and suspenders for extra protection from the elements.

Construction and Operation - Outerwear Shells

Outer shells are made from materials that are wind and water resistant. A common outer layer fabric is nylon (or a nylon blend), used for its durability and wind or water resistance. Nylon can be layered with other fabrics to create outerwear with greater flexibility or comfort. The closer the weave of the fabric fibers, the more resistant the fabric is to wind and water penetration. Nylon shells have the advantage of breathability, but if they have no additional coatings or membranes, or aren't made of very fine microfibers, they can only go so far in giving wind and water protection. A jacket or anorak made of a 60/40 blend of uncoated nylon and cotton can be a real heavyweight and next to useless in hard rain.

To be effective against wind and water penetration, the shell material must be made of one of the following: waterproof plastic; a non-breathable coated fabric; a breathable coated fabric (typically nylon with microporous inner coatings and additional water repellent outer coatings); layers of membrane fabric that are breathable and waterproof (such as Gore-Tex® or Sympatex® fabric bonded to layers of nylon or polyester); or one of the new microfibers that are so small and densely woven that they won't allow water molecules in, yet will allow body perspiration out.

Review Of Materials. A description of the various types of materials used for outer shells currently on the market is given below.

• *Single Layer Vinyl.* Pure "virgin" vinyl outerwear is dirt cheap, but doesn't hold up well since it lacks a layer of fabric to give it strength. It also doesn't even begin to breathe. For adventure travel, I'd skip this type altogether.

• *Uncoated nylon.* Simple nylon or nylon blend garments look and feel great, hold up to hard use well, and may give you some protection from wind and damp weather. Without waterproof coatings, however, they don't provide enough protection to be your only outer layer when traveling.

• *Non-Breathable Coated Fabrics.* These are a good value, a middle ground between cost and comfort. There are various types, from ultralight to heavyweight depending on material and thickness of coating. They are typically constructed of nylon fabric coated with PVC, urethane, or Hypalon® rubber. The heavier the fabric, or layers of fabric, the better suited they are to rugged conditions. They'll keep you dry, but also keep your body moisture in, so they are not as suitable for really active sports. Even though these garments don't breathe, the lightweight versions are comfortable enough for most outdoor activities in warm to cool climates. They also don't take up much weight or space; most lightweight outer shells can be rolled up and packed into a small pouch. Coated fabrics of lesser quality tend to lose their water-repelling effectiveness over time.

• *Breathable Coated Fabrics.* These fabrics rely on either microporous coatings or semi-permeable urethane to keep out the wind and water, yet allow body perspiration to pass through. The breathable coatings are typically applied to the inside of the outer fabric, and often additional water repellents are applied to the outside. These coatings include Helly-Hansen's Helly-Tech®, Columbia's Omni-Tech®, REI's Elements®, Patagonia's H2No® system, and Sierra Designs' HP Waterproof/Breathable® system.

• *Breathable Membranes.* Gore-Tex® is a widely used membrane fabric that is inherently breathable and waterproof. The membrane is laminated to a variety of abrasion resistant fabrics for use in outer layer garments. Other membranes include EMS's System III® membrane and Sympatex®.

• *Microfiber Fabrics.* These non-coated single layer fabrics such as Trevira® are made of densely packed microfilaments that allow body perspiration to pass through, but block the passage of wind and water from the outside. They are generally reputed to be less effective than membrane laminates, but adequate for most adventure travel needs.

Other Waterproofing Considerations. Other than the choice of material, there are additional considerations that outerwear manufacturers must address to ensure that their garments are waterproof. For a start, all seams must be well sealed, using either waterproof tape, a coating, or both. All pockets and zippers should be protected with correctly placed flaps. The cut of the jacket should be longer to provide more protection. Collar and cuff areas should also be designed to prevent water penetration. Be sure to check all of these features before purchasing.

Venting. Since no fabric by itself breathes enough to be totally comfortable in all conditions, outer shells usually come with some type of venting, from simple vent holes in the armpits to sophisticated zippered vent flaps.

Thermal Layers. Outer shells are also available with an internal layer of thermal insulation (either down, synthetic fill material, or fleece) providing extra warmth for extreme cold. This type of jacket is appropriate only for travelers going to cold weather destinations.

Inner Linings. Many outer shells have inner linings of soft fabric for an additional level of comfort.

Author's Recommendations - Outerwear Shells

New materials and methods of construction have allowed unprecedented comfort and protection in outerwear. They have also made for unprecedented price tags. It's up to you to decide how much you can afford to spend on outerwear. Comfort and durability are what you'll be paying the extra money for. For basic travel in moderate climates, you can easily get by with an inexpensive coated nylon shell. If weight is a major concern, try one of the lightweight packable shells. Many outdoor travelers seek warm, sunny destinations, keeping the necessity for good

REI's Ventana Outerwear

outerwear to a minimum. If you go where it's not so warm and sunny, to places with more rugged climates and conditions, you'll need additional protection. Recommended outerwear categorized by intended use and conditions are listed below.

Costs. The cost of an outer shell garment is directly related to its overall weight, comfort level, and durability. Ponchos cost from $15 to $40. You should be able to get a light-use, waterproof, coated nylon jacket for around $30 to $40, pants to match for $20 to $28. Moderate-use outer shells range from $26 to $45 for PVC-coated jacket and pants to $150 to $250 for waterproof/breathable jacket and pants. Outerwear for extreme use can cost $300 to $500 for jacket/pants combinations.

Author's Recommendations - Outerwear, Ponchos

Brand	Model	Style	Material
Campmor	Backpacker	backpack	urethane-coated nylon
Campmor	Regular	long/reg./child's	urethane-coated nylon
Cherry Tree	Omni-poncho	child and carrier	urethane-coated nylon
Log House	Backpacker	backpack	urethane-coated nylon
NxNE	St'n'd, Backpackers	long cut	urethane-coated nylon
NxNE	Cagoule, front pock't	long cut	urethane-coated nylon

Author's Recommendations - Outerwear, Light Use and Conditions

Brand	Model	Style	Material
Campmor	L'w't Backpacker	parka/pants	urethane-coated nylon
Cherry Tree	Shell jacket	jacket/pants	urethane-coated nylon
Columbia	Monsoon II	jacket/pants	urethane-coated nylon
EMS	Lightweight Rainsuit	jacket/pants	urethane-coated nylon
Helly-Hansen	Rainlight	jacket/pants	urethane-coated nylon
Sierra Designs	Microlight	j'ck't/an'r'k/p'nts	urethane-coated nylon
Sierra Designs	Minilight (child's)	jacket/pants	urethane-coated nylon

Author's Recommendations - Outerwear, Moderate Use and Conditions

Brand	Model	Style	Material
Campmor	Vagabond*	parka, pants	Gore-Tex, nylon taffeta
Campmor	Packaway*	parka	Gore-Tex, nylon taffeta
Campmor	Children's Rainsuit	jacket, pants	PVC-coated nylon
Columbia	Ibex Rainsuit, m, f, ch	jacket, pants	PVC-coated nylon
Columbia	Marsupial II*	parka, pants	Omni-Tech-coated nylon
Cannondale	Ultrex Rainwear*	jacket, pants	Ultrex, j'k't has bot'm flap
EMS	PVC Rainsuit	jacket, pants	PVC-coated nylon
Helly-Hansen	Lightning Rainwear*	parka, pants	Helly-Tech, coated nylon
Helly-Hansen	Rainbreaker	jacket, pants	urethane-coated nylon
L.L. Bean	Stowaway Raingear*	jacket, pants	Gore-Tex, nylon
Montbell	Cloudburst	jacket, pants	urethane-coated nylon
Patagonia	Raingear	jacket, pants	SealCoat-coated nylon
Performance	Cycling Suit	jacket, pants	Gore-Tex, nylon
REI	Ventana*	p'rka/an'r'k, p'nts	REI Elements system
REI	Cascade Rainwear	j'cket/p'rka, p'nts	Hypalon-coated nylon

Sierra Designs	HP Ripstop & Taffeta*	jacket, pants	HP W't'rpr'f/Br'thable, nyl'n
Sportif	Lightweight*	jacket, pants	Ultrex
The North Face	Stowaway I and III	jacket, pants	Gore-Tex, nylon

made of waterproof/breathable material.

Author's Recommendations - Outerwear Extreme Use and Conditions

Brand	Model	Style	Material
Campmor	Technical*	parka/pants	Gore-Tex, Supplex
Climb High	Summit Expedition*	parka	Gore-Tex, Primaloft, nylon
EMS	Weatherlite*	parka/pants	Gore-Tex, nylon
EMS	System III Storm*	parka/pants	System III coating, nylon
Helly-Hansen	Helly-Tech Pro*	jacket, pants	Helly-Tech coating, nylon
L.L. Bean	North Col*	parka, pants	Gore-Tex, supplex
L.L. Bean	North Col insulated*	parka, pants	G'-T'x, Thins'l'te, Suppl'x
Patagonia	Storm*	parka, pants	H2No coating, nylon
REI	Tawoche Alpine*	parka/pants	Gore-Tex, nylon
REI	Stormfront*	parka/pants	Gore-Tex, nylon
Sequel	Twilight Jacket*	jacket/pants	Gore-Tex, polyester
Sequel	Storm King Parka*	parka/pants	G'-Tex, Supplex, Hydrofil
Sierra Designs	HP Taslan	parka, bib pants	HP W't'rpr'f/Br'thable, nyl'n
The North Face	Mountain Light II*	jacket/pants	Gore-Tex, Supplex

made of waterproof/breathable material.

Maintenance and Repair - Outerwear

Since good outer shell garments are fairly expensive, it pays to take good care of them. Listed below are a few tips on routine care, as well as some suggestions concerning repair.

Keep Garments Clean. This maintains their performance in adverse conditions, especially waterproof/breathable fabrics where micro-pores can get clogged. A good cleaner such as *Sport-Wash* can restore breathability to any washable, waterproof/breathable fabric, including Gore-Tex®. A 16-ounce bottle of *Sport-Wash* costs around $5 and is good for up to 18 wash loads.

Water Repellents. You can also add water repellency to any washable garment with a product such as *Zepel Rain/Stain Repeller.* A six-ounce bottle costs around $7.50 and will treat three "average-size" garments. Rain and liquids that normally stain tend to bead up and roll off of fabrics treated with *Zepel.* Treatment does not affect breathability. Another good product for washing machine use is Kenyon's *Wash Cycle Water Repellent* (four-ounce bottle). Many silicon spray water repellents are also available, including *Camp Dry,* 3M's *Scotch Guard,* and Sno-Seal's *Silicone Water Guard.* Liquid waterproofers include K-Kote's *Recoat* (eight-ounce or 16-ounce size, replaces worn coating on nonbreathable rainwear) and a product called *Seam Stuff* ($4 for a two-ounce tube) made for sealing the seams on all Gore-Tex® garments.

Avoid Chemicals. Try to avoid contact with harsh chemicals, including stove and lantern fuel as well as many insect repellents; these chemicals can damage the fabric or decrease the performance of waterproof/breathable fabrics.

Rips and Tears. Rips or tears at the seams can be easily mended by hand or on a good sewing machine. Damage elsewhere in the fabric will have to be patched with spare material and a good adhesive. Ask the manufacturer what they recommend. Make the repair as neat as possible, and treat the new fabric with a water repellent coating or seam sealer as required.

Broken Zippers. This is the most common repair to jackets. Most professional cleaners, or any place that does alterations, can probably replace your broken zipper. Zipper styles and sizes vary widely, so it depends on whether they can match what you have.

Footwear

The last major category of clothing provides protection for your head, feet and hands. Don't underestimate the importance of these items. Having proper hats, shoes or boots, and gloves can often make all the difference between comfort and misery.

At home you typically have multiple pairs of shoes or boots, each specially suited for your climate and the various activities you like to do. On the road you can't afford this luxury. There's usually only room for one or two pairs of footgear, so the ones you choose should be versatile. In this section we'll take a look at footgear that is appropriate for general active travel. Shoes and boots for specific outdoor activities such as backpacking, bicycling or watersports are covered in the section on that activity.

Review of Generic Types - Footwear

Traditionally, the term "shoes" referred to footwear with a low cut (below the ankle), and "boots" to footgear with a high cut (above the ankle). Shoes were lightweight and worn for bicycling or walks around town, boots were heavy and worn on the trail. Several years ago a revolution in footwear took place. Shoes and boots became incredibly lightweight, a boon for the hiker and less damaging to the environment. "Trail shoes" started to appear (also called "light-weight hikers" or "rugged walkers" shoes) that are comfortable like running shoes, yet durable enough for a host of outdoor activities. There became less of a distinction between shoe and boot. Today, three basic styles are available: low-cut shoes, good for light hiking, bicycling, watersports, and general wear; high-cut boots, good for strenuous hiking and backpacking when extra support is needed; and a medium-cut version that is a hybrid between the two, good for moderately-rugged hiking, light trekking, and mountain biking. The top part of the medium-cut shoe is usually high in the front, sloping down to a back portion that is a bit lower for greater freedom of movement. Since the medium-cut version is somewhere between a shoe and a boot it is often referred to as a shoe-boot.

Materials and Construction - Footwear

Trail shoe and boot uppers are typically constructed of leather or a leather/fabric-mesh combination. They have a cushioned midsole, padded ankles, and a small-to-moderate size lug sole of lightweight rubber. For more information on construction, refer to the section on Backpacking Footgear.

Author's Recommendations - Footwear

I recommend taking one primary and one secondary pair of footwear on your travels. The primary pair should be a sturdy, comfortable, all-purpose pair of shoes or boots for active sports and general traveling. The secondary pair should be lightweight foot-wear for the beach, campsite or around town. When choosing footgear think about what types of activities you pursue and conditions you tend to encounter on your trips. No matter where or how you travel, you'll probably be doing a fair amount of walking, so footgear that is comfortable and durable is a must. You can always get by with sneakers or running shoes, but they won't stand up to hard use and don't have a good tread or support system for off-road hiking. If you tend to do a lot of walking on trails or in muddy conditions, try to find a pair of comfortable shoes or boots that have some extra reinforcement and a bit more tread for extra traction, and are more water resistant and easily cleaned. For bicycle travel, make sure the shoes have a low or medium cut (for freedom of movement) and that the tread isn't too deep (so it won't tend to get caught on the pedals).

In addition to your primary footwear, a second pair of light-weight thongs or sport sandals are nice for warmer climates and watersports. Slip-on "reef shoes" or "aqua socks" also make an excellent second pair of footgear for coastal or inland waterway travel, or for use around the campsite. Footwear well suited for watersports is covered in the section on Canoeing and Kayaking. Moccasins, "slipper socks", or thermal booties are also nice to slip into at the end of the day. Acorn Products offers a wide variety of indoor and camp footwear to choose from, including their ultra-comfortable Polar Pairs made of synthetic fleece uppers and padded leather soles. For colder climates, where your primary footgear is a heavier pair of boots, consider bringing a lightweight pair of walking or running shoes.

Primary Footgear. I've used lightweight trail shoes on many of our trips where we've combined walking, hiking, and bicycle touring, as well as other recreational sports. This type of low-cut shoe is convenient because it's lightweight and comfortable, versatile and durable, while also suitable for general wear. It represents a good compromise for active travel. Medium-cut versions are available for more ankle support during strenuous hiking and mountain biking. Keep in mind that medium or high-cut boots might be less comfortable for general wear and are generally not suitable for long-distance bicycle touring.

Tecnica's TKS   Merrell's Torrent   Acorn's Polar Pairs

Look for a comfortable fit and sturdy construction when choosing your primary footgear for active travel. The toe of the shoe should be well protected with a large strip of rubber, not a small flap like that found on running shoes. Some type of extra support should extend around the perimeter of the shoe where the uppers meet the sole. If the uppers are leather and there is no extra support, they may give out there prematurely.

Children's Considerations. Children present a different set of criteria when choosing shoes and boots. They need footgear that is good for outdoor activities as well as all the other things they do, like playing games, climbing trees, and kicking rocks down the road. Sneakers were the only choice until a few years ago. Now many models of lightweight trail and hiking footgear are offered in children's sizes. Children change shoe size so rapidly that outfitting can be a very expensive proposition. Considering the price of good quality sneakers, however, you're better off buying lightweight trail shoes for adventure travel. They'll stand up to an amazing amount of punishment and give them the support they need for long distance walking and hiking. If you pack heavier hiking boots for them, you should consider bringing along a lightweight pair of sneakers for general use.

Good children's models are offered by Hi-Tec, Merrell, Nike and Vasque. Vasque *Kids Klimbers*, a medium-cut boot, incorporate their "Variable Fit Child Growth System." This consists of a removable pad adhered to the underside of their variable fit insole. As the child's foot grows, the pad is removed and the usefulness of the boots extended for another season. This is the kind of practical design needed for all children's clothing.

Another good alternative for traveling children is leather indoor soccer shoes. Frustrated at how quickly ours wore out their sneakers, we turned to these on the recommendation of a friend who owns a sporting goods store. He told us they "wear like iron," and indeed they do. This one reasonably-priced pair of black shoes has served our children well for walking, light to moderate hiking, bicycling, boating, even dress up and general wear. Get a good pair and you'll inevitably hand them down to another child before they wear out. They are not suitable, however, for rough terrain, especially when carrying a load. For that you need true hiking shoes or boots.

Costs. Manufacturers of trail shoes offer a range of models to choose from. You should be able to get a good pair of trail shoes for around $40 to $75. For higher quality models that have better performance characteristics, expect to pay up to $100.

Author's Recommendations - Primary Footwear

Brand	Model	Sizes	Description
adidas	Adventure	m	active sports; lc, leather/mesh uppers
adidas	Bavaria low	m, f	active sports; lc, leather uppers
Hi-Tec	GT Series	m, f	all-purpose; mc, leather/mesh
Hi-Tec	B'ckp'ck'ng Series	m, f	Sierra Lite, Sierra Low, Diablo models
Hi-Tec	Trekking	m, f, ch	Teton, Topaz; hc, leather/mesh uppers
Merrell	Trek, Spirit	m, f	all-purpose; lc, leather/mesh uppers
Merrell	Taos, Lazer	m, f	all-purpose; mc, leather/mesh uppers
Merrell	Torrent	m, f	all-purpose; lc, rr, leather/mesh uppers

Merrell	Scout	child	all-purpose; mc, leather/mesh uppers
Nike	Tambura	m, f	cross terrain, lc, leather/mesh uppers
Nike	Caldera 3/4 Plus	m, f, ch	cross terrain; mc, leather/mesh uppers
Nike	Air Yewtah II	m, f	cross terrain; lc, leather/mesh uppers
One Sport	Sundance	m, f	cross terrain, lc, leather/mesh, low-imp'ct
One Sport	Base Camp	m, f	general travel; mc, leather/mesh uppers
Raichle	Trail Hikers	m, f	Telluride, Wasatch; lc, leather/mesh up.
Reebok	Sojurn	m, f	light hiking; mc, leather/mesh uppers
Reebok	Telos	m, f	hiking, cross; mc, leather/mesh uppers
Salomon	Outdoor low	m, f	all-purpose; lc, leather/mesh uppers
Tecnica	TKS	m, f	all-outdoors; hc, leather/nylon uppers
Tecnica	TKL	m, f	cross terrain; lc, leather/mesh uppers
Vasque	Terrain	m, f	all-purpose; lc, leather/nylon uppers
Vasque	Clarion III	m, f	hiking; lc, leather/Cordura uppers
Vasque	Rambler series	m, f	all-purpose; lc, leather uppers
Vasque	Kids Klimbers	child	all-purpose; mc, leather/Cordura uppers

DESCRIPTION: lc=low-cut, mc=medium-cut, hc=high-cut, rr=rubber rand.

Maintenance and Repair - Footwear

You can extend the life of your primary footgear by performing a little routine maintenance. It's simple to do, costs little, and you'll be rewarded with shoes and boots that last many seasons. Most trail shoe uppers are made of leather or a leather/mesh fabric combination. The three types of routine care for this type of shoe are cleaning, conditioning and waterproofing.

Cleaning. This removes dirt and oils from leather or fabric that cause stains and decrease material life. Select a good cleaner for your type of shoe and use it as needed. One recommended cleaner for fabric and leather uppers is Aquaseal's *Techniclean* (cleans and deodorizes), sold separately with a small bristle brush or included in the *Care-Kit* described below.

Conditioning. Leather tends to dry out with age, particularly if it's not adequately waterproofed. Conditioning restores suppleness to leather and increases its useful life. Most good leather sealers, such as those listed below, also condition while they waterproof.

Waterproofing. This is necessary to protect the shoe or boot from damage, and your socks and feet from frequent soakings. Waterproofing materials for leather usually come in paste form and are rubbed in and left to dry overnight. Recommended products include *Biwell, Aquaseal, Mink Oil, Bee Seal Plus* and *Sno-Seal*. The fabric mesh on shoe and boot uppers can be treated with any water-repellent product made for synthetic materials, such as *Camp Dry, Zepel, Scotch Guard,* or *Silicone Water Guard*. A complete kit for cleaning, conditioning and waterproofing shoes and boots is the

Fabric/Leather Care Kit from Aquaseal. It contains a four-ounce bottle of *Techniclean*, a four-ounce bottle of *Liquid Aquaseal* with dauber applicator, a small bristle scrub brush and detailed instructions for use.

Shoe Repair. The two most common repairs needed on trail shoes and boots are replacing worn or split soles and re-stitching or regluing the uppers where they meet the sole. On occasion I've re-stitched shoes and boots with a *Speedy Stitching Awl* (available through many outdoor retailers) and waxed synthetic thread, but any shoe repair shop will be able to assess the repair needed for your footgear and do a more professional job. The most annoying type of damage is a tear that occurs at the junction of the sole and uppers. There's usually not enough material showing to do an effective repair. That's why I recommend shoes and boots with a wide band of rubber or other protection around the perimeter where the sole meets the upper.

Hats

Hats provide protection from the elements or an element of style while adventuring. More so than other items of clothing, hats offer a chance to exhibit a little personal flair. Hats also serve important safety and comfort functions and, although not a necessity for mild weather, they are essential for head, face and neck protection in cold, rain and intense sun conditions. Everyone seems to have their own notions about correct headgear and manufacturers have responded accordingly. Hats for outdoor activities are offered in a multitude of styles and materials described below.

Review of Generic Types and General Features - Hats

Hat shape and construction varies to suit activity and weather conditions. Look for the following styles:

Wide Brim Style. This is the most popular style of hat, with a wide band of material encircling a center crown. These hats can assume a variety of configurations by adjusting the set of the brim: "sombrero" or "safari" (brim down), "Aussie" (one side of brim up), or "cowboy" (both sides up) styles are popular. The wide brim

Tilley Endurables Hat

gives the opportunity for good sun and rain protection, although the degree of protection depends on size of brim and material used. Wide brim hats are available in lightweight cotton, cotton canvas, canvas/polyester blend, felt, nylon, Gore-Tex®, and woven straw.

Narrow Brim Style. This style of hat is generally thought of as a "fishing" or "sport" hat. These are similar to wide brim hats, only with a narrow band of material around the center crown. Typically made of lightweight cotton or a cotton/synthetic blend, they offer only moderate sun and rain protection.

Extended Front Brim. Also known as "baseball" or "bicycling" hats, they have only an extended front brim (no side or rear brim) attached to a center crown. This style is usually lightweight and comes with an elastic headband to ensure a snug fit in windy conditions. The front brim gives additional face protection from sun and rain, but loses the ability to keep rain and sun from neck and collar areas without a neck flap. Some manufacturers adapt this style for use in extreme weather conditions by incorporating a waterproof/breathable fabric, a thermal lining, and ear flaps (see Outdoor Research's *Hat For All Seasons* and Columbia's *Yazoo Cap*). Another modified version of this type of hat is the sunshade, consisting of a front brim attached to a thin, adjustable headband for correct fit. Sunshades are suitable only as sun protection for the face as they leave the top of your head vulnerable to the elements.

Sailor's Cap. Also known as a "Greek sailor's" or "captain's" hat, this type has a small, stiff front brim with a low, flat crown and wide headband. Aptly named, these hats are comfortable and warm when you're out on the water. They offer a moderate degree of sun protection for the face. Some models with dark color and wool construction are not suitable in hot or intense sun conditions.

Cold Weather Hats. These include "watch" or "mountain" caps and ski hats. Hand-knitted hats made from good quality wool are hard to beat for comfort and warmth. Machine-made versions are available at any outdoor retail store.

Available Options - Hats

Look for these optional features when shopping for a hat:

Chinstrap or Collar Clip. Useful in windy conditions or during strenuous activity. Chinstraps can be sewn into the hat fabric (these usually include a cordlock for adjustment) or as a separate component attached with Velcro, as with Outdoor Research's *Hat For All Seasons*.

Flotation. A thin layer of insulating foam sewn into the top of the crown provides added warmth, a hidden pocket, flotation, and head protection. This option is available on several wide brim brands, including Tilley Endurables and the Ultimate hats.

Collar Attachment. Rear brim snaps or clips to coat to provide rain protection and prevents loss in windy conditions.

Neck Flap. Adapted from the legendary "Legioneer" hat, a neck flap provides great sun and wind protection.

Ear Flaps. Some hats incorporate ear flaps that come down over ears during cold conditions.

Sun Reflection/Absorption Layer. The Sequel *Desert Rhat* hat has a special material on the crown for reflecting the sun's ultraviolet and infrared radiation, while providing a dark layer under the brim that absorbs reflected light, reducing glare and eye strain.

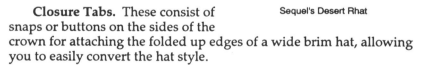

Adjustable Headband. Allows hat to be made in just a few sizes and adjusted for user comfort.

Closure Tabs. These consist of snaps or buttons on the sides of the

Sequel's Desert Rhat

crown for attaching the folded up edges of a wide brim hat, allowing you to easily convert the hat style.

Author's Recommendations - Hats

If you already have a water-resistant hood on your outer shell jacket you may only need a hat for sun protection. Inexpensive cotton or cotton/synthetic hats are available at most outdoor retail stores. Consider purchasing one with a neck flap or wide brim for hot, sunny climates. An extended front brim style is good for bicycling. Wide brim canvas hats are great for sailing. For complete rain protection in a lightweight hat, look for the Gore-Tex® models listed below. Finding a locally-made straw hat in places with hot climates is generally no problem. These are fun to collect and provide good sun protection. Their drawbacks, however, include being a bit bulky, useless in heavy rain, and hard to stow, but I've never let these minor considerations stand in the way of buying a hand-made straw hat wherever possible.

OR's Moonlite Pile Liner and Hat For All Seasons

Cost. Good quality hats for general wear run $10 to $25. Hats with Gore-Tex® run a bit higher. Wide brim canvas models like the Ocean Designs and Ultimate hats cost around $35, Tilley Endurables up to $55.

Author's Recommendations - Hot to Cool Weather Hats

Brand	Model	Style	Description	Material
A16	Backpacker's Sun	wb	wr, cs	cotton canvas
A16	Desert Hawg	efb	lwt, wr, nf	cotton canvas
A16	Mesh Breezer	efb	lwt, wr	Supplex
Cherry Tree	Desert Hat	wb	lwt, cs	cotton twill
Columbia	Booney	wb	wp/br, cs	Omni-Tech, nylon
Columbia	Matecumbe	ewb	wr, lwt, cs	cot., nylon, polyest'r
Columbia	Flats Stalker II	efb	wr, lwt, nf (med)	Supplex, nylon
EMS	Beau Geste	efb	lwt, nf (large)	cotton canvas
EMS	Flapback	efb	wr, lwt, nf (small)	nylon/cotton 60/40
Jansport	Desert Hat	efb	lwt, nf, g'd for sun	cotton
Ocean D's'gns	Canvas Hat	ewb	wr, cs, g'd for sail'g	cotton canvas
OR	All Seasons	efb	wp/br, wi, tl	Gore-Tex, nylon
OR	Sonora Sombrero	wb	wr, lwt, ahb, ct	Cordura nylon
OR	Seattle Sombrero	wb	wp/br, wi, ahb/ct/cs	Gore-Tex, polypro
REI	Safari Hat	wb	wr, leather band	Zepel-treated cotton
REI	Supplex Super	efb	lwt, wr	Supplex nylon
Sequel	Desert Rhat hat	efb	lwt, nf, cs, reflect'g	cot., mesh, met'l foil
TamCat	100 and 300	efb	lwt, wr, cs	nylon, fleece lining
Tilley	T1, T2, T3*	wb	wp, cs, ct, fl	cotton canvas
Ultimate	Ultimate hats**	ewb	wr, cs, ct (also wb)	cot. c'nv's, Supplex

*lifetime warranty on these hats. **lightweight model available.*
STYLE: *wb=wide brim, ewb=extra-wide brim, nb=narrow brim, efb=extended front brim.*
OPTIONS: *lwt=lightweight, wr=water resistant, wp=waterproof outer layer, br=breathable outer layer, wi=wickable inner layer, rl=reflective layer for sun protection, nf=neck flap, ef=ear flaps, ahb=adjustable headband, ct=closure tabs, cs=chin strap, fl=flotation, tl=thermal liner.*

Author's Recommendations - Cold Weather Hats

Brand	Model	Description	Material
A16	Bomber	fb, thermal ear/neck flaps	Ultrex, fleece
Columbia	Yazoo Cap	fb, thermal ear and neck flaps	Ultrex, thermal lining
EMS	Wool hat	all-purpose cold weather hat	wool
EMS	Pinnacle Fleece	good for under parka hood	synthetic fleece
Helly-Hansen	Lifa Prolite	good for under parka hood	polypropylene

L.L. Bean	Whittaker cap	waterpr'f, ear flaps, fl'ce lin'g	Gore-Tex, Supplex
Moonstone	Modern Peruvian	all-purpose cold weather hat	synthetic fleece
Moonstone	Polarlite Cap	good for under parka hood	synthetic fleece
NxNE	Snugazabug	waterpr'f, ear flaps, fl'ce lin'g	Gore-Tex, fleece
OR	Moonlite Pile	solo or liner for hats & hoods	synthetic pile
REI	Stripe Toque	all-purpose cold weather hat	wool, fleece lining
REI	Child's Astro Hat	parka hood-style with fb	nylon, fleece lining
TamCat	200 and 400	fb, folding ear flaps, strap	nylon, fleece lining
Wigwam	Ragg Wool cap	Inner liner helps wick m'sture	ragg wool, polypro

Gloves

Pack a pair of gloves if you plan on traveling to cooler climates. You'll find yourself wearing them at times when you wouldn't bother at home. You tend to feel the cold more when camping or pursuing outdoor sports. Gloves also protect your hands from rough objects and give you more gripping ability when you need it.

Review of Generic Types - Gloves

There are a variety of shapes and styles of gloves to choose from. The three basic types for active travel are described below.

Lightweight liner gloves are typically constructed of polypropylene or a wicking polyester that draws moisture away from your hands. They are intended to be worn under warm middle layer gloves, preventing that clammy feeling you can get during active sports. They can be worn alone in mild conditions.

Middle layer gloves of wool blends or synthetic fleece can be worn alone, over liners, or beneath outer mitts. They are available in different weights for use over a range of climates.

Outer shell mittens made of Gore-Tex® or treated nylon are highly water resistant and primarily used as a protective outer layer in extreme conditions. Wear over warm middle layer gloves or mittens.

Author's Recommendations - Gloves

Layering is just as important with gloves as it is with other clothing. Choose the style and material that best suits your needs. Good quality wool or fleece gloves (or mittens) should be used as all-purpose hand protection for

REI's M.T.S. Fleece Liners

general travel and outdoor activities. Some models come with friction palms to give extra grip during cold weather activities. You can also get finger-free gloves when you need added dexterity. You'll often only need wicking liner gloves with a thin outer protective layer for ski touring or other really active winter sports. Outer shell mittens are needed only for mountaineering or for extreme conditions.

Costs. Good quality gloves like the ones listed below run around $5 to $10 for liner gloves, $7 to $20 for middle layer gloves or mitts, up to $30 for outer shell mitts.

Author's Recommendations - Gloves

Brand	Model	Sizes	Description
Campmor	Ragg Gloves/Mitts	m, f	mid layer; ragg wool
Campmor	Silk liners	m, f	liners; ultra-thin yet warm
Climb High	Dachstein Mitts	m, f	mid or outer layer; oiled wool, wpf
EMS	Bergelene Liners	m, f	liners; wicking Bergelene material
EMS	Pinnacle Fleece	m, f	mid layer; Pinnacle fleece
Fox River	Ragg Gloves	m, f	mid layer; ragg wool
Helly-Hansen	Lifa Prolite	m, f	liners; polypro, 5% spandex
L.L. Bean	Polartec 200	m, f	mid layer; Polartec, nylon cuff
Manzella	Thermax liners	m, f	liners; thermax, 5% spandex
Manzella	Polartec 200	m, f	mid layer; sure grip palms, fleece
OR	Moonlite Pile	m, f	liners, syn. fleece; use overmitts
OR	Shell Overmitts	m, f	outer layer; G-Tex back, Cordura
Patagonia	Stretch Gloves*	m, f	mid layer; Synchilla, Lycra,
REI	M.T.S. fleece	m, f	liners or mid; M.T.S. polyester
REI	Marled Ragg	m, f	mid; ragg wool, leather palms
REI	Overmitts	m, f	outer; G'-Tex, coated nyl'n palms

These gloves have textured Clarino® palms.

OTHER OUTDOOR TRAVEL CLOTHING

Swimming Suits

You'll need some type of bathing apparel for outdoor trips with great beaches nearby, or other spots suitable for cooling off in the water. If you plan to spend a great deal of time swimming or relaxing at the beach, pack a regular swimming suit. You can cut down on weight by selecting lightweight briefs for men and boys (racing-type spandex suits) and bikini-style suits for women and girls. If your time in the water is limited, simply pack a pair of shorts made of quick-drying, lightweight material that can also serve as a swimming suit. Women can include a bikini top (or just wear a

T-shirt) to go with the shorts. Be respectful of the local dress codes when choosing swimwear.

Bandanas

Cotton bandanas come in handy as an all-purpose cloth when adventure traveling. Use them for keeping your neck cool, shading your head, keeping road dust or other airborne objects out of your mouth and nose, as a handkerchief, napkin or impromptu tablecloth, and dozens of other things. Bandanas come in a variety of colors and cost around $1.50 each.

ealth & Hygiene

- Toiletries Kit
- Towel
- Laundry Kit
- Sun Glasses
- Skin Care
- Insect Netting
- Insect Repellent
- Water Treatment
- First Aid Kit
- Medicine
- Emergency Kit

This is an important category of personal outdoor gear since it contains essential items that will help keep you and your fellow travelers healthy and happy. It will probably be your least expensive to outfit for, as much of the gear on the list can be found right at home. I recommend putting together a good health and hygiene kit that takes care of all your needs for the duration of a trip. Having the types of personal items you are used to at home means you'll have one less thing to worry about when arriving in a new place. You'll also know there's an allocated spot for them in your pack or pannier. As some version of these things can be found almost anywhere in the world, restocking during longer trips is no problem.

Some of the items in this category are for personal hygiene, including a toiletries kit, soap and shampoo, washcloth, towel, and a laundry kit. Keeping yourself and your clothing clean while traveling is important, especially in less developed countries or when traveling with little children. Besides the obvious benefits of increased comfort and decreased risk of transmitting disease when handling food, routine cleanliness can also provide a psychological boost to the adventurous traveler. Getting dirty and grubby while adventuring is inevitable. Cleaning up gives you a chance to refresh and renew yourself. You benefit mentally as well as physically. You'll find it helps to maintain rituals like having hot wash water for everyone in the morning and at night, even when far from civilization. It's surprising how simple things help you cope with the rigors of outdoor travel.

Other items on the health and hygiene list can be thought of as preventatives, things used occasionally to prevent discomfort or something of a more serious nature. They include sunglasses and sunscreen, hand cream, insect repellent and netting, water filters and purifiers. The old adage about "an ounce of prevention" serves as good advice for those on the road. While providing cures is most often the domain of the medical world, you have complete control over the simple methods of preventing discomfort or illness in the first place. Prevention gear should be supplemented with proper food handling techniques, good hygiene, and common sense.

There are also certain emergency items you'll want to pack for your own peace of mind. Adventure travel often takes you away from medical care that is easily accessible. You'll feel better knowing you're equipped to deal with minor first aid and emergency situations by having gear such as a well-stocked first aid kit, appropriate prescription medicines, and an emergency kit. The ready availability of items such as toilet paper and feminine pads is also a prudent precaution. I know that most advice could be tagged with the words "especially with children," but instant access to toilet paper takes on new meaning with young ones in tow.

If you plan to spend a large amount of time adventuring in the backcountry or on a boat, you might also consider taking a first-aid course. The Red Cross offers reasonably priced one-day courses nationwide. Try not to let the prospects of injury or emergencies dampen your enthusiasm for outdoor recreation. Just because you are prepared for a bad situation doesn't mean it is more likely to occur. Having the right equipment and being prepared is like having insurance—you probably won't need it, but it's nice to know it's there if you do.

PERSONAL HYGIENE GEAR

Toiletries Kit

A compact, easy-to-handle toiletries kit is a nice idea, whether for weekend getaways or long-term expeditions. It is a convenient way to store personal hygiene items, and affords easy access when you need them. We keep our kit in the top of a handlebar pack when bicycle touring, in a daypack for riding ferries (or other odd-hour activities), and in a carry-on bag on airplanes.

Review of Basic Items - Toiletries Kit

The basic items to include in the kit will be the same regardless of trip duration; only the amount you bring will vary. Try to keep the weight down, both for the kit itself and the types and amounts of items you place in it. Recommended items for the toiletries kit include:

Toothbrushes. The ones you use at home are fine. Find a place to store them where the bristles stay clean, keep their shape, and won't get other things wet. Collapsible toothbrushes that come apart and store in the handle are also widely available.

Toothpaste. Take your favorite brand along.

Dental Floss. These are lightweight, so we usually take enough for even long trips. Figure on one lasting an individual three to four months, a family of four about one month.

Body Soap. I highly recommend taking liquid soap instead of the bar variety. It saves on the mess of storing wet soap. Even those handy plastic soap holders can't prevent dripping soapy water from finding its way into your pack; they just aren't watertight, and wrapping them in baggies isn't a great solution. Concentrated liquid soap, on the other hand, comes in its own watertight container with a flip-out spout for easy pouring. You'll find it lasts quite a while since you only use a tiny amount each time. Many of the brands available at outdoor retailers and health food stores are organic, biodegradable, and multi-purpose for both body cleansing and shampooing, as well as dishwashing. The advantage of using this type of soap for dishes is that rinsing becomes less important, allowing you to conserve water when needed. Look for longtime favorites such as *Campsuds* (made by the company that produces Life Tree products), and *Dr. Bronner's* castile soaps. Other concentrated, all-purpose soaps now available include *Commonsense Soap* of Vermont, *Mountain Suds*, *Sea Suds* (for salt water), Kenyon's *Camp Soap*, Austin House's *Bio Suds*, and Sawyer's *Travel Soap*.

Washcloth. Try to find a lightweight washcloth to include in your kit. If you can't, and weight is a concern, cut down an old one to the desired size. This might seem like an extreme measure, but every little bit of weight saved helps. Washcloths are great for hot face washes, and for those times when a "sponge bath" has to take the place of a good shower. One washcloth per family is sufficient.

Shampoo. Except for short-term use, when a liquid body soap will do, you'll want an effective, biodegradable shampoo in your kit. I recommend brands such as *Tom's of Maine* and *Mill Creek* that are better for you and the environment. Take only the amount you need in a small and sturdy watertight plastic bottle. You can restock with local brands if necessary. Families might want to carry shampoo divided between two small containers so mothers and daughters can bathe at the same time as fathers and sons.

Shaving Kit. Pack one reusable razor for a small group, along with a small tray of individual blades. Include a small tube of liquid shaving cream, or simply use some of your concentrated, all-purpose liquid soap for shaving.

Deodorant. Try to find a small, lightweight stick deodorant for traveling. Sample sizes of most popular brands are sold in drug-stores and supermarkets. Outdoor Research also sells small replacement deodorants for their toiletries kit; check with your outdoor retailer for availability. Several natural brands of deodorant are now available, including *Tom's of Maine.*

Travel Mirror. This optional item is nice to have if you can spare the room. If you bring one, make sure it's small and light-weight. Some toiletries kits come with a mirror attached to the inner lining. You could also use one of those miniature mirrors that come with most cosmetics cases. Outdoor retailers usually have a light-weight version for sale, including the *Featherlight Traveler's Mirror* (one ounce) made of unbreakable acrylic, and the *Compact Travel Mirror* (2"x2", folding) that encases one regular and one magnifying mirror. Again, one for the group is sufficient.

Hair Brush and Comb. Bring your hair brush from home if it's small and lightweight, otherwise look for one better suited for travel. One per group is fine.

Nail Clippers, Scissors and Tweezers. Make sure to include a small pair of nail clippers or nail scissors. Tweezers are also indis-pensable when traveling. The scissors and tweezers could be part of your multi-purpose knife or sewing kit.

Toilet Paper and Feminine Pads. A small amount of these items should always be included in your travel kit. That way they'll be with you if and when you need them. Many places don't have public restrooms equipped with toilet paper, and feminine pads can be hard to find off the beaten track. Make sure to keep these items in their own plastic bag so they'll stay dry.

If this sounds like a lot of gear, don't worry—you'll be amazed at what fits into a small kit if the items are compact and well organized. Most trips only require a small amount of each item. Soap and shampoo can be packed in small plastic containers to reduce space. On longer trips, you can restock the small container from a larger one that gets left in the car, at a basecamp, or simply given away. Take several smaller tubes of toothpaste and dental floss, one in the kit and one or two for reserve. Except for toothbrushes, one of each of the listed items is sufficient for a family or small group.

OR's Standard Travel Kit

While you can easily make your own weatherproof toiletries kit with a small nylon stuff sack or heavy duty zip-lock plastic bag, there are some convenient, well-made kits on the market that unfold and hang up for easy access. These typically have bottle and tube pouches, plus a main pocket for additional items. The Eagle Creek *Wallaby* (made of Cordura® nylon) has a separate mesh bag for washcloth storage. Outdoor Research *Travel Kits* of nylon packcloth have a mesh main compartment, and come with a removable mirror as well as standard or optional travel items. The *Ditty Bag* from Caribou has a nylon webbing strap with quick-release buckle, separate waterproof pocket, and a mesh zippered pocket. Atwater Carey offers two sizes of travel kits, *Travel Pack* and *Travel Jr.*, available with or without individual travel items. REI, L.L. Bean, Camp Trails, and Jack Wolfskin also offer toiletries kits.

Costs. These inexpensive organizers cost around $18 to $30 depending on size and travel items included.

Author's Recommendations - Toiletries Kits

Brand	Model	Description
Atwater Carey	Travel Pack***	Packcloth, 6"x8"x2.5" closed,
Atwater Carey	Travel Jr.***	Packcloth, 6"x8"x2.5" closed
Caribou	Ditty Bag**	Packcloth, 4.5"x12" closed, 12"x17.5" open
Camp Trails	Travel Kit**	Packcloth, 5"x9" closed
Eagle Creek	Wallaby**	Packcloth, 7"x13" closed, 22"x13" open
Eagle Creek	Fold-Up Trip Kit**	Packcloth, 6"x10" closed, 10"x17" open
Jack Wolfskin	Washroom**	Packcloth, 7.5"x13" closed, 13"x21" open
Outdoor Res'rch	Compact*	Packcloth, 4.5 "x 9" closed, 9"x9" open
Outdoor Res'rch	Standard*	Packcloth, 5"x9.5"closed, 8"x20" open

OR also offers the Deluxe, a larger version of their standard kit. They also sell small refills of their travel items. Atwater Carey's Travel Jr. comes with Deet-free insect repellent.
*Basic travel items included. **Travel items not included. ***Travel items available separately.

Wash Basin

We've always used one of our large pots for washing up and dish water, but that's not necessary with the new *Folding Wash Basin* available through REI, Adventure 16 and other outdoor suppliers. This lightweight vinyl basin holds about 1.5 gallons of water and is self-supporting when full. It measures 5"x11", weighs four ounces, and costs about $2. Another lightweight alternative is the *Inflatable Kitchen* from Basic Designs. It measures 22"x22"x4"deep when inflated, then rolls up for easy storage. Use these basins for hot water sponge bathing, as a camp wash basin for hands and face, for freeing up your pots by holding dish water, or for soaking hand-laundries overnight.

Towel

You'll also need to include a towel in your personal hygiene inventory. Select one from home that is relatively small and light-weight. For traveling, we often use older towels, ones that have lost some of their bulk. While not as comfortable, they are much lighter and easier to pack. Two towels for a family of four is adequate; that way each adult will have one when showering with a child. If you can't find suitable ones at home, shop for something similar to the standard gym towel used in schools and health clubs. They are perfectly sized and moderately quick-drying.

If weight is of ultimate concern, try the innovative *Packtowl* from Pacific Dry Goods (formerly Hudco), which retails for about $6. Measuring 27" x 10", it is extremely compact and lightweight (1.5 ounces!), and absorbs ten times its weight in water. It is also quick-drying and washable. With these qualities you can afford to bring one for each person. Pacific Dry Goods just introduced two larger versions of their popular "chamois" towels, the *Aquatowl* and the *Megatowl*. Best suited for backcountry and general travel, they are probably not a good beach towel substitute for extended seaside visits.

Laundry Kit

If you have the room, it's not a bad idea to pack a small, light-weight laundry kit for occasional hand laundries and drying clothes. Here are a few hints for hand laundering:

• If you have a sink or small tub available, presoak your cloth-ing in soapy water overnight to help loosen up the dirt and lessen the amount of scrubbing necessary.

• Wring out the wet clothes well before hanging to dry.

Review of Basic Items - Laundry Kit

All you need for a good laundry kit are the following items:

Soap. The concentrated liquid soap you bring is probably fine for occasional clothes washing, too; check on its recommended uses. If one soap serves a variety of needs, make sure to pack an adequate supply. Convenient single-load boxes of powder detergents are available worldwide, but more ecologically suitable brands of powder and liquid detergents must be brought from home. These include products from Seventh Generation, Lifetree, Ecover, Biopac, and Arm and Hammer.

Small Brush. If you are taking an extended trip or washing for more than one person, and you have the room, consider packing a small wooden or nylon-handled brush for scrubbing clothes (similar to a brush for cleaning hands). While not necessary, it is the only way to get hand-laundered items really clean.

Clothesline. About 25 feet of one-eighth-inch nylon will do nicely; no need for a larger diameter line. This can serve as spare line for other needs as well. The length is for reaching between often hard-to-find tie-off points. If you're camping and no other point is available, tie one end to your tent and stake the other to the ground. Placing a short stick under the line near the stake raises it up a bit and keeps your clothes off the ground.

Clothespins. Pack about five plastic clothespins per person. They are lightweight and won't hold in moisture like wooden pins. For an alternative to clothespins, see the Innovative Product listing below.

Net bag. While an optional piece of gear, a medium-size net shopping bag is great for storing dirty laundry, especially when based at one place for a while. It allows the clothing to breathe and is perfect for transporting laundry to and from the wash place.

Innovation - The *Flexo-Line* Traveler's Clothesline

An alternative to standard clothesline is the innovative Flexo-Line. It consists of strands of elastic line braided together. There is no need for clothespins; clothes are attached by opening any point on the braid and inserting a portion of the material. It will not snag garments. The Flexo-Line comes in two versions, the *101 Traveler* (seven foot length stretched dimension, holds up to 12 pounds of wet laundry) and the *102 Backpacker* (seven foot length stretched dimension, holds up to 20 pounds of wet laundry). Cost is around $8; orders may be sent directly to Flexo-Line Company, Box 162, Dunbridge, OH 43414.

PREVENTATIVE GEAR

Sunglasses

This is an important piece of preventative gear for the active traveler, especially those with a low tolerance for bright sunlight. Wearing a hat with an extended front brim helps reduce the amount of light your eyes are exposed to, but good quality sunglasses provide additional protection from the sun's harmful rays, as well as from wind and airborne objects, including insects and road debris. Not only are they better for your eyes, they allow you to have good vision under harsh lighting conditions, times when you need it the most.

You don't have to spend a fortune to get appropriate sunglasses, but you should be careful about what you are buying. Really cheap models may do more harm than good by allowing you to look into bright sunlight without effectively blocking harmful rays. Better makes of sunglasses have specifications that tell how much UV and other radiation they block, as well as how much usable light they transmit. A higher percentage of usable light means better vision. Try to strike a balance by purchasing sunglasses that give good eye protection as well as adequate visibility. After reviewing the individual attributes of currently available sunglasses, select a pair that suit your travel needs, feel comfortable, and have the style you want.

Review of Generic Types - Sunglasses

Sunglasses fall into three general categories: sport, general use and fashion. We are only concerned here with sport models sold by reputable outdoor retailers. Sunglasses are categorized by frame type and by intended use.

By Frame Type. Sunglasses come in three basic frame types.

• *Frame-Style.* The most common is the frame-style, similar in look and construction to regular prescription glasses. You can get a non-prescription version from most outdoor retailers, or prescription sunglasses from your optometrist or specialty retailer.

• *Partial-Frame.* The second type is the partial-frame. On these sunglasses, the polycarbonate single-piece lens serves as part of the support. A partial nylon frame, including temples, is fitted only to the top or the bottom of the lens. On a few models the temples attach directly to the lens with no additional framework other than a nose piece.

• *Clip-On.* The other type is a clip-on version, made to be worn over prescription glasses. These models either clip directly onto the frame of the regular glasses, and can be easily flipped up or removed when not needed.

By Intended Use. Sunglasses are also categorized according to their intended use. By varying the materials and methods of construction, manufacturers can provide the following types of sunglasses:

• *Everyday.* This type is fine for general travel, most outdoor activities, and everyday use. A well-made everyday model will protect your eyes and give good vision under most conditions.

• *High-glare.* This type is best suited for outdoor activities such as canoeing, kayaking, sailing, ski touring or other sports where high-glare conditions are anticipated. These glasses typically have coatings or integral films that eliminate eye-discomforting surface reflection and glare.

• *Extreme Use or Mountaineering.* These sunglasses are made to high standards for extreme lighting situations. They are durable and have excellent optical characteristics under a wide range of conditions, plus optional features that give protection from the wind and cold.

Features and Options - Sunglasses

Features. Sunglasses have two basic components: a set of lenses, and a frame to house the lenses and hold them in position. Frames are available in standard, cateye, aviator, and the new partial-frame models. On partial-frame glasses a single-piece, polycarbonate lens is shaped like an M. A small, straight piece of frame is connected only to the top or bottom portion of the lens. Most sunglasses have a nose piece, or "bridge", located on the bottom of the frame (or lens on partial-frame models). Some models have padded nose pieces for comfort in cold conditions. The temples connect to the frame and hold the glasses on your head; they include the earpiece. Temples come in two earpiece designs, straight-style for general wear or cable-style for active sports. As with the bridge, some models are padded for comfort in cold conditions.

The following are available options:

Visor. Adventure 16 sells the *Sun Shark,* a neoprene visor that actually slips over the temples of your sunglasses, decreasing overhead lighting on your eyes and nose.

Side Shields. Removable leather pieces that attach to the temples and help block wind and unwanted reflected light.

Retainer Straps. These are thin strips of material designed to slip over straight-style temples and wrap securely around the back of your head. They keep sunglasses firmly in place during active sports, as well as accessible (around your neck) when not on your face. *Croakies* are made of fabric-covered neoprene that stretches to give a tight fit; *chums* are made of cotton knit in a continuous tube that has an adjustable length. Both are more comfortable and versatile than cable-style temples.

Case. It always a good idea to protect your sunglasses from abrasion and possible breakage by stowing them in a padded carrying case.

The Basics of Radiation - Sunglasses

The sun's energy comes to us in various wavelengths of solar radiation, categorized as invisible ultraviolet, visible light and infra-red.

Ultraviolet (or UV) is the radiation that can cause the most damage to our skin and eyes, as well as to tent flys and clothing. UV that reaches us on Earth comes as UVB or less harmful UVA (UVC is mostly blocked by the ozone layer). UVB ranges from 290 to 315 nanometers (nm) in wavelength. UVA ranges from 315 to 380 nm. The American National Standards Institute (ANSI) has specific standards for sunglasses: Sport-use models must protect against at least 99% of all UV. Most of the better makes block 100%. Since these standards are not monitored, you won't know if your sunglasses provide effective protection unless they clearly state it. Look for models that guarantee 99 to 100% block of UV up to 400 nm.

Visible Light exists in the range of 400 to 780 nm. It is less harmful than UV, but some evidence exists that blue light in the range of 400 to 450 nm can cause damage to the retina. The eye can not focus blue light easily, so a partial block of this wavelength actually increases vision while protecting your eyes. Visible light is needed in sufficient quantity for proper vision. Sunglasses that are too dark aren't appropriate for some conditions or activities. Lenses that block at least 75% of visible light also provide adequate protection from blue light.

Infra-red radiation exists in the form of heat. Although the eyes are adept at dissipating excess heat, a partial block is desirable, especially for those spending large amounts of time outdoors in sunny climates.

Construction and Operation - Sunglasses

There is quite a lot to this seemingly simple piece of gear. Knowing a little about methods of construction and how sunglasses operate should help you make the right choice.

Lens Material and Shape. Lenses are made from either ground and polished glass, or one of three types of plastics: polycarbonate, CR-39 resin or acrylic. Of the plastics, polycarbonate is much more durable and typically more expensive; CR-39 resin lenses are lightweight, and have good optical qualities and moderate scratch resistance; acrylic lenses scratch easily and are relatively inexpensive. Glass lenses tend to be more optically correct and are more scratch and abrasion-resistant, but are heavier and tend to fog up easily. Polycarbonate lenses are lightweight and more shatter-resistant, with less tendency to fog, but probably won't last as long as glass lenses. "Six-base" refers to a lens design where the curvature is equal to that of the surface of your eyeball, giving minimal light refraction and distortion. Look for this type when buying lenses. Inexpensive sunglasses that don't give true images can cause headaches and potentially can be a safety hazard.

Lens Color and Characteristics. Lenses come in various colors to meet different sunlight conditions. The most common are gray and amber. Occasionally you'll see other tints like green, brown or bronze. A gray tint gives the truest color representation and is good for high levels of sunlight. Polarized gray is the term used for a gray-tinted lens with a polarizing effect. Polarized lenses allow only vertical light waves to pass, eliminating what we refer to as glare. These are best for snow and water sports. Amber-tinted lenses give better contrast and are good for changing conditions, when low light levels or haze may be encountered.

Lens Coatings and Films. There are also a variety of coatings and films to enhance performance. Coatings can be applied to increase scratch resistance (hard coatings), decrease fogging tendency (hard, water-repellent or all-weather coatings), or decrease unwanted reflected light. "Double-gradient" means that the upper and lower portions of the lens receive more coating than the center for a further reduction of reflected light. Some high quality sunglass lenses have an integral photosensitive plate that allow the lens to change color as lighting conditions change.

Author's Recommendations - Sunglasses

I recommend you find sunglasses that filter out 99% to 100% of all UV up to 400 nm. If you are going to be spending much time on the water or snow, make sure to have sunglasses with polarizing lenses. Sideflaps are good for blocking wind and reflected light, but since they also cut down on your peripheral vision, the user should be conscious of this when wearing them. If you currently wear prescription glasses, ask your optometrist or outdoor retailer about prescription sunglasses.

L.L. Bean's Mountain Glasses

Costs. The cost of sunglasses is most often determined by lens material, optical precision, applied coatings, as well as frame material and included options; occasionally it has more to do with a brand name. You can easily pay $100 or more for a good pair of non-prescription sunglasses, but I don't feel it's necessary to pay over $50 for everyday or multi-activity sunglasses, or over $75 for extreme-use sunglasses. Listed below are some of the more reasonably priced, high-quality sunglasses on the market.

Author's Recommendations - Sunglasses for Everyday or Multi-activity

Brand	Model	Lens	Frame	Options
Bolle	Sportglasses	pc, bz; hc, ar	ny, ce and av, st	
Bolle	Mountaineering	ac, br;	ny, ce, st and ct	it, ss, ca
Bolle	Polycarbonate	pc, gr;	ny(ce)/me(av), st	
CEBE	System	pc, br	ny, ce, st	ss, rt
EMS	Trail	pc, gr, hc, ar	ny, ce and av, st	ss
EMS	Timberline	gl, am, hc, ar	ny, ce and av, st	ss
L.L. Bean	Bean/Bolle	ac, gr and am	ny, ce and av, st	ca
L.L. Bean	Double L	pc, gr and am	ny, ce, av, cl	ca
Martin	Econo Everest	pc, gr	ny, ce, ct	ss, rt
REI	Mountain Sport	pc, gr	me, av, st	ss
Smith	Navigator	gl, gr	ny, av, st	

Author's Recommendations - Sunglasses for High-glare Conditions

Brand	Model	Lens	Frame	Options
Bolle	Polarisant	pc, gr, po	ny, ce and av, st	
EMS	Ridge	pc, gr, po, hc, ar	ny, ce and av, st	ss
L.L. Bean	Double L Polar	pc, gr, po	ny, ce, av, cl, st	ca
Martin	Everest Polaroid	pc, gr and am	ny, ce, ct	ss, rt
REI	Polarized Glacier	gl; gr; po	ny, ce, ct	ss, ca
Smith	Polar'd Navigator	gl, gr, po	ny, av, st	

Author's Recommendations - Sunglasses for Extreme Conditions

Brand	Model	Lens	Frame	Options
Bolle	Irex 100 Mtn.	pc, br, hc	ny, ce, st and ct	it, ss, ca
CEBE	Special Mountain	pc, br, ar	me and ny, ro, ct	ss, rt
CEBE	Cecchinel	pc and gl, br, gn	me and ny, av, ct	ss, rt
EMS	Timberline	gl, am, hc, ar	ny, ce and av, st	ss
EMS	Summit	gl, ph, hc, ar	ny, ce and av, st	ss
Julbo	Glacier Glasses	pc, dark am	me, ro and av	ss, ca
L.L. Bean	Mountain Glasses	pc, gr and am	ny, ce	it, ss, ca
Martin	Everest Ultrasafe	pc, gr, ar	ny, ce	ca, rt
REI	SP Glacier	gl and pc,	ny, ce, ct	ss
REI	Karakoram	gl/pc, gr	ny, ce, st	ss, rt, ca
REI	Summit II	gl, ph; dg	ny, ce, ct	ss, rt

LENS TYPE: gl=ground and polished glass, pc=polycarbonate, ac=acrylic; ph=photosensitive.
LENS COLOR: gr=gray, am=amber, gn=green, br=brown, bz=bronze.
FILMS and COATINGS: po=polarized, hc=hard coating, ar=anti-reflective coating, dg=double gradient coating.
FRAME MATERIAL: ny=nylon, me=metal. FRAME STYLE: st=standard, ce=cateye, av=aviator, ro=round, cl=clip-on, st=straight temples, ct=cable temples. OPTIONS: it=interchangeable temples (straight and cable), ss=side shields, ca=case, rt=retainer strap

Sunscreen

Make certain to pack some type of sunscreen. It provides the necessary protection your skin needs when spending time outdoors, especially in conditions of high reflectivity on the water or on snow. For those traveling south for the winter, prodigious use of sunscreen allows your skin to tan slowly and safely. Combine sunscreen use with common sense—cover up during peak hours (10 a.m. to 2 p.m.); wear a hat to shade your face when possible; and don't forget critical places like lips, nose, ears and the backs of hands when sunscreening.

Sunscreens are rated with an SPF number according to the protection they provide from harmful UVB radiation. A sunscreen with an SPF 15 or higher is recommended for general use, and an SPF 20-36 for sensitive areas like nose, lips and ears. There are many good brands of sunscreen currently available. One of the best brands on the market is Chattem's *Bullfrog* sunscreen. PABA-free and available in either gel or lotion, it comes in SPF ratings of 18 or 36. *Bullfrog* sunscreens are virtually waterproof and sweatproof for all-day protection during active sports, and are the sun protection used by the U.S. Navy SEALS. There is now an SPF 18 *Bullfrog* gel just for kids.

I also recommend non-oily, PABA-free sunscreens loaded with moisturizing aloe vera, such as *Bullfrog Moisturizing Gel, Aloe Up, Burn-Off, Dr. Outdoors* and *Sun Stuff*. These brands provide sun protection and skin care in one product. A good broad-spectrum sunscreen to look for is *Photoplex Cream*. Other good sunscreens include REI's *Ultrascreen* (SPF 22 and 29) and Banana Boat's *Regular Sunblock* (SPF 15) and *Baby Sunblock* lotion (SPF 29).

Carry enough sunscreen for your whole trip if you can. At this time, it's hard to find brands rated more than SPF 8 outside the U.S. Keep a small separate tube of sunscreen specially for lips in a convenient spot; lips tend to need frequent reapplications of sunscreen. For good lip protection try *Vaseline Lipscreen* (SPF 15), or products with the brand names listed above.

Skin Cream

Being outdoors in the elements tends to create chapped, dry skin that can be uncomfortable. Find a brand of skin cream that you like that can be used on both hands and face. If you buy a large container for home use, pack some in a small plastic bottle (preferably with a tilt-out spout) for traveling. To prevent chapped lips on your travels, try a good lip balm such as Quantum's *Supple Lips*, a natural cream made of 100% natural ingredients.

Insect Repellent

You may want to bring along some type of insect repellent on your travels if you plan to camp or spend a lot of time outdoors. Some people are more affected by bugs than others, and some destinations are relatively bug-free, while others are notorious for biting pests. Different locations have different insects to combat, the common ones being no-see-ums or midges, typically found in marshy, wet locations; mosquitoes, a universal pest; ticks, including some varieties that transmit Lyme disease; and black flies, prevalent in the woods of Canada and the northern U.S. Exotic destinations seem to have their share of exotic pests. Try to find out what the local conditions are like beforehand and come prepared.

Author's Recommendations - Insect Repellent

Most brands of insect repellent on the market are made from chemicals such as DEET, potentially harmful to humans when absorbed through the skin. Admittedly, they are effective repellents, but products made from harsh chemicals don't make sense for routine use, especially for children. If you're wondering if safe, effective insect repellents are too much to ask for, the answer is definitely not. Several good brands costing around $4 to $7 are now on the market.

Tender Corp.'s Natrapel

Author's Recommendations - Insect Repellents Without DEET

Brand	Model	Description
Avon	Skin-So-Soft	bath oil effective for sand flies, others; pump spray
Kiss My Face	Kiss Off	No DEET; citronella sunscreen (SPF 15), repell'nt
Lakon Herbals*	Bygone Bugs	No DEET or citronella, essential oils; antiseptic
Quantum	Buzz Away**	No DEET; contains pure ess'ntial oils, pump spray
Tender Corp	Natrapel	No DEET; 10% citronella, aloe vera; pump spray

*Distributed by Kenyon. **Also available with an SPF 15 sunscreen for sun protection.*

Author's Recommendations - Insect Repellents With Reduced DEET

Brand	Model	Description
Skedaddle	Child repellent	10% DEET; reduced skin absorption.
3M	Ultrathon	35% DEET; polymer prevents skin absorption
Ben's	Backyard	24% DEET; pump or eco-spray are ozone friendly

Keep in mind that insect repellent is fine for short-term protection, but won't take the place of good netting for sleeping or long-term use in the woods (see Insect Netting below). You can lower your exposure to biting insects by following a few simple rules.

1. Camp in open areas with good exposure to sun and wind.

2. Use only non-perfumed soaps and shampoos.

3. Make sure you have proper netting on your tent or over your bedding. Fine-mesh netting effective against no-see-ums is best.

4. In buggy areas, try to be prepared for the inevitable invasion around dusk each evening. Have your meal preparations done and sleeping arrangements set if possible.

Insect Netting

The use of netting is the most effective way to avoid bites during extended exposure to insects, including while sleeping. Most destinations have low levels of biting insects. For those that have higher levels, the netting on your tent usually provides sufficient protection when camping. For those traveling without a tent, or to places where biting insects are prevalent, other netting options described below are recommended.

Review of Generic Types - Insect Netting

Head nets. Bugs in your face can drive you crazy, especially when trying to concentrate on setting up your tent or other pressing needs. These nets are made to drape over your head for complete face and neck protection. Some have ultra-fine mesh for protection against no-see-ums. Most models have a drawstring to snug them at the bottom and come with or without an integral hat. They look a bit strange, but are invaluable in the deep woods or in black fly country during peak season. Average cost is around $6.

Body suits. Stranger-looking still, net jackets and pants are available for total body protection. They offer the advantage of being able to apply insect repellent to the net suit instead of directly to your skin. For the backwoods traveler only. Average cost for jacket or pants is around $25.

Bed nets. Reminiscent of safari sleeping quarters, these portable nets are truly ingenious, invaluable to those traveling to buggy destinations without tents. Most use the pole technology of light-weight tents to provide a self-supporting net enclosure for one or two sleeping persons. The nice feature of these nets is that they can be set up quickly and used most anywhere—under the stars or inside rooms without screens (including most low-budget accommodations around the world). They also provide much more ventilation than you get when using a regular tent for bug protection.

Author's Recommendations - Insect Bed Netting

EPCO's *Sleepscreen*, available in one or two person models ($35, $50), has a tent-like, self-supported netting over the head and chest area only; additional fabric drapes over bedding. This is the same idea behind Adventure 16's single person *Bug Bivy* ($30), only a continuous, collapsible wire is used instead of poles; this makes it very lightweight and packable. EPCO's spacious *Tropicscreen* ($60) completely encloses two people on the ground or in a bed, or one person in a cot. Long Road's *Indoor Travel Tents* ($99, $109) are similar to the Tropicscreen one and two-person models, only with an integral floor, making them effective protection against ticks, fleas, and other crawling insects. Their one-person *Travel Tent II* is made completely of netting, reducing weight and cost ($49). Long Road also offers their new *Skeeter Defeater*, a lightweight one-person net tent with no floor ($39). Thai Occidental's *The Spider* ($70) is a complete bed netting that hangs from the ceiling and drapes over

EPCO's Sleepscreen I

Long Road's Travel Tent II

the floor instead of being supported with poles, thereby being suitable for all bed sizes.

Author's Recommendations - Insect Bed Netting

Brand	Mode	Description
Adventure 16	Bug Bivy	single person; continuous wire; 6.5 oz.
EPCO	Sleepscreen I	one person; corded poles, stuff sack; 10 oz.
EPCO	Sleepscreen II	two person; corded poles; stuff sack; 23 oz.
EPCO	Tropicscreen	two person; corded poles; stuff sack; 37 oz.
Long Road	Travel Tent single	single bed; net tent with nylon floor; 2.3 lbs
Long Road	Travel Tent double	double bed; net tent with nylon floor; 2.8 lbs.
Long Road	Travel Tent II	single bed; net tent with net floor; 20 oz.
Long Road	Skeeter Defeater	single bed; net tent without floor; 16 oz.
Thai Occidental	The Spider	fits all bed sizes; nylon with stuff sack; 18 oz.

Water Treatment Gear

Having safe drinking water is a real concern for travelers and outdoor enthusiasts. Even when the drinking water is supposedly good, some people are more susceptible to minor stomach disorders caused by unfamiliar, yet essentially harmless bacteria.   In addition, water that is labeled "good for drinking" may have large amounts of chemicals present, including the chlorine that makes the water "good", pesticides, or herbicides. Some destinations have the potential for more serious waterborne microorganisms to be present in local water supplies, making it essential for adventurers to adopt precautionary measures.

Outdoor enthusiasts in the backwoods are presented with a different set of conditions. Even though they may be in a pristine wilderness, the seemingly clean water from ponds and streams may be infested with microorganisms that can cause serious illness. If there is grazing or agricultural land nearby, the possibility exists of water contamination from animal wastes, as well as from pesticides and herbicides.

How to Avoid Contaminated Water

Regardless of how and where you travel, it makes sense to investigate the various ways of avoiding illness due to contaminated drinking water.

You can choose from the following options:

Bottled Water. Using bottled water may be the best bet for short-term travelers. Just remember it tends to be liberally chlorinated. For those on longer trips, the cost of bottled water adds up, as does the number of throw-away plastic bottles. Alternative sources of clean water are needed when traveling to places where bottled water might not be available.

Boiling Water. Choosing this method to kill living organisms in suspect drinking water is in some respects the safest option, but you must have at your disposal some way of heating water. For those travelers carrying stoves, the added fuel use and inconvenience, the length of time required (particularly at high altitude), the poor taste of boiled water, along with the remaining possibility of chemical contamination cause many outdoor enthusiasts to look for other alternatives.

Chemical Disinfectants (Iodine Crystals or Tablets). Iodine crystals or tablets have been used by outdoor travelers for many years. They are relatively inexpensive and easy to carry, yet the nature of chemical additives makes them better suited for emergencies or occasional short-term use rather than repeated or extended use. Some of their drawbacks include the fact that their effectiveness against waterborne organisms depends on water pH and temperature, water clarity, and length of contact time; colder water slows the disinfecting process, particulate matter tends to neutralize the iodine, and effective treatment times may be hard to determine. The look and taste of the water is also affected by chemical use, and the particulate matter remains after treatment.

By its nature, when iodine is used in solution (as opposed to a resin matrix now used in water purifiers), some of the chemical is bound to be present in the water after treatment, often more than is commonly regarded as healthy. Specific health risks are still undetermined at this time, but iodine additives are not considered a good alternative for lengthy trips or use by pregnant women, young children or those with a thyroid disorder. One exception to this is the use of iodine in combination with a water filter as a precaution against viral infection; the iodine kills the virus and the filter takes out the remaining free iodine, as well as any odor or taste.

There are two good brands of iodine disinfectant currently on the market, *Polar Pure* crystals and *Potable Aqua* tablets. Since the proper proportion of iodine crystals required varies with temperature, *Polar Pure* comes in a bottle with an integral thermometer. *Potable Aqua* iodine comes in a convenient tablet form; under normal conditions, one tablet purifies one liter of water using a 10 minute contact time. For very cold or discolored water, two tablets and a 20 minute contact time are recommended. Iodine crystals or tablets begin to lose their effectiveness after opening the bottle, so it's best to restock for each season or trip. Keep in mind that iodine will not remove (some feel it even contributes) to chemical contamination of the water.

Water Treatment Gear. Fortunately for outdoor enthusiasts, there is now a wide choice in effective water filtration and purification gear. They differ widely in operation and cost. Some use mechanical filtration, some use chemical purification, while others offer a combination of the two. To better understand which type is best suited to your needs, let's first examine the various water contaminants, then review the generic types of treatment gear now available.

Water Contaminants

Adventurers and outdoor enthusiasts potentially have four categories of water contaminants to be concerned with. The first three are microorganisms (too small to see with the naked eye) that are enteric (they enter the body via the intestinal tract) and pathogenic (cause illness). These include protozoa and helminths, bacteria and viruses. The fourth category is chemicals.

Protozoa and Helminths. In this category, Giardia protozoa pose the most common threat in temperate climates worldwide, while the larger-size helminths cause concern in tropical climates. These organisms are most often found in backcountry water supplies. Even the smaller protozoa can be effectively removed with a one to two micron filter. They can also be chemically inactivated, but Giardia is a thick-walled cyst that requires adequate contact time to kill when using iodine crystals or tablets.

Bacteria. Microorganisms that cause typhoid, dysentery, and cholera, along with other bacteria that are enteric pathogens, are more typically found in less developed countries. That doesn't mean they can't pose a health hazard elsewhere, especially in the aftermath of a natural disaster. Bacteria multiply readily in surface water. In reality, harmful bacteria can exist anywhere, especially when raw sewage from human settlement finds its way into the drinking water supply. Bacteria can be effectively removed with a 0.1 to 0.4 micron (absolute) filter or killed with proper chemical treatment.

Viruses. Hepatitis A (HAV) and B, herpes, polio and other illnesses caused by viruses are also more commonly a threat in less developed countries. Waterborne viruses can live a long time in water, but require the presence of a host to reproduce. Waterborne viral infections are almost always the result of sewage contamination. At 0.003 to 0.1 microns, they are too small to be effectively filtered. While it's true that viruses typically cling to a host and are often filtered out along with bacteria, there is no guarantee they will remain trapped in the filter. They are only effectively inactivated with proper chemical treatment.

Chemicals. Water can also be contaminated by synthetic organic chemicals such as herbicides and pesticides (including the chlorine used in public water supplies), and volatile organic chemicals such as benzene and carbon tetrachloride. These chemicals can be removed by a properly functioning activated carbon filter. Inorganic chemicals such as arsenic, lead and mercury may also be present. The danger from chemical contamination is often more imagined than real. Short of accidentally ingesting a high concentration of such chemicals, it is generally believed that harmful side effects from trace chemicals usually result from long-term exposure, making it less of a concern to travelers. My personal feeling is that most of the world still has little awareness of, or control over, the dangers of herbicides and pesticides; anything you can do to reduce the risk should be done (including becoming an advocate of pesticide-free lawns). In addition to removing many chemicals, the greatest value of an activated carbon filter is to improve water taste and odor.

Review of Generic Types - Water Treatment Gear

It's important to distinguish one type of water treatment device from another. They perform quite differently and are effective against different types of contaminants. They also vary in cost according to quality and craftsmanship, ease of use, as well as what contaminants they remove.

Filter vs. Purifier. Much confusion has arisen over the liberal use of the terms filter and purifier. There seems to be no industry standard; both terms are used regardless of how the gear functions or what type of contaminants are removed or neutralized. I feel the consumer deserves clarification, so for the purposes of this book water treatment gear that use only mechanical filtration are labeled as water filters, and gear that use only a chemical disinfectant or a combination of filtration and chemical disinfectant are called purifiers.

Small Capacity Travel Cups and Straws. Designed for light use and compact storage, these filters and purifiers are especially handy for single, short-term travelers. They have a more limited capacity than larger capacity versions, but their sleek appearance makes them equally at home at a fine hotel or in the backcountry. These units are relatively low-cost, available as either filter or purifier, and typically have a convenient drinking cup or straw included.

Larger Capacity Hand Pump and Water Carrier Models. These are designed for longer trips by families or other small groups. They typically have a faster rate of treatment or a larger storage capacity, as well as a longer service life. They are still relatively lightweight and compact. The water carrier models can serve double duty as standard water storage devices.

Mechanical Filtration Only. True water filters rely only on very fine filtration to do the job of treating water. These filters are rated by the smallest size contaminant they can remove. Ratings are often given as nominal (not 100% effective at this level), and absolute (level at which unit is 100% effective). When comparing filters, make sure you look for the absolute rating. The size and type of the filter medium varies according to what contaminants that unit is trying to remove. Some inexpensive models currently available only filter to one to two microns absolute since they are mainly concerned with protozoans present in backcountry water. Other models filter down to 0.1 to 0.4 microns absolute. While inherently more expensive, this makes them very effective against protozoans and bacteria. These filters are available as travel cup, hand pump, or water carrier models.

Chemical-Only Purification. The WTC and Accuventure *PentaPure* purifiers currently on the market have no means of mechanical filtration, relying instead on the passing of contaminated water over an iodinated resin for purification. The process is de-mand-release, unlike using iodine in solution. Iodine is used only when contaminants are present. If the supply water is pure, no iodine is released. This is a major safety improvement over crystals or tablets. The basis for this process is naturally occurring electro-static attraction. The contaminants are negatively charged and the resin is positively charged, ensuring contact between the two. These purifiers are reputed to be effective against protozoans, bacteria and viruses. They are conveniently available as straws, travel cups or water jugs. They will not remove chemicals, and may need to be supplemented with some sort of straining device when using turbid water.

Mechanical Filtration Plus Chemical Purification. Several Pur models are also available that use a combination of mechanical filtration to about one micron, effectively removing particulates and protozoans, and an iodinated resin treatment (similar to the *PentaPure* resin) that claims to be effective against all bacteria and viruses. These are currently available as travel cups and in hand pump models.

Features and Options - Water Treatment Gear

Here are the things to look for when shopping for a water filter.

Prefilter. This is usually a separate surface filter that removes larger particles and protects the main filter element from clogging. Prefilters are usually easy to clean. They are either included with the unit or sold as an option.

Pump. Filters require the use of pressure to force the water through in an acceptable amount of time. Most filters have an ergonomically designed pump that is easy to use. Some pumps are integral to the filter, making them easier to use, while others are a separate component from the filter element. All water carrier-style filters and all chemical-only purifiers simply rely on gravity (or suction through a straw) to provide the required pressure.

Body or Housing. This serves as protection for the main cartridge and a convenient place to hold on to during operation. Different models vary in size and shape.

Main Filter/Purifying Cartridge. Water filters and purifiers rely on their main element or cartridge to do the bulk of the work. These cartridges are good for a specific number of gallons of water before they require cleaning or replacement. Some are definitely more easily serviced than others. Most filter cartridges are depth filters, which trap contaminants as they travel through a complex matrix. The matrix can usually be backwashed occasionally to extend its life, but will eventually require replacement. One exception is the Katadyn *Pocket Filter* matrix, which can be scrubbed and reused many times before replacement. The MSR *Waterworks* also employs a final stage membrane with precisely sized holes to complement the depth filter and two-stage prefilter. Surface filters and membranes tend to clog, but are also cleaned quite easily.

Tubing. Most models have tubing that connects the water intake point with the main cartridge, and often the main cartridge with the potable water container. Some units connect directly to a water container, eliminating the need for secondary tubing. Some optional or replacement items are listed below:

Replacement Cartridges. Most units have replacement cartridges in the event that the main element is damaged or has simply exhausted its useful life. The cost of these cartridges varies; replacement cost and frequency should be taken into account when purchasing water treatment gear.

Water Carriers. Some models offer optional water carrying devices that connect to the unit for ease of operation.

Carbon Filters. Some of the purifiers on the market offer optional carbon filters that can be attached for improved taste and removal of trace chemicals and odor.

Bottle Adapters. Some models, such as the Pur *Scout* and *Explorer*, have optional adapters so the treated water can flow directly into a wide-mouth Nalgene bottle.

Spares and Repair Kit. These are available for most filters on the market.

Construction and Operation - Water Treatment Gear

Water treatment gear housings and tubing are typically made of plastic or rubber. On water filters the main cartridge is usually constructed of either ceramic or a special carbon matrix. Water purifier cartridges are either iodinated resin-impregnated fiber, as in all Pur models, or simply encapsulated iodinated resin as in the case of all *PentaPure* products. Despite their differences, operation is similar for all filters and purifiers. For small capacity travel cups, suspect water is poured into an integral cup or holding area. The water is then drawn through the main cartridge by hand pumping or gravity feed. Travel straws are used just like regular straws. Suspect water is drawn in and purified as it passes through the tube. Larger capacity models use either an intake hose and hand pump to draw water directly from a stream, pond, or storage container, or they use an integral water carrier and rely on gravity to do the work. Treated water is then fed into a potable water container directly or through additional tubing. If the gravity feed unit is filtering the water (two of the Basic Designs models) as opposed to chemically purifying it (as with the WTC models) treatment time will be much greater. This is usually no problem since the unit can be hanging in camp and working while you do other things.

Keep in mind that the effectiveness of water purifiers relying on chemical treatment varies with temperature in the same way, but to a much lesser degree, as iodine crystals or tablets. Very cold water may have to be purified more slowly (more contact time) and sometimes more than once. Check with the manufacturer for their recommendations. Refer to Maintenance and Repair for main cartridge cleaning procedure.

Author's Recommendations - Water Treatment Gear

Taking all this information into account, which type of unit is best for your needs? I feel the units described below are well designed, practical and reasonably priced.

Single Travelers. Single travelers can take their choice of the low-cost, light-use travel purifiers in the form of straws (extremely lightweight and compact) or travel cups that make a cup of pure water at a time without the need for pumping.

Backcountry and General Travel. For backcountry and general travel, I'd use any of those listed below. Of the filters listed, I like the superb engineering of the MSR and Katadyn, the size and price tag of the First Need, the price and easy operation of the Basic Designs models, the design and effectiveness of the Pur models, and the easy, worry-free operation of the WTC models. Any of the models listed that rely strictly on filtration could provide complete protection if supplemented with the use of iodine tablets when needed, including the Basic Designs models which are intended primarily for larger bacteria and protozoa.

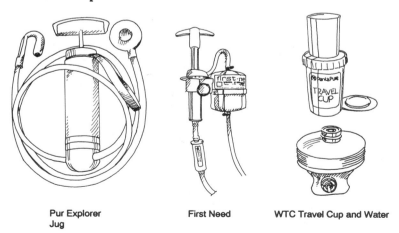

| Pur Explorer Jug | First Need | WTC Travel Cup and Water |

Extended World Travel. For extended world travel, I'd ultimately choose a purifier that employs filtration for particulates, protozoa and larger bacteria; the point-of-contact chemical treatment of an iodinated resin matrix for smaller bacteria and viruses; and a carbon filter to remove residual tastes and chemicals. The only two models currently available that claim to do all that are the Pur *Scout* and Pur *Explorer* (with their optional carbon filter attached). Another intriguing option is the WTC water jug—just pour water into the carrier and purified water can be drawn out of the built-in spigot. WTC claims their iodinated resin is effective against all waterborne organisms. Side benefits are that no pumping is required and the fact that the collapsible jug can double as your water storage container. Even though it employs no filtering mechanism, it does have a sediment trap at the bottom of the jug. WTC recommends using a coffee filter or cheesecloth to catch larger particulates. The replaceable cartridge has carbon filter material built in to improve taste.

Costs. The light use travel purifiers vary widely in cost, from $25 for WTC's simple cup up to $60 for Pur's elegant *Traveler.* Heavy use water filters also vary, from $40 for the *First Need,* $60 to $75 for the Basic Designs and Pur *Scout* models, around $130 for MSR's *Waterworks* and Pur's *Explorer,* to the high-end Katadyn *Pocket Filter* at around $240.

Author's Recommendations - Light-Use Travel Purifiers

Brand	Model	Type	Main Purifier	Cartridge Life	Wgt.
Accufilter	Straw	chem.	iodine resin	50 gal.	0.75 oz.
Accufilter	Sport Bottle	chem.	iodine resin	65 gal.	2.75 oz.
Gen Ecology	Trav-L-Pure	.01 mic. mech.	carbon matrix	100 gal	22 oz.
Pur	Traveler	mech. and chem.	resin in fiber	100 gal.	13 oz.
WTC	Cup Purifier	chem. **	iodine resin	100 gal.	4 oz.

Author's Recommendations - Heavy-Use Water Treatment Gear

Brand	Model	Type	Main Purifier	Cartridge Life	Wgt.
Basic Designs	Ceramic filter	1.0 mic. mech.	ceramic, int.	1,000 gal.	12 oz.
Basic Designs	High Flow	1.0 mic. mech.	ceramic, ext.	1,000 gal.	12 oz.
Basic Designs	Filter Pump	0.9 mic. mech.	ceramic, ext.	500 gal.	N/A
Gen. Ecology	First Need	0.1 mic. mech.	carbon matrix	100 gal.	15 oz.
Katadyn	Pocket Filter	0.2 mic. mech.	ceramic	reusable	23 oz.
MSR	Waterworks***	0.1 mic. mech.	4-stage filter	varies	18 oz.
Pur*	Scout*	mech. and chem.	resin in fiber	200 gal.	12 oz.
Pur	Explorer*	mech. andchem.	resin in fiber	300-500 gal.	21 oz.
WTC	Water Jug**	chem.	iodine resin	100 gal.	16 oz.

*Optional carbon filter. **Optional mech. filter to 20 microns. ***Optional ceramic filter replaces metal screen and carbon filter (stage 2 and 3).*

The Pur models have a 1.0 micron mechanical filter. The Basic Designs Ceramic Filter and High Flow models (3 gal. water carrier included), as well as all WTC models, use gravity feed.

Maintenance and Repair - Water Treatment Gear

Here are six things you can do to keep your filter in good working order.

Use Clear Supply Water. Try to use supply water that is relatively clear of particulate matter; if possible, take water from near the surface of lakes and ponds, in a relatively calm area without stirring up the bottom. This reduces time spent on cleaning the prefilter and extends cartridge life. Buy the optional prefilter when available.

Pump Slowly. On hand pump models, pump slowly and smoothly. This increases effectiveness and decreases risk of damage.

Clean or Replace Cartridge. Clean the cartridge as required according to manufacturers recommended procedure. Some units can be backwashed to extend cartridge life (General Ecology and Pur models), others require disassembly for cleaning (Basic Designs, Katadyn, and MSR models). Pur *Scout* and *Explorer* models require less cleaning since they don't use as fine a filter. When they do need cleaning they have a convenient backwash procedure—simply twist the handle and continue pumping. The iodinated resin inactivates contaminants used in the backwashing procedure. General Ecology units must be backwashed using filtered water with a few drops of household bleach (for the chlorine content) or iodine tablets added. Some disassembly is required. Ceramic filters can typically be removed and cleaned, and even scrubbed a bit to expose a new layer of filter. This can greatly extend cartridge life. WTC purifiers require no backwashing or cleaning since they employ no filter.

Sanitize if Necessary. Some filters that employ no chemical treatment should be sanitized after cleaning or before storage. This includes General Ecology, MSR and Basic Designs models. The Katadyn unit has a silver impregnated inner core in the main cartridge that inhibits bacterial growth, so no sanitizing is required.

Keep it Clean. Wipe clean and dry your filter or purifier before storage.

Protect it. Take care not to drop your filter if possible, and be careful how you pack it for travel. The main cartridge can be damaged and require replacement. Be especially careful of ceramic elements. General Ecology offers a dye kit that allows you to test the integrity of their compressed carbon cartridge. This is less of a concern for the MSR, Pur and WTC models.

EMERGENCY GEAR

The final category under health and hygiene is emergency gear, items you'll be glad you have but hope you don't have to use. A little forethought and preparation can give you much peace of mind when traveling.

First Aid Kits

Every adventurer should pack a well-stocked first aid kit, regardless of how and where you travel. You can buy one of the many preassembled first aid kits on the market, or prepare your own. For many years we have put together our own kit, buying what we need at discount drugstores and carrying them in strong zip-lock plastic bags. This low-cost solution has allowed us to tailor the type and amount of the included items to our destination, climate and children's ages. There are several disadvantages, however, to making up your own kit. In the first place, you must determine what items are important for your needs and spend time shopping for them. Secondly, your first aid kit tends to look like other things in your pack or pannier when stored in a plastic bag. Ideally, it should be instantly recognizable during emergencies. Placing it in a red nylon bag will help, as will storing it in a separate, easily accessible pocket of your pack. The last consideration is that you may spend valuable time searching through the contents of a plastic or nylon bag looking for what you need. Kits that fold out or open up completely, such as the travel organizers from Outdoor Research, are much better. There are some wonderful preassembled kits on the market that solve these problems and take the guesswork out of what to bring with you.

Author's Recommendations - First Aid Kits

I feel the best kits on the market are made by Adventure Medical Kits, Atwater Carey and Outdoor Research. All three companies offer rugged, lightweight kits that are perfect for oudoor traveling.

Adventure Medical Kits. Adventure Medical Kits was founded by Dr. Eric A. Weiss, an assistant professor of Emergency Medicine at Stamford University. Each kit they supply comes with a copy of *A Comprehensive Guide to Wilderness and Travel Medicine* written by Dr. Weiss. They offer five versions of their Adventure Kits, from the basic *Optimist* (cost around $16) to the *Comprehensive* (cost around $120). Adventure Medical Kits now offers their new *Traveler Kit*, one of the most complete first aid kits available for worldwide travel. They also have special models geared for whitewater paddlers, as well as other kits made just for cyclists. All of their kits are well designed and produced. I especially like the detachable inner bag that comes with the Comprehensive Kit. It has belt loops and can be used separately for day trips.

AMK's Backcountry First Aid Kit

Adventure Medical kits are made of tough water resistant nylon and sturdy nylon handles for carrying. This company also sells the empty bags and individual components so you can build your own first aid kit. They also market *Oral Rehydration Packets,* formulated to help replace fluids in diarrheal illness and dehydration.

Atwater Carey. Buck Tilton, Director of the Wilderness Medicine Institute and noted author, heads up product development for Atwater Carey. This company offers a wide range of medical kits, from general kits such as the *Family, Trekker II,* and *Expedition,* to the compact sport-specific first aid packages such as the *Day Hiker, Walkabout,* and the *All-Terrain Bicycle,* to the watertight *Whitewater* and *Wilderness Canoe* kits, to professional medical backpacks such as the *EMT Mini* and the *Mountain Rescue.* They also offer innovative *First Aid Modules* that enhance existing kits by upgrading content inventories to target a specific need, or serve to refill depleted items in kits returned from the field.

Outdoor Research. OR makes a series of five first aid kits for backcountry and general use, from their *Basic, Compact,* and *Standard* units ($25-$50) to their *Advanced* and *Expedition* models ($75-$110). These are intended for times when you might be far from a doctor. They also offer three sizes of what they call *Traveler's Health Kits* ($21-$60). These concentrate on supplying the basics, plus allow you to cope with common travel ailments like fever, cough, indigestion and diarrhea. They leave out some of the heavy-duty items such as wire splints and bandage compresses. Each kit is accompanied by *The Pocket Doctor,* a small invaluable reference for the traveler.

Outdoor Research (OR) kits are made of tough nylon pack cloth with a waterproof coating, a nice touch if you have to spread it out on wet ground or snow. You can buy OR organizer bags separately if you care to create your own first aid kit.

For those inclined to assemble their own first aid kit, the chart below lists the items included in two of OR's kits of appropriate size for a family or small group. It is not necessarily a complete list of what you need, but it does give an idea of the various types of items you should be considering for your kit. You should carefully examine your own requirements before purchasing or creating a first aid kit. Any of the models on the market can be added to or modified to suit your needs.

Items Included	Traveller's Health Kit	First Aid Kit (standard)
water purification tablets	50	—
anti-diarrheal tablets	24	—
electrolyte replacement tablets	20	—
analgesic tablets	24	12
antacid tablets	12	6
decongestant tablets	12	—
antihistamine tablets	6	6
cough-control lozenges	8	—
sore throat lozenges	4	—
pill vials with labels	4	4
3/4" bandages	8	—
1" bandages	8	—
XL bandages	4	—
adhesive bandages, 1"x3"	—	12
fingertip bandages	4	—
knuckle bandages	4	—
butterfly bandages	6	6
triangular bandage	—	1
wire mesh splint	—	1
3"x3" gauze pads	4	6 (4"x4")
3"x4" Telfa pads	4	—
eye pads	2	—
2" x 5 yrd gauze roll	1	2
1" adhesive tape	1	—
2" adhesive tape	—	1
moleskin, 3.5"x3.5"	2	2
3" elastic bandage	1	—
needle	1	1
tweezers	1	1
scissors	—	1
razor blade	1	1
thermometer	1	1
anti-bacterial towelettes	6	6
antibiotic ointment pkts	6	6
cortisone cream, 1 oz.	1	—

tincture of benzoin, 1 oz.	—	1
providone iodine cleanser, 1 oz.	—	1
zip-top plastic bags	—	2
accident report form	—	1
pencil	—	1
first aid manual	1	1

Babies and Toddlers. Babies and toddlers require a little extra care in planning a first aid kit. Include the following in your kit, or in a special baby travel bag, when adventuring with little ones: corn starch, A and D or Desitin ointment, bacitracin, baby Tylenol, Pepto-Bismol, aloe vera gel, hydrogen peroxide, sunscreen, thermometer, ipecac syrup and amoxycillin (2 courses).

Prescription Medicines

Many preassembled first aid kits on the market come with empty pill vials for prescription medicines. Besides packing medication that you might currently be taking, it's a good idea to include one general antibiotic for the rare emergency. We favor amoxycillin, an excellent all-purpose drug used to treat ear, nose, throat, sinus, respiratory, and urinary tract infections. Amoxycillin is appropriate for both children and adults. Carry enough for two courses (or 20 days). Beyond that, only extended backcountry or remote travel would warrant the need for a more comprehensive medical list.

Since customs officials and local gendarmes can be highly suspicious of prescription drugs you are carrying, it's a good idea to store them in your first aid kit. This will help to convince them that these are medical necessities. Even better is to make sure the kit is well marked as such, with the international Red Cross symbol or other recognizable markings.

Emergency Kit

There are times when some simple emergency items can give us extra peace of mind. It is a good idea to have a few emergency items in addition to your usual first aid kit, especially for day outings in the backcountry when you've left the majority of your gear back at your camp or base. Day trips of hiking, bicycling, canoeing, or ski touring can often take you away from the security of the basic equipment you left behind—things like a tent, sleeping bag, stove, water purification gear, and food. In the case of an accident or the onset of bad weather, you should be prepared to cope until you can get back to safety. I want to emphasize again that bad things don't happen any more often on the road than they do at home. All this talk of first aid and emergency kits shouldn't put you off traveling in the outdoors. These kits should help you feel confident that you can deal with unexpected situations. Of course, the knowledge of how to use them is also important.

One way to be prepared for emergencies is to include a few additional survival items in with your first aid kit. If you can't fit them in, buy or make a separate little pouch that holds basic emergency gear. Carry this stuff in a small cooking pot and you'll be able to make a warm drink, undeniably comforting in troubled times. Make sure to take both first aid and emergency gear with you on all day trips to remote areas, even on easy outings in nice weather. The one time you leave them behind might be the time you really need them. The following is a list of recommended emergency items. This is in addition to sensible items like adequate clothing, rain protection, and ample food and water.

Author's Recommendations - Emergency Kit
Basic Items to Include:

Compass	High energy food, drink
Damp-proof matches	Water bottle and purifying tablets
Fire starting tabs	Small pot, tea bags, broth
Needle and thread	Emergency shelter, all weather blanket
Small diameter cord	Safety pins
Rescue whistle	Razor blade
Signal mirror	Fishing line, hooks (optional)

One alternative to making your own emergency kit is to purchase one of the small cannisters produced by MPI Outdoor Safety Products. These sealed waterproof cannisters not only hold most necessary emergency items, they double as a pot or drinking cup when opened. Look for *You Can Survive* and *You Can Survive Two*.

Specialty Gear

- Sewing Kits
- Utility Knives
- Clocks, Watches
- Cameras
- Binoculars
- Compasses
- Maps
- Flashlights
- Daypacks
- Duffels
- Sleeping Gear
- Travel Pouches
- Eating Utensils
- Recreation
- Net Bags

In addition to your clothing and health and hygiene gear, there are some other items that can make outdoor recreation and travel more comfortable and enjoyable. I've lumped this equipment into one category called Specialty Gear. It's up to you which ones to include for any given trip, but be ruthless when selecting them in order to maintain a comfortable packing size and weight. It's easy to allow those harmless ounces to become backbreaking pounds.

SEWING KITS

This category straddles the line between sewing and general repair. I feel it's essential that you equip yourself for basic repairs to clothing and other gear while traveling in the outdoors. The sewing kit and the expertise you acquire with it will serve you equally well at home or on the road. It wasn't so long ago that our ancestors had the basic skills to repair almost everything they owned. Over the years more complex possessions, more disposable income and a throwaway culture have combined to make us thoughtless consumers in what is termed a "growth economy". The notion of repairing, reusing and making do have fallen out of fashion temporarily, but it's expensive and wasteful not to perform simple repairs to your gear. There is a good feeling that comes from this degree of self-sufficiency, and the real point for adventurers is that there may be no replacement gear available at your destination.

Most of the pre-assembled kits on the market are more appropriate for the car glove compartment on weekend jaunts than for a backpack or pannier during extended active travel. A few light-duty needles, a few small spools of weak thread and some buttons in a breakable plastic box is not my idea of being prepared. There are a few models currently marketed as tent or backcountry repair kits. These have the more durable needles and thread you'll need for repairing outdoor gear, but many leave out some of the general sewing items you'll want to bring along. If you find a kit that suits your needs and the type of trip you're planning, by all means buy it; you can always supplement it. If not, it's easy enough to prepare your own.

Author's Recommendations - Sewing Kits

I recommend carrying a kit that can deal with more than just a torn shirt or a loose button. One of the better ones I've seen for active travel is Safesport's *Expedition Sewing Kit*, available from many outdoor retailers. At just 1.5 ounces, it has the standard sewing items plus heavy duty needles and thread, and an awl for making thread holes in leather and really tough fabrics. The awl is needed because a thimble just won't work for those materials. Sailors use a leather sewing palm to force sturdy needles through tough fabrics; it's based on the idea of a thimble, only worn on the hand, with a hard contact area on the palm for pushing the needle. While a little bulky for single travelers, one could be packed for extended group travel.

Another good sewing kit is the *Murphy's Law Backcountry Repair Kit* by Outdoor Essentials. Its 4"x6" waterproof pouch is resealable and the total kit weighs only 3.5 ounces. Other good alternatives are Kenyon's *Hiker's* and *Camper's Nylon Tent Repair Kits*.

If you want to put together one kit that will handle all your repair needs, a good solution is to buy a lightweight travel pouch such as the smallest *Outdoor Organizer* from Outdoor Research; it folds out and has multiple compartments. Then buy one of the sewing kits available and supplement it with other things you'll need. Or buy one of the larger size organizers and combine first aid, emergency and repair kits in one; keep it handy and you'll be prepared for almost anything.

The following list of repair items would serve a family or small group on an extended trip.

Basic Sewing and Fabric Repair Items

2	light-duty needles	8	buttons
2	heavy-duty needles	4	snaps
25	yds regular colored thread	4	straight pins
15	yds nylon thread	4	small safety pins
15	yds waxed polyester thread	4	large safety pins

1	thimble	2	3"x12" strips of repair tape
1	needle threader	2	nylon fabric patches
1	lightweight scissors	1	no-see-um netting patch (optional)
1	small sewing awl	1	small amount of light gauge wire

MULTI-PURPOSE KNIVES

The term "multi-purpose" is used to distinguish this type of knife from the regular variety limited to only one or two blades. You may carry a small pocket knife for general use, but consider packing a multi-purpose knife when you go traveling. We always keep ours handy, including on day trips and shorter excursions. It's truly amazing how often it gets used. Cutting line, carving wood, repairing gear, driving screws, opening bottles and cans, uncorking wine bottles, preparing meals, trimming paper, cutting fingernails, removing splinters, punching holes in leather, reaming holes in wood, and stripping wire are just some of its uses.

You can choose from many of the various multi-purpose knives on the market. Different models offer different accessories. I'd steer clear of the old fork, knife and spoon models—too heavy and bulky. Stick with small, lightweight versions that give you just the accessories you need. Standard items offered include several flat blades for cutting (one small and one large), bottle and can opening blades with slot screwdriver ends, collapsible scissors, reaming tool, Phillips screwdriver, corkscrew, toothpick, tweezers, even items like a saw blade, pliers, and a fish cleaning tool. Not everyone on the trip needs to carry a multi-purpose knife. One per family or small group is sufficient.

Author's Recommendations - Multi-Purpose Knives

The Swiss Army knives by the Swiss companies of Victorinox and Wenger, as well as the SwissBuck models by Buck Knives, are the most practical, durable knives you can buy. They are moderately priced, versatile, lightweight and superbly crafted. Their most practical versions for travelers are listed below.

Victorinox. I recommend the *Climber* ($26) and the *Super Tinker* ($29). Both have two cutting blades, can and bottle openers with slot screwdriver ends, scissors, reamer, toothpick and tweezers. The fun-loving *Climber* also has a corkscrew, while the more earnest *Super Tinker* substitutes a Phillips screwdriver and pliers. My only wish is that they offered a version of this knife with all three—a corkscrew,

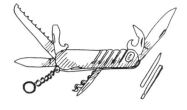

Victorinox's Climber   Buck Knives' Trekker

pliers, and a Phillips screwdriver. Other good Victorinox models for
active travelers include the "lockback" knives—full size, with longer
blades and locking mechanism to prevent accidental opening. The
Rucksack ($26), has one blade, a bottle and can opener, a flathead
screwdriver, a corkscrew, a reamer, a saw blade, a toothpick and
tweezers.

Wenger. This company has similar models to those described
above. The *Hunter* and the *Traveler* have the corkscrew, the *Backpacker II* substitutes a saw blade for the scissors, and the *Handyman*
substitutes a Phillips screwdriver for the corkscrew and adds a saw
blade.

Buck Knives. Buck Knives also has a good line of multi-purpose
knives called SwissBuck. Their most practical SwissBuck models for
active travelers include the *Trekker* (similar to the *Backpacker II*
described above) and *The Remedy* (similar to the *Handyman* described
above).

CLOCKS AND WATCHES

Despite the desire to get away from it all when traveling, it's nice
to have the option of knowing what time it is. You might want to
time yourself on a hike or other outing, or you might want to set the
alarm so you can get up and break camp in time for the sunrise.

Author's Recommendations - Clocks and Watches

Travelers have the option of carrying a watch with an alarm or
packing one of the compact travel alarm clocks now on the market.

Travel Clocks. If you prefer a travel clock, find one that is
lightweight, durable and a miser on batteries. Some travel clocks
operate on small watch or camera batteries, others on one or two

AAs. It should also have a protective cover that folds open for stand-up use, then closes over the face during storage and travel. Lorus offers a great travel clock, the *International Travel Alarm* ($20), marketed through L.L. Bean and other retailers. It's rotating bezel shows time in 19 major international cities and indicates 24 time zones for global reference. This clock is powered by a small battery that reportedly lasts one year.

Radio Shack offers a similar version of this type of travel clock, the *LCD World Time* ($20). They also have other models to choose from, including the *LCD Travel Alarm* ($18) and the *LCD Micro Travel Alarm* ($13). We've used one of their travel clocks for years without a problem. They include liquid crystal display, on-demand light, and an alarm. Most models run on a small watch battery. Adventure 16 carries two models of travel clocks from Jean Clement, the *Travel Alarm Clock* (requires one AA) and the *Travel Flashlight/Alarm* (requires two AAs). Remington also makes a nice little travel alarm clock, available through Campmor and other retailers, that runs on one AA battery.

Watches. For single travelers a lightweight watch with a reliable alarm is probably the best option. Keep it in your daypack or travel pouch if you don't like wearing it on your wrist. Liquid crystal displays are most efficient, but battery life can vary. Lithium batteries have a longer life, a consideration on extended trips. There are many models suitable for active travel. If you'd rather have a watch with a classic analog display (not digital), and an alarm isn't something you feel the need for, REI and Early Winter both offer handsome, yet rugged, active sports watches with quartz movement for around $80. The *Sportsman's Watch* by Casio has both digital and analog readout, plus an alarm and built-in compass for about $70. Timex offers both digital and analog watches for active travelers, including models in their *Guide Series* and their *Adventure/Aviator Collection*. Many models come equipped with Timex's *Indiglow* electroluminescent technology.

CAMERAS

It is a natural inclination to want to preserve outdoor memories on film, and there are many good 35mm cameras to choose from. You may also be entertaining thoughts of writing about your adventures, in which case accompanying photographs can be helpful. In either case you'll be richly rewarded if, in addition to the gear you buy, you take the time to learn some proper photo techniques, as well as how to be a courteous and discriminating photographer.

Basic Outdoor Photography Hints

Here's some basic hints that should help you get off on the right foot.

Be Selective. Resist the urge to record everything you see on film. Some situations produce good photographs, while other are best visualized in your memory. Be selective when choosing what and how much to film.

Lighting. As this is the most important condition for good photography, learn what to look for. Early morning or late afternoon, when the sun's angle is lowest in the sky, is the best time for proper lighting, resulting in exceptional photographs.

Contrasts. A scene where everything is washed out will look washed out on film. Look for contrasts between light and dark, or supply some yourself (a bright backpack in a wooded scene, a colorful door against a pale building, flowers in a subdued surrounding).

Get Close. Try to close in on your subject. Most poor photography looks disappointingly distant, with the focal point lost in the surroundings. Use a telephoto lens or bring your camera very close to whatever it is you want to film. Photographing people is always best up close. Even scenery shots are best limited to one area rather than trying to capture an entire vista.

Frame Your Shot. Take the time to frame your shot first. Avoid things like too much sky, unbalanced shots of people, or objects cut off at the wrong spot.

Author's Recommendations - Cameras

Any good 35mm camera now available is fine for outdoor photography. Once the basic techniques are mastered, you can increase your effectiveness with optional lenses and accessories. If you tend to travel with a hiking stick, try a lightweight, aluminum telescoping model such as the Tracks *Sherlock Travel Staff,* or the wooden, two-part Wind River *Hiking Staff* marketed by Adventure 16. Both models break down for travel and can also serve as a camera monopod for increased steadiness while shooting, something that's especially helpful when using a heavy telephoto lens or when shooting in reduced lighting conditions. Automatic cameras are easier to use, although manually-operated models allow for greater user adjustment, are less prone to disrepair, and don't run through batteries as easily (the only battery use on a manually-operated camera is for the light meter and flash).

If traveling light is your main concern, choose from the many featherweight, automatic travel cameras now available. Prices range from $150 for good quality basic models to $275 for high-end cameras. These practically foolproof wonders are equipped with automatic everything—focus, exposure settings, wind and rewind, even zoom capability.

Olympus Super Zoom 3000

Author's Recommendations - Compact Travel Cameras

Brand	Model	Description
Minolta	Zoom 90	35mm, autofocus, 38-90mm autozoom
Minolta	Weathermatic	35mm, fully automatic, waterproof
Nikon	Zoom Touch 800	35mm, autofocus, 37-105mm autozoom
Nikon	Sport Touch	35mm, autofocus, splashproof
Olympus	Super Zoom 3000	35mm, autofocus, 38-110mm autozoom
Olympus	Infinity Zoom 220*	35mm, autofocus, 28-56mm autozoom
Pentax	IQ Zoom 90	35mm, autofocus, 35-90mm autozoom

Includes panoramic wide angle lens.

Camera Accessories

There are a few additional items you might want to consider when traveling with your camera.

Camera Bag. Always carry your camera in a well-padded camera bag to protect your investment. Camera bags are typically made of tough, water repellent nylon with an internal lining of soft fabric. Most large models have universal sizing and are capable of holding a full-size 35 mm camera and an additional lens. In addition to great backpacks, Lowe makes a good line of camera bags: their petite *AF-1* and *Shoulder Pouch* are for compact models; the *Top Load Zoom* holds a full size camera with zoom attached; the *Orion Belt Pack* is carried around your waist and holds a full size camera and several lenses; the *Elite Convertible* holds a full size camera and up to four lenses and can be worn as either a shoulder bag or belt pack; and the *Photo Trekker* is a daypack-size camera bag for your photo items, lunch and other gear. L.L. Bean and Caribou offer nice padded camera cases for compact models.

Film Protector. You may also want to protect your film from airport security X-rays. The *Filmshield,* sold by many camera and outdoor retailers, protects up to 22 rolls of film (or a small camera) in a 6"x12.5" lead-lined pouch. There are two models, one for up to 400 speed film (approximately 4.5 ounces, around $10), and one for up to 1000 speed film (approximately seven ounces, around $15).

Monopod. A monopod is a one-legged stand that serves to steady the camera for shooting in poor lighting or with heavy lenses attached. It weighs much less than a tripod and can double as a hiking stick. For more information on combination hiking sticks/ camera monopods, refer to the Specialty Gear section of Backpacking.

BINOCULARS

For the avid birder or inquisitive budding naturalist, binoculars can help make explorations more fun and educational. Outdoor travelers can't afford to pack a heavy, bulky piece of gear, and therefore must find binoculars that are lightweight, compact and able to withstand the rigors of the outdoors. In addition to comparing the size and weight of various compact models when shopping for binoculars, compare the features listed below.

Features and Options - Binoculars

Look for the following features when comparing binoculars:

Magnification Factor or Power. This is a number that tells how much closer an image will seem when looking through the binoculars than it actually is. Typical magnification factors are 7x, 8x, or

10x. This means that if you are looking at a bird 100 feet away, it will seem 10 feet away with a 10x pair of binoculars.

Lens Size. There are two lenses in a pair of binoculars. The ocular lens is the smaller one closest to your eyes, and the objective lens is the larger one at the end farther away from your eyes. It is the diameter in millimeters of the objective lens that is specified by manufacturers. Lens size is typically in the range of 21 to 25 millimeters. A larger lens lets in more light and gives a brighter image.

Field of View. The field of view is the width of the area seen through the binoculars for a given distance. Since this number changes with distance, it is usually specified as field of view in feet at a distance of 1000 yards. There is a wide range of fields of view among the various compact travel binoculars available.

Prism Type. All binoculars use prisms to help increase their power without the need for large lenses with long focal lengths. Prisms bend light without distorting it; this makes light travel a greater distance and increases the focal length in another way. This, in turn, increases power. Conventional binoculars use porro prisms, which allow more brightness, while compact versions use roof prisms for their light weight.

Focusing. Center focusing is currently the most common method employed. Focusing is quickly accomplished by using a single dial centered between the two lenses. Setting the proper pupil distance for each user is done by swinging the binocular barrels either closer together or farther apart.

Body Styles. There are three basic body styles: European, American and compact. The European version uses separate barrels to house the objective lens and prisms. The American style houses both the objective lens and prisms in one body piece. This is somewhat sturdier but also more expensive. Compact travel binoculars use a single body similar to the American style, but they reduce size by using roof prisms and reduce weight by using lighter body materials.

Eye Cups. These are the soft rubber cups that surround each ocular lens. Be sure to have eye cups that roll back if you plan to wear sunglasses or corrective lenses while viewing.

Armor Coating. A coating of rubber on the outside of the binoculars protects them from scratches and bumps, and makes

Author's Recommendations - Binoculars

Some of my favorite compact binoculars for active travel are listed below. I also like the single lens *Armored Monocular* (viewed with one eye) sold by REI. It is featherweight and reasonably priced (three ounces, around $50).

Cost. You'll spend anywhere from $90 to over $200 for a good quality pair of travel binoculars, including the models listed below. While you could spend much, much more on high quality optical masterpieces, most people don't need that level of craftsmanship for general use. If you do want something more precise, try higher quality models from these manufacturers, or other brands such as Leica, Steiner, Swarovski or Zeiss.

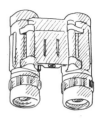

L.L. Bean's
Compact Binoculars

Author's Recommendations - Compact Binoculars

Brand	Model	Magn.	Lens Size	Field of View	Wgt.
Binolux	Wide-Angle	8	21	372 ft.	N/A
Binolux	10x25	10	25	288 ft.	N/A
Brunton	8x21 Lite-Tech	8	21	315 ft.	7.5 oz.
Brunton	8x25 Waterproof	8	25	315 ft.	14.8 oz.
EMS	8x21	8	21	367 ft.	6.7 oz.
EMS	10x24	10	24	315 ft.	12.7 oz.
L.L. Bean	Compact Binoc.	8	25	430 ft.	10 oz.
L.L. Bean	Compact Binoc.	10	25	289 ft.	12 oz.
L.L. Bean	Waterproof	8	25	315 ft.	12 oz.
Minolta	8x22	8	22	432 ft.	10.5 oz.
Minolta	10x25	10	25	341 ft.	10.7 oz.
Nikon	Travelite III	7	20	373 ft.	7.4 oz.
Nikon	Travelite III	9	25	294 ft.	9.3 oz.
Nikon	Sportstar	8	20	330 ft.	7.5 oz.
Pentax	UCF	8	24	393 ft.	9.9 oz.
Pentax	UCF	10	24	315 ft.	9.9 oz.
Pentax	UCF	12	24	236 ft.	9.9 oz.

Field of view is given for a distance of 1000 yards.

COMPASSES

Anyone who has spent time in the backcountry knows the value of a good compass. It's not all that difficult to miss a trail or route and lose your way when traveling in unfamiliar territory. Many times this is just an inconvenience. By retracing your track, watching for landmarks and using the position of the sun to provide approximate bearings, you can usually figure out where you went wrong.

times this is just an inconvenience. By retracing your track, watching for landmarks and using the position of the sun to provide approximate bearings, you can usually figure out where you went wrong. But it isn't always so easy. Sometimes you can't find the place where you left the trail or route, no distinguishing landmarks are present, and the sun is obscured by clouds or fog. Without a compass, map, and some basic knowledge of orienteering, a simple mistake might lead to a potentially hazardous situation. With a compass, you'll be able to travel off the beaten track with confidence.

Review of Generic Types - Compasses

There are many styles of good quality compasses, but only two different types are suitable for the outdoors: those for orienteering use and those that are strictly used as hand bearing compasses. They are all hand-held versions that are precise and easy to use.

Orienteering Compass. This is the type where the compass mechanism is mounted on a flat, clear sheet of plastic (the base) that includes some type of scale for use with maps. Most backcountry travelers choose this type.

Hand Bearing Compass. This type has the compass mechanism mounted in a protective case that can be held in the hand or mounted on a wrist band and worn like a watch. This type is good for general use, but is not as well suited for map work.

Features and Options - Compasses

Look for the following features when comparing compasses:

Base. This is what the compass and most of the features are mounted on. Orienteering compasses usually have a flat, clear plastic base suitable for map work.

Capsule. The capsule contains the magnetic needle. In most good quality compasses, the capsule is liquid-filled to dampen needle movement and make it easier to read.

Needle. This is the thin piece of magnetized metal that points its tip toward the Earth's magnetic North Pole.

Dampening Fluid. Better compasses are filled with a liquid to steady the needle movement so the compass can be read accurately. Less expensive models have only air surrounding the needle, causing erratic movement that makes reading difficult.

Graduated Points. A compass has a graduated scale around the perimeter of a moveable bezel, divided into points that correspond to degrees of a circle, from zero to 360 degrees. On better compasses each point represents two degrees. The four basic directions of the compass are also indicated on the bezel, as are the four additional quarter directions on some models.

Protective Case. Some compasses have a sighting mirror that forms an integral protective case when it is closed. Others have optional cases available.

Lanyard. Most compasses have an attached lanyard that makes them easy to handle and prevents accidental dropping which could cause damage.

Sighting Mirror. This is a flip-up device that allows you to accurately plot positions. The mirror reflects the image of the compass. A sighting notch on the top of the mirror allows you to accurately pinpoint your object. A hairline on the mirror, and in line with the notch, indicates the direction of your object with great accuracy.

Scales. Additional distance scales are often located across the sides, top or bottom of the compass housing. This makes it convenient to work with maps of various scales.

Alignment Lines and Arrows. Lines and arrows running the length of the clear plastic base make it easy to plot directions on a map. Lines inside the compass capsule are aligned with the North arrow, allowing you to place the base on a map and rotate the bezel until the lines and the North arrow are aligned with the North lines on the map.

Magnifying Lens. On some models you'll find a small magnifying lens on the clear plastic housing to aid in reading small scale maps.

Declination Adjustment. Some compasses include a means of adjusting for local declination from true North so you don't have to add or subtract from your reading.

Clinometer. A useful feature located on the base for measuring slope angles.

Thermometer. Some models have a built-in thermometer on the base.

Operation - Compasses

The basics of compass operation are simple, but proficiency requires practice. You can use a compass to find the bearing of an object in the distance, or use it to orient your way toward an unseen place using information from a map. One thing you must always remember is that compasses give readings relative to the magnetic North Pole, which is hundreds of miles from the geographical, or true, North Pole. The difference between true North on a map and your compass reading is known as declination.

Declination varies widely around the world, and it is slowly changing. Declination can be to the East or West, and can be anywhere from zero to 45 degrees depending on location. The compass rose located on a map should give the amount of declination present in that area, and, to be accurate, you should find out the date of the map and the amount and direction (East or West) of yearly declination change.

Bearing of an Object. If you want to determine the bearing of an object in the distance, place the compass face-up in your hand and face the object. Point the direction arrow on the compass base at the object. Turn the bezel until the North arrow on the capsule lines up with the North (red) part of the needle. The compass point (heading) that is adjacent to the direction arrow on the base indicates the magnetic heading of the object. Now you must adjust this magnetic reading for local declination to get a true reading. If local declination is West, add it to your reading. If it is East, you must subtract this from your reading.

Orienteering from a Map. In this procedure you are using a known bearing on a map to guide you toward an unseen point. Place the compass base on the map so that one edge runs in a parallel line from your current position to your destination. Rotate the capsule so that the inner lines and the North arrow are parallel with the North lines of the map. The compass point adjacent to the direction arrow on the base indicates the direction you should go in. Now adjust for declination to get a magnetic bearing to follow. Going from a true reading to a magnetic reading you must add Easterly declination and subtract Westerly declination. Holding the compass in front of you, line up the North point on the needle with the North arrow on the bezel. The direction arrow on the base indicates the course you should follow.

Author's Recommendations - Compasses

I recommend that you find a small, lightweight orienteering compass with two degree increments and liquid dampening. Choose one that is in your price range and has the features you want. Many of the world's best compasses for active travel come from Scandinavia—Silva compasses are made in Sweden, Suunto compasses in Finland. Brunton also makes excellent compasses for active travel. A few of the most practical models available are listed in the chart below.

Suunto MC1-D

Costs. Small pocket models such as the Brunton *Tag-A-Long* retail around $6 to $10. Most of the lightweight compasses for active travel cost between $10 to $25 depending on their features. Higher quality models such as the Brunton *Elite Survival*, the Silva *Ranger* or the Suunto *Professional* cost anywhere from $35 to $70.

Author's Recommendations - Compasses for Active Travel

Brand	Model	Description
Brunton	Tag-A-Long	hb, lf, is=5, th, small zipper pull compass
Brunton	Advanced Map	ot, lf, is=2, cb, da, ly
Brunton	Elite Survival	ot, lf, is=2, cb, sm=3, ly, cl, th
Silva	Explorer 3	ot, lf, is=2, cb, lp, sc=3, mg, ly
Silva	Trekker Type 20	ot, lf, is=2, cb, sc=2, sm
Silva	Guide Type 26	ot, lf, is=2, cb=semi, sc=3, sm
Silva	Ranger	ot, lf, is=2, cb, lp, sc=2, sm, da, ly, cl
Suunto	A-1000	ot, lf, is=2, cb, lp, sc=3, sm=optional, da
Suunto	A-2000	ot, lf, is=2, cb, lp, sc=4, da, ly
Suunto	MC1-D	ot, lf, is=2, cb, lp, sc=3, sm, da, ly
Suunto	Professional	ot, lf, is=2, cb, lp, sc=3, sm, da, ly, cl
Suunto	TK-3	hb, lf, is=2, cb, lp, mg, pocket compass

DESCRIPTION: ot=orienteering, hb=hand bearing, lf=liquid filled, is=increment size (in degrees), cb=clear base, lp=luminous points, sc=scale markings (in degrees), sm=sighting mirror, da=declination adjustment, mg=magnifying glass, ly=lanyard, cl=clinometer, th=thermometer.

MAPS AND GUIDES

While some adventurers find it more stimulating and spontaneous to travel without these items, most are inclined to pack them along to help sort out destinations or backcountry routes. They are not only helpful while actually on the move, but great fun to study while temporarily based somewhere. A map serves as a constant reference on where you are going, as well as where you've been, and can provide valuable information on topography and route planning. You quickly become adept at identifying the backroads and scenic routes to travel.

Author's Recommendations - Maps

Maps. For travel within the U.S., the DeLorme Mapping Company of Maine has a great selection of map/guides that include interesting backroads and many trails. They come in large-format booklets for handy reference at home or on the road. Trails Illustrated also has fantastic maps with high accuracy for backcountry travel in U.S. national parks. These maps are made of a paper-like plastic that is waterproof and tearproof. Folded size is 4" x 9"; cost per map is around $7.

Map Cases. A good way to keep your maps dry yet accessible is to use a clear plastic map case such as Granite Gear's *Thunderhead* or *Stormshield*. These optional cases attach to panniers, backpacks or portage packs with adjustable hook and loop fastenings. They are made of clear vinyl and nylon packcloth and are well suited to active travel.

FLASHLIGHTS

You may also want to carry a small flashlight while traveling in the outdoors, especially if you plan to spend some time camping. I couldn't count the number of times we've had to sort out equipment or find some elusive item in the dark. Over the years, we've tried just about every type of compact flashlight, so I can tell you with certainty that, even at discount prices, the hardware store variety is usually not worth the money. Most of the ones I've used quit working long before the trip was over. They just are not made for rough treatment or wet conditions. Problems typically occur at the internal contacts. How many times have you had to shake your flashlight to get it to work?

Author's Recommendations - Flashlights

What's needed for active travel is a flashlight that is small, shock-resistant, highly resistant to moisture penetration, and provides a bright light with little battery drain. It sounds like a lot to ask, but several good models that operate on two AA batteries are now on the market at an affordable cost. Don't travel abroad with a flashlight that requires odd size batteries (such as AAA) as it will be difficult to find replacements. All of the models listed below are well designed, and have energy conserving bulbs. The BLI from Tekna even has a built-in battery life indicator. One flashlight per small group is adequate. Prices range from $7 to $15.

Author's Recommendations - Compact Flashlights

Brand	Model	Description
A16	Ultra Brute AA	thermoplastic rubber, krypton bulb, 2 AA
A16	Backpacker AA	reusable light, 2 AA
EMS	Hitch Lites	Tekna 1 and 2 models with attached versalink
L.L. Bean	2 AA Legend	alum., d'ble seal'd, sp't-to-fl'd foc's'ng beam, 2 AA
Mag Lite	Mini-MagLite	alum., waterpr'f, sp't-to-flood foc's'ng beam, 2 AA
Tekna	2 AA BLI	ABS plastic, integral battery life indicator, 2 AA
Tekna	1 AA	ABS plastic, 4" overall length, lanyard, 1 AA

You can also get a small solar charger that will recharge Nicad batteries, available from Real Goods and many specialty retailers. Be sure to check with the manufacturer of your flashlight before buying— some models such as the *Mini Mag Lite* are not compatible with rechargeable batteries. You could also purchase a flashlight that has a built-in solar charger such as the *Solar Flashlight* from Real Goods ($19, charges 2 AA's at a time). The combination flashlight/charger is the more compact option for travelers. If battery-operated flashlights don't excite you, try the *Dynalite* flashlight from Real Goods. A continuous hand-squeezing action generates enough power to produce a small steady light. It's not as bright as a conventional flashlight, but it won't let you down in an emergency.

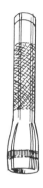

Mini-MagLite

Flashlight Accessories

Here are a few items you might want to carry along with your flashlight:

Headband. There are times when you don't have a free hand available to hold your flashlight, and that's when headbands such as the Adventure 16 *Light Header* come in handy. This one-inch elastic band accommodates most AA models. The light rests comfortably alongside your head. Velcro adjustment makes sizing universal.

Spare Bulb. Efficient flashlight bulbs have a limited lifespan and are hard to find in less developed countries. It's a good idea to carry a spare for good measure when traveling.

Spare Batteries. If your flashlight uses AA batteries, there is really no need to carry spares unless you are really going to a remote location. AA batteries are available worldwide.

DAYPACKS

Some sort of small pack or rucksack should be considered for the many day outings and side trips you'll be likely to take. They also come in handy for carrying groceries, laundry and other items to and from your base. For most travelers, their main pack is too bulky for comfortable day trips. What's needed is something small and lightweight that can be easily tucked away until needed.

Eagle Creek's Half Trek

Several options are available. You can: buy a large travel pack that has a detachable daypack or lumbar pack included (see section on Backpacking); select a component pack system where smaller packs, suitable for day use, strap on to larger packs (see section on Backpacking); use bicycle panniers that convert to daypacks (see section on Bicycling), or just include a lightweight daypack along with your other outdoor travel gear.

Author's Recommendations - Daypacks

This is one category where it is almost impossible to recommend one manufacturer's daypack over another; there are simply too many good packs on the market. I will say that I'm partial to packs that provide the following: travel organizer compartments for all the little items you want to keep track of; padded backs that give protection from water bottles, cameras, and other hard objects; comfortable shoulder straps with ample padding; and functional, well positioned waist belts. The trick is to find one that has these features, yet is lightweight and can still be easily stowed when not in use. These and other types of daypacks are offered by a host of equipment suppliers. Some popular models now available are listed below.

Costs. Expect to pay anywhere from $20 to $40 for a lightweight, non-technical daypack, $40 to $65 for models with more support and heavier construction.

Author's Recommendations - Daypacks

Brand	Model	Capacity	Wgt.	Description
Camp Trails	Touring Pack	1850 cu. in.	1.3 lbs.	pl, pss, pb, wb, 2 ep, lash tabs
Caribou	Potomac	1550 cu. in.	1.4 lbs.	pl, pss, pb, wb, 2 ep
Dana Designs	Colter	1760 cu. in.	2.3 lbs.	tl, ash, pss, wb, 1 ep
Eagle Creek	Half Trek	1350 cu. in.	N/A	pl, pss, pb, wb, 1 op
EMS	Morthana	1400 cu. in.	N/A	pl, pss, pb, wb, 1 ep
Eastpak	Padded Packer	1385 cu. in.	13 oz.	tl, pss, pb, wb, 1 ep
Gregory	Day Pack	1365 cu. in.	1. 5 lbs.	pl, pss, pb, 1 ep
Jack Wolfskin	Fred	1342 cu. in.	1.2 lbs.	tl, pss, pb, wb, 1 ep
Jansport	Chesapeake	1846 cu. in.	1.0 lbs.	pl, pss, 1 ep, 1 op
Kelty	Trailhead	1800 cu. in.	1.3 lbs.	pl, pss, pb, wb, 1 ep, zod
L.L. Bean	Rucksack	1700 cu. in.	1.5 lbs.	tl, pss, pb, wb, 2 ep
Lowe	Jitterbug	1750 cu. in.	1.5 lbs.	pl, pss, pb, wb, 2 ep, io
Madden	Getaway**	1500 cu. in.	1.9 lbs.	pl, pss, 2 ep
MEI	Reflection	1430 cu. in.	N/A	pl, pss, wb, 1 ep
Mount'nsm'th	Day Pack*	1254 cu. in.	1.6 lbs.	pl, wb, 1 ep
Osprey	Simplex	1850 cu. in.	2.0 lbs.	pl, pss, pb, wb, 1 ep
Outbound	Stormcloud	1650 cu. in.	N/A	pl, pss, pb, wb, 3 ep
Patagonia	Alpine Pack	850 cu. in.	N/A	pl, pss, pb, wb, io
Quest	Grand Teton	2200 cu. in.	N/A	pl, pss, pb, wb, 2 ep
REI	Bookpacker	1659 cu. in.	1.4 lbs.	pl, pss, pb, wb, 1 op
Tragar	Organizer	2025 cu. in.	N/A	pl, pss, pb, 1 ep, 1 op

This model is a lumbar pack that also serves as an accessory pocket for larger packs.
**This model converts from a functional daypack to an elegant carry-on piece of luggage.*
DESCRIPTION: pl=panel loading, tl=top loading, ash=adjustable shoulder harness, pss=padded shoulder straps, pb=padded back, wb=waist belt, ep=external pockets, mp=mesh pocket, op=organizer pocket, io=internal organizer, zod=zip-out divider.

Daypack Variations

The models described above are mostly classic daypack designs. If you don't see one that fits your needs, take a look at the many daypack variations now on the market.

Ultra-Lightweight Daypacks. If you only have the room for an ultra-lightweight daypack, try one of the self-stowing models on the market. They don't have the padding and support of heavier models, but they weigh little and roll up to fit in their own handy pocket. One recommended model is the Eagle Creek *Pack-It* (16" x 22", around $22). Another is the *Jet Stream* from Mountain Tools. It has a capacity of 1,625 cubic inches, stows in its own 4"x12" stuff sack, weighs only 14 ounces, and costs around $50.

Variable Volume Daypacks. For those who want more flexibility from a daypack, Jack Wolfskin has recently introduced the *Falter*, a daypack that expands to suit your load. On this top-loading pack, the top flap folds down and clips to two quick-release buckles, similar to the way you seal waterproof stuff sacks. The *Falter* expands from 1,240 cubic inches to 1,740 cubic inches, weighs 1.6 pounds, and has a removable foam back pad.

Fanny and Lumbar Packs. Backpacks with shoulder straps aren't the only type of load carrier useful for day outings. Fanny packs that rest on your hips, and lumbar packs that hug the lumbar region of your back, are also available. Fanny packs are lightweight and unobtrusive, great for carrying a few small travel items. Lumbar packs are typically more comfortable and capable of much more substantial loads than fanny packs. Mountainsmith makes several lumbar packs, including the *Day Pack* listed above, that are rugged, incredibly comfortable, and even fit together with other models in a total component system for backpacking or bicycling.

Gregory also offers a component-style lumbar model, the *Rumper Room*, that can be attached to a larger pack. Dana Design offers four models of *Hipsacs* that range from 400 to 960 cubic inches of load capacity. Ultimate Direction's torso packs, such as their smaller *Voyager* (1,450 cubic inches) and MEI's *Big Bubba* lumbar pack (1,200 cubic inches) provide innovative side pouches for water bottles, eliminating the hassle of stopping and digging through your pack for a drink. Caribou's *Back Draft* fanny pack (330 cubic inches) has the same idea, only with two water bottles located just inside the main zipper. Madden's *Outback* lumbar pack (600 cubic inches) has padded back and attachment points for water bottles. These packs allow you to keep hydrated on the move just as frame-mounted water bottles on a bicycle do.

DUFFEL BAGS

There are times when you need an extra load carrier above and beyond your main pack or pannier. There have been several times in our travels where a duffel provided just the right amount of additional carrying capacity. Duffels can be used for car or van travel, canoe trips, or general travel.

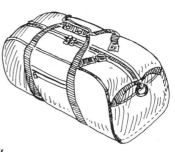

Caribou's Mighty Duffel

Author's Recommendations - Duffel Bags

Many good makes of duffels are currently on the market. Select a model that suits your budget and style of travel, and make sure to get a comfortable shoulder strap if you plan on carrying it any distance. Duffels with zip-out, padded shoulder straps (so you can carry them like packs) are available on some models.

Innovation - Granite Gear's *Hudson Bay*

One of the most useful duffels on the market is the *Hudson Bay* from Granite Gear (6,000 cubic inches, around $110). This bag is shaped like a duffel, yet functions more like a backpack. Instead of zippers, it has compression straps that enable you to compress the bag to fit the load. A drawstring and velcro top closure are covered by a sturdy flap with nylon straps, a system guaranteed to protect your gear. This duffel opens like a chest for good accessibility, while the carry handles convert to shoulder straps for easy transport. If you like the concept, but want something smaller, try their 4,000 cubic inch *James Bay*.

If you just need something for carrying modest loads, and want to be able to pack it away easily when not in use, all you need is a basic duffel made of lightweight nylon. Inexpensive generic duffels are available from most outdoor equipment suppliers. But if you want something that can withstand more abuse and hold up well on repeated adventures, I recommend one of the models listed below. These duffels range in price from $55 to $125.

Author's Recommendations - Heavy-Duty Duffels

Brand	Model	Capacity (cu. in.)
Campmor	Expedition Cargo	1 size: 7238
Camp Trails	Adventure Travel	3 sizes: 2130, 4050, 5500
Caribou	Mighty Duffels	3 sizes: 2000, 4250, and 7500
Dana Design	Roadmaster	2 sizes: 4125, 7514
Dana Design	South Pole Overland	2 sizes: 10,080 and27,648
Dana Design	Travel Pocket	2 sizes: 6480, 8400
Eagle Creek	Cargo Duffels	5 sizes: 2000, 3400, 6700, 8100, and12100
Eagle Creek	Expedition Duffels**	2 sizes: 5880, 6880
Granite Gear	Hudson andJames Bay**	2 sizes: 6000, 4000
Gregory	Duffel Bags	3 sizes: 2052, 2717, 3500
Jack Wolfskin	Fasser I andII	2 sizes: 2600, 4030
Jansport	Cargo Bags	3 sizes: 4700, 7300, 11300
L.L. Bean	Everest Duffels andBags	5 sizes: 2000, 2093, 3525, 4500, 6075
L.L. Bean	Ballistics Gear Bags**	2 sizes: 6300, 8300
Lowe	Travel Tote	1 size: 7800
Madden	Duffels	3 sizes: 1350, 2400, 3300
Madden	Firefighter Duffel	1 size: 7000
MEI	Duffel andGear Bags**	5 sizes: 2640, 4608, 4680, 6630, 10880

Millet	Croisiere*	1 size: 5492
Mountainsm'th	Travel Trunks	3 sizes: 3292, 6506, 9759
Osprey	Transporter	1 size: 8000
Outd'r Pr'd'cts	Gear Duffels	4 sizes: 1458, 2900, 5070, 8704
Overland	#71	1 size: 7888
Quest	Gearbag II, III andIV	3 sizes: 2175, 4900, 8200
REI	Bear Bags	3 sizes: 2080, 3725, 7680
Wild Country	Kong	1 size: 8600
Wild Things	Burro Bag	1 size: 6500

*Has removeable daypack. **Has zip-out shoulder straps
Dana Designs' Travel Pocket also serves as a raincover for a large backpack and it stows in its own pocket.

SLEEPING GEAR

Even if you don't plan on camping during your travels, you may want to bring along a few items to ensure a clean, comfortable place to bed down. For children, it's additional security. They are comforted by familiar things like their own pillow or sleeping bag. Pillowcases can be stuffed with clothes to serve as a pillow, whether camping, hosteling or on public transportation.

Author's Recommendations - Sleeping Gear

If you are not restricted by weight and room, I highly recommend that you at least take along a pillowcase, and possibly a lightweight sleeping bag liner for each person. Pillowcases can be brought from home, bag liners can be purchased or easily made by sewing up cotton linen or flannel sheets folded in half lengthwise. Children's liners can be easily cut down to the appropriate dimensions. Cocoons offers a line of cotton or silk travel sheets and bag liners that are perfect for globetrotters. They have pillow pockets and can be used on their own or to provide an extra layer of warmth for regular bags. Great fleece combination bag liner/blankets are available from North by Northeast. Campmor offers bag liners in cotton flannel ($15) or Polartec™ 300 fleece ($45). The Polartec™ version unzips for use as a blanket. Log House Designs offers a cotton/polyester bag liner (around $16) with an extra layer at the head that can serve as a pillow when stuffed with clothing.

It's up to you whether you feel the need to bring a sleeping bag and pad along if you don't plan to camp. Currently available makes and models of sleeping bags and pads are discussed in the Lightweight Camping section.

The other sleeping gear item you may want to pack when heading for warm weather destinations is a lightweight hammock. Slung between two trees, it provides a really comfortable place to sleep. Combine a hammock with some mosquito netting in buggy locations. Look for the *Hiker's Hammock* (15 ounces, around $20) and the compact *Mini Pack Hammock* (only 10 ounces, around $10).

TRAVEL POUCHES

A proper travel wallet or money pouch is another nice addition to your travel gear. They are a great way to carry valuables like your wallet, car keys or identification when traveling in the outdoors.

Author's Recommendations - Travel Pouches

Traveler's pouches are made to be worn around your neck, waist, or even strapped to your leg. Austin House makes a series of carriers for travelers—*Waist Safe, Neck Safe, Sock Safe* (slips onto the calf and hides valuables under a pant leg), and *Le Holster* (worn like a detective's gun). Eagle Creek offers a wide range of traveler's pouches, including their *Undercover Deluxe Security Belt* (for waist use), the *Undercover Hidden Pocket* (slip the outer loop through your belt and tuck the pocket under the waistband of your pants), and the *Undercover Passport Carrier* (a larger pouch for either waist or shoulder use). Caribou offers their around-the-neck *Passport Pouch* and *Walkin' Wallet*, or their on-the-hip *Maui Hip Pack* for carrying larger loads securely. Madden offers the handy *Field Office*, a versatile travel pouch for neck or waist. Jack Wolfskin also makes a line of good travel wallets and pouches, including their *Traveller* that is worn below the armpit, completely hidden from view under a jacket or shirt.

EATING UTENSILS

Active travelers will appreciate the inclusion of a few eating and drinking items tucked in with their other gear. Regardless of whether you are camping or not, there are bound to be many times when you are preparing and eating your own meals. A multi-purpose knife, water bottle, drinking cup, bowl, fork and spoon can make these times much easier without adding an appreciable amount of weight. Some recommended eating and drinking gear is described below.

Water Bottle. A one-quart (or one-liter) capacity plastic water bottle for each person is nice to have, both for day outings and times on the move. Choose from high quality models such as the Open Country *Faceted* or Nalgene *Loop Top* water bottles. Both these versions have a captive top that can't be misplaced. Nalgene also offers a range of standard wide-mouth models with molded ring seals. If you have bicycling gear with you, you can just use one of the water bottles from your bike. They don't usually have as positive a sealing mechanism as regular water bottles, but they work just fine in a rucksack for day trips.

Drinking Cup. Any type of lightweight cup or mug will do, although something that keeps drinks hot without burning your hands is desirable. You'll be using it for all types of drinks, so find one that works equally well for hot or cold liquids. Olicamp makes a nice insulated stainless steel mug (10 oz. capacity) that will stand up to rough treatment. We each typically each carry an unbreakable plastic mug on our trips for their light weight, durability and versatility. Choose one such as the *Dinex Cup* (8 oz. capacity)

Dinex Cup and Bowl

carried by Adventure 16. Adventure 16 also offers a new *Lexan Backpacker's Cup* (12 oz. capacity) that looks promising. Try to pack cloth napkins, dishcloth or other lightweight items inside the cup, then nest the cup into other gear to avoid wasted space when packing.

Bowl. One lightweight, durable plastic bowl also comes in handy. Make certain it is stable and doesn't tend to tip. What works for the dining room table might not be appropriate on tipsy or uneven camp tables, laps or other make-shift surfaces. A nice choice for traveling and a good companion to the cup above is the *Dinex Bowl* (9 oz. capacity). Another good option is Campmor's deep plastic *Soup Bowl*. It weighs only three ounces, holds 30 ounces, and costs around $3.

Fork, Spoon and Knife. You have three choices here—lightweight stainless steel cutlery sets, ultra-lightweight lexan tableware, or a combination fork and spoon with knife edge for cutting. Use the lexan where weight is critical. If you buy a cutlery set and weight is a concern, I suggest you leave the knife at home. Your galley paring knife (if camping) or multi-purpose knife will be adequate for all cutting needs. Lightweight, high quality stainless steel cutlery sets such as the *Mountaineer's Silver*, PEAK 1's *Nesting Cutlery*, and Olicamp's *Utensil Set* are recommended (two to three ounces, $3 to $4). The time-honored *Chow Set* that locks together via tabs on the spoon and slots on the fork and knife brings back fond memories of scout camp. It is perfectly serviceable, although not as comfortable to handle as the other sets. Lexan cutlery holds up surprisingly well and costs around $3 to $4 for a four-piece service. The combination utensils include the *KFS Utensil* (less than $3) that is shaped like a spoon with short prongs at the tip to serve as a fork, and the larger *Hungry Camper* (around $5) that has a spoon at one end and a fork at the other, with an integral bottle and can opener. One edge of the spoon on both models is ground to serve as a table knife. Chopsticks are a lightweight alternative to cutlery sets.

Mountaineer's SilverDinex Cup and Bowl

Cloth Napkin. You may scoff at the thought of including a cloth napkin on your travels, but consider this: you're going to need some type of napkin to use while eating, and the alternatives to cloth are throw away paper products. Why not pack something elegant as well as reusable? Lightweight cloth napkins are readily available, inexpensive and easy to launder. One per person is recommended.

RECREATION GEAR

Make sure to include something just for fun in your travel kit. It helps to pass the time on camp evenings or while waiting for inclement weather to depart.

Books. Reading books is our favorite pastime while traveling. We always have three or four paperbacks tucked into each pack. Try to bring books that have some substance and will last a while. We shop around at second-hand bookstores for paperback classics, small print books that take some time to read. Make sure the books you bring are good ones. It's terrible to settle down to one of the few books you brought on a trip, only to discover you hate it. Couples should choose books that they both want to read, effectively doubling the amount of reading material.

Games. Unlike books, games get used again and again. Small combination chess, checkers and backgammon travel sets such as Caribou's *Packgames* (rolls up into a 4"x14" zippered pouch) and REI's *Travel Games II* (self-contained in a nylon pouch) are popular, as is the ubiquitous deck of cards. A small ball to kick or toss at the campsite or beach is another handy item. Kites provide a great

Caribou's Packgames

way to pass a beautiful day in the countryside, but most are just too big and bulky to pack on a trip. One exception is the *Packable Parafoil* (5.5 ounces, around $20), marketed by many outdoor retailers. This model is a frameless nylon kite that flies like a champ and stuffs into its own carrying sack for travel.

Music. If you have musical inclinations, or want to develop them, pack a lightweight musical instrument such as a harmonica, penny whistle or recorder. There is something magical about music by firelight that brings people together. Leave your bulky acoustic guitar at home in favor of a smaller instrument, or take one of the new compact acoustic travel guitars that are starting to hit the market.

NET BAGS

We find a few net bags invaluable at home or on the road. Lightweight, durable, and compact, they make great shopping bags, eliminating throw-away paper or plastic. Most of the world seems to have adopted a policy of handing out plastic bags at shops and markets. You can do your part to curb this waste by carrying your own reusable bags. Don't be put off if you get strange looks and comments from check-out persons; attitudes are changing rapidly and you'll soon be in the majority.

Net bags are useful even if you carry a daypack. They are easily washed and therefore great for loading up dirty vegetables at the market. In the backcountry, food can be hung up in the net bags to protect it from animals. Net bags can also be filled with your favorite beverages and lowered into a stream to provide cool drinks. They are available at most outdoor retailers, health food stores and numerous grocery stores for about $5.

Children's Gear

While children bring exciting new dimensions to adventure travel and outdoor activities, they also bring the need for some additional gear. Your time in the outdoors can be great fun, developing strong family bonds that carry over into your everyday life. Proper equipment helps make the transition from home easier, the notion of adventuring less intimidating. Outdoor gear that pertains to adults as well as children is covered elsewhere in the book. Only gear specifically designed for kids is presented in this section.

CHILD CARRIERS

By far the most important piece of children's gear for active travel is a good child carrier. Being able to wear a child comfortably on your front or back gives you freedom and mobility to go almost anywhere. The child carriers available today are truly amazing.

Review of Generic Types - Child Carriers

Listed below are the criteria used to classify the various generic types of carriers now available.

By How it's Worn. Child carriers come in two basic types, soft carriers that are initially worn on the front and then on the back as the infant grows, and frame carriers that are worn on the back. Soft carriers are typically only suited for young infants up to around nine months old. Frame carriers are intended for older infants, toddlers, and young children up to the manufacturers recommended age and weight.

By Child's Age and Weight. One way to distinguish between the various models of child carriers is by the manufacturer's rating of maximum allowable weight and/or by the recommended age range the product is intended for. All carriers have these ratings stated clearly in their sales literature. Some soft carriers such as the Tough Traveler *Pony Ride* and the Gerry *Snugli II* are made for infants up to about nine months old. Typically worn on the front, these soft carriers are intended for use with infants too young to sit up easily. After that they become very interested in the scenery and should be transferred to a back carrier. Back carriers have a wide range of ages and weights that they are useful for, starting with sitting infants and including children up to four to five years of age and 60 pounds.

By Intended Use. Child carriers are also categorized by their intended use. They can be rated for general use around town, light day hiking, all day hiking, and extended trekking. The more extended the use, the more features and options are available.

Features and Options - Child Carriers

These are the things to look for when shopping for a child carrier.

Frame. Soft carriers don't need one, but all models for older children have some sort of frame. Frames can be internal or external as with other backpacks. They can also be made of tubular or flat stock aluminum, or molded plastic that conforms to your body.

Seat. All models have a soft seat that supports the child from below. Most often, it is a suspended piece of fabric that provides freedom of movement and is adjustable according to child size.

Headrest. A padded headrest is available on most models to protect the back of the child's head during sudden motion (either by the wearer or the child).

Padded Shoulder Straps. All good quality child carriers have padded shoulder straps, a necessity for larger children or extended use. On some models the shoulder straps are incorporated into a rapid-adjustment system that allows wearers of different heights to switch easily.

Padded Hipbelt. A hipbelt allows you to transfer the load from your shoulders to your hips, easing strap tension and stress on your lower back. As with the padded shoulder straps, a padded hipbelt is a necessity when carrying larger children or during periods of extended use.

Sternum Strap. This is a simple piece of adjustable nylon webbing that connects the shoulder straps at the sternum (that hard bone in the front of your chest), keeping them from slipping off your shoulders during strenuous hiking.

Storage Space. All child carriers intended for extended use have some provisions for carrying light gear below the child. This usually takes the form of a weather resistant zippered bag, often detachable from the carrier, for storing food, diapers and other baby gear you want to keep handy.

Foot Stirrups. Any parent who has carried a child knows one of their favorite activities while riding is to swing their legs. Foot stirrups give some restraint to their movements, making any hike easier for the parent and more comfortable for the child.

Storage Pockets. A few child carrier suppliers also offer optional storage pockets that attach to the carrier frame for extra carrying capacity.

Rain and Sun Hood. This is a great convenience for travelers and outdoor enthusiasts. It provides protection from rain and intense sun when you need it, and stows easily out of the way when you don't. Another option for foul weather is the *Child Poncho* from Cherry Tree. This functional poncho is sized to provide protection when used alone or with a stroller or child carrier.

Construction and Operation - Child Carriers

Child carriers are made either completely of heavy duty fabric (all soft carrier models), or they consist of a combination of a fabric outer shell and metal or plastic support frame. Shoulder straps and hipbelts are usually padded with foam.

Operation. Despite great advances in child carrier technology, you still can't overlook the fact that it's a child you'll be carrying. Unlike an inanimate load that stays put once packed, children can behave in an amazingly lively fashion, even when confined to a pack. While some will sit in angelic docility, others will stand up, lean perilously from side to side, grab hair, play with earrings, tilt backwards, and talk incessantly. Fortunately, children generally love riding in a pack, reveling in their new, superior vantage point. The following few tips should help eliminate any trouble spots when carrying an infant or child.

Load the child or baby into the carrier before putting it on your back. This applies to both soft and hard frame types. Next, lift the carrier up, balancing it on your raised knee (brace your foot on something), then gently swing the carrier across one shoulder. Even soft frame carriers such as the *Snugli II* can be put on your back this way without harming the child.

Women should avoid wearing things that tempt curious babies, including earrings, necklaces, and long hair within easy reach. Position the child's feet out through the side straps so he can't brace them on the lower bar of the pack and stand up. This can be an irritating, yet easily discouraged habit. Using stirrups can help. Bring along a good supply of nibble food to tide over a fussy baby or toddler. Despite all that inactivity, they seem to develop a powerful hunger. Try rice cakes, crackers, zwieback or similar foods. If embarking on a long hike, remember that a child is bound to nap at some time. While pleasantly restful for parents, it does make your load seem heavier. Reserve this time for your strongest load carrier to do the work.

Author's Recommendations - Child Carriers

Plan on needing two carriers to cover the time from infancy to the age when your child can walk sufficient distances alone. Begin with a soft carrier to wear on the front, then switch to the back as the weight becomes uncomfortable. Next, select a frame type that can carry a baby from about nine months on. The best all-around choice is a model that stows fairly easily, has sufficient extra carrying capacity (for diapers, food, clothing, changing pad, etc.), and covers a large age span. Being avid hikers and travelers ourselves, we favor a pack that can carry a child up to four or five years of age, such as Tough Traveler's *Kid Carrier* or *Stallion* , Gerry's *Trail Blazer* or L.L. Bean's *Child Carrier*. Although experienced children of that age can walk well, the option of giving them periodic spells in a carrier will greatly increase your mobility.

Think seriously about how you plan to use the carrier. Ask yourself if you intend to use it for general travel or in the backcountry, on weekends for day hikes or on the Grand Tour. Storage capacity is another serious consideration, determined by intended use. Some carriers are designed with spacious lower compartments, suitable for carrying practically everything an infant would need on a trip or outing. Others are better suited for short-term use.

In general I look for the following in a child carrier:

Comfort. Try out as many child carriers as you can before you buy one. Pick one that provides the most comfort for you. Models with molded plastic internal frames such as the Lafuma *660* use the same type of support system found on technical backpacks. It

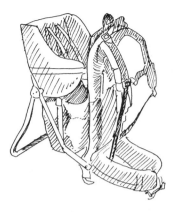

Tough Traveler's Stallion

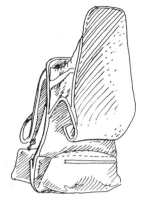

Lafuma's 660

conforms more easily to your body shape than models with tubular frames.

Extended Use. Try to avoid the added expense of buying two frame carriers. If you are planning some long-range backpacking, choose a good load carrier, even if your infant looks silly in it at first (just fill up the extra space with spare paraphernalia). If your trips will always be shorter, then go with a simpler, less expensive model.

Easy Size Adjustment. Try to choose a pack that is easily adjustable to different wearers, a great asset when carrying an older child. On a recent hike our three-year-old niece in her Tough Traveler *Stallion* was shared between four people, from her six-foot-tall father to our thirteen-year-old son. Only a carrier with height adjustment in the shoulder straps could have covered that size differential comfortably. Another carrier that makes adjustment a breeze is the Lafuma *660* with its sliding *Fast Back* system. It's nice if the seat of the carrier also adjusts easily to suit the size of the child.

Free-Standing Frames. Free-standing carriers allow easier loading and can double as a high-chair, sleeping place or just somewhere confining to put a baby. This leaves out carriers with molded frames such as the Lafuma *660*. Be sure to match the carrier to the height of the person who will be doing the bulk of the carrying. Despite adjustable strap systems, a five-foot mother is hardly going to want a pack designed for a six-foot man, or visa versa. Again, the ones with the greatest flexibility in height range are going to be best for serious hikers and travelers.

Cost. Good quality soft carriers currently cost around $50 to $60, frame models for moderate use range from $75 to $100, and high quality carriers for extended use and heavy loads cost up to $160.

Author's Recommendations - Soft Front Carriers

Brand	Model	Description	Weight
Gerry	Snugli II	Adj. inner seat, outer pouch for security	N/A
Gerry	Snugli Escort	Inexpensive, lightweight carrier; waistbelt	N/A
Tough Traveler	Pony Ride	Infant-9 months; seat cradles; waistbelt	3.5 oz.

Author's Recommendations - Frame Back Carriers

Brand	Model	Age/Weight	Description	Weight
Gerry	Kiddie Pack	5 months to 40 lbs.	light use carrier	N/A
Gerry	Ultra Deluxe	5 months to 40 lbs.	gsu; abs; as; ss; phr	N/A
Gerry	Trail Blazer	5 months to 45 lbs.	gsu; abs; as; ss; phr	N/A
Kelty	Child Carrier	6-36 months, 35 lbs.	lrg. gsu; abs; as; phr	4.8 lbs.
Lafuma	Model 840	9-36 months	light use carrier	3.5 lbs.
Lafuma	Model 660*	9-36 months	gsu; abs; as;	2.9 lbs.
L.L. Bean	Child Carrier	up to 40 lbs.	gsu; abs; as; phr	N/A
Outbound	Baby Carrier	6-36 months	gsu; abs; as;	N/A
Tough Traveler	Stallion	up to 4-5 yrs., 60 lbs.	gsu; abs; ss; phr	4.6 lbs.
Tough Traveler	Kid Carrier	up to 4 years, 50 lbs.	gsu; abs; ss; phr	4.0 lbs.
Tough Traveler	Bronco	up to 4 years, 40 lbs.	gsu; abs; ss; phr	3.0 lbs.
vauDe	Hopper	N/A	gsu; ss; phr	3.5 lbs.
vauDe	Jolly	N/A	gsu; as; ss	4.4 lbs.

*I recommend this model over the 650 which only serves children up to 24 months of age.

**Other models by Tough Traveler include The Montana and The Colt.

DESCRIPTION: gsu=gear storage under; abs=adjustable back support; as=adjustable seat; ss=sternum strap; phr=padded head rest

Innovation - The *Stroller Pack*

The typical child stroller is heavy, bulky, and has tiny wheels that can barely hold up to long-term use on smooth sidewalks, let alone rough roads or tracks often encountered when traveling. This is why child carriers have become so popular— they go where strollers can not. Wouldn't it be nice if a stroller was available that was easily transportable, went over rugged terrain like it was child's play, yet could turn into a back carrier at the drop of a diaper pin? The *Stroller Pack* from Skaggs and Ingalls does just that. Its two 12" wheels (pneumatic or plastic) and sturdy aluminum frame allow it to traverse the most demanding terrain. Then the quick-release wheels pop off, the frame folds flat, the shoulder straps and padded waist belt unpack, and it converts to a back child carrier.

It also works well as a cart for transporting gear. In some ways, *Stroller Pack* does for pedestrians what bicycle trailers do for bicyclists; it easily transports a child or lots of gear on two wheels. You'll be using it as a cart long after your children are grown. Total carrying capacity of this sturdy unit in the stroller/cart mode is a staggering 150 pounds. It should be pointed out that this product is intended for those who want the advantages of a stroller, child carrier and utility cart in one product. If you're just interested in a good child carrier, you'll get more comfort and performance from some of the models listed previously. With a $300 price tag (pneumatic wheel version $50 more) and a total weight of 10 pounds (weight is only 4.8 pounds as a child carrier), this product may not be for everyone, yet it offers many new possibilities for active travelers. Options include a sun bonnet, rain fly and accessory bag.

BABY TRAVEL KIT

Despite their seeming helplessness, babies need little in the way of gear, a definite asset on any trip and one of the many reasons they travel so well. How far or long you plan to travel is irrelevant. A weekend trip to the nearest park takes basically the same amount of gear as a three-month trek abroad.

Author's Recommendations - Baby Travel Kit

The following is a list of items recommended for a child from infancy through the toddler years:

- cloth diapers (14 for infants, 8-9 for toddlers)
- rubber pants (6 for infants, 3 for toddlers)
- corn starch (a baby powder substitute)
- A and D or desitin ointment
- cup, bowl, spoon
- baby hair brush and comb
- baby food grinder
- washcloth
- lightweight changing pad

If you have room in your backpack, pannier or child carrier for these items, then you don't need an additional travel bag; just use a daypack for short outings. If you'd rather stow this gear in its own travel bag, there are currently two great models on the market. My favorite is the *Diaper Pack* from Eagle Creek, a baby bag that converts into a comfortable daypack. You can substitute this pack for one of the adult's personal daypacks. It holds 1,300 cubic inches of gear, has an integral fold-out changing pad, side bottle pockets, organizer panel and regular carrying handles. Another good option is one of Tough Traveler's *Diaper Bags/Carry-Alls*. They come in large or small sizes and include lots of pockets and a removable changing pad. Large size is 16"x12"x6", holds 1,400 cubic inches and weighs 14.5 ounces. The smaller version is 14"x11.5"x6", holds 1,200 cubic inches of gear and weighs 13 ounces.

Eagle Creek's Diaper Pack

TRAVEL TOYS

Despite the abundance of toys in most homes today, children need few sources of entertainment on an adventurous trip. The very nature of outdoor-oriented travel lends itself to imaginative and active play, with little dependence on supplied toys. It's always a good idea to bring along a few choice items for the occasional rainy day, vehicle travel or other confining times. Choose toys that have the most versatility and lasting appeal.

The following are some tried and true things for keeping children entertained.

- Leggos (Duplos for toddlers)
- Fisher Price "little people" sets
- action figures
- drawing paper, colored pencils
- scissors, tape
- soccer ball or other small ball

- paper dolls
- dollhouse items
- stuffed animals
- matchbox cars
- playing cards

CHILD'S SLEEPING GEAR

Babies have a remarkable ability to sleep anywhere, given a few familiar objects to make them feel at home. Always pack some nightwear, even when traveling lightweight. This helps impart the message that it's time to go to sleep, no matter how unorthodox the surroundings. Other recommended sleeping gear includes a small pillow, blanket, or other familiar bedding and one or two treasured "sleepy friends." Most babies and toddlers (not to mention older children) are fondly devoted to some type of security object. By no means leave it behind. With these few things, most little children will happily bed down anywhere.

II LIGHTWEIGHT CAMPING

The word camping has come to represent several different, philosophically diverging ways of enjoying a stay in the outdoors. Highway signs present a convincing argument that camping is an activity primarily for people driving or pulling large vehicles. Some would have you believe that the word is actually *kamping* and synonymous with a low-cost holiday, complete with swimming pool and game room. To myself and many outdoor enthusiasts, it represents the temporary opportunity to live simply and appreciate the wonders of the natural world, something impossible to do in *kampgrounds,* and difficult to do in many standard camping areas where the sites and sounds of nature are often overshadowed by the noise of people reluctant to leave their mechanized gadgets at home.

Fortunately, lightweight camping, or camping with gear that is easily carried on your back, bike, or boat, allows you to escape the crowds and seek less visited places where nature rules. Many parks offer walk-in camp sites for tenters, located just far enough away from the other sites to make a difference, but close enough so you can use the common facilities. Some parks offer wilderness sites further afield where, with a little extra effort, you can enjoy the pleasures of backcountry camping that few experience.

World travelers also appreciate the freedom that lightweight camping gear gives them. With a tent, sleeping bag and cooking gear, your home is literally always with you; you'll never lack a place to sleep or something to eat.

Camping is especially good for families. It allows children the freedom to run about and play without parental worries of disturbing the hotel management or the guests in the room next door.

Children find endless things to do in a campground or in the countryside. They still should be considerate of fellow campers, but it's much easier to keep everyone happy when outdoors.

You'll need the same basic types of lightweight camping equipment regardless of when or where you go traveling. Precisely what items you decide to take on any particular trip is a personal decision based on your destination, its climate, your mode of travel, how many in your group and so on. Wilderness camping is far different from a stay in an organized campground, and backpacking has slightly different parameters than bicycle touring, for instance. This chapter will give you the information you need to choose and purchase the right lightweight camping equipment for your trip.

- Tents
- Dining Shelters

Shelter

A shelter can be thought of as anything that protects you from the discomforts of cold, wind, rain, sun or biting insects. We don't often think of it in these terms, but it also refers to a psychological shelter, a temporary home, a source of privacy and succor or a place to gather and socialize. The practical concerns of the former are paramount, but the intangible comforts of the latter can be equally important.

The shelters presented in this section are designed for active outdoor travelers and must have certain physical characteristics. They must be lightweight, easy to pack and carry, and durable. They should also be affordable. It's not surprising that there are many good makes and models available that meet all these criteria. What may surprise you is how pleasant the modern shelters are to be in. New materials and designs have allowed them to be light and airy in moderate conditions, warm and dry in foul weather.

TENTS

When we talk about providing shelter away from home, we are most often referring to tents—shelters that use fabric and a light-weight skeletal framework to create comfortable, protective spaces. There is an intangible magic to be experienced inside a small fabric dwelling, something relating to the proportion and scale, the filtered light and subtle shade, the safety of being inside and the freedom of being in the outdoors. Those new to camping often fret over the thought of being cooped up in a tent, especially with children or in bad weather. When viewed as a house, a tent does indeed seem small and cramped. When viewed as an outdoor sanctuary, how-ever, a shelter offering comfort in the midst of nature, time in a tent becomes something eagerly anticipated.

Tent choices these days are wide-ranging. If you haven't taken a close look at tents lately, you'll find things have changed dramati-cally over the past several years. Let's first take a look at the various types currently on the market.

Review of Generic Types - Tents

Tents are classified in several different ways. The primary classification is based on intended use. Manufacturers label their tents according to the conditions they are designed and built for. The intended use influences the basic shape and features of the tent, along with what materials are used. The other ways of classifying tents are by shape, by sleeping capacity, and by whether they are free-standing or require stakes and guy lines to hold their shape. Most tents on the market are free-standing, although they still need corner stakes to assume their correct shape and prevent movement, and a guy line or two to hold them steady in high winds.

By Shape. It used to be easy to classify tents by shape; there were A-frame, dome, hoop, umbrella and wall/cabin tents. New designs make these basic shapes less distinct, yet still recognizable, with the preface "modified" thrown in to cover all variations. Lightweight, collapsible poles, connected together by shock cord to form flexible supports, have helped create tents with unusual shapes and superior strength. Some modified A-frame tents now use a center hoop to give a dome-like impression, with greatly increased usable space and strength. Others flatten the top of the A with additional framework to give steeper walls and more interior room. Many dome models have become geodesic sculptures in fabric with criss-crossing hoops in wild arrays. Some have rectangular floors, others have floors with five, six, or eight sides. Umbrella designs, now with their attached flys and vestibules, are only remotely recognizable. When shopping for a tent these days you'll still hear the traditional terms used; they've just taken on new meaning.

By Sleeping Capacity. In each category a manufacturer may offer various sizes, the most common for lightweight camping being one, two, three, four, and six-person models. Six-person tents are generally only suitable for lightweight camping if the tent's components (and thus the weight) are distributed among group members, or the weight is otherwise compensated for. Each tent shape has its own characteristics that help define the number of occupants comfortably accommodated. Other factors include size of occupants (short or tall person, adult or child) and whether or not gear is to be stored inside. The only way for you to tell if the rated capacity is adequate for your needs is to get inside and try it.

By Intended Use. The basic classifications are as follows:

• *Summer Tents* are useful in hot climates and when fair

weather prevails. They concentrate primarily on ventilation and air movement. A light-colored fly provides moderate rain protection and a barrier against the unrelenting sun.

• *Three Season Tents* are intended to provide comfort in light to moderate conditions relating to spring through fall weather. Equal emphasis is placed on ventilation for hot weather as on wind and water resistance. These models are usually adequately waterproof, but don't have the capability to withstand extreme weather, high winds, and snow loads potentially encountered in winter conditions. Three season tents can be successfully used in the winter if your site is sheltered and the conditions are moderate.

• *Four Season Tents* have more inherent strength because of their design and construction. Stronger, more durable pole and fabric materials are used. The shape of the tent is typically stronger and more aerodynamic for less wind resistance. The stress points have extra reinforcing, while the external guy lines are more frequent and better positioned. Don't think that a four season tent is needed only if you go winter camping. You may encounter extreme conditions in the middle of summer in some locations, particularly at high altitudes and other notoriously windy areas. Other features on four season tents include double doors for easy exits and additional gear space inside.

• *Mountaineering Tents* are lighter in weight, yet made to handle the extremes of high-altitude weather and heavy snow loads. They typically have a lower profile for minimal wind resistance and compact floor plans so they can fit on a mountain ledge.

• *Expedition Tents* are a bit heavier and expected to stand up to rugged conditions and long-term use by professionals or groups of independent travelers. Although they are often simply modified versions of a standard tent model, typically all materials and critical stress points have been upgraded. Many manufacturers offer this type of tent in addition to their standard line.

• *Bicycling/Backpacking Tents* are usually synonymous with the lightest weight version of a given tent model, with shorter pole sections utilized if possible so the packed length is minimal. Compact, easy to stow models marketed as bicycling or backpacking tents can be used for any activity. Conversely, almost any lightweight tent can be used for bicycle touring and backpacking.

• *Family Camping Tents* have traditionally been models that you could stand up in, were large enough for a family, and solid enough that you could repeatedly spend your vacation comfortably ensconced in one. Not formerly intended for self-propelled travel, they used to be quite heavy and required half the car's trunk space for storage. Times have changed. The same materials and design ingenuity that make the smaller lightweight models desirable are now used to create larger versions for families or small groups. Some four and six-person models aren't much heavier than their two and three-person counterparts. When you calculate tent weight per person in the group, one large tent often comes out weighing less.

• *Bivy Shelters* refer to single layer, low profile, waterproof hoop tents. They are usually free-standing, narrow enough to be set up on a mountain ledge, and typically only slightly bigger than your sleeping bag. The portion above the chest and head areas is raised to provide room to sit up in. These come in one-person and two-person models, either single layer waterproof (sometimes waterproof and breathable) or double layer with canopy and fly.

Features and Options - Tents

Listed below are the features and options you can expect to find on currently available tents:

Waterproof Floor and Lower Sidewalls. This ensures protection from rain and water runoff. The tent fly covers the upper section of the tent and extends below this waterproofed material.

Breathable Canopy. Most of the upper surface of a tent is made of breathable nylon. Its job is to allow air movement and prevent condensation by forming a dual layer of fabric when used with a tent fly.

Door and Window Ventilation. Most tents have one or two zippered doors for entering and egress, plus some combination of opening windows. Tents with large doors at opposite ends usually dispense with the windows.

Insect Netting. The industry standard is to use netting that keeps out no-see-ums, that tiny creature with the large bite. This finer mesh netting cuts down on air flow a bit, but is well worth it for the job it does. Zippered netting is provided at all door and window openings.

Internal Gear Storage. A relatively new feature on tents is a place to stow small personal items. These storage places come in the form of mesh pockets down near sleeping level, optional gear "lofts" made of fabric that suspend up near the peak, or loops that accept a length of line for hanging clothes or a flashlight.

External Support System. Almost all tents currently made have an external framework. The main tent material is suspended underneath the system of poles, allowing it to retain its waterproof integrity. The tent fly is stretched over the framework to protect the upper sections of breathable fabric.

Waterproof Fly. A waterproof fly is the key to providing comfort and preventing condensation on the inside of the tent. The single component fly also takes most of the abuse from ultraviolet rays, and is easily replaceable if it eventually degrades. It generally has guy line points in critical locations to secure the tent in strong winds.

Stakes and Guy Lines. Stakes and guy lines provide structural integrity on models that are not free-standing, as well as additional security and a tighter "set" on free-standing models. Stakes come in a variety of configurations, with different models better suited for certain types of ground. There is usually a stake for every corner of the tent, plus several for guy lines and a few for the optional vestibule.

Packing Bag. This keeps the tent components neatly packed and protects them while traveling. You may elect to split up components between group members and reserve the packing bag for just the main section of the tent.

Groundcloth. This is an optional piece of waterproof fabric that goes under the tent floor. It is meant to give an additional line of defense against water penetration, as well as to protect the tent floor. Many manufacturers offer groundcloth options. Reinforced blue plastic tarps cut to size also make economical, lasting groundcloths.

Optional Vestibule. These are invaluable in wet weather. Once you use one you'll never leave it behind. Attached to the tent over one of the doors, vestibules provide a waterproof place outside the main tent to store gear, cook, remove shoes and raingear before entering the tent, and a dozen other things. It helps keep the tent free of grass, sand and dirt. On most tents, this is an option that slips over one end of the pole system before the fly is installed. On a few, it is standard equipment and integral to the fly itself.

Internal Guy Lines. Several tents make provisions for internal guy lines that criss-cross at the tent ends to provide additional support in extreme conditions.

Construction and Operation - Tents

Most tents are constructed of nylon fabric. The floor is a heavier weight material, able to hold up against abrasion and rough ground. It is typically coated with a generous layer of waterproof material. More expensive tents use a stronger fabric and better coating techniques. The upper canopy is also made of nylon fabric, with a looser weave that allows air to pass through easily. This upper mesh is only moderately water resistant, and should not be confused with the breathable, waterproof fabrics used on clothing; it relies heavily on the waterproof fabric fly above it. Some companies now offer high-end, single layer tents made of breathable, waterproof material to reduce weight and bulk. On some tents sections of the canopy are replaced with insect netting to allow for star gazing with the fly removed. Fabric seams are kept to a minimum on floor and lower sidewall sections, as well as on the fly.

Moss's Netting Deltoid
shown with and without fly

Modern tents are almost exclusively supported by external pole systems. The poles are constructed of either fiberglass or aluminum, with a select few made of light-gauge stainless steel. The aluminum and steel versions are stronger and usually lighter, the fiberglass poles have greater flexibility. Individual pole sections have one male and one female end. They join together to form the appropriate length pole. Sections are typically connected by an internal length of elastic shock cord, greatly assisting in erecting and disassembling the tent. Pole systems gracefully arch over the tent, which connects to this framework in a variety of ways. The tent either has external sleeves of materials that the poles slide through, small external loops of material with clips that snap onto the poles, or a combination of the two. The sleeves can be continuous or simply short sections for the poles to pass through. There are small loops of material around the tent perimeter with holes or tabs to accept the ends of the poles. These sleeves or loops take most of the stress exerted on a tent, so they should be adequately reinforced.

Pitching the Tent. The typical scenario for erecting a free-standing tent, by far the most popular, is to unroll the main section and place it on the ground with the waterproof floor face down. If you are using a groundcloth (highly recommended to protect the bottom of your tent from rough ground) place it down first with the tent on top. It helps to put a stake in each tent corner just to hold it in position, but this isn't necessary. If the tent has pole sleeves, pass the poles through the sleeves in the order recommended by the manufacturer; sometimes it makes a difference which pole is underneath and which one is on top. After passing through the sleeve, place one end of the poles in the perimeter holes provided on the tent. Gently push the pole through the material and place the other end in its perimeter hole (it may take some effort to get it into its final position). This bows the pole so that it and the fabric assume their correct shape. If the tent has no sleeves, simply erect the pole system, then clip on the tent starting from the bottom and working your way up. It's unbelievable how easy this system is to erect.

Once the poles and clips are in position, you can pick up the entire tent and place it where you want it. Then stake out the tent corners (even if you already did this, you may have to reposition them slightly for correct tensioning). Place the fly over the pole system and attach as required. If you have a vestibule, attach the upper end under the fly first. Stake out the vestibule if available, then pull out the guy lines and stake them down as far away from the tent as is practical (the further from the tent, the better the angle and the more effective they'll be). Since groundcloths can trap water as well as shed it, make certain all corners are tucked well under the tent.

A few tents on the market with clip-on systems allow you to set up the groundcloth, poles, and fly first, then erect the tent under a dry canopy.

Breaking Camp. Take down the tent in reverse order of assembly. For morning departures, allow the tent fly to dry out a bit before packing. Draped over a bush or picnic table and faced toward the sun, it will dry in no time. For departures in the rain, you might be able to leave the fly and pole system in place while you take

down and pack up your tent (Noall, Lafuma, and some others with
clip-on pole systems). It may take a little practice, but if done
correctly, it will keep you and your tent dry during disassembly.

Innovation - *No-Hitch-Pitch* by The North Face

Several years ago The North Face introduced their innovative *No-Hitch-Pitch* system that makes tent-pitching a breeze, even in the wind, the
dark, or when you're alone. In the *NHP* system every pole is pre-
attached to one floor grommet and already threaded through the
correct canopy rings. All that's left for you to do is spread out the floor,
push the poles into position, and snap the free ends into the remaining
grommets. To take down the tent, simply reverse the process. All of
the poles fold up and stow right along with the tent canopy. The *NHP*
system is available on the *Tadpole* and *Bullfrog* models, and a partial
NHP system is incorporated into the *Hotel-46*.

Author's Recommendations - Tents

Your choice of which tent to buy will be influenced by many
things: your budget, desired sleeping capacity, personal taste, as well
as how and where you plan to use it. Here are some general recommendations to keep in mind while browsing:

Give Yourself Plenty of Space. Select a tent that gives you
adequate sleeping capacity without squeezing someone up against a
potentially damp sidewall. Figure on an average of 12 to 16 square
feet per person to be comfortable. If you want to store gear inside
the tent instead of in a vestibule, it pays to move up one in rated
capacity (i.e. three people plus gear should get a four person tent).
I've never heard anyone complain about having too much room in
their tent, only too much weight to carry. The only exception to this
might be someone winter camping and trying to keep the heated
area to a minimum.

Balance Space with Size and Weight. Try to balance interior
spaciousness with reduced size and weight, comfort with mobility.
Select designs that give you extra space where you need it most.
Designs that slope up to provide headroom and down toward your
feet are ideal for saving weight yet providing the necessary room.

When Bicycle Touring. Choose tents with short pole sections
and compact packing dimensions for bicycle touring or lightweight
backpacking. Longer tents packages can be cumbersome on a bike
or narrow trail.

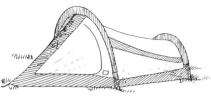

Sierra Designs' Flash Magic   Kelty's Windfoil Ultralight

For Long Term Use. Look for a tent that can stand up to long periods of use. Expedition or professional series tents are best.

Low Wind Resistance. Select tents with aerodynamic shapes (in other words without steep, flat walls). You'll undoubtedly be forced to camp in exposed areas once in a while. You'll notice I haven't listed any standard A-frame tents because of their poor wind resistance.

Full-Coverage Fly. Check out tents that offer full coverage flys for maximum weather protection. Shorter flys may look fine on the showroom floor, but fall short in wind and driving rain.

Clip-On/Continuous Sleeve Systems. Look for pole systems that attach to the tent with clips or continuous sleeves. The clips are easiest to use by far, but provide only single stress points. Continuous sleeves are still easier to use than multiple-section sleeves. They allow you to insert the pole end and feed it through without having to keep finding the start of the next sleeve, a difficult task in the cold or dark. Continuous sleeves are also stronger and provide a better wind block between fly and canopy.

Vestibules. I highly recommend you find a tent that offers an integral or optional vestibule. That protected space outside the tent is almost as valuable as the space inside. Ideally, you should be able to enter the vestibule and close the door without soaking your gear, sit down to remove your shoes, and get into the tent without crawling over everything. Vestibules with a small hoop pole and side entry are more easily accessed than ones just staked out straight. You should also be able to fit the vestibule over either door in two-door models.

Diamond Brand's Mountain Creek

Multiple Tents for Families. Families should consider carrying several tents, one larger one for the parents and young children, and a smaller tent for older children. The larger tent serves as the gathering place in the evening and when waiting out bad weather, the smaller tent allows parents and children to have some privacy. If you are concerned about security, you can place the tents so the doors are almost touching. In fact, it isn't too difficult to fashion a piece of waterproof material between the two to form a dry place for entering the tents and cooking.

Avoid Sagging Flys. Look at the fly of the tent you are considering. Does the design pull it away from the sidewall of the tent or allow it to sag toward it? Picture what it would be like in strong winds. If it sags into the sidewall during a rainstorm you'll have water coming in for sure. Standard A-frames are notorious for this in heavy rains. I had to sew loops onto the fly of one A-frame tent so I could attach a guy line and pull it out to prevent leaking.

Good Ventilation. Consider ventilation as important as weather protection. On most trips you'll be spending the majority of your time in dry weather (or if not you'll be spending the majority of your time asking why you chose that destination). Choose a design that allows you to really open up the tent during hot, humid weather.

Cost. Tent prices go up with the quality of materials and construction, and with increased protection or decreased weight. Single layer tents made of waterproof and breathable materials will also cost more. Expect to pay around $100 to $200 for a good quality one to two-person bivy shelter for moderate conditions, up to $450 for mountaineering models. You should be able to get a nice three-season, two to three-person tent for $200 to $350, four to six-person models for $250 to $450. Four season/mountaineering two- to three-person tents will cost from $350 to $550, four-person models up to $750.

Other than following these recommendations, choose a tent that appeals to your sense of aesthetics and is priced right. If you hope to use it long-term, find a manufacturer with a reputation for quality. Some offer lifetime guarantees on poles and defects in workmanship. Listed below are what I feel are the best lightweight, reasonably-priced tents available for active travelers.

Author's Recommendations - 1-2 Person Tents/Bivy Shelters

Brand	Model	Style	Sleeps	Packed Size	Wgt. (lbs)
Adventure 16	Nylon Shelter**	ho	1	N/A	1.6
Bibler	Solo Dome***	do, fs	1	NA	2.6
Blue Ridge	Camp Hammock**	ho	1	6"x22"	4.0
EMS	Gore-Tex Bivy***	ho	1	5"x12"	1.1
Eureka	Gossamer	ho	1	5"x18"	2.9
Kelty	Windfoil Ultralt.	ho	2	5"x20"	4.1
Moss	Outland	mod, fs	1	5"x16"	5.0
Moss	Starlet	mod, fs	1-2	5"x16"	6.0
Noall	Equinox**	ho	2	NA	3.8
Outbound	Clip Andromeda	ho	2	NA	4.9 *
Quest	Seescape	ho	2	5"x19.5"	4.1
Sierra Designs	Divine Light***	ho	1	4"x17"	2.1
Sierra Designs	Flash Magic***	ho	2	4.5"x17"	2.9
The North Face	Leafhopper	ho	2	N/A	4.3
The North Face	Tadpole NHP	mod, fs	2	N/A	4.3

**Single layer waterproof material; ***Single layer waterproof/breathable material.
STYLE: mod=modified dome, moa=modified A-frame, ho=hoop, fs=free-standing

Author's Recommendations - 2-4 Person Summer/Three Season Tents

Brand	Model	Style	Sleeps	Packed Size	Wgt. (lbs)
Diamond Brand	Mountain Creek	dom, fs	2/4	6"/8"x26"	8.8/10.9
EMS	Absaroka	dom, fs	2-3	NA	7.3
Eureka	Alpine Meadows	moa, fs	2/4	7/8"x26"	7.7/10.4
Eureka	Aurora	moa, fs	2/4	7/9"x22/24"	10.5/13.5
Jack Wolfskin	Temite	mod, fs	2	N/A	5.3
Kelty	Quattro	mod, fs	2/4	8/10"x24"	8.2/12.2
Kelty	Domolite	mod, fs	2/4	7/9"x24"	7.5/10.8
Lafuma	Connemara	mod	2/4	NA	8.2/9.8
L.L. Bean	Dome Tent	do, fs	2/4/6	7-8"x30-32"	7.5,11,14
Moss	Netting Deltoid	mod,fs	2-3	6"x21"	7.0
Outbound	Clip Pegasus	do, fs	3	NA	7.8
Quest	Preying Mantis	moa, fs	2	5"x20"	5.7
Quest	Conquest IV	mod, fs	4	8"x28"	11.0
REI	Trail Dome	do, fs	2	7"x27"	6.5
Sierra Designs	Meteor/Comet	mod, fs	2/3	6.5/7.5"x20"	5.8/7
Sierra Designs	Mondo Condo	mod, fs	4/6	8/10"x24/31"	10/13.7
The North Face	Hotel-46	do, fs	4	NA	10.1
The North Face	Bigfrog NHP	mod, fs	3	6"x21"	6.6
vauDe	Tenere	mod, fs	4	5.5"x18.5"	6.0 lbs.

* aluminum pole version; **Single layer waterproof material; ***Single layer waterproof and breathable material.
STYLE: mod=modified dome, moa=modified A-frame, ho=hoop, fs=free-standing

Author's Recommendations - 2-4 Person Four Season /Mountaineering Tents

Brand	Model	Style	Sleeps	Packed Size	Wt.(lbs)
Bibler	Kiva***	do, fs	4	NA	5.8
Bibler	I-Tent***	do, fs	2	NA	3.5
Diamond Brand	Mountain Home	mod, fs	2/4	6/7"x28/27"	7.9/11
EMS	Roadhouse	do, fs	4	NA	11.4
Eureka	Equinox	umbr.	2-3/4	8/10"x22/24"	8.9/11.6

To The Best Outdoor & Recreation Equipment

Eureka	Geom Ex-3	do, fs	3	8"x30"	9.2
Jack Wolfskin	Pocket Hotel	ho, fs	3	N/A	5.8
Kelty	Jetstream	mod, fs	2-3	9"x22"	9.6
Kelty	Windfoil	ho	2/4	5"x20"	4.1
Lafuma	Camp 2	mod	2	NA	7.4
L.L. Bean	Geodesic	mod, fs	2/4	7"x30"	7.8/11
L.L. Bean	Backpacker's	do, fs	2	9"x19"	7.3
Moss	Olympic	mod, fs	2-3	6"x21"	7.9
Moss	Deltoid	mod, fs	2-3	6"x21"	8 lbs
Moss	Dipper	mod, fs	3/4	7"x21"	10.8/12
Mountainsmith	Mountainshelter	pyramid	4	NA	6.6
Noall	Harmony Base	mod, fs	2	7"x22"	7.8
Outbound	Golden ears	mod, fs	4	NA	12.5*
Outbound	Black Tusk	mod, fs	2/3	NA	7.4/9*
Quest	Preying Mantis 4S	mod, fs	2	6"x21"	7.1
Quest	Headwall	mod, fs	2-3	6"x23	8.1
REI	Geodome	mod, fs	2/4	7/9.5"x29/30"	7.7/10
Sierra Designs	Stretch Dome	do, fs	2-3	6"x20"	7.7
Sierra Designs	Stretch Prelude	do, fs	4	7"x25"	9.9
The North Face	Oval-25	mod, fs	2	NA	7.6
The North Face	Aerohead	mod, fs	2	9"x30"	6.8
vauDe	Space Explorer	mod, fs	3	7"x18.5"	8.0

*aluminum pole version; *** Single layer waterproof and breathable material.*
STYLE: mod=modified dome, moa=modified A-frame, ho=hoop, fs=free-standing, umbr=umbrella

The North Face's Oval-25
A strong four season tent.

Eureka's Equinox
A lightweight umbrella tent.

Innovation - *Wing Shelters* From Moss

Vestibules are great, but they don't give you all that much room for taking off your raingear and boots; some wind and wet still comes in every time your enter or exit. Wouldn't it be nice if you had a bit of sheltered space outside your tent, over the entry door like the porch on a house? Moss Tents has solved the problem with their *Tentwing* and the new *Heptawing*, versatile canopies with compound curves to spill wind and rain.

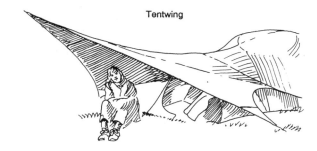
Tentwing

Originally designed for their tents with hoop vestibules, new models fit almost all Moss tents, as well as most other tents on the market with hooped vestibules. They erect over the vestibule and can be pitched in a variety of configurations to suit changing weather conditions. The *Wings* can also be erected separately as stand-alone shelters, either by using support lines tied to convenient spots, or by using Moss's optional poles. They work well as sunshades or outdoor seating areas to relieve the confinement of being in a tent. The *Tentwing* covers 35 square feet, packs to 4"x19", and weighs 1.5 pounds. The *Heptawing* covers 65 square feet, packs to 4"x17", and weighs 2.8 pounds.

Maintenance and Repair - Tents

Even though it is a tough piece of gear, there are a few things you can do to help protect your investment and extend the life of your tent.

Seal the Seams. When you first purchase your tent, chances are the seams have not been sealed. Some manufacturers supply a tube of seam sealer as part of the package. Pick a nice day and pitch your tent in the yard. Seal the floor, sidewall and door seams from the inside. Leave the doors and windows open for ventilation. Now reverse the fly and seal those seams. When applying sealer, several thin coats are better than one thick one. Allow 12 hours drying time before repacking. Reapply sealer each season.

Keep it Clean. Having a vestibule or outer canopy where you can remove shoes and store gear is a good way to prevent dirt inside the tent. Clean out any dirt that does find its way in each time you break camp. Unstake the tent and either shake overhead (small tents), or have a person hold up one end, forcing the dirt toward the door, while another person sweeps out the dirt (larger tents). A whisk broom makes the job a little easier, but is not a necessity. Wash off any muddy spots with water, a rag or sponge, and a bit of concentrated liquid soap. Don't ever use abrasive powders or stiff brushes on tent fabric.

Keep it Dry. If possible, allow the sun to dry off your tent and fly before packing up in the morning. This helps prevent mildew from forming. Set up your tent after a trip to make sure it is dry and clean before storing.

Use a Groundcloth. A groundcloth is not a necessity on tents with waterproof "bathtub" floors, but I still recommend that you bring one along. It protects the floor from rough ground, increasing your selection of suitable tent sites.

No Sharp Items. Keep open knives and other sharp objects out of the tent if possible. Tent fabric stands up really well to tension and abrasion, but can't cope with sharp points or blades. Canopy and netted sections are especially vulnerable. The same applies for packed tents; keep sharp stakes and poles well away from the tent or fly.

Don't Store Sweets. Don't store chocolate or other sweets (including dried fruit) inside a tent, unless they are in a sealed, airtight container, as it may attract ants. They can eat right through a tent floor, as they did to us in Turkey one time in search of our coconut-covered apricot bars. Rodents can also damage your tent in search of stored food.

Watch those Claws. Dog or cat claws can also do a number on your tent. We awoke one morning in Nova Scotia to discover a local cat sitting on top of our tent canopy under the fly. Imagining the worst, I tried to gently to dislodge the intruder, only to helplessly watch as it extended its claws and left symmetrical tears up one side of the tent and down the other.

Stay in the Shade. Do your tent a favor and pick shady areas for extended camp sites. Long-term exposure to ultraviolet rays will damage the fly, vestibule and other exposed sections. This isn't a concern for short-term campers.

Stuff, Don't Fold. You'll get more life out of your tent if you stuff it into its bag instead of folding it. Repeated stress on the same folds will eventually cause the coating to peel.

Lubricate Zippers and Poles. Periodically apply silicon lubricant on the door and window zippers, and a bit on the male end of all pole sections to keep them in good working order.

If your tent does encounter a mishap while traveling, make sure you have the proper tools, materials and know-how to cope with it. Field repairs can usually be handled with a well-stocked sewing kit and a few spare parts.

Tent Repair Kit. Tent repair items can simply be part of a travel sewing kit that serves for all general repairs (see Sewing Kit under Specialty Gear, this section). The nylon fabric on tents can easily be repaired with adhesive nylon tape, heavy duty needles and thread, and a thimble or sewing palm. Adhesive tape can be applied directly over small holes or abrasion tears. Larger tears should be taped to hold the fabric in place short-term, then sewn for a lasting repair. Guy line or tent pole nylon loops can be resewn if necessary. Sewn repairs should always be sealed to keep moisture out of the needle holes. Zippers are almost impossible to field repair, and so should be treated with care (see Maintenance above). Children should be taught to open and close them with a slow, steady motion. This is a good reason to opt for a tent with two doors, in case the zipper on one becomes inoperable. If you can't fix the problem in the field, it's best to secure it until you can take it to a seamstress or local service center. Tent pole sections can be temporarily splinted with a pliable stick and duct tape, but probably won't assume their proper bend with this type of repair.

Spare Parts. Other than items in the repair kit, some spare guy line, and an extra stake or two, you might want to carry a pole section splint if one is available for your tent. Most suppliers offer emergency pole splints that are quite effective. If not, one can be fashioned out of aluminum or light gage stainless steel tubing with an inside diameter slightly larger than the outer diameter of the poles.

DINING SHELTERS

This piece of gear is associated more with car camping than self-propelled travel, but a lightweight version can be particularly useful to families and small groups where the extra load is distributed

among several people.
One thing that can ruin
a camping trip is not
having a good place to
cook or relax outdoors
in foul weather. A
dining shelter, set up
over a picnic table or

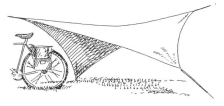

Moss' 12' Parawing

just covering a sheltered piece of ground, can make a big difference.
In addition to their *Tentwing* and *Heptawing* described previously,
Moss Tents offers the 12' *Parawing*, a 1.8-pound ripstop nylon fly that
is a vast improvement over traditional tarps. Its hyperbolic paraboloid shape (you know what that is, don't you?) gives more protection
by easily spilling wind and rain. Two of the four corners are made
to be tied up high to trees, the other two corners staked to the
ground. Cost is around $120. Moss offers optional, collapsible poles
for this model, similar to those provided for their larger 19' *Parawing*.
Poles give a lot more freedom when choosing pitching sites, especially in environmentally sensitive areas. Moss' 19' *Parawing*, their
new *Outfitterwing*, and other large dining shelters are covered in the
chapter on Car and Van Travel.

Other paraboloid dining flys are offered by Jack Wolfskin and
Campmor. The waterproof polyester *Moonshadow* by Jack Wolfskin
measures about 13'x13', weighs just over six pounds, and comes
without poles. The *Nylon Parafly* by Campmor measures 13.5'x13.5',
weighs five pounds, costs around $90, and has optional poles
available.

Eureka also offers the compact *Nylon Lean-To* (2.25 pounds,
about $70) that could serve as a dining fly or extra sleeping area. It
can be erected between two trees with a few corner stakes, or you
can use two Eureka aluminum poles and two more stakes and pitch
it anywhere. A version with screen netting (around $100) is also
available for insect protection.

If you'd rather fashion your own dining shelter to best suit your
requirements, get some lightweight coated nylon fabric (often
available at outdoor retail stores or material stores), some heavy
duty needles for your sewing machine, and some polyester thread.
It may not have the professional appearance of a store-bought fly,
but could save money and provide exactly what you need. I recommend that you design it such that with minor modification in how
it's pitched, it can also serve as a shelter over your tent door. Proper
shape and guy line locations are the key to a successful fly.

Sleeping

- Sleeping Bags
- Stuff Sacks
- Sleeping Pads
- Pillows

When choosing lightweight camping gear, the equipment you pack for sleeping is second in importance only to your shelter. Providing your own sleeping bag and pad gives you a clean, comfortable place to sleep wherever you are. It used to be only hardy souls with strong backs slept on the ground and enjoyed it, but with the gear available today anyone can experience sound sleeping away from a bed.

SLEEPING BAGS

Over time, a good sleeping bag gets to be like an old friend; protective, comforting, always there when you need it. Long after you've returned home from the trip, pleasant memories linger of curling up in the coziness of a warm bag. You don't even need to be camping to appreciate the convenience and comfort of having a sleeping bag tucked into your travel pack.

Review of Generic Types - Sleeping Bags

Sleeping bags come in a variety of models, each well suited for a specific set of conditions. There are so many good brands available, the selection process often comes down to finding one that feels right because it fits your body and how you like to sleep. Let's take a look at the different types of bags currently available and how they are classified.

By Intended Use. As with tents, sleeping bags are primarily categorized by the conditions they are intended for. This in turn affects their shape, as well as the materials and construction techniques employed.

• *Summer/Liner Bags* are inexpensive, lightweight, and can be used on their own in warm weather or as an inner lining to your existing bag for some extra warmth in cold weather. Liner bags can be made of single-layer poly/cotton or synthetic fleece, or constructed like regular sleeping bags with shell, lining, and fill material. Some have fill material in the top section only, with a soft fabric sheath on the bottom that accepts a sleeping pad. Liner bags are all you need camping in the tropics, when traveling light in warm weather, or when staying in accommodations such as hostels where warmer layers of bedding are supplied.

• *Three Season Bags* keep you comfortable over a fairly large range of conditions. They are the best choice for most travelers and outdoor enthusiasts who try to choose destinations where moderate weather conditions prevail. Liner bags can be added for cold weather comfort.

• *Cold Climate/Mountaineering Bags* are for winter campers, mountaineers or those whose metabolism keeps them from ever really being warm. Tapered to your body, these bags sacrifice roominess for ultimate comfort in cold weather.

By Shape. Sleeping bags are also categorized by their shape, with rectangular, semi-rectangular and mummy being the popular configurations. Keep in mind that with all the different cuts and configurations currently offered in sleeping bags, the distinction between categories is often unclear.

• *Rectangular.* Truly rectangular bags, seen more often in the camping goods section of department stores than in outdoor specialty shops, are reminiscent of scout troops and childhood sleepovers. They have the same spacious width at the bottom as they do at the top, but with all that room they tend to be heavy, bulky to pack, and offer much less ability to keep you warm in cold weather. Full zippers (along one side and the bottom) make it easy to zip bags together, and also allows them to open up for use as comforters at home or on the road. There are some very good lightweight rectangular bags on the market, but in general they are more suitable for car camping than self-propelled travel.

• *Semi-rectangular and Barrel.* This covers a lot of territory. These bags vary greatly in how they are tapered toward the bottom and a bit at the shoulders to cut weight and bulk, and to increase heat retention. Zippers can be mid-length to cut down on drafts or full length for ease of joining bags. Opposing zippers are needed for some models. Semi-rectangular bags are a good compromise between mummy and rectangular styles; there's still space to toss and turn in, yet in general they are warm, lightweight and packable.

• *Mummy and Modified Mummy.* The mummy bag has a more pronounced taper toward the feet and head areas, conforming more accurately to body shape (at least to that of a mummy in repose!). Being more confining, they take a bit of getting used to initially, but their advantages of warmth and weight savings can be worth the effort. Modified mummy bags give a little increased elbow room between the waist and the shoulders. Mummy bags typically have just enough zipper to allow comfortable entering and exiting, and an insulated hood to snug down with. Couples must get bags with opposing zippers so the hoods end up on the same side. When joined, the bags lay side by side so your lower legs remain in your own bag, ideal for those of us who suffer from bedmates with cold toes.

By Temperature Rating. You'll find that all bags are rated according to the temperature down to which the occupant remains comfortable. Below this temperature (in theory, anyway) you'll begin to feel the cold. The rating for liner bags typically ranges from 40-60°F depending on material used; three season bags are usually rated in the 20-40°F range; temperature ratings for cold climate/mountaineering bags can go down to well below 0°F. As you can imagine, there are so many factors that affect one's comfort level that this rating, prepared separately by each manufacturer, should only be regarded as a general indicator, most useful for comparison shopping. The temperature rating is determined not just by the shape of the bag as described above, but also by the type and amount of fill material used, how the bag is put together, and what additional features are included.

Features and Options - Sleeping Bags

Listed below are the typical features and options you'll find on currently available sleeping bags.

Outer Shell. A bag's outer shell keeps the fill material contained from the outside, helps prevent wind and moisture from entering and heat from escaping, and protects the bag from damage. By nature the outer shell must also be breathable to allow body moisture to escape. On most bags the outer shell is made of taffeta or ripstop nylon that is only moderately water resistant, fine for most cases where you are also protected by a bivy shelter or tent.

Inner Lining. The inner nylon lining contains the fill material from the inside, and provides a comfortable layer against your skin.

Fill Material. Bags appropriate for lightweight camping are typically made of natural duck or goose down, or a synthetic substitute. Fill materials must have good lofting ability when opened, yet compress to a small package when stuffed in a carrying sack. Synthetic fill materials include time-tested Hollofil®, Quallofil®, and Polarguard®, as well as relatively new synthetics with more down-like qualities such as Primaloft™, Polarguard® HV, Micro-Loft®, and Thinsulate™ Lite Loft.

*Note: Hollofil, Hollofil II, Quallofil, and Micro-Loft are trade names of Dupont. Thinsulate Lite Loft is a trade name of 3M. Primaloft is a trade name of Albany International. Polarguard and Polarguard HV are trade names of Hoechst Celanese.

Goose down is still the material of choice for providing ultimate warmth in the smallest, lightest bag. It is rated by its "fill power" or loft; 550-fill is the standard, 650 or 700-fill down is the best you can buy. If your down bag is cared for and kept dry, it will keep its loft and temperature rating for many years. Down does, however, tend to temporarily lose its loft and insulating ability in wet conditions, and can take forever to hang-dry. The synthetics tend to be a good bit heavier and bulkier for an equivalent temperature rating, and their loft doesn't usually hold up as well over the years, but they also don't tend to absorb moisture, retaining much of their insulating ability when wet and allowing them to dry more easily.

Zipper and Draft Tube. Most sleeping bags use durable, reliable YKK coil zippers. Better bags incorporate an internal insulated tube running the length of the zipper that seals it from drafts and heat loss.

Drawstring. Almost all sleeping bags come with a perimeter drawstring so the top (and hood if available) can be drawn tightly to keep in the warmth.

Insulated Hood. Insulated hoods are found on most mummy and some semi-rectangular sleeping bags. They provide a convenient spot to lay your pillow in moderate conditions, or can be drawn up around your head to help prevent what could amount to as much as 85% of your total heat loss. Some bags have removable hoods that can be stowed when not needed.

Sleeping Pad Sheath. Manufacturers are finally waking up to the fact that pads are an integral part of a good sleep system, and that provisions should be made for them. If you've ever strayed off your pad in the middle of the night, you'll appreciate the sheath built into the under side of the outer shell on some new bags. Children are especially prone to nocturnal wandering, so expect to see sheaths appear on small person bags in the near future.

Pillow Pocket. Some models have an integral pocket at the head of the bag where you can tuck your jacket or sweater, making a convenient pillow. The nice thing about this arrangement is that your pillow stays put during the night and you can leave your pillowcase at home.

Utility Pocket. A number of bags even come with a small pocket built into the outer shell for storing personal items, making them easy to find in the middle of the night.

Waterproof/Breathable Shell. Various manufacturers now offer the option of having the outer shell made of Gore-Tex or other waterproof/breathable material that is much more capable of protecting you from drafts and wetness while adding about five degrees to the temperature rating. You can also get a waterproof/ breathable overbag or bivy sack to enclose your existing sleeping bag.

Top-fitting Liner. Some sleeping bags allow you to snap in an additional insulated lining to the top inside layer for extra warmth.

Overbag. Insulated overbags do the same thing for the bag you own as internal liners, only from the outside. They provide additional water resistance and can add up to 30 degrees of warmth to your existing bag.

Innovation - A Bottom Sheath For Double Comfort

For those of you who enjoy zipping bags together with a mate, and are conscious of every bit of extra weight and bulk, this product is for you. Moonstone has come up with the *Doubler*, a lightweight (15-ounce) fabric sheath that holds two pads firmly in place while eliminating the need for a bottom bag. This allows couples to save weight, bulk, and expense by carrying just one bag for the top layer; simply open up any one of Moonstone's compatible models and zip it onto the *Doubler* for a comfortable night's rest. This product also solves the problem of ending up between your two pads during the night.

Moonstone's Doubler

Caribou Mountaineering has a similar product called the *Joint Venture*, available in two sizes with a tri-blend lining, coated nylon shell, and pillow pockets. The *Joint Venture I* holds *Therm-A-Rest* sleeping pads, the *Joint Venture II* accommodates the *Camp Rest* pads. The *Joint Venture* fits most sleeping bags that have a #7 YKK separating zipper. Western Mountaineering offers its own version of a bottom sheath called the *SummerLite Coupler*, made of cotton tri-blend.

Construction and Operation - Sleeping Bags

Sleeping bags mainly consist of fill material sandwiched between two layers of fabric, an outer shell and an inner lining. The goal when designing and constructing a sleeping bag is to sew these three parts together and provide a zipper for access without creating cold spots. A great deal of effort has gone into accomplishing this in creative ways, mostly having to do with internal baffles of lightweight netting sewn to the shell and liner independently. Manufacturers position these baffles in unique ways to achieve the desired results—holding the fill material in place while eliminating the thin cold spots you'd get with sewn-through construction. Better quality down bags even use baffles inside the draft tube to prevent fill material from shifting.

A few more heat-saving techniques used on high quality mummy bags for winter use include boxed foot sections to allow the fill material to loft freely around your feet; a differential cut where the lining is smaller than the outer shell so you can't compress the fill material from the inside; filled collars and insulated shoulder yokes that prevent drafts; and double insulated draft tubes around the zipper. Some sleeping bags are made with less fill material on one side than the other. This allows you to put the heavy side up to prevent more heat loss during cold weather and the light side up to give more comfort in warm weather.

Your sleeping bag should be taken out of its stuff sack and spread out in the tent upon arrival in camp. This gives it a chance to achieve some loft before you climb in, and the less time a bag spends compressed in a sack the longer it will retain its lofting ability. Pull the drawstring closed to prevent heat loss, open it up to allow more heat to escape.

If you want to zip two together, unzip both bags completely and feed the top section of the zipper from one bag into the bottom section of the zipper from the other. Pull slowly to prevent catching the draft tube material in the zipper. When bags with full-length zippers are joined, the zippers end up on the sides and one bag is positioned on top of the other. This is convenient for using bags of different weights when you want to switch between cold and warm weather use. When mummy bags are zipped together the zippers end up in the middle with the two bags sitting side by side. This allows each hood to remain positioned properly under the head area.

Author's Recommendations - Sleeping Bags

Most of us can only afford one main sleeping bag, so it's important to choose one that is versatile. You should select a bag style that is suitable for the way you sleep, then select the temperature rating you need to stay comfortable over a fairly wide range of conditions. Finally, shop around until you find what you're looking for in your price range. Be generous with your budget if you can. A good sleeping bag will last a long time, and should be thought of as an investment in comfort. Other recommendations when selecting a sleeping bag include:

View it with Room. Make sure you get plenty of room to sleep comfortably, but not more room than you need. Extra room means extra weight and bulk, and more space to heat. Modified mummy and semi-rectangular (or barrel) bags are my first choice. I'd steer clear of square-cut rectangular bags for lightweight travel. If you are less concerned about weight and warmth and like the space of a rectangular bag, by all means get one; it'll also make a great comforter at home.

Reduce Weight and Bulk. Get the lightest bag you can afford that has your desired temperature rating. Then make sure its stuffed size is acceptable. You'll never regret placing importance on reduced weight and bulk.

Layer for Warmth. You can layer sleeping components just as you would clothing. Choose a bag that gives you good three-season comfort, then keep a liner bag or overbag handy for those cold weather outings.

Damp Conditions. If you plan to use the bag for sailing or other water sports, or in humid climates, you should most certainly consider selecting one with synthetic fill. Down bags can be protected from wetness with waterproof/breathable shells, but that won't keep the fill from getting soggy in really humid conditions.

Changing Conditions. Another good way to attain flexibility is to select a bag with one side heavier than the other. This is great for trips where you'll encounter a wide range of conditions. Many bags are manufactured with this in mind. The same thing can be accomplished by using lightweight liners that snap into just the top side of the bag. Couples can bring one heavy and one lightweight bag, zipped together with the appropriate side up depending on the climate.

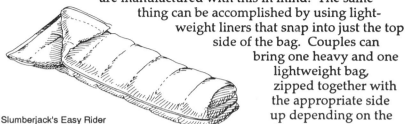

Slumberjack's Easy Rider

Especially for Women. Women are made differently from men, so wouldn't it make sense to have some bags cut with a woman's shape in mind? Well, yes and no. First of all, as with men, female figures vary widely. It's hard to offer a cut of bag to fit them all. Also, shape is really only an issue in mummy bags that tend to be confining. Modified mummies usually have ample hip and chest room. With so many models of bags to choose from, you'll undoubtedly find what you need in a unisex bag. Some good women's bags are available, however, and you'll have to try them out for yourself to see if they make a difference to you.

Children. There used to be only a few high-performance bags available for children. Now, most manufacturers offer technical sleeping bags for small people. Babies and toddlers can snuggle in with their parents, share a bag with each other, or have a small bag of their own. To keep them from heating extra space, get the smallest mummy bag you can find, then fold it at the appropriate length and sew a few ties in place to keep it there. Adjust the length as they grow. For an even better solution, see Tough Traveler's *Growing Bear* sleeping bag described on the following page.

Costs. In general, expect to pay more for down bags and those that are lightweight yet have low temperature ratings. You'll pay a good bit more for bags that have waterproof/breathable outer shells or are extremely lightweight. You can get good quality single layer fleece or poly-cotton liners for under $50, summer or liner bags for under $100. Three-season bags range between $85 and $225, cold climate bags can cost anywhere from $175 to $450, and true mountaineering bags with waterproof/breathable shells and temperature ratings to 30 degrees below zero can cost up to $700.

Innovation - The *Growing Bear* Bag

Tough Traveler has been making wonderful children's gear for a long time, but they really made a hit with their *Growing Bear* sleeping bag. This modular sleeping system allows one bag to adjust in length so it fits a child from ages three to eleven. The basic bag fits ages three to seven, while two extensions ensure a good fit up to age eleven. The foot area is boxed for extra room and a hood is included to keep in warmth. Hollofil II® fill material is currently used. The bag weighs 3.5 pounds complete, costs around $85, and is rated at 35°F. Use a lightweight liner bag for added warmth. Tough Traveler will be introducing a new Primaloft™ version of this children's bag this year. Weight and bulk will be substantially reduced, although the price will jump to $150.

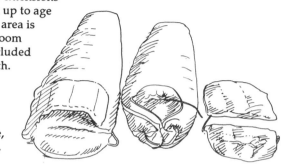

Author's Recommendations - Summer/Liner Bags

Brand	Model	Shape	Rating (°F)	Fill	Length	Wgt. (lbs)
EMS	Light Tour	R	60	DN	77"	1.0
Jack Wolfskin	One Kilo Bag	SR	N/A	PG	82"/90"	2.2/2.4
Kelty	Light Top	R	55	HF	75/80"	2.2/2.5
L.L. Bean	Ultralight	MU	60	DN	76"	1.8
L.L. Bean	Polarfleece liner	R	60	FL	60/76"	1.5/2.3
Montbell	Summer Breeze	MU	45	QF	75"	1.5
Moonstone	Starlite*	SR	25	LL	76"	2.9
MZH	Biker	MU	40	QU	80"	2.0
Outbound	Travelite 8/16	R	48/39	PG	78"	2.5/3.0
Performance	+40 Overbag	MU	40	LL	72/78"	2.8
REI	Starlite*	SR	30	QF	76/80	2.6
Sierra Designs	Summerlite	SR	30	LL	81/87"	2.9
Slumberjack	Summer Hummer*	R	45	HF, FL	82"	2.8
Slumberjack	Super Liner	MU	40	QF	80/86"	2.0/2.4
Western Mt.	MityLite	SR	40	DN	72"	1.5

These bags are reversible for changing conditions.
**These bags have a waterproof/breathable outer shell.*
BAG SHAPE: R=Rectangular, SR=Semi-rectangular, MU=Mummy. FILL MATERIAL: DN=Down, HF=Hollofil, LL=LiteLoft, ML=MicroLoft, PG=Polarguard or Polarguard HV, QF=Quallofil, PL=PrimaLoft, FL=Fleece

Author's Recommendations - Three Season/General Touring Bags

Brand	Model	Shape	Rating (°F)	Fill	Length	Wgt. (lbs)
Caribou	Light Tour	SR	25	PL	78"	3.1
Caribou	Early Frost	MU	20	ML	71/78"	N/A
EMS	Light Flight	SR	20	PG	78"	4.0
EMS	Light Cruiser	MU	40	PG	72/77"	2.5/2.7
Feath'd Friends	Penguin**	SR	10	DN	72/78"	3.1
Feath'd Friends	Swallow**	MU	20	DN	84/90"	2.1
Jack Wolfskin	Ayer's Rock	MU	N/A	DN	82/90"	2.9/3.0
Kelty	Philmont	SR	20/15	HF	75/80"	3.8/4.9
Kelty	Soft Touch	MU	20	LL	80/86"	3.2/3.5
L.L. Bean	Lite Loft	SR	20	LL	75/80"	3.8/4.0
L.L. Bean	Lite Loft	MU	20	LL	75/80"	2.9/3.0
Marmot Mt.	Quail	SR	25	DN	70/76"	2.6
Marmot Mt.	Swift	MU	20	DN	70/76"	2.8
Montbell	Main Squeeze	MU	15	HF	77"	3.1
Moonstone	Geko	SR	25	PG	76"	3.4
Moonstone	Upside D'nside*	MU	20	LL	76"	3.3
MZH	Traveler	MU	20	QU	90"	4.0
Outbound	Skagit	MU	15	HF	92"	4.25
Outbound	Cheakamus	MU	9	PG	86"	5.0
PEAK 1	Peaklite II	SR	35	TL	82"	4.2
PEAK 1	Peaklite II	MU	30	TL	85"	4.0
Performance	+20	MU/SR	20	LL	72/78"	3.2
REI	Starlite	SR	30	QF	76"	2.6
REI	Radiator	MU	20	QF	78/84"	3.5
Sierra Designs	Varilite*	SR	10	LL	81/87"	4.3
Sierra Designs	Wide Mummy	MU	20	PG	84/90"	4.5/4.7
Slumberjack	Easy Rider*	SR	20	HF	82/88"	4.1/4.4
Slumberjack	Down Under	MU	20	DN	82/88"	3.0/3.2
The North Face	Chysalis	SR	25	DN	78"	2.5
The North Face	Cat's Meow	MU	20	PG	80/86"	3.5
Western Mt.	Aspen	SR	25	DN	72/78"	2.2/2.4
Western Mt.	Ponderosa	SR	10	DN	72/84"	3.2/3.6

*These bags are reversible for changing conditions.
**These bags have a waterproof/breathable outer shell.
BAG SHAPE: R=Rectangular, SR=Semi-rectangular, MU=Mummy. FILL MATERIAL: DN=Down,
HF=Hollofil, LL=LiteLoft, ML=MicroLoft, PG=Polarguard or Polarguard HV, QF=Quallofil,
PL=PrimaLoft, FL=Fleece

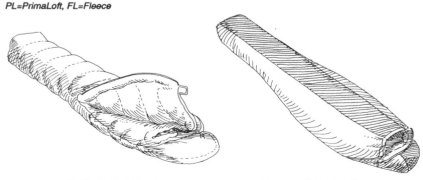

Caribou's Early Frost   Moonstone's Maxima XL

REI's Nod Pod

L.L. Bean's Ultralight

Author's Recommendations - Cold Climate/Mountaineering Bags

Brand	Model	Shape	Rating (°F)	Fill	Length	Wgt. (lbs)
Caribou	Big Chill	MU	-30	ML	71/78"	N/A
EMS	Mountain Micro	MU	-20	DN	72/78"	4.5/4.8
Feath'd Friends	Puffin III	MU	-30	DN	86/92"	4.1
Jack Wolfskin	Kingfisher	MU	N/A	DN	82/90"	3.0/3.3
Kelty	Soft Touch	MU	-15	LL	80/88"	4.6/4.9
L.L. Bean	North Col	MU	-10/-30	DN	82"	3.9/5.0
L.L. Bean	Down Series	MU/SR	0/-15	DN	80/88"	1.5/2.13
Marmot Mt.	Gopher GTX	MU	-20	DN	70/76"	3.8
Marmot Mt.	Penguin GTX	MU	-30	DN	70/76"	4.6
Montbell	Polar Furnace	MU	-30	QF	78"	5.9
Moonstone	Maxima XL	MU	-5	LL	69/76"	3.5/3.9
Outbound	Noosak	MU	-18	PG/HF	92"	5.75
PEAK 1	Peakloft	MU	-5/-25	QF	85"	4.4/5.6
Performance	+20 and +40	MU	5	LL	72"/78"	6.0
REI	Nod Pod	MU	0/-15	QF	78/84"	4.3/5.3
Sierra Designs	Fire Lite	MU	-15	LL	84/90"	4.8/5.1
Slumberjack	Down Range	MU	-20	QF	80/86"	4.2/4.5
The North Face	Igloo HV	MU	-25	PG	80/86"	5.4
The North Face	Curlew**	MU	-35	DN	85"	5.3
Western Mt.	Puma Super **	MU	-20	DN	76/82"	3.4
Western Mt.	Bison V**	MU	-40	DN	76/82"	4.5

These bags are reversible for changing conditions.
**These bags have a waterproof/breathable outer shell.*
BAG SHAPE: R=Rectangular, SR=Semi-rectangular, MU=Mummy. FILL MATERIAL:
DN=Down, HF=Hollofil, LL=LiteLoft, ML=MicroLoft, PG=Polarguard or Polarguard HV,
QF=Quallofil, PL=PrimaLoft, FL=Fleece

Maintenance and Repair - Sleeping Bags

Listed below are a few things you can do to help keep your sleeping bag in top shape.

Packing Up. If you have never used a down or synthetic fill sleeping bag, you'll soon learn that the way to pack it for traveling is to stuff it in a small nylon sack. This protects the bag and allows you to reduce it to a manageable size. When stuffing, place one hand on the outer lip of the stuff sack and start feeding material in one handful at a time. Rotate the sack so it fills evenly. With about half the bag stuffed in, it will appear as if the sack is full, but just keep stuffing and pressing it down until the entire bag is in. Cover the end with the dust flap and press down with one hand while you close the drawstring with the other. Stuffing in no way harms the bag, and in fact is actually better for it than rolling. It's also the only way to get the bag into a reasonable size for packing.

Don't Keep it Stuffed. Do your sleeping bag a favor, though, and take it out of its stuff sack whenever possible. This will help keep the fill material lofting as it should. The best way to stow your bag after a trip is to wash it or just give it a good airing, then place it in a large breathable sack that allows the fill material to loft to its natural size. Many bags come with such a storage sack included. You can also buy them at any outdoor retailer or make one yourself from a large pillowcase or piece of cotton cloth.

Clean it Regularly. Dirt and body oils reduce the loft and performance of the fill material. This is especially the case with down. Special soaps for cleaning down products are widely available. It is recommended that you wash sleeping bags by hand in a set tub (or bathtub) with warm water. Agitate the sleeping bag gently with your hands, rinse thoroughly until all soap is removed, then squeeze out the water by hand. Keep the bag supported when wet to prevent the damp, heavy fill material from damaging the internal baffles. Air dry on a slanting board, or in a large tumble dryer on low heat with a sneaker tossed in to help agitate the fill. If the bag has a waterproof/breathable outer shell, follow the manufacturer's directions for cleaning.

Use a Liner. Fleece or poly-cotton liners not only keep you warm, they also protect your sleeping bag from dirt and body oils. You'll find them much easier to clean than your sleeping bag.

Repairs. Minor splits in the seams of the internal lining may occur over time, exposing fill material. These can easily be repaired in the field with needle and thread. Larger rips or tears to the lining or shell should be properly patched.

STUFF SACKS

Many sleeping bags come with an appropriately-sized stuff sack. These are typically cylindrical in shape with a drawstring at the top, a dust flap sewn to the inside upper edge to cover the contents as you draw the sack closed, and a webbing handle on the outer bottom for carrying. For the most part they are simple nylon sacks with little compressibility or water resistance. You can improve on this standard item with some of the new stuff sacks now on the market.

Waterproof Stuff Sacks

You'll really appreciate a stuff sack that keeps out wetness, especially if you stow your bag outside your pack or pannier, or pursue water sports. You can always use a plastic garbage bag to give some temporary protection for a stuffed sleeping bag, but why not get something that looks good and does the job properly? Waterproof bags are reasonably priced and will last a long time.

• *Outdoor Research* has a line of *Hydroseal Stuff Sacks* ranging in size from 6"x11" (300 cubic inches, approximately $10) to 13"x19" (2500 cubic inches, approximately $20). These bags have a drawstring closure with generous dustcover, a webbing bottom handle, and a row of webbing loops on the side for lashing onto packs. The heavy duty nylon cloth is sealed with a highly waterproof elastomeric coating and all seams are taped.

• *Gymwell Corporation* has a line of *Gymtech Stuff Sacks* that are guaranteed to be waterproof. They use a tough nylon fabric with a lightweight urethane coating and an additional water repellant. Sack tops are rolled and then clipped to hold them in place. They are available in a variety of sizes.

• *Moonstone* offers their *AC Stuff Sacks*, rectangular-shaped waterproof sacks that feature coated fabric, taped seams, and a roll top closure (like that used on river bags) for absolute waterproofness. A compression strap is included to cinch the sack into the most compact size. As the size decreases, simply roll the top down as needed. Available in small, medium and large sizes.

• *Log House Designs* also makes a line of waterproof stuff sacks from heavy-duty pack cloth coated with a generous urethane coating. A special nylon sleeve extension seals the opening when twisted and shut with a cord lock.

• *Jack Wolfskin* offers their *Waterproof Packsacks* in four sizes: extra-small, small, medium and large.

Compression Stuff Sacks

A compression sack has a strap, or series of straps, that allows you to cinch the sack down to 60% of the size you can achieve with just your hands. This stabilizes the load inside of a pack or pannier, and is important when attempting to store your bag inside a moderately-sized load carrier. Compression stuff sacks cost around $15 to $20. Some of the most popular compression sacks are listed below.

• *Contour Compression Sacks* from Gregory come in three sizes and compress your sleeping bag with the pull of one strap.

• *Telecompressor Stuff Sacks* from Lowe use a series of four cinch straps around the bag to provide compression.

• *AC Sacks* from Moonstone described above have a single strap running length-wise to compress the sleeping bag downward.

• *Compression Sacks* from Slumberjack come in three sizes (9"x21", 12x22" and 15"x22"), each with a series of straps around the circumference.

• *The North Col* from L.L. Bean offers a unique type of compression stuff sack that has four straps running length-wise, sewn into waterproof collars at either end. Once the bag is stuffed, the collars are set in place and cinched down tightly and evenly.

L.L.Bean's North Col

• *Compression Stuff Sacks* from Jack Wolfskin are sacks that are similar in concept to the L.L. Bean model described above.

Other good compression stuff sacks are offered by A16, Gregory, The North Face, and Lowe.

SLEEPING PADS

In addition to a comfortable sleeping bag, it's imperative that you have something that insulates and isolates you from the cold, hard ground when sleeping. A good sleeping pad provides that necessary layer of comfort.

Review Of Generic Types - Sleeping Pads

Sleeping pads have gone through an amazing revolution in the past few years. Thin, rigid foam pads used to be the only choice for lightweight camping and travel. Air mattresses took forever to inflate and were too heavy; thick foam pads were too bulky. Consumers pleaded for a new type of design that could provide more comfort in a small package. Enter the truly remarkable self-inflating sleeping mattresses, a new generation of compact pads that compete with your mattress at home for giving a good night's rest. Closed cell versions still serve as inexpensive, lightweight alternatives for those on tight budgets or counting every ounce, but most campers agree that the performance of the self-inflating pads makes them well worth the extra weight and cost.

Closed Cell Foam Pads. Pads made from closed cell foam come in two varieties, rigid and non-rigid. Rigid pads are quite thin, usually between 3/8" and 3/4". They compress only slightly, relying on their rigid construction to keep rough objects from penetrating. Some models are flat on both sides, while some have ridges or bumps to trap warm air and conform more easily to your body and the ground. They can be rolled up tightly for packing, but since they don't compress can be quite bulky. Non-rigid foam pads must be much thicker since they compress more easily. The result is they are more comfortable, but are even heavier and bulkier to stow, making them generally not suitable for lightweight camping or travel. They come in both 3/4-length and full-length models.

Therm-A-Rest's Ridge Rest

Self-Inflating Mattresses. These pads combine the use of compressible foam with the advantages of an air mattress. When open, the foam expands to give it shape, and a surrounding airtight envelope seals so it can maintain that shape. They come in short or long, standard or deluxe models. They can be anywhere from one to two inches thick when inflated, giving ample protection from rough 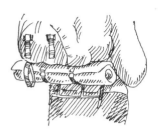 ground. The big advantage over regular air mattresses is that, other than a puff or two at the end, you don't have to blow into them for inflation—the expanding foam does that for you. Air pressure is adjustable to yield the desired degree of stiffness. They can be rolled tightly, compressing down to a surprisingly small packing size. They are available in both 3/4-length and full-length versions.

Features and Options - Sleeping Pads

Rigid foam pads don't have much in the way of features and options. They are simple, reliable, no-frills pieces of gear. About the closest thing you'll find to an intentional design feature is apparent on the *Ridge Rest* from Cascade Designs. It has a symmetric ridge pattern molded into the EVA closed-cell foam to give superior warmth and comfort. The self-inflating mattresses are more complex. The features and options to look for when shopping for sleeping pads are listed below.

Outer Shell. The outer shell forms an airtight chamber around the foam. Although it stands up well to normal amounts of abrasion, a stuff sack is recommended for extended travel.

Air Valve. The air valve is a more sophisticated version of what is used on standard air mattresses. It is typically located in one corner at the head of the pad.

Ergonomic Shapes. Look for a variety of shapes available today. Standard single-thickness, single-chamber rectangles have been assaulted by variable-thickness, multiple-chambered versions that conform more accurately to your body.

Built-in Pillow. Some models have a small section of greater thickness at the head of the pad that serves as a pillow. It usually inflates and deflates along with the rest of the pad.

Built-in Storage Straps. Other models have nylon straps sewn to the head of the pad (or the end with the air valve) so that when the air has been expelled, you simply loop the straps to keep the pad tightly rolled.

Coupler. This simple nylon strap is great for couples since it holds two pads firmly in place. I can attest that without it you end up between pads more often than not.

Stuff Sack. A coated nylon stuff sack will help protect your investment, especially when traveling and storing the pad on the outside of a pack. If you have a pack pocket to store the pad in, a stuff sack is not necessary.

Repair Kit. This is really too important to be just an option; every self-inflating pad should come with one. Any inflatable object is prone to puncture. While these pads are wonders when inflated, a deflated pad is next to useless.

Chair Conversion. An amazing new option for almost any self-inflating mattress is a lightweight harness and sheath that converts it into a flexible seat similar to the original Crazy Creek chair (see camp chairs in the chapter on Specialty Gear, Lightweight Camping).

Friction Coating. A spray-on high-friction coating to reduce slippage is also available.

Construction and Operation - Sleeping Pads

Rigid pads are either cut from rolls of flat, single-piece foam material, or individually molded as with the *Ridge Rest* described above. Closed cell foam is used since it can't absorb moisture. The operation is simply unrolling them for sleeping and rolling them back up tightly for storage. Nylon webbing straps secure them to your other gear. Self-inflating pads have more to them. They start with a one- to two-inch layer of compressible, open-cell foam that is bonded to a tough airtight/waterproof outer fabric. The composite is then sealed to make an airtight chamber. Some pads use foam with a waffle pattern on the upper surface to increase comfort and lessen the chance of your body slipping off during use. An air valve receptacle is always provided, typically in the upper corner.

Inflation. When the pad is unrolled and the valve opened, inflation is automatic. You won't believe how easy it is the first time you try it. The inner foam has a memory. As it returns to its non-compressed shape, air is drawn in through the valve. You can open up the pad and valve in your tent upon arrival at camp. In a short time, the inflation is complete. If you like your pad a bit stiff, add a few puffs of air as desired.

Deflation. This takes a bit more effort unless you have a high-flow air valve. When you are ready to break camp, open the air valve and slowly roll the pad up from the bottom. You are forcing air out the valve as you work your way up to the top. The trick is to roll it tightly enough to fit back in the stuff sack. Sometimes you have to return to the bottom to roll the last bit of air out. I use a combination of rolling with both hands and pressing down with my knee—roll a section and press until no more air escapes, roll another section and press, and so on until I reach the top and can turn the valve to keep it from inflating again. The new high-flow valves available on most current self-inflating sleeping pads make this a much more pleasant procedure.

Author's Recommendations - Sleeping Pads

I offer the following advice for choosing a sleeping pad:

When to Buy Self-Inflating. Even though they are two to three times heavier than a rigid pad, and are about three times as expensive, I highly recommend the self-inflating pads for anyone who can afford the extra weight and cost. Perhaps this is because when we travel we tend to go for longer periods of time, too long to settle for nightly discomfort. It could also be because I had back trouble before using the self-inflating pads and have had no trouble since. The pad shouldn't get all the credit, but it certainly did help. If you travel frequently or for extended periods of time, or if you suffer from back problems, the self-inflating pads are for you.

When to Buy Rigid Foam. Rigid foam pads are the best bet for ultralight or infrequent travel, for people with tight budgets, and for those who are relatively unaffected by sleeping on harder surfaces. They have some distinct advantages. They are inexpensive; they can't be punctured or deflate; they are extremely rugged; and as a rule they don't absorb moisture so you can strap them to the outside of your pack without worrying about the rain.

Short vs. Long Styles. You can cut down on some of the weight by getting a pad with a mid-length cut. At around 48" long, it does the job of cushioning your upper body while leaving your lower legs to fend for themselves. I find this style of pad to be fine for everything except winter camping, when you need the extra length for insulation.

Thin vs. Thick Styles. You can also cut down on weight and bulk by choosing the thinnest self-inflating pad that is still comfortable for your needs. Cascade Designs offers their *Ultra Lite* in regular or long styles. It inflates to one-inch thickness, and packs to an incredible 4.5" or 5.5"x11". The standard pad thickness is around 1.5 inches, while deluxe pads measure about two inches thick.

Ergonomic Shapes. I've used standard rectangular pads for years and have been very happy, but I'm starting to get interested in the new ergonomic models, especially ones with integrated pillow sections. The shape and price are right, the only drawback might be the extra weight. REI's full-length *Ergomat* has four different inflatable sections and is tapered top and bottom like a mummy bag. The top section is just an air chamber for use as a pillow; the middle two sections, covering shoulder to hip area, use an egg carton-shaped foam that conforms to your body and prevents slipping; the lower chamber has a thinner foam core.

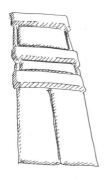

Basic Designs' Equalizer

Basic Designs has several ergonomic models. Their *Equalizer* not only self-inflates, but also self-adjusts by allowing air to transfer between inflated sections as you change position. Their *Foam•Air•Mat* is similar to REI's version with multiple chambers of varying thickness and a pillow section for your head. Gymwell Corporation offers two versions of their *Insul-A-Mat* that have unusual shapes, the *Plus* which has a built-in three-inch pillow section, and the *Wave* with its ridges of foam for greater comfort and reduced tendency for slipping.

My only complaint about ergonomic sleeping pads is that they only fit your body one way, so the 3/4-length versions with an included pillow section seem too short—your head is comfortable, but your upper legs are left unprotected. With standard pads you can slide the pad down and make a pillow out of a pile of clothing. My recommendation is that if you get an ergonomic pad, make certain it's long enough for your needs.

Costs. Rigid foam pads cost around $10 to $15 for short and $15 to $20 for long models. Self-inflating pads start at around $40 for standard models and go up to $80 for a deluxe version. Some models do not include a repair kit and stuff sack, a $10 investment.

Innovation - Sleeping Pads That Double As Chairs

This is almost reason enough to get a self-inflating sleeping pad in the first place. Crazy Creek started the whole idea of packing along a lightweight, flexible camp chair when you go camping. Their fabric and foam chairs have some cushioning so you can sit right on the ground, and nylon side straps that connect to the back to keep you in an upright position. Not long ago someone figured out that it didn't make sense to carry both a flexible chair and a self-inflating sleeping pad. They asked, "Why not combine the two?" and the idea of a chair/pad combination was born.

There are several models that are primarily intended to be used as camp chairs, yet also work nicely as sleeping pads when you unfasten the side straps and lay them flat. These include the *Powerlounger* from Crazy Creek and the *Insul-A-Seat* from Gymwell Corporation. The *Powerlounger* is only 1/2" thick and not inflatable, but as a seat with the flaps folded double it has one full inch of cushioning. It also sports two pockets that can be stuffed with clothes to serve as a pillow. The *Insul-A-Seat* is 1.5" thick and a true self-inflating sleeping mattress. It has two side straps so the pad can be folded in the middle to form a comfortable seat.

The other option is to buy a separate harness and sheath assembly that uses your existing self-inflating pad to form a chair. These models include the *Therm-A-Rest'R Lite* from Cascade Designs (10 oz., fits all 20" wide *Therm-A-Rest* models) or Crazy Creek's *Thermalounger* (three different models allow use with all *Therm-A-Rest* pads).

Something to remember about chair/sleeping pad combinations is that in most campgrounds the bottom of the pad is going to get dirty unless housed in a fabric sheath. Clean it off well before putting it back into the tent.

Crazy Creek's Thermalounger

I recommend the sleeping pads listed below for lightweight camping and active travel.

Author's Recommendations - Sleeping Pads

Brand	Model	Type	Width	Length	Depth	Wgt. (lbs)
Basic Designs	Equalizer	full length	22"	73"	1.5"/3"	3.3
Basic Designs	Equalizer	3/4 length	20	48	1.5"/3"	2.0
Basic Designs	Foam•Air•Mat	3/4 length	21"	48"	1.5"/1"	1.8
Basic Designs	Foam•Air•Mat	compact	21"	73"	1"	2.4
Cascade Designs	Therm-A-Rest	standard	20"	48"/72"	1.5"	1.5/2.3
Cascade Designs	Therm-A-Rest	Ultra Lite	20	48"/72"	1"	1.0/1.8
Cascade Designs	Therm-A-Rest	Ridge R'st*	20"	48"/72"	5/8"/3/4"	0.5-1.1
Crazy Creek	Powerlounger**	standard	20.5"	69"	0.5"	2.1
Gemini	Earthpad Twill	st'd long	20"	60"/72"	3/8"/1/2"	1.0
Gymwell Corp	Insul-A-Mat	Plus	20"/26"	72"	1.5"	2.8/3.5

Gymwell Corp	Insul-A-Mat	Wave	24"	72"	1.5"	2.8
Gymwell Corp	Insul-A-Mat	Alpha Plus	20"26"	48"/72"	1"-2"	1.3-2.7
Gymwell Corp	Insul-A-Mat	standard	20"/26"	48"/72"	1"-2"	1.3-2.7
Gymwell Corp	Insul-A-Seat	st'd long	18"/20"	48"/72"	1.5"	2.5/3.3
REI	Ergomat	tapered	22"/14"	77"	1.5"/1"	2.5

*Rigid closed cell foam pad. **Made with closed cell foam; not inflatable. Primarily intended for use as a chair or lounger, it also serves as a sleeping pad.

Note: The Insul-A-Mat Plus has a 3" pillow section at the top of the pad; the Alfa Plus has a tough, puncture resistant bottom fabric and high-density foam core; and the Wave utilizes a foam core with ridges for greater comfort.

Maintenance and Repairs - Sleeping Pads

Here are a few suggestions on how to keep your self-inflating sleeping pad in good shape:

Keep it Clean. Used solely in a tent, your sleeping pad will rarely need cleaning. If you use it as a cushion, lounger, or for sleeping outside of the tent, it's bound to get dirty. If it does, take some warm water and a mild liquid camp soap to wash off any accumulated dirt or grime; just don't scrub too hard with a stiff-bristled brush.

Store it Dry. It's fine if your pad gets wet during use; the outer fabric is usually waterproof. You should dry it before packing if possible, though, to prevent the growth of mildew. If you can't do it the morning you're packing up, take it out and dry it later in the day. The nylon material dries quickly in the sun. It should be totally dry before storing it when you return home.

Inflate for Storage. Don't store your pad long term with it deflated and rolled. This will eventually reduce inflation time and final thickness the foam can achieve. When you return home from a trip, allow the pad to self-inflate, then make sure it's clean and dry before storing. It takes up more room to store it this way, but will greatly increase its useful life.

Use a Stuff Sack. It is probably redundant to use an additional sack to store your sleeping pad if you only carry it protected in a pack, pannier or duffel. More often than not, however, the pad is strapped to the outside of your other gear and subject to damage from abrasion. This is especially true for air travel. I suggest you use a stuff sack whenever you can; it's better to replace an inexpensive sack than a costly pad.

Other Helpful Hints. Don't store an inflated pad in a car on a hot day. Don't allow spilled solvents and insect repellants to remain on the pad; wash them off immediately with concentrated camp soap. Keep the pad away from fires and stoves or pet teeth and claws. You can use your mattress for occasional floating on a lake or pond, but chlorine, salt water, or extended exposure to the sun should be avoided.

Repairs. The most common repairs to a self-inflating pad are punctures and tears from some sharp object underneath you on the ground or encountered while traveling. All manufacturers of these pads also sell easy-to-use repair kits that include a tube of adhesive and self-adhering fabric patches. Punctures are easiest to fix; simply deflate the pad, place a thin layer of glue around the hole in an area as big as the patch. When this is tacky to the touch, place the patch firmly over the hole and allow to dry. Tears require more extensive patching. It is rare, but occasionally an air valve may become defective. On most pads this is easy to fix. The valves are screwed into a rigid piece of material bonded to the fabric. Unscrew the old valve and apply some rubber adhesive (that comes with the new valve) to the threads of the new valve. Screw it tightly into position and you are ready to go. You can also use the new high-flow valve kit from Therm-A-Rest to update their old pads.

PILLOWS

Pillows have generally been regarded as an unnecessary luxury for backcountry campers and lightweight travelers. It's true that they aren't really needed; it's easy enough to stack a few clothes in a neat pile and cover them with your parka, or stuff clothes inside a pillowcase. But for those times when you left your parka and other cushioning clothing at home, or you just want some extra comfort, a few good lightweight pillow options are now available.

Review of Generic Types - Pillows

Listed below are the currently available types of lightweight pillows for campers and travelers.

Integrated with a Pad. A few models of self-inflating sleeping pads have a slightly thicker section up at the head to serve as a pillow when inflated. This is one of the nicest options since the pillow is always there, serviceable without the need for clothing.

Inflating Pillows. Some manufacturers of self-inflating pads also offer small versions to be used as pillows. These are very compact, don't rely on clothing, and can also be used as a cushion or backrest for a variety of activities.

Compressible Pillows. A few lightweight, compact camp pillows are available that have a soft outer shell and cushioning synthetic fill material. They stuff just like a tiny sleeping bag. These can be also be used at home or on public transportation.

Sleeping Bag Pockets. Some sleeping bags come equipped with pockets that can be stuffed with clothing to form a comfortable pillow. There is virtually no extra weight and the pillow stays in place through the night.

Pillowcase or Shell. Whether from home or purchased through an outdoor retailer, this lightweight option can be stuffed with clothing to form a suitable pillow. They weigh little and are easily cleaned.

Author's Recommendations - Pillows

Over the years we have mainly used pillowcases from home with a few clothes placed inside to serve as our pillows. This type of pillow is still the preferred choice for lightweight travelers. If you prefer not to take a pillowcase from home, try the *Therm-A-Rest Pocket Pillow*. It has flannel-like softness on the outside, weighs 1.25 ounces, and costs around $6. Stuff it with a few clothes for a great makeshift pillow. You can also create a nice pillow by placing clothing in the pocket provided on many sleeping bags and bag couplers. All of these options give you a serviceable pillow with very little additional weight.

If you can spare a few more ounces, try the *Self-Inflating Pillow* from Basic Designs (seven ounces, 12"x16"), or the *Back Rest* from Cascade Designs (five ounces, 8"x16"). The *Back Rest* is intended to be a lumbar cushion, but works well as a lightweight pillow. These pillows are produced using the same construction as self-inflating sleeping pads. They can double as multipurpose cushions at home or on the road, weigh five or six ounces, and cost around $15.

I'd also recommend any of the compressible Quallofil® pillows on the market, including the *Therm-A-Rest Deluxe Pillow* (13"x17"), the Slumberjack *Quallofil Pillow* (10"x20"), or the MZH *Camp Pillow* (14"x19"). These soft fluffy pillows weigh about half a pound and cost around $15.

Food and Water

- Staples
- Camping Food
- Food Containers
- Water Carriers
- Water Treatment Gear

Having adequate supplies of food and water, as well as adequate methods of storing and packing them, is an important consideration when traveling without a vehicle. This becomes more important the further afield you go on your travels. Sometimes getting supplies will be easy, with a well-stocked store and a convenient water spigot within reach. Other times places to provision will be harder to find, so it pays to be prepared by having some basic food staples, containers for packing and storing your provisions, and a means for securing safe drinking water.

Foods are either staples you always try to have a small supply of, local food that you buy as you travel, or packaged dehydrated foods for backpacking or bicycle touring when weight is critical and stores are not easily accessible.

STAPLES

There are some lightweight, easily-packed food staples that ensure you'll always be able to prepare a simple yet filling meal on the road. Staples for lightweight camping include:

Tea and coffee	Ovaltine or hot chocolate
Honey or sugar	Powdered milk
Herbs and spices	Small bottle of cooking oil
Small container of mayonnaise	Bouillon cubes and powdered soups
Butter or peanut butter	Dried fruit
Crackers	

CAMPING FOOD

Lightweight dehydrated camping food is also available for travelers. The variety of dishes is staggering, from bountiful breakfasts and soups to gourmet dinners and desserts. In addition to entrees, you'll also find items such as lightweight butter, hot spiced cider and even ice cream. While camping foods tend to be quite pricey, they really come into their own for extended backcountry travel where weight must be kept to a minimum and opportunities to restock are nonexistent.

Preparation - Camping Food

Most camping foods are packaged in dry form with the water removed to reduce and increase shelf-life. Add water and cook according to the manufacturers instructions on the package, then add spices to taste. Camping foods typically require very little cooking, offsetting their initial cost with savings in cooking time and fuel.

Author's Recommendations - Camping Food

The best camping foods available are offered from the following suppliers: Mountain House, Backpacker's Pantry, Harvest Foodworks, AlpineAire, and Richmoor. Meal type and taste vary considerably, so make certain to try some meals at home before you order in quantity for a trip. Look for dishes that have no MSG, preservatives, or artificial colors and flavors. Entrees can be complemented with soups, side dishes, desserts and drinks.

Costs. You'll pay around $3 per serving for one to two-serving entrees, less for breakfasts and soups or when dishes are packaged for groups of four to six. Desserts, vegetables and other extras are in the range of $1.50 per serving. Costs are reduced on complete prepackaged meals (entree, soups, dessert, and drink included), and discounts are usually available on quantity purchases.

A sampling of some popular main dishes is listed below:

Author's Recommendations - Camping Foods

Brand	Dish	Servings	Weight
AlpineAire	Leonardo De Fettucini	2	5.5 oz.
AlpineAire	Brown Rice Pilaf w/ Vegetables	2	7 oz.
Backpacker's Pantry	Spinach Noodle Stroganoff	2	6 oz.
Backpacker's Pantry	Cajun Rice w/ Chicken	2	7 oz.
Harvest Foodworks	Couscous Almondine	2, 4, 6	10, 19, 28 oz.
Harvest Foodworks	Bountiful Veg. Pasta w/ Ch'se	2, 4, 6	8.6, 18, 26 oz.
Mountain House	Sweet and Sour Pork w/ Rice	2	4.9 oz.
Mountain House	Turkey Tetrazzini	2	3.3 oz.
Richmoor	Mexican Bean Tostada	2	7.8 oz.
Richmoor	Mandarin Orange Chicken	2	5.5 oz.

FOOD CONTAINERS

You should also give some consideration to how you're going to carry and store food while traveling. You need containers that have adequate seals and are sturdy enough to be stuffed in a pack or pannier, yet are lightweight and easy to stow. There are different types of containers for different consistencies of food. Most travelers use a wide assortment of sizes and shapes to cover their needs.

Author's Recommendations - Food Containers

You'll find the following types of food containers to be the best available for lightweight camping.

Tupperware. You may have to suffer through a "Tupperware party" to get some of this fantastic plasticware, but then nothing worthwhile comes easily in this life. Tupperware is available in a multitude of sizes and is almost indestructible, as its lifetime warranty illustrates. Particularly useful are the little spice containers that have served our family well for many years.

Spice containers. Other than the Tupperware ones mentioned above, try any of the small food-grade plastic bottles available at outdoor retail stores If you'd rather have all your spices in one container, try the *Dial-A-Spice*. It has room for six of your favorite spices in one easy-to-pour bottle. Just twist the top to the one you want to use. Don't worry if the names on the outside don't correspond completely with the spices you carry; it's easy to reassign names with some pieces of tape. The one problem you'll have is that the slots of the *Dial-A-Spice* are equal sizes, and some spices are used more rapidly than others. On longer trips carry extra supplies of more commonly used spices in a zip-seal bag.

There are also a few good combination salt and pepper shakers. My favorites are Coglan's ultra-lightweight *Backpacker's Salt and Pepper Shaker* and the larger *Camper's Salt and Pepper Shaker* that is more appropriate for families. If you don't use much salt in your diet, use that space for some other favorite spice, such as curry or garlic. You'll also see small plastic lids for sale that turn used film cannisters into spice containers. I don't recommend their use. The plastic used for the cannisters is not food-grade, and articles have appeared that suggest traces of toxic chemicals from the film may be able to leach into the spices. That's enough for me to want to seek alternatives.

Freezer Containers. These containers are rugged and inexpensive, although they won't last as long as Tupperware. Make sure to find brands with good seals to keep the food and your pack safe while traveling.

Squeeze Tubes. Several good brands of squeeze tubes are available, including models from Coglan's and REI. They operate similar to toothpaste tubes. The bottom opens up for filling and cleaning, then reseals for use. The top incorporates a small dispenser with a screw cap. The tube is rolled up as food is used. These are particularly nice for peanut butter and other spreadables.

Nalgene Bottles. The Nagle Company offers a great selection of durable plastic bottles and jars for all travel and outdoor needs. Types that are suitable for foods include their vials, dropper bottles, lexan and polypropylene jars, narrow-mouth and wide-mouth bottles, rectangular bottles, and lexan wide-mouth loop-top bottles. Choose sizes that are appropriate for the type of provisions you carry.

Zip-Seal Bags. These locking baggies are great for powdered food and other items. They come in a wide variety of sizes, including 2x3, 3x5, 5x8, 9x12, and 12x15 inches. To ensure a good seal, roll them so the unused part of the bag is wrapped around the part holding the food. Make sure the extra air has escaped. Then zip the seal closed and use a rubber band to keep the bags rolled tightly.

WATER CARRIERS

Water carriers come in handy for hauling water as well as providing an easy means of storing and dispensing water at your campsite. There are two basic types available for lightweight campers, soft water bags and collapsible jugs.

Collapsible Jugs. These types of water carriers have been around for a long time. They come in a variety of sizes, although the most convenient to fill and carry are the 2 to 2.5-gallon models.

We've used this type of water container for many years, but there are better alternatives available now. The plastic collapsible jugs are lightweight, but they are bulky, hard to fold up, tend to fall off their perch during use, and seem to develop leaks with unfortunate regularity. The soft water carriers described below are a much better option for active travelers. The only exception to this is if your water treatment gear includes a collapsible jug, such as the WTC *Pentapure Water Jug*. In this case, having a jug makes sense, since it doubles as both treatment gear and carrier. This simple device holds about two gallons expanded and one gallon collapsed.

Soft Water Bags. Soft water bags usually have an inner lining of food-grade material that is water-tight and a tough outer shell that is abrasion resistant. On some models, such as the REI and Basic Designs water bags, the inner liner is an inexpensive food-grade plastic bag that is replaceable. On others, such as the MSR *Dromedary Bag*, it is a high-quality material that is laminated to the outer shell. A few models consist of only one layer of tough food-grade plastic. Soft water bags usually have a large mouth fill point with a removable screw cap/pour spout. They are easy to use, can be hung up or used free-standing on almost any surface, and roll up to almost nothing when it's time to break camp. Some models have shower attachments for bathing or washing dishes, and even connect directly to the outlet of water treatment gear.

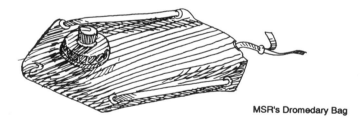

MSR's Dromedary Bag

Author's Recommendations - Water Carriers

I highly recommend the following soft water carriers for light-
veight camping:

Basic Designs' *Water Carrier* holds about three gallons yet weighs only four ounces dry. It has replaceable inner liners, a nylon outer cover, a nylon carrying handle, a shower attachment, and attaches directly to the Basic Designs water filters. Cost is around $7.

REI's *Water Bag* is about the same as that described above. It also costs around $7, and has a convenient shower attachment that is great for doing dishes.

MSR's *Dromedary Bag* is made of a watertight inner lining laminated to a durable Cordura nylon outer shell. It is extremely high quality, as the price reflects. This sturdy bag comes in two, four and ten-liter sizes, weighs three, four and ten ounces respectively, and costs from $15 to $28. These bags are more expensive, but will last many seasons. They attach directly to MSR's *Waterworks* water filter. You can get models that have brass grommets laced with webbing for hanging or securing the carrier to your pack.

EMS stores typically carry an inexpensive, single-layer version of a soft water carrier, a flexible clear plastic bag with spout that doubles as fill point, and an integral plastic handle for carrying and hanging.

WATER TREATMENT GEAR

Even though water filters and purifiers really come into their own during lightweight camping, they are primarily health items, and as such I have described them in the Health and Hygiene chapter of Personal Gear. Please refer to that section for complete product reviews and recommendations.

C ooking

- Stove
- Cook Set
- Baking Gear
- Grill
- Other Cooking Gear
- Dishes and Cutlery
- Clean-up Gear

In this section, we'll examine the lightweight cooking gear currently on the market for travelers and outdoor enthusiasts. Those who frequent the backcountry are probably more familiar with the basic types of equipment available, since the ability to prepare meals, as with the ability to provide your own shelter, is a must when adventuring far from civilization.

STOVES

The primary item in a lightweight cooking kit is a one-burner "backpacking" stove. These stoves are compact and incredibly well designed pieces of gear. Putting them to use for preparing a complete meal takes a bit of practice. After all, they are temporarily supplanting your four-burner range, oven, toaster, and other cooking apparatus at your disposal in a house. Cooking on one burner may seem daunting at first, but you'll soon gain proficiency at it and may even begin wondering why you need all that other gear at home.

Many of us started our outdoor cooking careers on stoves like the Swedish *SVEA 123*. These simple little stoves have been around for ages. They don't have much in the way of controls or features, and when operating they sound like a jet during take-off, but our little SVEA always got us through a camping trip in fine style. Stoves have come a long way over the years. More sophistication, greater control and efficiency, multi-fuel capability, and easier operation head the list of recent changes.

Review of Generic Types - Stoves

Lightweight stoves are all similar in size and construction, but they can be quite different in design and operation. Listed below are the generic types of lightweight stoves currently on the market, along with their general classifications.

By Fuel Type. The most distinguishing characteristic of a lightweight stove is probably what fuel it runs on. All stoves convert the stored energy in solid, liquid, or gaseous fuels into heat for cooking. Gaseous fuels must be compressed and stored in liquid form in pressurized bottles or cannisters. They vaporize as they leave the cannister, entering the stove as a combustible gas and making them very easy to operate. Liquid fuels store easily in unpressurized containers, but the fuel must be pressurized or preheated before it can be burned to produce a hot, controllable flame. There are also a few solid-fuel stoves on the market that burn wood and other organic matter for cooking.

*Note: There is often some confusion surrounding the use of the word gas. Gas can refer to a state of matter, as with the gaseous fuels of propane and butane, or it can be a colloquial word for the liquid fuel gasoline, as with white gas and auto gas.

• *Propane Gas.* At home, a good choice for cooking is either natural or propane gas. Although propane gas burns well at cold temperatures and is widely available in the U.S. for camping, the self-sealing containers it comes in must be constructed of fairly thick steel to keep it stored in liquified form under pressure. This makes straight propane a good choice for domestic travel in a vehicle or boat, and a less desirable choice for self-propelled travel when weight is a big consideration.

• *Butane Gas.* The preferred compressed gas for lightweight travelers and outdoor enthusiasts has been butane, since it can be stored in relatively thin-walled cannisters. Operation of a butane cannister stove is simple, almost like using a gas stove at home. The only drawback is that straight butane has trouble vaporizing in cold weather at low altitudes. High altitude operation is improved because of the reduced atmospheric pressure, but many fuel suppliers are now switching to a blended gas mixture—butane with up to 20% propane added to give better cold-weather performance. Butane and butane blends are widely available outside the U.S.

• *White Gas* is a highly volatile liquid fuel that is primarily marketed in North America. It burns cleanly and produces a relatively hot flame. White gas stoves come in two different versions, those with integral fuel storage and increasingly popular models where fuel is remotely stored in a bottle and fed to the stove through a thin piece of tubing.

- *Kerosene* is another liquid fuel that can be used in some lightweight stoves. Its major advantages are low cost, worldwide availability and the hot cooking flame it produces. This fuel is not very volatile, making it safer to use but harder to clean up since it doesn't evaporate easily. Lightweight stoves that use kerosene typically can also use white gas by changing the fuel jet; some can also use other liquid fuels.

- *Solid Fuel.* These lightweight backpacking stoves are the result of modifying an old concept to yield a simple yet efficient cooking apparatus. Twigs, wood chips, pine cones, animal dung or other organic debris is ignited in a small chamber in the stove. Battery-powered ventilation provides a concentrated blast of oxygen that promotes combustion and produces a hot flame. Solid fuel stoves' advantages include simplicity of design and operation, a hot cooking flame, plus the fact that free organic material is available everywhere.

- *Alcohol.* A few stoves on the market use alcohol. This fuel is not a by-product of the petroleum industry. It is made from renewable sources such as corn, grain and wood, and therefore the fuel of choice for many environmentalists. It is widely available in a variety of forms, including denatured alcohol, shellac thinner, methanol/ethanol, Everclear, boat stove fuel, even gas line anti-freeze. Alcohol has some other good points: it has low volatility and only a simple lightweight burner assembly with no priming or preheating required. Yet alcohol can be quite expensive (especially boat fuel), and you'll only get about half the heat output for its weight as you do with some other liquid fuels.

- *Other Fuels.* In addition to kerosene and white gas, a few multi-fuel stoves can also run on auto fuel (gasoline and diesel) as well as more exotic fuels such as jet fuel, Stoddard solvent, and AV gas. While this amazing line-up of potential fuels sounds impressive, the truth is that between kerosene and white gas you'll be able to operate your stove almost anywhere in the world. Auto fuels have additives that tend to clog the stove easily and make their operation a smoky affair. Unleaded gasoline can be a good low-cost substitute fuel, but it is only available in some locations outside the U.S. and Canada. Leaded gasoline is not recommended at all since it produces toxic fumes and residues. And how many travelers come into contact with jet fuel and Stoddard solvent?

By Fuel Storage Location. Stoves are also classified according to how they are designed.

• *Integrated* stoves have the fuel storage tank attached directly to the burner assembly, usually on the bottom so the tank can also serve as a base.

• *Component* stoves separate the burner from the fuel storage. The fuel is typically stored in a remote bottle, connected to the stove by a flexible hose or thin metal tube.

By Intended Use. Stoves are also classified according to how and where they are to be used. The three major categories are listed below:

• *Three Season* stoves operate most efficiently in above freezing conditions. Generally speaking, the only stoves that are rated as three season are a few models that use straight butane gas. Butane has a hard time vaporizing in the cold.

• *Four Season* stoves operate admirably in cold climates, and this covers almost all stoves on the market. What is most affected by temperature is the vaporization of gas and liquid fuels. Four season stoves make provisions to ease fuel vaporization, as well as improved wind and weather protection.

• *Mountaineering* stoves are made to perform well at high altitudes and in extreme conditions. Most models run on blended gaseous fuel and are sold as kits complete with hanging mount, pots and windscreen.

Features and Options - Stoves

Listed below are the features and options to look for when shopping for a lightweight backpacking stove.

Burner. This is the assembly where fuel combustion takes place. It typically consists of a fuel jet and a flame spreader.

Fuel Jet. Sometimes included in a more elaborate component and called a generator, the fuel jet is typically just a piece of metal with a small hole drilled in the center. The hole is sized exactly for the type of fuel to be used. It acts as a restriction, keeping the fuel flowing at a regulated rate. On multi-fuel stoves, jets are usually threaded brass inserts that must be exchanged when switching between white gas or gasoline and kerosene. Jets must be free of dirt and debris for the stove to operate properly. Some stoves, such as MSR's *Whisperlite Internationale,* come equipped with an integral cleaning wire for consistent operation.

Flame Spreader. This allows the flame to assume an efficient configuration. It is either integrated with the burner assembly or fastened above the flame as a separate component.

Vaporization Tube. Some liquid-fuel stoves help the vaporization process by winding the last bit of metal fuel feed tube right near the burner assembly. This allows the incoming fuel to heat up and vaporize soon after lighting, reducing the priming time required.

Pump. Some liquid-fuel stoves integrate a small air pump that pressurizes the fuel before it leaves the storage tank. This is especially important on four season models. In some cases, this is all that is necessary before lighting, as with the PEAK1 *Apex* and *Multi-fuel* stoves. Most other liquid-fuel stoves require a little preheating before the fuel vaporizes completely and smooth combustion takes place.

Priming Cup. This is where you place a little priming fuel to burn, preheating the incoming fuel until the hot stove can vaporize it on its own.

Fuel Control. Every stove has a small knob or lever that allows you to control the flow of fuel. Most stoves with gas cannisters allow for easy adjustment from simmer to high, just like your stove at home. Some liquid fuel stoves have a hard time with the simmer stage, tending to be either off or on full blast.

Fuel Storage. Fuel is either stored remotely in a bottle or cannister that is connected to the stove by a tube or hose, or in an integral tank or cannister under the burner. Gas fuel cannisters either have self-sealing threads so you can remove them from the stove and store them separately, or they are simply punctured as they initially seal with the stove, in which case you must leave the cannister attached until it is used up.

Main Housing. This metal structure provides a point of attachment for all other components. It sometimes serves other purposes, such as a windscreen or heat containment area.

Base. The base provides a means of steadying the stove, a contact surface with the ground, and sometimes a heat reflector. The base either consists of a flat bottom pan or adjustable legs that form a tripod, or it is formed by the fuel storage tank itself, as with some gas cannister stoves and a few liquid fuel models.

Windscreen. This is a very important component of a good stove system. It can be built-in as part of the main housing or pot support, or it can be a separate component. In some instances, the windscreen also forms a directed heat path up the side of the cooking pot, increasing heat exchange and efficiency. In all cases, it surrounds the burner and blocks wind that can disrupt the flame and rob heat from the bottom of the cooking pot.

Heat Reflector. Sometimes built into the unit, sometimes a separate component, this part is usually located under the burner to make sure that escaping heat is reflected up toward the bottom of the cooking pot.

Pot Support. This simple piece (or pieces) of metal extends up from the housing, holding the pot or pan at a measured height above the burner. The pot support is often mobile so it can swing out for better support during operation, then swing back in for compact storage.

Construction and Operation - Stoves

Stove components are typically constructed of brass, aluminum and stainless or coated steel. Gas fuel cannisters are typically made of coated steel; they are not reusable and therefore should be recycled where possible. The pump assembly on remote fuel storage bottles is usually made of aluminum and high-impact plastic, along with rubber for all pressure seals.

Stove operation varies widely, so it will be discussed according to the various models available.

Gaseous Fuel Stoves. If the stove uses self-sealing gas cannisters, then the cannister is simply connected to the fuel control valve (either attached to the stove itself, or a remote component connected to the stove through a flexible hose). A needle in the fuel control assembly is either inserted through a rubber seal in the cannister, similar to inserting an air pump needle into an inflatable ball, or it depresses a spring-loaded internal valve in the cannister. With the cannister firmly in place, gas is able to flow to the burner anytime the fuel control is opened. Adjust the fuel control to get the desired flame. To remove the cannister, simply close the fuel control and unscrew the fuel control assembly. The needle gradually withdraws from the rubber seal, or the spring-loaded internal valve reseats, and the cannister is free to be packed for travel.

Stoves that use cannisters that are not self-sealing generally have the fuel control assembly attached directly to the bottom of the stove. As the cannister is pressed tightly to the bottom of the fuel control assembly, a sharp needle point actually punctures a tiny hole in the steel cannister. No gas escapes since a rubber gasket becomes compressed around the puncture as the cannister is installed and held in place. The only anxious moments are after you've punctured the cannister and before you actually secure it in place, usually with spring-loaded legs that grab onto the bottom of the cannister. Once the cannister is punctured and securely fastened, the stove behaves the same as that described above. The only difference is that you can't remove the cannister until all the fuel is consumed. This is generally no problem since you can pack the stove and cannister as one unit for local travel. If you ever have to travel by airplane, though, make sure the fuel is gone before it's time to board. No combustible fuels of any kind are allowed on commercial flights. Several times before a flight we've had to light off our stove and burn half a cannister or so of fuel so we could separate it from the stove.

Liquid Fuel Stoves. Stoves that use liquid fuel function a little differently. There are several distinct stages of operation.

• *Pressurization.* Pressure is needed to force fuel into the burner assembly. First make sure the fuel storage area is filled no more than 2/3 full with fuel. Don't overfill the fuel tank; the space at the top is required to allow air to become pressurized. This is true for both integral and remote fuel storage containers. The fill cap on integral tank models is placed so that with the stove on level ground, fuel can't be filled above the bottom of the cap. With remote bottles you just have to guess; they fill in the vertical position, then lie horizontally during operation. Many models, including all component stoves with remote storage bottles, rely on a pump to initially pressurize the fuel. Too little pumping will mean insufficient pressure, too much can cause the stove to burn erratically. You'll soon find out what works best for your stove. Some stoves with integral fuel storage don't use a priming pump; they get adequate pressure just by burning a bit of fuel on a priming cup. As the burning fuel warms the fuel storage area, the air inside expands and forms pressure. Although a little harder to execute, this pressurizes and vaporizes the fuel in one step. Because of the added difficulty, Optimus offers optional priming pumps for their liquid-fuel stoves.

• *Vaporization.* Once the fuel is under pressure and able to flow to the burner, it must be vaporized (changed into a gaseous form), or at least well atomized (dispersed in a fine spray) in order to burn cleanly and smoothly. Preheating is typically the method used to vaporize fuel. Failure to preheat adequately may cause dramatic flare-ups. The fuel feed tube is usually looped through the burner assembly so it becomes hot soon after the priming fuel is lit, then stays hot during operation. In some cases, the same preheating technique described above for pressurization also serves to vaporize liquid fuel once the feed tube or burner is hot enough. The design of some liquid-fuel stoves with pressure pumps, such as the PEAK 1 *Apex* or *Multi-Fuel* models, is such that they require no preheating before lighting. Atomized fuel burns initially, and soon after start-up, once the stove is hot, the incoming fuel becomes fully vaporized and burns smoothly.

Note: Another source of confusion for stove users in the use of the term priming. To prime a stove literally means to get it ready for operation. That is why the term is used to describe the pump and the act of pressurizing the fuel, as well as the preheating fuel cup and the preheating process.

• *Starting the Stove.* A typical starting scenario goes like this: Attach the fuel bottle if fuel storage is remote. If a priming pump is used, pump the required number of times to get initial pressurization. Place some priming fuel in the appropriate location and light it (if preheating is required). Wait until the fuel feed tube has a chance to get hot. Before the priming flame is gone, open the fuel control valve until fuel begins to be forced through the burner. If the preheating sequence was a success and vaporization is complete, the fuel will burn with a clean blue flame. If not the flame will sputter, spurt, and may flare up as liquid fuel ignites. Shut down the control valve immediately. Allow the stove to calm down and burn the fuel already in the fuel feed tube. The flame will quickly die out. Slowly open the control valve again before the flame goes out. This time it should burn smoothly; a flare-up usually provides enough preheating for full vaporization. You'll soon get used to how much priming fuel and time is required to start your stove.

Solid Fuel Stoves. The solid fuel stoves on the market operate much the way a blacksmith's forge works. A small fire is made in the main combustion chamber (a simple metal cannister) with tinder and a match. Twigs or other organic matter are added. Once the fire is going oxygen is forced into the chamber by a small fan, producing a very hot fire. The fan speed is variable so you can adjust the heat output; be careful, it can be double that of other stoves. One "AA" battery will last up to six hours of operation. Cooking on this type of stove is less controlled than with some other models, more like cooking over an open fire. Watch your meal since this stove can burn very hot. You need to keep track of the fuel level during cooking. When you start to run low just add organic matter and allow it to begin burning properly.

Storage. After your meal is cooked, shut off the stove and allow it to cool thoroughly before packing it away. Make sure all seals and shut-offs are tightly closed. You can usually store the pump assembly in place on remote liquid-fuel bottles; no need to pack it separately.

Author's Recommendations - Stoves

I offer the following recommendations on lightweight cooking stoves for outdoor enthusiasts:

GASEOUS-FUEL STOVES

There is no question about the convenience of stoves that use butane or blended-fuel cannisters. They are simple pieces of gear and incredibly easy to use; no priming, just turn on the fuel control valve and light it. The flame size is almost always totally adjustable, so more complicated meals that require simmering can be easily accommodated. They are quiet and require almost no maintenance. These stoves are perfect for many travelers and campers, but after using one for several years I have three reservations about recommending this type of stove.

First of all, cooking time is usually increased with gas cannister stoves, making it harder to prepare meals for families and small groups with a one-burner stove. Using blended-fuel or propane cannisters diminishes the time difference, but if you are used to liquid-fuel stoves you'll still find most gas cannister models slow. This is illustrated by the four MSR stoves now available. The three liquid-fuel models boil water about 30% faster than MSR's gaseous-fuel model. Some gas cannister stoves do have faster boil times, including the EPIgas and Bibler models.

The second reservation I have is the availability of fuel cannisters. Not only do you have to find places that sell gas cannisters, you have to find gas cannisters to fit your particular stove. It might be available in one region, totally unheard of in another. The self-sealing cannisters from MSR, EPIgas, Optimus, and Markill/Apex (Husch) have threads that only match certain stoves. Camping Gaz's large *CV470* self-sealing cannisters fit their *Ultra S470* and Bleuet *470 HP* model stoves. Hank Roberts and some Optimus cannisters have a rubber tip instead of threads, and only fit those types of stoves. Gas cannisters that don't self-seal, like Camping Gaz's *C206* (or any of the foreign equivalents you'll find), can only operate on specially made stoves. I've had trouble locating cannisters for lightweight stoves both in the U.S. and abroad. In the U.S., they are sold only at specialty retailers. This is no problem if you live near a supplier and can pack what you need for short trips, but if you are traveling light and for longer periods of time, you'll undoubtedly spend time searching out gas cannister retailers. Finding the cannisters outside the U.S. can also be hit or miss; just because they are available in a country doesn't mean that you can find them easily.

My last reservation is the environmental concern of all those empty gas cannisters. If you conscientiously recycle them, then they are no different than any other disposable metal containers, including those used for canned food. But in many countries there are no metal recycling facilities, and use of gas cannisters (and canned food) just adds material to the local landfill, often the nearest ravine.

Having voiced these concerns, I would still recommend gas cannister stoves to anyone who wanted or needed the convenience of operation they give; wasn't trying to cook for a large group or on a long-term basis; made sure that the fuel for their type of stove was available at their intended destination; and was able to recycle the cannisters easily. This encompasses a great many outdoor travelers and campers.

As for specific recommendations on gas cannister stoves, I offer the following:

Self-Sealing Cannisters. I prefer stoves that use self-sealing cannisters such as the EPIgas models, MSR's *Rapidfire*, Olicamp's *Scorpion*, and Camping Gaz's *Bleuet 470 HP*.

Large Size Cannisters. I also recommend that you buy the largest size cannisters that you can pack comfortably; they give you the best value for your money (often not much more expensive than the small cannisters) and cut down on disposable material. Six-ounce cannisters are fine for short to medium-length outings; larger cannisters can be purchased for longer outings or when using gaseous fuel for both cooking and lighting. Camping Gaz calls their *CV470* cannister their *Family Camping* series. With 16 ounces of gas fuel and a total cannister weight of 22 ounces, they are a bit heavy for one or two persons, but not bad for a family or small group where the total load can be distributed.

Readily Available Cannisters. The 14.1-ounce and 16.4-ounce Coleman propane bottles with a total weight of around 32 ounces are really not much heavier than the Camping Gaz *CV470*, and you can find them at almost any discount, hardware or outdoor retail store in the U.S. and Canada. Their availability might be worth the extra weight when traveling in a group and/or using gaseous fuel for both cooking and lighting. Currently, the cannisters that are not self-sealing are more widespread abroad, with the most prevalent being the Camping Gaz *C206* (or similar size foreign equivalent). Packing along a stove to fit this size cannister, such as the *Bleuet 206*, would probably give you the greatest chance of finding fuel. In time, the *CV470* will have equally wide distribution. The EPIgas cannisters are widely available in the British Isles and Europe.

Component Stoves. Tiny stoves that fit right onto a fuel cannister, such as the *Bleuet 206* and *470 HP*, the Hank Roberts *Mini-Stove*, or all but one of the EPIgas models, are the lightest, most compact stoves available. These make sense for most applications. You can also find component gaseous-fuel stoves, such as the MSR *Rapidfire* or the EPIgas *Alpine Stove*, where the fuel container is mounted separately. Component stoves typically have legs that create a more stable, level cooking platform.

EPIgas 3140HP Micro   Camping Gaz's Bleuet 206 and 470HP

Costs. The stoves that use gas cannisters or bottles are by far the cheapest to purchase initially, but the fuel makes them the more expensive option in the long run. You can buy a good quality gaseous-fuel stove for $20 to $40. The small cannisters of fuel run between $0.50 and $1 per day when cooking for two to four persons, the large cannisters about half of that. The following comparison on Coleman's Dual-Fuel Lantern illustrates the disparity in operating costs for various fuels: For 100 hours of operation you pay around $4.25 for unleaded auto fuel at $1.20 per gallon (or kerosene where applicable), $15.75 for white gas at $4.00 per gallon, and about $60 for propane at $3.30 per 16.4-ounce bottle.

LIQUID FUEL STOVES

Liquid-fuel stoves also have their advantages. They are dependable, produce a hot flame for short cooking times, and fuel is easy to find. I have the following specific recommendations:

North American Travel. White gas is clean and evaporates quickly, making it a desirable fuel if your travels are limited to the U.S. and Canada. You'll save money and reduce disposable waste if you buy white gas by the gallon, though this isn't always practical. When bicycle touring or hiking you can only carry a limited amount, so quart or liter sizes are more convenient. It's just as well, since those sizes are more readily available in small towns, particularly in Canada.

World Travel. Multi-fuel stoves are definitely the way to go when traveling abroad, particularly to more exotic destinations. Models that burn kerosene in addition to white gas and unleaded gasoline are the best. Without the ability to use kerosene, you'll still be stuck abroad trying to find unleaded gasoline. My three favorites are the MSR *XGK-II*, the MSR *Whisperlite Internationale,* and the PEAK 1 *Apex* component stoves. They embody all that I look for in a lightweight one-burner stove for world travel.

MSR's Whisperlite International   PEAK 1 Apex

Mountaineering. There are several good choices for high altitude mountaineering in extreme conditions. The gaseous-fuel stoves with blended-fuel cannisters are really easy to operate in cold weather. They are no trouble to light and require almost no maintenance (who wants to be unclogging fuel jets when it's below zero?). The other intriguing option is the Denali International stoves that burn alcohol. They're also easy to use and operate well at high altitude. Even though the heat content of alcohol is relatively low, Denali's windscreen and pot design keep heat loss to a minimum. Their stove systems typically include a burner, windscreen, and complete cooking pot set. A butane burner is available for some models. Adventure 16 carries the *Deluxe Alcohol Stove* for high-altitude travelers. It weighs less than nine ounces, boils a pint of water in five minutes, and comes with a zippered pouch.

Component Stoves. I always prefer component stoves when burning liquid fuels. The fuel bottles hold a lot more than integral storage tanks and they are so much more convenient to fill. Component stoves are also easier to pack (you can store stove and fuel bottle separately) and adapt better to uneven cooking surfaces.

Good Windscreens. Look for models that have effective, foolproof windscreens. This is an important consideration. Without a good windscreen, it's like trying to heat an uninsulated house; even with a good heating system it is still inefficient. The best are types that go all the way to the ground, or that force heat up the sides of the pot for greater heat transfer. If your stove doesn't come with one, try Olicamp's Collapsible Windscreen (9.5 ounces, around $12).

No Preheating. I have to admit that I'm intrigued by the PEAK 1 stoves that require no preheating, though I'm pessimistic that their system works flawlessly when using kerosene. Even though preheating is not much of a chore, it can get tiresome if you frequently use the stove for drinks as well as meals. This is especially true when preheating with kerosene fuel that smokes and throws some soot if burned when not vaporized.

Costs. Liquid-fuel stoves vary widely in cost, running anywhere from $40 to $80 for good quality models. Add to this the price of a fuel bottle or two, and your initial investment is much higher than with a gaseous-fuel model. In the long run, however, the low cost of fuel will make this option the bargain. If you buy white gas fuel by the gallon it could work out to about $0.25 per day, and you can cut this cost by two-thirds if you use kerosene or auto fuel.

Author's Recommendations - Lightweight Liquid-Fuel Stoves

Brand	Model	Type	Fuel	Weight	Boil Time
Adventure 16	Deluxe Alcohol	FS	al	9 oz.	5 min.
Denali Intern'l	Triangia 27	FS/CO	al	37 oz.*	7-8 min.
Denali Intern'l	Triangia 25	FS/CO	al	48 oz.*	7-8 min.
MSR	Whisperlite	FS, CO	wg	14 oz.	3.7 min.
MSR	International	FS/CO	wg, ker, jf	14 oz.	3.5 min.
MSR	XGK -II	FS/MT/CO	wg, ker, ug, jf	16 oz.	3.4 min.
Optimus	Hiker III	FS/CO	wg, ug, ker, al	52 oz.	5.5 min.
Optimus	Huner 8R	FS	wg, ug	21 oz.	8.0 min.
PEAK 1	Multi-Fuel	FS/MT/IN	wg, ker	20 oz.	4.8 min.
PEAK 1	Feather 442	FS/IN	wg, ug	22 oz.	3.8 min.
PEAK 1	Apex	FS/CO	wg, ker	19 oz.	4.8 min.

*Denali stoves come with a complete set of cooking pots. The weight given is for burner and stainless steel cook set, including tea kettle.

TYPE: FS=four season, MT=mountaineering, IN=integral fuel tank, CO=component stove. FUEL: wg=white gas; ker=kerosene; ug=unleaded gas; jf=jet fuel; al=alcohol; bu=butane gas; bf=blended gas fuel; wo=wood or organic matter.

Author's Recommendations - Lightweight Gaseous-Fuel Stoves

Brand	Model	Type	Fuel	Weight	Boil Time
Bibler Tents	Hanging Stove	FS/MT/IN	bf	29 oz.	3.0 min.
Camping Gaz	Bleuet 206	FS/IN	bf	16 oz.	5.5 min.
Camping Gaz	Bleuet 470 HP	FS/IN	bf	8.5 oz.	4 min.
Camping Gaz	Ultra S470*	FS/IN	bf	10 oz.	5.0 min.
EPIgas	3140HP Micro	FS/IN	bf	5 oz.	4.0 min.
EPIgas	3005HP*	FS/IN	bf	10 oz.	4.0 min.
EPIgas	3002HP	FS/IN	bf	7 oz.	4.0 min.
Hank Roberts	Mini-Stove	TS/IN	bu	7 oz.	7.0 min.
Markill/Apex	Gas Cooker	FS/CO	bf	11 oz.	5.0 min.
Markill/Apex	Storm Cooker	FS/CO	bf	39 oz.**	5.0 min.
MSR	Rapidfire	TS/CO	bu	13 oz.	5.0 min.
Olicamp	Scorpion	FS/CO	bu	8 oz.	5.0 min.

Camping Gaz and Optimus are distributed by Suunto USA. EPIgas stoves are available from Taymar Inc. and Climb High.

*This stove is available with piezo-electric starting. **This stove's weight takes into account an integrated stainless steel cook set.

TYPE: FS=four season, MT=mountaineering, IN=integral fuel tank, CO=component stove. FUEL: wg=white gas; ker=kerosene; ug=unleaded gas; jf=jet fuel; al=alcohol; bu=butane gas; bf=blended gas fuel; wo=wood or organic matter.

Author's Recommendations - Lightweight Solid-Fuel Stoves

Brand	Model	Type	Fuel	Weight	Boil Time
Markill/Apex*	Wilderness	FS/IN	wo	18 oz.	4.0 min.
Sierra	Zip-Stove	FS/IN	wo	15 oz.	4.0 min.

*This stove has an optional solar electric panel that operates an internal fan or recharges the battery.

TYPE: FS=four season, MT=mountaineering, IN=integral fuel tank, CO=component stove. FUEL: wg=white gas; ker=kerosene; ug=unleaded gas; jf=jet fuel; al=alcohol; bu=butane gas; bf=blended gas fuel; wo=wood or organic matter.

Note for all stoves: Boil times are approximate, published by individual manufacturers stating the time it takes one quart of room-temperature water to come to a boil at sea level. Use these numbers for comparison only. Actual boil times will vary with outdoor temperature and windspeed, how sheltered the cooking area is, what type and grade of fuel is used, cleanliness of fuel jet, and other factors.

The Optimus Hiker III

Sierra's Zip-Stove

Maintenance and Repair - Stoves

Gas cannister stoves require little maintenance since the fuel burns so cleanly. Stoves that burn organic matter also place relatively few demands on the user. One-burner, liquid-fuel stoves, on the other hand, can be the most temperamental of all travel and outdoor gear. Most models require care during lighting and operation, as well as periodic maintenance to keep them performing as they should. Listed below are some easy maintenance tips to keep your liquid-fuel stove operating smoothly.

Burn Clean Fuel. Burn the cleanest liquid fuel you can find. If the fuel source is questionable, use a small strainer to catch particulates that could clog the fuel jet. Clean out the bottom of your fuel bottle regularly to remove accumulated particles.

Clear the Fuel Jet. Do this as often as you can. Some stoves have a built-in needle to clear the jet, others require the use of a separate tool. Carry spare cleaning tools in your repair kit.

Keep Burner Assembly Clean. On some models, a small flame remains for a while after you shut off the stove. Blow out the flame to prevent soot build-up on the burner or flame spreader. Clean the flame spreader regularly; if the underside is rough, it will cause the flame to burn erratically.

Preheat with Volatile Fuel. When using kerosene as a fuel, try to preheat the stove with white or unleaded gas. This will burn more cleanly and prevent soot build-up.

Lube Priming Pump. Keep the pump leather and shaft well lubed for smooth operation. You'll know when it is dry—pumping will become harder and you'll have a hard time maintaining pressure.

Check all Gaskets. Check the seals around the stove and fuel bottle for cracks or worn places. It's hard to maintain adequate pressure unless they are in good condition. Replace them as necessary.

Most stoves are easy to field repair if you have the necessary spare parts. Manufacturers usually supply "maintenance and repair kits" that contain items such as gaskets and 0-rings, fuel jet, flame spreader, pump seals, and other commonly replaceable parts, as well as any tools that are required. A method for cleaning or clearing the fuel jet is always provided, either integral to the stove or included as a separate tool. Carry these items in your general repair kit.

COOKSETS

Once you have your stove, you'll need to select a good cooking set that will adequately serve the number in your group. Having a cooking set along on a trip can be truly liberating. With the many sizes and types of lightweight cookware available, there's no reason to suffer culinary deprivation away from home. A typical cooking set for travel or outdoor use consists of lightweight pots of various sizes, a frying pan or two, an adequate number of pot lids, and some means of handling the pots and pans when hot.

Review of Generic Types - Cooksets

There are several different types of cook sets on the market that are suitable for active travel. They are classified in the following ways:

By Material. Camping cook sets are available in either stainless steel, aluminum or steel coated with baked enamel. Only stainless steel or aluminum are practical for lightweight travel, and of the two stainless steel is preferred for its durability and reputed health advantages. The use of aluminum cookware is not recommended because of the suspected long-term harmful effects of ingesting small amounts of aluminum that leach into the food.

By Content. Cooking sets are often labeled according to the number of persons they are best suited for. Compact "solo" sets are available for single travelers, two-person and four-person sets serve those numbers, and larger sets are available for larger groups.

By Intended Use. Although most are for general travel and outdoor use, some cooking sets are made specifically for a certain type of stove. Combination stove-cook sets include the Denali *Trangia*, Bibler's *Hanging Stove*, and certain MarKill/Apex units. These are usually mountaineering models that incorporate windscreens and specially-designed pots for efficient heat transfer.

By Component or Complete Set. You can buy cookware as complete sets or as individual components. There are advantages both ways, but the sets are usually the best bargain. The individual components most often used are pots ranging from half a quart up to five quarts, and pot lids (they often double as frying pans on larger pots).

Features and Options - Cooksets

Listed below are the key features and options to look for when shopping for lightweight cookware:

Nesting Pots. Most lightweight cookware is made to nest together for compact storage. Pot handles can pose a problem for nesting, but manufacturers have several ways of conveniently keeping them out of the way.

Frypan/Lid Combination. On some cooking sets the pot lids also serve as frypans. On other sets only the largest pot can be used in this way. To function as a frypan, the lid must be deep and have some type of handle.

Pour Spouts. Some of the smaller pots come with a small spout to one side for ease of pouring. This type of pot can also be used as a bowl suitable for mixing.

Handles. Pot and frypans typically come with either some type of integral handle that folds or collapses for packing, or a single pot/pan lifter capable of lifting and holding any commonly available piece of camp cookware.

Rounded Bottoms. Many lightweight pots come with rounded bottoms. On these pots, the sidewalls curve gently into the flat bottom instead of ending abruptly as with those of the household variety. The curved bottom aids in heat transfer and allows for easy clean up.

Copper Bottoms. Many of the stainless steel cooking pots you'll find on the market have a thin layer of copper on the bottom for greater heat transfer.

Windscreen. Some cooksets, such as the PEAK 1 *Trekker Cook Kit* come with a small windscreen that will fit certain stoves.

Stuff Sack. This consists of a nylon bag with a drawstring that covers the cookset when not in use.

Tea Kettle/Coffee Pot. A nice addition to any cook set is a separate lightweight tea kettle. Looking more like a pot than a kettle, they typically have a pouring spout, a small lid, and a flip-up handle.

Pot Lifter. This ingenious item allows you to grab onto the top of any size pot (with lid removed) without burning yourself or spilling the contents. It consists of a set of handles and clamping jaws that allow you to firmly grip the pot lip using only one hand.

Innovation - MSR's *Heat Exchanger*

Now you can increase fuel efficiency and reduce cooking time with one simple piece of gear. MSR offers a removable heat exchanger that wraps around the outside of your pot, serving as both a windscreen and a means of channeling heat up the sides of the pot. The inner layer of metal is corrugated to increase surface area, an outer band of stainless steel serves to clamp the heat exchanger tightly to the pot for more efficient heat transfer. A heat exchanger is included with MSR's *XPD Cookset*, is an option for their *Alpine Cookset*, and can be used with many other brands of pots. Cost is around $27.

Author's Recommendations - Cooksets

The following are my recommendations based on years of trying various types of lightweight cookware:

Use Stainless Steel. My first recommendation is that if you are buying a cookset you hope to use for many years, get one made of stainless steel. It is usually marginally heavier than aluminum, but it's much more pleasant to work with and doesn't have the potentially harmful side effects associated with long-term use.

Supplement Sets with Individual Components. Complete cooking sets are usually your best bargain, yet buying individual components allows you to tailor cookware to your exact needs. Perhaps the best way to buy is to purchase a basic cookset and supplement it with the additional items you need. We've had to do this over the years as our children have grown, mostly in the form of adding larger pots and a separate tea kettle. Make sure your individual components can still nest with the main cookset. In our case, the tea kettle fits inside our smallest pot and the extra large pot holds the whole set. Eastern Mountain Sports sells all its nesting cookware in component form, offering a discount when purchasing multiple items.

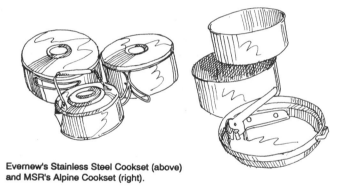

Evernew's Stainless Steel Cookset (above)
and MSR's Alpine Cookset (right).

Select an Appropriate Size. Pack the amount of cookware you need to adequately serve your group. Solo travelers know that friendships are easily made on the road, so they usually have cookware that allows them to share a meal now and then. Families and small groups should have one large pot for cooking a meal's worth of noodles, rice, potatoes, or soup, and a selection of smaller pots for other components of the meal.

Use a Separate Tea Kettle. Tea or coffee made with water heated in a cooking pot can have some unappetizing traces of last night's dinner. This problem is solved with a lightweight tea kettle that nests in your cookset. Since boiling water is the only thing you do with the pot, it will also serve for heating odor-free wash water for face and hands.

Use a Pot Lifter. Most cooking pots have handles that either swing out from the pot sides, or swing up in bail fashion and lock in place. The fact that they are made to move makes both types rather tipsy. The handles also make them harder to nest. A better solution is to carry pots without attached handles and use a pot lifter. This tool is fine for most pots, but is only recommended for frypan/lids such as MSR's and others that can be grabbed easily when covering a pot. Otherwise use the handles that come with the frypan/lid.

A Lid for Every Pot. I recommend that you have some type of lid for every pot. They don't all have to double as frypans, as long as they function as a cover to keep in heat or keep out bugs and dirt while cooking or serving dinner. Supplement compact sets, where one lid serves for multiple pots, with some type of lightweight covers.

Use a Stuff Sack. Carrying a nylon bag to store your stove in may seem unnecessary for the cookset, but it really helps to keep other gear clean. Allowing the outside of your pots to assume a dark color actually aids in transferring heat, which is just as well since it is hard to prevent. A nylon sack ensures that pot grime stays on the pot and not in your pack or pannier.

Store Your Stove Separately. I know that a lot of sales literature claims you can fit a compact stove right in with the pots, but unless you like "oatmeal au kerosene" or "rice white gas" I recommend you find some other place to stow it.

Costs. Solo stainless steel cooksets cost around $20 to $25, two to four-person sets between $30 and $40. You'll spend a bit more if you buy individual components. Expedition quality cooking sets cost $50 or more. You can add a tea kettle to your set for around $12.

Author's Recommendations - Stainless Steel Cooking Sets

Brand	Model	Description
Evernew*	S.S. Cookset	0.8 teapot, 1.4, 1.7, 2.1 quart pots with lids; stuff sack
Evernew*	Nesting Pots	1.0, 2.0, 3.0 quart pots with frypan/lids; sold separately
EMS	S.S. Cookware	various size pots, frypans/lids, tea kettle; components only
L.L. Bean	Stacker	1.0, 1.5 quart pots, 1 lid, 1 frypan/lid; windscreen; stuff sack
L.L. Bean	Combo Set	1.5 2.0, 3.0 quart pots with 2 lids; large frypan/lid; stuff sack
MSR	Alpine	1.5, 2.0 liter pots; 1 frypan/lid for both; pot lifter, stuff sack
MSR	XPD	same as above with heat exchanger included
MSR	Cascade	1.0, 2.0, 3.0 liter pots; 3 frypan/lids; pot lifter, stuff sack
PEAK 1	Short Stack	0.25, 0.4, 0.5 quart bowls/pots; .4 quart frypan; stuff sack
PEAK 1	Solo	0.25, 0.5, 1.0 quart bowls/pots; 0.4 qt. frypan/lid; stuff sack
PEAK 1	Trekker	1.3, 2.0 quart pots; lid, 1.0 qt. frypan/lid; windscr'n; stuff sack
PEAK 1	Outfitter	1.3, 2.0, 3.0 quart pots; 0.5, 0.9, 1.5 qt. frypan/lids; stuff sack
Olicamp*	Mess Kit	1.0 quart pot with lid; frypan; deep dish
Olicamp*	Small Cookset	0.75, 1.0 qt. pots with lids; frypan; measur'g cup; stuff sack
Olicamp*	Large Cookset	1.5, 2.0 qt. pots with lids; frypan; 3 measur'g cups; stuff sack
Open Country*	Standard	0.75, 1.0 qt. pots with lids; frypan; measur'g cup; stuff sack
Open Country*	3-Person	1.5, 2.0 pots with lids; frypan; 3 measur'g cups; stuff sack
REI	S.S. Stack Pots	1.3, 2.0, 3.0 pots, each with frypan/lid; components only
Sigg	Tourist	same as MSR Alpine cookset above

Other models are available.

Maintenance and Repair - Cooksets

There isn't much to do to maintain your cookset in good condition. Just keep it free of dirt and grime. Stow your cookset in a stuff sack to protect other items in your pack.

The pot handles are the only components we've had problems with over the years, making me a firm believer in using a separate pot lifter. Bail-type and swing-out handles are typically spot welded to the pot. This connection is subject to stress over time and can eventually break. You usually have some warning, although it could just as easily happen as you're lifting off your completed dinner from the stove. I once tried to get a pot handle welded back on while on a bicycle tour in Canada. The owner of a local machine shop said he could fix it, and I watched as he stuck the light-gage steel pot under a high-current tack welder better suited for thick steel plate. One zap later, the handle was attached just above a new hole his machine had made in the side of the pot. The handle worked fine, but after that every time we tried to cook with the pot, water would run out of the hole and extinguish the stove.

Innovation - Lightweight Baking Gear

The lightweight camper now has several innovative options for baking while on the road or trail. The *Bakepacker* allows you to bake right in your existing cooking pot over any one-burner stove. Items to be baked are mixed up and placed in a special plastic baggie suitable for cooking. The baggie is placed on the *Bakepacker*, an aluminum grid that rests on the bottom of the pot. This keeps baked goods from burning. Put on the lid and adjust the stove to a low flame setting. In no time you'll be enjoying breads, cakes and other goodies. *Bakepackers* come in two sizes for either a 6" pot (4 ounces, $13) or a 7.5" pot (8 ounces, $15).

Another way for travelers and outdoor enthusiasts to bake away from home is with the *Outback Oven* from Traveling Light, Inc. This temperature-controlled portable oven lets you add pizza, breads, cookies and other baked goods to your menu. It comes in two sizes, the *Ultralight* and the *Plus 10*. The *Plus 10* comes with a 2" high x 10" diameter pan that also doubles as a no-stick frypan, perfect for Asian cooking. The pan lid has a built-in thermometer so you can keep track of baking conditions. The pan and lid rest on a heat deflector that sits on top of any one-burner stove and forces hot air up the sides and top of the pan. A fire-proof flexible cover surrounds the oven similar to a loose-fitting tea cozy, trapping heat inside to create the oven effect. The flexible cover may be used with other pans to keep food hot. The *Ultralight*, an *Outback Oven* without the 10" pan, has all of the components necessary to convert most cooksets on the market into a functional oven. The *Plus 10* weighs 1.5 pounds and costs about $40. The *Ultralight* weighs only nine ounces and costs $20.

Traveling Light's Outback Oven

GRILL

There will always be outdoor enthusiasts who feel no trip is complete without the opportunity to cook over an open fire. The problem is that most metal grills are simply too heavy for lightweight camping. Now there are two good lightweight options available. The featherweight *Backpacker's Adjustable Grill* is a flat frame of stainless steel tubing that extends from 13" to 22". The grill is ready for use by supporting the two ends on rocks around the campfire. Packing size is 5" x 13", weight is 4.5 ounces, the cost is around $10. A few heavier alternatives are the *Backpacker's Grid* and the *Folding Camp Grill*. These grills consist of a three-part metal frame - a top grid (the former is rectangular, the latter round) and two hinged side legs that support it. These units weigh about one pound, cost around $10, and fold flat for packing. The grills described above are available from most outdoor retailers.

OTHER COOKING GEAR

You'll undoubtedly need a few other culinary items to complement your cookset. Some of them can be utensils you use at home, others are lightweight versions especially for travel. They include:

Paring Knife. Your multipurpose knife will work fine for short trips and outings, but if you cook on the road frequently, or for extended periods of time, you'll want to pack a sharp paring knife for cutting and peeling vegetables. Try to choose the smallest, lightest version you can find that does the job. A good paring knife in your cooking kit eliminates the need for a peeler unless you eat lots of carrots.

Cutting Board. Cutting boards are great for meal preparation and can double as a serving tray. Most commercially available cutting boards are too heavy, so we travel with an improvised, lightweight, home-made plastic version. It provides a much easier surface to cut on than dishes or pans and it prevents cut marks on your cookware. Traveling Light offers two great round plastic cutting boards to go with their *Outback Ovens* (10" diameter, five ounces, costs around $6; or 7" diameter, 2.5 ounces, costs around $5). As with the paring knife, a cutting board is nice, but not absolutely necessary for short trips.

Hot Mat. I highly recommend that you include a small hot mat in your cooking kit, especially if you're using pots with swing-out or bail-type handles; they can get very hot over a one-burner stove. A pot lifter stays cooler since it only touches the pot when you are actually lifting it. An added benefit of having a hot mat is that it also serves as a place to set hot pots and pans when camping. Make sure to select a dark color that won't show pot grime.

Spatula. Outdoor retail stores usually carry several types of lightweight plastic spatulas, though I find most too big or too flimsy for practical use. I like the *Backpacker's Spatula* (pancake turner) from

Outdoor Research. It is included in OR's *Kitchen Kits,* and you'll often see it sold as a set with OR's serving spoon described below. Another nice option is the small *Gourmet Spatula* sold by Adventure 16 and many outdoor retailers. This item is easily recognizable by its silver handle and brown plastic blade. It is very stiff and compact, and works nicely for spreading butter, peanut butter and the like. A new product from Traveling Light is their *UTU Spatula/Knife* made of sturdy carved bamboo. One edge of the handle is sharpened into a knife blade. It weighs only one ounce and costs around $4.

Serving Spoon. The best I've seen is OR's lightweight companion to the backpacker's spatula described above. It is perfect as an all-purpose serving and stirring spoon.

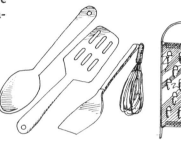

Whisk. The best on the market is a tiny version called the *Gourmet Whisk,* a great companion to the *Gourmet Spatula* described above.

Grater. There are two options for lightweight campers. The first is the stainless steel *Camp Grater* from Adventure 16. Ultra-light-weight and compact, it can fit into any pack or pannier. The other option is to carry a cheese shaver and use it for grating as well. It won't work as well as a grater, but it really makes a piece of cheese last by allowing you to cut very thin slices.

Can Opener. A can opener that can completely remove a can lid is an indispensable item for cooking no matter where you are. On the road or trail, you must have a compact, lightweight version, and several options are available. My favorite is to carry a multi-purpose knife that has this attachment. The knife handle gives the needed leverage and grip for easy can-opening. In lieu of that, or as an emergency spare, try the tiny *G.I.* can opener (one ounce, $1 each) made of hardened steel. An improved version of the G.I. is the compact *British* can opener (0.75 ounces, $1 each). It opens the most difficult cans, opens bottles, and the end may be used as a spoon.

Matches. Any camper needs to have a ready supply of dry matches for lighting stoves, lanterns and open fires. You can purchase regular kitchen matches and place them in a small watertight container (don't pack them tightly), or buy any of the waterproof matches sold by outdoor retailers.

Innovation - One Cup Coffee Brewer

If you enjoy a cup of freshly-brewed coffee while relaxing in camp, yet don't want to carry the weight and bulk of a coffee pot, you'll love the *One Cup Coffee Brewer* from T-Mos (4" high x 4" max. diameter, cost around $3). This featherweight plastic brewer fits easily into your backpack or pannier and allows you to make one perfect cup of coffee at a time using no paper filters. It consists of a funnel-shaped reservoir that holds the water. A wide lip around the bottom allows the unit to sit on top of any common mug. One small section of the lip is cut out so you can watch the brewing process. A removable brewing basket with permanent filter fits on to the bottom of the reservoir. Simply place one small scoop of coffee in the brewing basket, screw it in place, 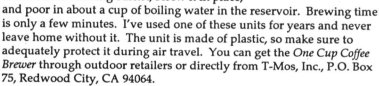 and poor in about a cup of boiling water in the reservoir. Brewing time is only a few minutes. I've used one of these units for years and never leave home without it. The unit is made of plastic, so make sure to adequately protect it during air travel. You can get the *One Cup Coffee Brewer* through outdoor retailers or directly from T-Mos, Inc., P.O. Box 75, Redwood City, CA 94064.

DISHES AND CUTLERY

Dishes and cutlery for lightweight travel are covered in the Personal Gear section under Specialty Equipment. In general, for each person in the group I recommend a good sturdy mug that is lightweight and good for cold drinks, yet won't burn your hands when it's full of a hot liquid; a multi-purpose deep dish or bowl that eliminates the need for a plate; a lightweight fork and spoon, with lexan the choice when weight is critical; and a cloth napkin. Lexan cutlery can be purchased separately or as part of Outdoor Research's complete *Kitchen Kits*. Small wooden chopsticks can also replace a fork and table knife when camping, but you'll still need a spoon.

CLEAN-UP GEAR

Make sure to pack some lightweight gear for cleaning up after a meal. You can put together your own clean-up kit, on its own or stowed with other cooking gear, or purchase one of the preassembled *Kitchen Kits* from Outdoor Research (see Innovative Product review below). The following items are recommended:

Dish Soap. A small container of liquid soap such as Camp Suds, Dr. Bronner's, or any of the others listed under Toiletries in the section in Personal Gear will work well for dish washing. They are all biodegradable and cut grease easily. Since they are concentrated you need only carry a small portion for most trips (a two-ounce squirt container is recommended). Larger containers can be used for longer trips.

Dish Pan. A separate dish pan is really unnecessary for most travels. Your large cooking pot will do nicely once it is rinsed out. We usually heat up dishwater in a small pot or tea kettle after the cooking is complete. This way we don't have to relight the stove, and the water is ready by the time the meal is done. Temper the hot water with a little cold water in the large pot, add some liquid soap, and you're ready for dish duty. Most liquid camp soaps don't tend to stay on the dishes after washing, eliminating the need for rinsing. If you'd like the added convenience of a separate dishpan, try the *Folding Wash Basin* available from REI, Adventure 16, and other outdoor retailers. This lightweight freestanding vinyl basin holds over a gallon of water and can be used for dishes or for washing hands and face. Filled dimensions are 5" height x 11" diameter, weight is four ounces, cost is just $2.

Rubber Gloves. The secret to getting dishes really clean when camping or at home is to use dishwater near the boiling point, too hot for unprotected hands. A pair of rubber gloves, available at most grocery stores, allows you to do dishes in comfort.

Scouring Pad or Sponge. A good scouring pad or sponge is recommended since food tends to stick to the inside bottom of pots when cooking on a one-burner stove. The flame is usually concentrated in the center of the pot, causing a hot spot that can be troublesome, and the flame is typically more difficult to regulate than your stove at home. Practice helps, but even camp cooking pros find themselves scouring regularly. Sponges that have one rough side and the other smooth are good for most short trips, but they don't last long. We usually take a good copper scouring pad packed in a plastic baggie on longer trips.

Dishrag. While a dishrag might be redundant if you have a sponge for dishes, it comes in handy for so many other things— wiping up spills, wiping hands, and wiping pots and pans dry so you don't ruin your dishtowel. Lightweight cotton dishrags are available at most kitchen shops and department stores.

Dish Towel. A lightweight cotton dishtowel is also included in our clean-up kit. It doesn't have to be large, just big enough to dry dishes and cutlery for one meal. We hang the dishtowel and handtowel from a line suspended inside the tent and they are usually dry by morning.

Innovation - Preassembled Kitchen Kits

Pre-assembled kitchen kits have taken the hassle out of putting together practical, easily accessible items for meal preparation and clean-up away from home. Two very good kits currently on the market are available from Outdoor Research and Atwater Carey. These kitchen kits are similar in style and function to the travel and first aid kits offered by both companies. They include a nylon pouch that zips open and unfolds for easy access, mesh inner compartments for storing damp items, and a clip for hanging. All components are right at the cook's fingertips, including utensils, cutlery, spices, condiments, and clean-up gear. Outdoor Research offers two models, the *Compact* (perfect for one or two persons) and the *Deluxe* (can accommodate up to four persons easily). OR sells pouches and individual items separately so you can customize your own kitchen kit. Atwater Carey offers two similar models, the *Campside Kitchen* and the *Campside Jr.*, and also sells pouches separately. Costs including utensils are around $23 for the small kits, $35 for the larger versions. Pouches without utensils cost $15 to $24.

The components for OR's kits are listed below (similar items are found in Atwater Carey's kits).

Compact (Open dimensions: 4.5" x 9" x 2"). Lexan cutlery (two knives, two forks, two spoons), can opener, wire whisk, scrubber sponge, salt and pepper shakers, spatula, and plastic containers (two half-ounce polycons, two 1-ounce round bottles, two 2-ounce squirt bottles).

Deluxe (Open dimensions: 6.5" x 11.5" x 2"). Lexan cutlery (two knives, two forks, two spoons), can opener, wire whisk, scrubber sponge, salt and pepper shakers, spatula, serving spoon, measuring spoons, and plastic containers (two half-ounce polycons, two 1-ounce round bottles, two 2-ounce squirt bottles, two 2-ounce oval bottles, four 5-dram vials).

L ighting & Other Gear

- Compact Lanterns
- Fuel Bottles & Cannisters
- Nylon Cord
- Camp Chairs
- Lightweight Saws

In addition to tents, sleeping bags, provisions and cooking gear, there are a few other items to consider for any lightweight outdoor adventure. The first is a compact source of lighting, and the others are specialty items you might need such as stove and lantern fuel, fuel bottles, nylon cord (for a variety of uses), comfortable yet lightweight camp chairs, and a lightweight saw. First let's take a look at the sources of lighting available for lightweight camping.

COMPACT LANTERNS

One of the nicest times when camping is after sunset, when the stars come out and the sound of nocturnal creatures fills the air. Most adventurers eagerly anticipate nightfall in the great outdoors, particularly if they remembered to pack along a good source of lighting. Even though the tendency is to go to bed earlier when camping, on most trips you'll still spend a fair number of waking hours after dark. If you have an open fire and are camping short term, the need for other illumination can be greatly diminished. Many places don't allow open fires, however, and, even when they do, trying to cook, read or work in the dark gets old quickly without some additional light source.

While proper lighting is something that concerns any camper, it becomes paramount to those without vehicles and on a strict weight allowance. When you travel with a vehicle, it's easy to bring lanterns and plenty of fuel, or simply use the vehicle's battery to power any of the 12-volt electric lights available. In a pinch the vehicle's headlights can provide illumination for setting up a tent or the interior lights used for reading. Without a vehicle, however, your options for good lighting are limited. Light sources currently available to the lightweight camper are reviewed below.

Review of Generic Types - Compact Lanterns

There are only three reliable choices for lighting available to lightweight campers. They are compact candle and oil lanterns, high-performance lanterns that burn vaporized liquid or gaseous fuel, and electric battery-powered lanterns (flashlights are covered under Personal Gear). All of these options serve the lightweight camper well on short trips, although I must confess that most of them are not ideal for extended travel, especially if you like to read in the tent before bedtime as I do.

Candle lanterns don't throw off a great deal of light, require a fair amount of attention to keep them burning properly, and the safety of a flame in a tent, even one well protected in a small lantern, is questionable. High-performance lanterns and the fuel to run them can be fairly heavy and bulky to pack, and since they pose a much greater fire hazard than candle or oil lanterns, their use in a tent is highly discouraged. Most electric lanterns go through disposable batteries in a hurry and always seem to quit working when you need them the most. Despite this gloomy general appraisal, there are some promising lighting alternatives on the market for both short-term campers and global travelers. Before we look into specific models, though, let's review in depth the three basic generic types of lighting now available for lightweight camping.

Candle and Oil Lanterns. Candle lanterns are just what they sound like, small lanterns that use long-burning candles for fuel. These handy little lanterns are an evolutionary leap above just using candles or old-fashioned oil lamps, mostly due to their compact size, good performance in windy situations, and their ease of use. They are typically about 2" in diameter, 4" to 5" in length when closed, and 6" to 7" in length when open. With a flat base and pivoting hanger these units can operate free-standing on a table or hanging from any convenient spot. Candle lanterns burn special long-burning candles (eight to nine hours per candle), usually sold at outdoor retailers in a package of three. Oil-burning models, almost identical to candle lanterns, have recently been introduced. In these units, the candle is replaced with high-grade lamp oil (kerosene can be substituted abroad). You can buy oil inserts to replace the candle assembly in many existing candle lanterns, or buy lanterns made exclusively for oil burning.

High-Performance Lanterns. These units burn vaporized liquid or gaseous fuel. Their brightness distinguishes them from candle and oil lanterns that have relatively low levels of illumination. They achieve their performance through the vaporization of fuel, similar to one-burner camp stoves, and the use of a special mantle that glows brightly when in the presence of fuel combustion. Models are available that operate on white gas or naptha, gaseous-fuel cannisters, and even on kerosene. As with their candle lantern counterparts, they operate either free-standing on a table or other flat surface, or hung from any convenient spot.

Electric Lanterns. Electric lanterns that run on battery power are the third alternative for travelers and outdoor enthusiasts. They come in a variety of shapes and sizes, yet all operate similar to a flashlight. One or more batteries, usually located in the base to provide stability, power an efficient lamp. They are the easiest to use and the safest lighting option inside a tent.

Features and Options - Compact Lanterns

These are the features to look for when purchasing a lantern for lightweight camping. Lantern features vary widely according to type.

Outer Housing or Frame. All lanterns have some type of protective outer housing or frame to protect the inner components. The housing also provides a base to make the units free-standing.

Glass Globe or Lens. Candle, oil and high-performance lanterns have a clear or opaque glass globe to enhance light output and provide wind protection. Electric lanterns typically have a glass lens (similar to a globe) that protects the lamp and serves to cut the glare produced by a bare bulb.

Optional Globe Protector. Some high-performance models have an optional protective cover or case that protects the globe from breakage.

Burner Assembly. This is where the fuel is actually consumed. It can be a very simple candle tip or wick in candle and oil lanterns, a sophisticated burner assembly with mantle on high-performance lanterns, or an efficient lamp in electric lanterns.

Heat Reflector. Candle, oil and high-performance lanterns all have a heat reflector at the top of the globe to protect hands and materials located above the flame. This is essential for use when the lantern is hung below combustible materials.

Fuel Storage Compartment. The inner sleeve on candle lanterns acts as a storage place for fuel (the candle itself). Oil lanterns have a small reservoir of fuel directly below the wick. High-performance lanterns have a larger fuel tank located under the burner assembly, and electric lanterns store their fuel in batteries located in the base.

Fuel Control. Candle lanterns have no way to control their burn rate other than what is inherent in the design. High-performance and oil lanterns have an adjustable fuel control knob to allow for settings between high and low. Electric lanterns have a simple on/ off switch.

Hanger and Lanyard. All lanterns come equipped with a metal chain or rigid hanger so the unit may be suspended in a convenient location.

Optional Hanging Stand. Hanging lanterns from trees in environmentally sensitive areas is highly discouraged. Some camp-grounds in these areas provide lantern hangers to avoid damage to tree limbs, but many do not. One option to not hanging your lantern is to pack a lantern hook or stand. The *Lantern Hanger* (weight about 11 ounces, cost $8) attaches directly to any tree or post without harm. For outdoor travelers less conscious of weight, The *Lantern Sky Hook* is a nifty solution. Simply drive a steel stake in the ground and slip the aluminum pole and hook assembly over it. It extends from 41" to 72", weighs 1.5 pounds, and costs about $10. A well-engineered alternative is the *Firefly Lantern Stand*. It uses a three-pole tripod to create a secure hanging spot. Pole sections are shock-corded to-gether. In use, it stands five feet high with base dimensions of three feet, weighs 2.8 pounds, costs about $17, and packs into a convenient storage sack.

Construction and Operation - Compact Lanterns

The information below describes how lanterns for lightweight travel are constructed, and recommends proper methods of opera-tion.

Candle and Oil Lanterns. Candle lanterns are the most widely available of the two. A protective cylindrical housing of high-impact plastic or aluminum surrounds a cylindrical glass globe during storage to prevent breakage. The globe extends above the housing during use to enhance the light from the flame and serve as a windscreen. An internal metal sleeve actually holds the candle. A captive large-coil spring sits in the base of the sleeve and pushes against a round metal plate under the candle, forcing the candle upwards as it burns. A metal hanger attaches to the top of the outer housing and loops above the globe to hang the unit from any conve-nient spot.

To use most candle lanterns, simply unscrew and remove the inner metal sleeve and base assembly from the outer housing. Now unscrew the base from the sleeve; the spring and round metal plate usually come out with the base. Insert the candle tip upwards into the sleeve; it will poke out through a hole in the top. Place the round piece of metal against the bottom of the candle (don't forget this!), compress the spring and reassemble the base. The spring is under maximum compression at this point. As the candle burns the coil expands, keeping a fresh portion of the candle available for burning. You'll find it's most convenient to light the candle before the sleeve has been reinserted into the outer housing. Keeping the candle and sleeve in an upright position, lower the outer housing with globe extended for use over the burning candle and screw the sleeve base tightly onto the housing so it can't come loose during operation.

You'll get best performance if the top of the candle can maintain a conical shape. If it starts to form a crater where melted wax collects, it tends to drown the flame and can drastically reduce light output. You'll have to allow the wax to cool, remove the candle and trim it back into shape. Unfortunately, you lose a fair portion of wax each time you trim. You're supposed to get eight to nine hours of burn time per candle, but the need to trim can reduce candle life substantially. When the candle is nearly gone, the round metal base begins to be visible through the partially melted wax that is left. Allow the wax to burn completely, or until the flame is no longer useful. Allow the wax to cool, then remove the inner sleeve, clean out any wax that has dripped down inside (this happens frequently), and insert a new candle. Try not to bump the lantern during operation as spilled wax can make a mess on the globe and inside the sleeve.

Lightweight oil-burning models differ slightly in construction and use from the candle-burning variety. The inner sleeve and spring is replaced by a small container to house the oil. An adjustable wick is placed into the container and extends up through a threaded metal piece on the top. Suggested wick height is around 1/16" to produce a flame no larger than 3/4". A cap with a rubber gasket screws onto the threads and seals the container when the lantern is not in use. Oil lanterns are much easier to use. There is no dripping wax or trimming of candles, only an occasional trim of the wick is all that is required. The flame is also adjustable, allowing for a little brighter flame when needed. For operation just adjust the wick height—not too high as excess heat could damage the lantern—and light with a match. When the fuel reservoir is empty, remove it from the lantern and fill with high-grade lamp oil for best operation. You can use high-grade kerosene in these units if you don't mind a moderate amount of smell and smoking.

High-Performance Lanterns. The two major types of high-performance lanterns on the market are those that use white gas and those that use gaseous-fuel cannisters. They both operate similar to their cookstove counterparts, although lantern fuel consumption is less than half that of a one-burner stove.

The base of high-performance lanterns burning liquid fuel is also the fuel tank, typically holding around eight ounces of fuel with a burn time of around three to four hours. A priming pump pressurizes the fuel before use. Once pressurized, the fuel control is opened and atomized fuel flows to the burner assembly. A single mantle is suspended below the fuel jet. Light the escaping fuel with a match in the vicinity of the mantle. During combustion the mantle glows brightly to produce illumination. The fuel is vaporized by the heat of the lantern, and therefore burns cleanly and smoothly. On models that burn kerosene (only one or two currently exist), you must first preheat the burner assembly with a small primer cup filled with alcohol. Flare-ups can occur if the fuel is not sufficiently atomized before lighting. If this happens to you, shut off the fuel control immediately and try again. You may have to pump during operation if the fuel tank pressure runs low during long periods of use. Reduced illumination or a pulsating glow alerts you to this condition. You should also be aware of over pumping; too much pressure causes the lantern to burn erratically.

As with one-burner stoves, lanterns that use gas cannisters are much easier to operate and adjust. All models operate in the same way. These small units consist of a fuel control, burner assembly, glass globe, and protective wire frame, all mounted directly above a gas cannister. It is recommended that you use only resealable cannisters for lanterns. For use, fit the lantern assembly onto the cannister. Tighten securely. Set the lantern on a flat surface or suspend it by the hanger. Turn on the fuel control and light in the vicinity of the mantle. Adjust the brightness to suit. The gas will already be properly vaporized and the lantern should run smoothly right from the beginning.

*Note for all mantle lamps: Mantles can be easily handled without harm during installation. Once installed, light the mantle WITHOUT the gas on to burn off the protective coating. It will flare and smoke a bit. Mantles change characteristics and become very fragile after lighting. Don't touch or try to manually adjust them at this point; they'll just flake off in your hand and be ruined. After "burn-off," the mantle is ready for use.

Electric Lanterns. The construction and operation of lightweight electric lanterns is very simple. The base assembly provides stability and a convenient place to house the batteries. Wire leads connect the batteries to an efficient krypton, halogen or fluorescent lamp. Efficiency is needed to prolong the battery life and cut down on disposable batteries. Krypton and halogen lamps are big improvements over regular incandescent bulbs, and fluorescents are more than twice as miserly with electricity as krypton and halogen lamps. An on/off switch is placed in the circuit for control. Just insert the appropriate batteries, flip the on/off switch and it is ready for use.

Author's Recommendations - Compact Lanterns

We have tried just about every type of lantern over the years. They all seem to have their good and bad points, so you have to find one that best suits your needs. In general, I would make the following recommendations:

For Simplicity. Candle lanterns, available by brand name or under private label from many large outdoor retail chains, have been our main source of light on many adventures. Among their strong points are the fact that they are inexpensive to buy, reliable, simple to operate and repair, and at around six to eight ounces are feather-

Candle Lantern

weights compared to other lanterns. Candle lanterns have almost no smell associated with their use. They are great for short trips, or when only low light levels are needed. They also have some bad points. Single units don't really put out enough light to read by, especially on a long term basis. You'll only get good light right next to the lantern. The four of us usually end up crowding around two lanterns hung by a suspended line so we can read in the tent. It also seems as though one candle or the other always needs to be trimmed so it will produce maximum flame, and therefore maximum light output. An inadvertent bump and hot wax sprays on the globe and down the inner sleeve. Chances are you won't find the special long-burning candles away from North American outdoor retail stores, so you have to bring a full supply with you for trips to other destinations.

For Lightweight World Travel. Compact oil-burning versions of the above are recommended for global travelers and others who prefer not to mess with candles. They have all of the good points of candle lanterns with few of the bad, and are my personal favorites.

They are easier to use, have a greater light output and longer burn time with each fill; they eliminate the candle-trimming and the risk of spilled wax, and the fuel (lamp oil or kerosene) can be purchased almost anywhere in the world. The only drawbacks are the smell and smoke you get from using oil kerosene, and the fact that their use in the tent is slightly risky due to the flame.

The *Ultralight* from Northern Lights is the best unit I've seen. It promises to set the standard for compact oil-burning lanterns. Cost is around $28, weight filled is eight ounces, packed size is a tiny 2.5" x 4", burn time up to 17 hours per fill. An optional heat ring converts the lantern into a small warming stove. Pure lamp oil or citronella oil to discourage bugs are both available from the manufacturer at around $3 for eight ounces. Another good oil-burning alternative from Northern Lights is their *Cand Oil* that replaces the insert in most standard candle lanterns. Similar in operation to the *Ultralight*, cost is around $15, burn time is up to 14 hours per fill. I hope that with future improvements, kerosene can be used in these units without smoking. It would be a great convenience to those already carrying kerosene for their cooking stove.

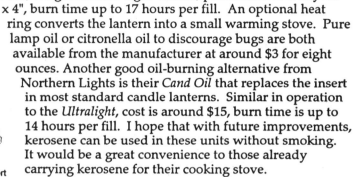

Cand Oil Insert

For High Light Output. The only choice you have if you want lots of light and don't want to carry much weight is one of the compact high-performance lanterns. Which one you choose depends to some extent on what type of cooking stove you have (see below). They'll work well in almost any conditions, but they are not recommended for use in a tent. This means carrying an additional source of light for tent use; a flashlight is fine for short trips, but unless it is solar-powered (see the Innovative Product that follows) the number of disposable batteries you'll go through on longer trips is a problem.

Use Like Fuels. Try to carry only one type of fuel for both cooking and lighting. The best for use in North America is white gas, so using the *PEAK 1 Lantern* and any one-burner stove that uses that fuel is a good combination. The *PEAK 1* (9.5" tall, costs about $37) adds an additional 30 ounces to your load and consumes about eight ounces of fuel in three and a half hours. Force 10 used to carry a tiny lantern that was a beauty, similar to the *PEAK 1* only it was brass and operated on kerosene fuel. It was a bit heavy, but I always thought that would be a nice companion to a kerosene stove if you could afford a little extra weight. Force 10 no longer carries that

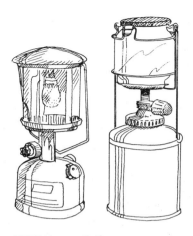

PEAK 1 Lantern (left) and Lumogaz

model, but I hope some manufacturer fills this need for outdoor travelers and boaters who want the safety and availability of kerosene in a high-performance lantern.

Likewise, if you use gas cannisters for cooking, then carry one of the lanterns that also uses gaseous fuel. As stated in the stove section, gas cannisters can be hard to find and should be recycled if you are going to feel good about their use. My favorite gas lanterns are the *Lumogaz 470* from Camping Gaz (about $27) and the *Backpacker Lantern* (about $35) from EPIgas/Taymar. They add less than ten ounces to your load if you are already carrying the cannister, and put out sufficient light for camping. In my opinion, most larger lanterns are too bright and consume too much fuel. When weight is a concern, one large cannister can serve for both cooking and lighting. Remove the stove after the evening meal is over and replace it with the lantern. Groups on longer trips should carry two cannisters, one for each appliance, so they'll always have a spare available.

For Safety and Convenience. Electric lanterns are by far the most convenient and safest for use in a tent. When we are traveling with a vehicle we use a 12-volt version that we can hook up to the car battery. A length of light gauge wire is run from there to the tent and the illumination is great. Without a vehicle your options are limited, especially if you hate disposable batteries as I do. The best solution for shorter trips would be an electric lantern that is rechargeable, such as the *Lighthawk* available at REI and other outdoor equipment suppliers. It comes with its own battery that can be recharged up to 2,200 times, weighs 2.5 pounds, and costs around $45. Light intensity adjusts between 10 and 40 watts, and it will run ten hours on the low

REI's Lighthawk

setting. One solution for long-term travelers might be the use of an electric lantern with a solar charger and rechargeable batteries. A good choice of lantern would be any of the compact models that use an efficient halogen or four-watt fluorescent bulb.

Costs. Candle lanterns are the bargain here, typically costing under $15. The candles are sold in sets of three for around $2. Compact oil lanterns are twice that price at around $28. You'll save money over time if you use kerosene that presently costs about ten cents for eight ounces, but not if you buy the cannisters of high-grade lamp oil that cost $3 for eight ounces. High-performance lanterns range between $25 and $40, electric lanterns range anywhere from $10 for basic units up to $45 for rechargeable models (the *Lighthawk*), to over $100 for good quality solar electric models (see below).

Innovative Product - Solar Electric Lights

A durable, reliable light source that can be used safely in a tent, produce its own non-polluting fuel, have a long life, and works anywhere in the world would be a boon to travelers and outdoor enthusiasts, to say the least. It sounds a bit far-fetched, but products actually exist that do just that. Solar electric flashlights and lanterns are now available that convert sunlight directly into electricity. Solar cells integrated into the surface of the unit create the power, a small rechargeable battery provides storage for later use. The best on the market is the *Solar-Powered Lantern* available from Real Goods. It has 2.5 watts of solar cells laminated to the side, a 4-volt, 6-amp-hour battery, and provides about five hours of light from one solar charge. Unfortunately, at 3.3 pounds and a price tag of $109 it is still out of range for most lightweight campers. Real Goods also sells the *Solar Flashlight* that provides one to one-and-a-half hours of light and fully recharges its two AA Nicad batteries in seven to eight hours of full sun. It is featherweight, costs only $19, and can be used to recharge other batteries. The products described above are good, but for active lightweight travelers there should be something between the two—a smaller lantern that weighs a pound or so with batteries, recharges in one day of average sunshine, and gives two to three reliable hours of light each night.

Solar-Powered Lantern

Maintenance and Repair - Compact Lanterns

There are a few things you need to do to keep your lantern operating the way it should. Maintenance and repair suggestions are itemized below by lantern type.

Candle Lantern. Clean the globe regularly with a soft rag or tissue paper, and scrape off any accumulated wax so the unit assembles easily. Keep track of the copper spring when changing candles; it's hard to find in dirt or tall grass. The globes are well protected in candle and oil lanterns, but you might take a spare globe on longer trips. One of ours once broke and I had to use cellophane tape to hold it together until we got home.

Oil Lantern. There should be almost no maintenance with this lantern other than occasionally trimming the wick and cleaning the globe. Burning kerosene will increase the frequency of globe cleanings considerably.

High-Pressure Lantern. Those using gas cannisters burn so cleanly you won't have to clean the globe very often. Liquid-fuel models have more tendency to flare and smoke a bit. The most important thing to remember is to keep the fuel jet clear. Most models come with a built-in needle that clears the jet with each use. Both gaseous and liquid-fuel lanterns have maintenance and repair kits available for them. It's a good idea to carry these on longer trips. It's not really feasible to carry spare globes when traveling light; just take care to pack it well, or use one of the optional globe protection pads or cases.

Electric Lanterns. Protect your lantern from moisture to avoid shorts and corroded circuits. Check the contacts regularly, clean as needed. Don't store batteries in the lantern if it is to be unused for long periods of time. Carry an extra bulb in your spare parts kit.

FUEL BOTTLES AND CANNISTERS

Chances are that for most camping trips you'll be packing a fuel bottle or gas cannister for your cooking stove and lantern. All gaseous-fuel stoves and lanterns, either component models or those with the fuel storage directly attached, operate on disposable gas cannisters. Since it's best to pack gas cannisters separately from stove or lantern, you'll need to find room for one or more cannisters when using that type of gear. The size and quantity you pack depends on trip length and your load-carrying ability.

All liquid-fuel component stoves require the use of a separate fuel bottle. Even when you carry a liquid-fuel stove with an integrated fuel tank (such as some of the PEAK 1 or Optimus models) and a similar type of lantern (such as the PEAK 1), you'll still probably need to carry a spare fuel bottle to refill the integrated tanks on all but short weekend trips.

Listed below are the types of fuel bottles and cannisters currently available, along with some operational recommendations and any optional pieces of gear that make their use a little easier.

Gas Cannisters

Gas cannisters come in two basic types, resealable and non-resealable. Resealable cannisters can be removed from the stove or lantern at any time. They either have a threaded connection or a rubber tip connection. There are also three different fuels available, propane, butane, and a butane blend (80% butane and 20% propane). For more information on cannisters, refer to the section on stoves.

The most widely available non-resealable models in North America are Camping Gaz's *C106* (just over three ounces) and the *C206* (6.5-ounce) cannisters. Abroad you'll see many other brand names. Resealable cannisters are much more popular, with the most common size being around six ounces. Optimus, Primus, Markill/Apex (Husch), MSR, Olicamp (Scorpion), and EPIgas all offer cannisters in the six-ounce range with similar threads on the connection, making them interchangeable. Hank Roberts and Optimus offer six-ounce rubber-tipped cannisters that are interchangeable. Camping Gaz and EPIgas both make large butane or butane blend cannisters in the 16-ounce range. All EPIgas cannisters, regardless of size, are interchangeable. (Threads on the large *CV470* (16-ounce) cannister from Camping Gaz are not compatible with other cannisters presently available. Coleman offers propane bottles in both 14.1 and 16.4- ounce sizes. Threads on Coleman bottles are not compatible with other types of cannisters. Cost is around $2 to $3 for the smaller cannisters, $3 to $4 for those in the 16-ounce range.

Below is a chart that compares size and weight of the most commonly used gas cannisters and bottles.

Brand	Model	Connection	Fuel	Capacity
Camping Gaz	C106	puncture	butane blend	3+ oz.
Camping Gaz	C206	puncture	butane blend	6.5 oz.
Camping Gaz	CV470	threaded	butane blend	16 oz.
Coleman	14.1	threaded	propane	14.1 oz.

Coleman	16.4	threaded	propane	16.4 oz.
EPIgas	100	threaded	butane blend	3.5 oz.
EPIgas	185	threaded	butane blend	6.5 oz.
EPIgas	250	threaded	butane blend	7.5 oz.
EPIgas	500	threaded	butane blend	15.5 oz.
Hank Roberts	Gas Cartridge	rubber tip	butane	6 oz.
MSR	Isobutane Fuel	threaded	butane	6 oz.
Olicamp	Scorpion	threaded	butane	6 oz.
Optimus	702	rubber tip	propane	6 oz.
Optimus	808	threaded	butane	6 oz.

Liquid-Fuel Bottles

Liquid fuel is best carried in a container specially designed for that purpose. Fuel bottles for camping use are available from most outdoor retailers in a variety of sizes, constructed of either aluminum or nylon. They all come with a tight-sealing cap and can hold any type of liquid fuel commonly used in stoves or lanterns, including white gas, unleaded auto gas, kerosene, and alcohol. Remember never to mix fuels or use fuel bottles for consumable beverages.

MSR aluminum fuel bottles come in 11-ounce, 22-ounce, and 33-ounce models. Sigg fuel bottles are also aluminum and come in 16-ounce, 32-ounce, and 48-ounce sizes. We carry two 22-ounce bottles when we travel; one with the stove pump attached and the other for spare fuel. Those two bottles last about eight days when cooking for a family of four. MSR and Sigg bottles include a screw cap and O-ring for safe transport. You can replace this cap with an easy-pour spout found at most outdoor retailers. Choose from the *Ulti-Mate* or the *Fuel Faucet*, both designed to make refilling a breeze. Cost of aluminum fuel bottles ranges from $8 to $12 depending on size; the

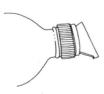

Nagle's Plastic Fuel Bottles
and the Fuel Faucet

cost of easy-pour spouts is around $4. In lieu of an easy-pour spout, or to aid in filling fuel bottles, you can get a small plastic fuel funnel sold at most outdoor retailers for $2 to $3.

The Nagle Company offers an alternative to the aluminum fuel bottle. They manufacture plastic versions made from 100% nylon in either a 16-ounce or 32-ounce size. All Nagle bottles come with a leakproof cap and a dripless spout for easy pouring. Cost is around $6 to $8 depending on size.

NYLON CORD

It's always a good idea to carry some lightweight cord or line when camping. You'll find a multitude of uses for it—spare boot laces, clotheslines, tent guy-lines, hanging line in the tent, strapping and securing gear, hanging food, and many other things. Weight is a consideration, so you want small diameter cord that is strong for its size. The best type to carry for general use is 1/8" nylon cord. It packs tightly and is easy to work with, even in cold weather. Determine how much you need for each particular trip. 1/8" cord is usually sold in 50 or 100 foot bundles. Cut it to length and burn the ends to prevent fraying.

CAMP SEATING

If you camp in the backcountry, or travel anywhere outside the U.S. and Canada, you'll rarely have a convenient picnic table or seating at your campsite. You can get by without a seat for a weekend trip here and there, but those who camp frequently know that sitting on the ground, especially when cooking and eating, has a limited appeal.

Grass Mats. One of the most convenient options for outdoor enthusiasts is to carry a simple grass mat, the kind found at most beach areas anywhere in the world. They provide a clean surface for sitting, cooking, eating, or removing shoes beside the tent. They can also be used in the tent annex to keep gear protected from ground moisture. Grass mats roll up compactly for storage and clean off with a few shakes in the air. They can be a bit heavy, especially when wet, but we've found them to be well worth their weight.

Camp Chairs. Grass mats are great, but they give no back support. Camp chairs give back support, but most types are much too heavy for lightweight travel. What's the solution? Collapsible fabric and foam chairs, of course. These compact, lightweight seats have given comfort to thousands of travelers and outdoor enthusiasts alike. Crazy Creek started the revolution in camp seating many years ago with their *Original Chair* (weighs 20 ounces, costs around $40). It is basically a 15.5" x 33.5" pad of 1/2" closed cell foam that folds in half to form a seat. Adjustable nylon side straps keep the seat in position and allow for a perfect fit for all users. Crazy Creek enhanced their line with the *Power Lounger* (weighs 34 ounces, costs around $55), a longer version of the *Original Chair* that also serves as a sleeping pad. The extra length is gained by additional sections at the top and bottom. Fold these flaps in for a seat with double thickness and comfort. The weight of the *Powerlounger* makes it only practical if used for both seat and sleeping pad. Gymwell Corporation also offers the *Insul-A-Seat*, a self-inflating camp seat that comes in three sizes—15.5" x 33", 18" x 36", and 18" x 48". All of these pads are 1.5" thick when inflated. The largest model doubles nicely as a 3/4-length sleeping pad.

Gymwell's Insul-A-Seat

Another seating option is the simple fabric sheaths that are able to turn any self-inflating sleeping pad into a camp chair. A pad just slips into the sheath pockets top and bottom. Side straps secure the chair in position as with the models described above. This concept was a breakthrough for lightweight travelers; the sheath is very lightweight and in most cases they already carried the pad. The additional cushioning of self-inflating pads (typically 1.5" thick when inflated) makes for a very comfortable seat. The lightest on the market is the *Therm-a-Rest'R Lite Chair Kit* from Cascade Designs (weighs only ten ounces and costs around $35), made to accept all 20" wide 3/4-length and full-length pads. The *Therm-a-Rest'R Long Chair Kit* is basically the same, only it fully encases the pad instead of just the top and bottom section. Crazy Creek's *Thermalounger* also fully encases any pad from Cascade Designs. The 3/4-length version weighs 22 ounces and costs around $35, the full length version weighs 26 ounces and costs around $40.

LIGHTWEIGHT SAWS

Those camping in campgrounds or the backcountry where open fires are permitted will find a saw a convenience. There are several models to choose from.

By far the lightest and most compact is the 18" *Campers Pocket Saw* (weighs only one-half ounce, costs around $3). It consists of a rough metal cord with finger rings at each end. It cuts by grasping finger rings and pulling in a back-and-forth motion. It works well

Sierra Saw

on logs up to 6" to 8" in diameter. A second option is to carry a multi-purpose knife that has a saw blade as one of the attachments, although its usefulness will be limited by the blade length. You can probably break limbs by hand or foot almost as easily. A third option is the *Sierra Folding Saw* (weighs 5.5 ounces, costs around $15). Its 7" tempered steel blade allows you to cut larger limbs; it never needs sharpening, and folds neatly into the handle for storage. Total length when closed is 9.5". Similar versions are the *Prozig Folding Saw* (6" blade that folds into handle) and the Gerber *Sport Saw* (5.25" serrated blade that folds into handle). Saws larger and heavier than these are better suited for vehicle travel.

III CAR & VAN TRAVEL

Certain destinations spanning a large territory or lacking widespread public transportation are often best experienced with a car or van. This is true in many parts of North, Central and South America, as well as in parts of Australia, New Zealand and North Africa. Although many campgrounds abroad are within easy walking distance of a train or bus station, particularly in Europe, a vehicle makes it much easier to explore rural countryside and to camp away from well-traveled routes. Many people find this mode of travel convenient since it offers a large degree of independence and self-sufficiency, greater mobility and load-carrying capacity, and in the case of camping vans the potential for improvised cooking and sleeping accommodations.

Even though there are some obvious advantages to vehicle travel, in some ways it places you at a disadvantage when attempting to travel adventurously. It's hard to have the same type of experience in a vehicle as you would when traveling under your own steam. A vehicle makes the journey more comfortable, but tends to insulate you from the challenges and pleasures that can make outdoor travel so memorable. There is a temptation to cover large distances in a vehicle, even though it's bound to be less interesting than exploring a smaller amount of territory on foot, by bicycle, in a canoe or on a cruising sailboat. You also tend to miss much of what a destination has to offer by traveling in a vehicle—it all goes by so fast. You can even feel this way on bicycles at times— that you are practically past a place before realizing you should slow down and investigate its potential.

Another pitfall of vehicle travel is the tendency to overpack once you have all that carrying space at your disposal. This not only ties you down, it takes away from some of the excitement of adventure travel. You'll be wondering why you ever left home if you attempt to bring everything with you. It's not only the quantity of what you bring, it's the size and weight of the individual pieces of gear that can make a difference. Vehicles allow you to upgrade from light-weight backpacking or bicycling gear to regular camping gear. While this equipment is often less expensive, and in some cases easier to use, you'll be tied to it when you arrive at a destination. Larger tents, sleeping bags, cooking stoves, lanterns, camp chairs, and other gear may make your time in camp more comfortable, but won't be of much use for making short-term explorations by foot, bicycle, canoe, or kayak.

Author's Recommendations - Vehicle Travel

Everyone seems to have their own account of a nightmare car trip, one that didn't live up to expectations or was so exhausting that a second vacation was needed just to recover from it. In most cases, the trip could have been a success if a different attitude was adopted from the beginning. Vehicle travel can be very pleasant if you are aware of its strengths and limitations, and are careful to avoid common pitfalls. Here are some simple solutions to making travel with a car or van a rewarding experience.

Cover Less Territory. The first recommendation for vehicular travel is to try not to take in too much territory. This is sage advice for all travelers, but is especially important for those in a car or van. Be less concerned with how much you see than how well you see it. Be more conservative when planning an itinerary. Just because the tourist guide tells you a recommended route can be driven in a day, don't feel compelled to do so. Some of the best experiences are missed this way. Take in less territory and everyone on board will be happier. You'll have a much richer experience and the money you save on fuel can be used for more interesting things.

Slow the Pace. This goes hand-in-hand with covering less territory. Don't be in such a hurry that you miss the less publicized points of interest. Stop and explore places that look inviting. Take the time to go for a walk, stop and chat with the locals, and enjoy what the surrounding area has to offer. You'd do this if hiking, bicycling or taking public transportation, so why not with a vehicle. You can also help the cause by covering those long stretches in a vehicle during foul weather, or later in the day after you've had a chance to pursue some outdoor activity.

Leave Your Vehicle Behind When Possible. Having your own car or van doesn't mean that you can't strike off on your own when you feel like it. Use your vehicle as a base or to cover the long distances, then don't hesitate to leave it behind while you explore an area in a more exciting, less obtrusive and less expensive manner. Take ferries to outer islands, bicycles to out-of-the-way villages, hiking trails to wilderness sites, canoes or kayaks to hidden waterways. Everyone in your group will benefit by being more active. If you plan to rent a car or van, limit it to just part of your vacation if possible. This allows some time for more adventurous modes of travel.

Don't Overpack. Try to resist the temptation to bring an excessive amount of gear, even though your vehicle may well be capable of carrying the load. Be selective about how much to take, as well as the size and weight of the individual components. Take advantage of the fact that a vehicle allows you to stock up on provisions, but if you plan to periodically leave your vehicle behind I recommend packing lightweight travel and outdoor items such as tents, sleeping bags and personal items. This affords you the freedom to travel light whenever the opportunity arises.

Choosing a Vehicle. Select a fuel-efficient, modest-size vehicle, one that provides for no more than your basic needs. This applies to traveling with your own vehicle or renting one at your destination. A smaller vehicle keeps some of the sense of adventure intact and helps reduce your impact on the places you visit. It also reduces your initial outfitting costs, as well as the continuing cost of fuel and servicing.

Station wagons or hatchback model cars provide good storage space and easy access to travel and camping gear. They are appropriate if you don't need to cook or sleep in the vehicle. Even relatively small cars can be quite effective in coping with additional gear by using a good roof rack system or a small trailer. Both roof rack systems and trailers free up interior space and increase comfort for passengers.

To illustrate the point that no vehicle is too small, we once made a six-week tour of the Canadian Maritimes in a Honda Civic loaded with two adults, two children, four bicycles (two on a roof rack system and two on a back rack), our touring and lightweight camping gear, and some basic provisions. It was a tight fit, and we all wished for more room at times, but traveling that way made car travel a little more interesting, and helped us to focus on the outdoors and the short hitches of backpacking and bicycle touring that we were ultimately after. It was also remarkably fuel-efficient, an important consideration in a country where gas prices were over twice that of the U.S.

The next year we traveled to Newfoundland in a Dodge Colt Vista, a compact seven-passenger micro-van that, while not as efficient as the Civic, was also miserly on fuel. It had much more room for equipment, but we resisted the temptation to increase our gear load. Instead, we increased our staple food provisions a little and our driving comfort a great deal. The Vista has middle seats and two additional rear seats. With the middle seats folded down, and gear stowed underneath and between the seats, you can create a comfortable bed for travel.

A moderate-size van of some type is needed if you want the ability to cook and sleep inside the vehicle. Any mini or mid-sized van can be modified into an expedition vehicle. These vans get reasonably good gas mileage and can be used with their rear seats in place for carrying passengers, or removed for carrying gear and providing camping accommodations. Possible modifications include a pop-up roof to give standing headroom, skylights for light and ventilation, convertible beds, a convertible table, and a small galley complete with stove, storage for provisions and fuel, even a small 12-volt or propane refrigerator. Standard vans are less fuel-efficient but offer greater space and load-carrying capacity. You can buy camping vans completely set up or have them modified by van conversion companies, although most conversion firms specialize more in the "bordello" look (shag carpeting and a big bed) than in serious adventure travel accommodations. If you can't find something suitable, buy a stripped van and create your own camping vehicle. The outfitting process can be great fun and you'll end up saving money.

Volkswagen continues to lead the way in factory-direct compact camping vans. Their spacious new *Eurovan MV* comes standard with tons of storage space, two removable rear-facing middle bucket seats, a folding table, and a three-person rear seat that folds down into a 72" x 55" double bed. In the past, Volkswagen would contract Westfalia to convert their vans into camping vehicles, but now they offer their own *Weekender Package*. This optional package includes a "pop-top" roof that gives standing headroom and an additional two-person bed; fixed driver's side middle seat with a 12-volt refrigerator underneath; an auxiliary battery; gathered window curtains; and side window and rear hatch screens. Base price on a stripped version of the *Eurovan* is around $17,000, the *Eurovan MV* is around $21,000, and the *Weekender Package* costs an additional $2,500.

L oad Carriers

- Cargo Duffels
- Roof Rack Systems
- Trailers

Your vehicle itself may be able to carry all the equipment you need, but if interior space is at a premium you may want to consider getting creative with ancillary load carriers. There are basically three choices for carrying additional outdoor and recreation gear with a vehicle: simple cargo duffels strapped to the roof, a complete roof rack system for storing a variety of specialty gear, or a small trailer that can be hauled.

CARGO DUFFELS

The simplest type of load carrier for vehicle travel is a large cargo duffel. These reasonably-priced bags can hold mountains of gear, yet can also be folded up and easily stowed when not in use. They work just as well inside the vehicle (stuffed in the back or under seats), outside the vehicle (strapped up on the roof), or away from the vehicle (when carrying gear to your tent or hotel). Placing a duffel up on the roof allows you to carry really bulky items, while increasing the interior space for passengers. Cargo duffels can be strapped to a factory-installed roof rack, a set of crossbars or luggage racks from a complete roof rack system (described below), or to any improvised framework.

There are many sizes and styles of cargo duffels to choose from. Since duffels are used in a variety of outdoor and recreational activities, specific models are discussed in the Personal Gear section under Specialty Equipment.

Innovation - The *Kanga RoofPouch* Cartop Carrier

Providing extra storage space when traveling with a vehicle has traditionally meant choosing between a soft cargo duffel strapped to the roof or a rigid open rack or enclosed storage box made for a complete roof rack system. The duffels are inexpensive and easy to handle, yet their capacity is limited and strapping them down can be a chore. The storage boxes have large capacities and are simple to use, but they are bulky when not in use and are more expensive. If you are looking for something different, try the *Kanga RoofPouch* from the Kanga Company. They make two sizes of soft yet durable roof pouches made of waterproof nylon packcloth. These large storage pouches rest on the roof or a standard luggage rack and are held in

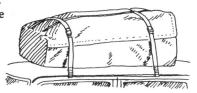

place with four convenient nylon straps (you must have raingutters or some type of roof rack to mount the pouches). They protect your gear from the elements and are aerodynamically shaped for minimal air resistance. The 10 cubic foot model, recommended for most sedans, costs around $115 and measures 36"x40", with the height varying between 8" (front) and 16" (rear). The 15 cubic foot model is more suitable for mini-vans and larger utility vehicles, costs around $135, and measures 40"x48" with the height varying from 9" to 18".

ROOF RACK SYSTEMS

Probably the single most important piece of gear you'll need for car and van travel is a versatile roof rack system. The new rack systems are engineering marvels that increase available interior room by utilizing the unused space on top of your vehicle. Roof rack systems are great for carrying everything from spare equipment and extra provisions to bicycles, skis, canoes, kayaks, rowboats and dinghies, and even small sailboats and sailboards.

Review of Available Types - Roof Rack Systems

While you'll find many types of car-top racks on the market, from simple crossbar sets and standard luggage racks to aerodynamic rooftop storage containers, there are only a few brands of complete roof rack systems available for active travelers. Roof rack systems are by far the most popular method of carrying extra gear since they are so amazingly versatile and easy to use. Not only are they practical, but their sleek design can enhance the appearance of any vehicle. The two most widely marketed systems are those manufactured by Yakima of California and Thule (pronounced "too-lay") of Sweden.

These two roof rack systems are actually variations on the same theme. They both start with black tubular metal crossbars that are held firmly in place off the roof surface by various types of mounting "feet." There are two feet per crossbar, one on each side of the vehicle. Foot type is determined by vehicle model and whether or not it has raingutters. With a few elastic tie-down straps, these crossbar sets alone are pretty good at carrying household items and building supplies, but for travelers and outdoor enthusiasts they merely provide a foundation for storing a wide variety of gear. Their real beauty lies in the myriad optional components that are available. Attach one or more of these options to the crossbars and you have a serious load-carrying system tailored to the way you like to travel.

Features and Options - Roof Rack Systems

The features on the Yakima and Thule systems are similar in approach, although quite different in execution. Both offer a wide range of optional attachments for carrying various types of gear. Look for these features and options when comparing roof rack systems.

Crossbars. These tubes of steel provide a structure for carrying general loads, or for mounting optional attachments capable of carrying specialty recreational gear. Yakima uses round tubes while Thule's are rectangular. Crossbars come in various lengths to suit car width or gear requirements.

Mounting Feet. The load on the crossbars is transferred equally to four individual mounting feet (two per crossbar) that sit on the roof. They in turn transmit the weight directly to the framework of your vehicle. A soft rubber pad on the bottom of each foot protects the vehicle's finish. There are three basic types of mounting feet: 1) those that attach to doorjambs on vehicles with flush trim styles; 2) those that attach to existing roof racks; and 3) those that attach to raingutters, or to brackets that form "artificial raingutters" when no raingutter, doorjamb or existing roof rack is available. Special mounting feet (Thule) or feet extensions (Yakima) are available to raise the crossbars on vans, mini-buses or other vehicles with high-roof profiles.

Locking Mechanisms. All types of mounting feet, as well as most optional components, have small yet effective integral locking mechanisms available to prevent theft. Locks can be purchased in sets so that one key fits all. Wire cables are also available to secure additional gear.

Stretch Kits. *Stretch Kit* is Yakima's term, one that aptly describes a means of extending the distance between crossbars on two-door vehicles that have short rooflines. Thule calls theirs the *SRA* (Short Roofline Adapter). By any name, the kit consists of two spreader bars (one each side between fore and aft mounting feet) and a middle set of feet that grabs the same raingutter or doorjamb as the front set, allowing the rear set to just rest on the roof. Spreading the crossbars creates a more stable platform for the load.

Luggage Carriers. Luggage carriers are sturdy open-frame racks or baskets that attach to the crossbars. They can accommodate almost any type of luggage or bulky gear. Thule offers four sizes of tubular steel *Luggage Baskets* that rest above the crossbars.

Yakima's Basket Case

The end bars on each rack adjust to create either a flatbed or cradle-type carrier. Thule offers heavy-duty straps for securing loads. Yakima opts for an actual basket-shaped luggage carrier (2.5' x 3.5' x 2" deep) of steel wire that hangs below the crossbars, allowing additional loads such as canoes and kayaks to be placed above it. Yakima also offers the *StretchNet*, a high-quality elastic net that stretches over almost any load and secures to the *BasketCase* with nylon hooks.

Storage Containers. Modern roof-top storage containers aren't even remotely like the old strap-on versions available at rental places. These new units have aerodynamic profiles and sleek Euro-styling for efficient load-carrying. Storage containers mount directly to the top of the crossbars. The top swings open with hinges on the side, front or rear. Gas struts keep the top open on larger models. Storage containers are typically made of polyethylene or ABS plastic, and have integral locks. Thule offers two sizes of *Combi Boxes*, low profile containers for ski and general gear. They also have three additional models of storage containers, the *Alpine*, *Adventurer* and *Weekender*, for a wide variety of travel loads.

Thule's Weekender

Yakima offers the *RocketBox* and the shorter, higher profile *SpaceCadet*. Another good storage container option is any one of the new *Packasport* roof boxes from Packasport Systems. They offer a complete range of sleek, well-designed fiberglass gear carriers that mount directly to the crossbars of any roof rack system.

Bicycle Carriers. Bicycles have traditionally been the hardest items to transport on the roof; you either damaged your car, your bike or yourself in the attempt. Now Thule and Yakima have made bicycles one of the easiest types of gear to carry, with a variety of well-engineered mounting styles to choose from.

• *Upright Mount Carriers.* These keep your bicycle standing upright with no need to remove the front wheel. These carriers

typically have a straight track fastened across the crossbars (running lengthwise for the tires to rest in) to carry the load, and a down tube clamp (that pivots up from the track and attaches to a convenient spot on the bike's down tube) for holding the bike in position. A set of clamps or straps keep the bike wheels firmly in place on the track.

Thule's Premier Upright Carrier

• *Upside Down Mount Carriers.* Thule used to offer an inexpensive mounting kit that held a bicycle upside down above the crossbars. The front mount locked the handlebars in place while the rear mount provided a padded cradle with tie straps for the seat. There are no mounts of this type currently being marketed.

• *Fork Mount Carriers.* Fork mount carriers are probably the best for the bike and the most efficient for travel—they don't grab onto the bike's finish and they lower the profile exposed to the air stream. On these models, the bike's front wheel is removed and the fork placed into a simulated wheel axle down near the front crossbar. The rear wheel is held firmly by either a short section of track attached to the rear crossbar or a longer track able to accommodate a variety of bike lengths. The removed front wheel can be carried inside the vehicle, strapped to the bike frame, or on a front wheel carrier described below.

Yakima's 2A Standard Bike Carrier

• *Front Wheel Carriers.* These simple U-shaped brackets mount to any convenient spot on the crossbar and hold the front wheel on a simulated bike axle.

• *Rear Deck Carriers.* Bicycles can also be carried on a special bicycle carrier that mounts to the back of almost any vehicle. Rhode Gear offer several models with a patented design that makes them one of the leaders in this style of bicycle carrier.

• *Hitch Carriers.* Another popular carrier is the type that attaches to any car or truck hitch. Performance's *MaxRac* is a well-designed model that carries up to three bicycles firmly in the upright position. The entire carrier can then be pivoted down for easy trunk or rear hatch access when the bikes have been removed.

• *Spare Tire Carriers.* A modification of either the rear deck or hitch style carriers for vehicles that have a spare tire mounted on the back surface.

• *Truck Mount Carriers.* Both Thule and Yakima offer bike carriers that mount to the front of any truck bed. They typically consist of a long metal tube that straddles the bed and pairs of fork mounts and front wheel mounts for the desired number of bicycles. Rhode Gear has a model that attaches to the side of any truck bed.

• *Tandem Carriers.* Both companies also offer fork mount carriers for tandem bicycles. The front mount is the same as on standard versions, but the rear mount either grabs the bike's rear axle (Thule's approach; rear wheel stays on), or it attaches to the tandem's bottom bracket stanchion with a heavy-duty T-bolt (Yakima's approach). Due to the length of tandems, it is usually necessary to use an extended track so that the fork attachment point and the rear attachment point can be located beyond the crossbars.

• *Bug Shields.* Yakima offers a piece of spandex fabric called a *B-String* that stretches over the front of a fork-mounted bike, similar to a wind fairing. It protects the bike from grime, dust, bugs, and weather.

Water Sports Carriers. Any set of roof top crossbars provides enough support to carry lightweight recreational boats and accessories, but without special water sports carriers it will undoubtedly be a struggle. These handy options give you unsurpassed convenience and safety. Both Thule and Yakima offer a carrier model for almost any type of boat or boat gear.

• *Crossbar Pads.* The most economical way to protect your boat, board or other gear, these fabric-covered foam pads slip over the crossbars to provide cushioning and enough friction to prevent side-slip. Use them on their own with a few tie-down straps or with kayak stacking mounts to provide edge protection for your kayak.

• *Gunwale Brackets.* Canoes, dinghies, dories and other small boats are best transported in an inverted position on the crossbars. Adjustable brackets that snug up to the boat's gunwale (the upper perimeter edge) provide some modest cushioning and keep the boat perfectly positioned while driving. Two sets of brackets (one set per crossbar; one bracket to port and one to starboard) are required. Gunwale brackets should always be used in conjunction with adequate tie-down straps.

• *Saddle Mounts.* The most sophisticated of the water sports carriers, adjustable saddle mounts protect and hold your kayak or sail board firmly in place during transport. Two sets of these soft, gently sloping brackets (one set per crossbar; one bracket to port and one to starboard) are required. They can fit most hull shapes by adjusting the distance between brackets on the crossbar. Tie-down straps for each set of brackets is included with the carrier.

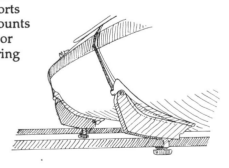

Thule's Kayak Carrier

• *Kayak Stacking Mounts.* Another good way to carry kayaks on the roof, particularly if transporting more than one, is with stacking mounts. A straight tube, or set of tubes, stands upright from each crossbar to provide a point of support and lateral stability for kayaks. Resting on their sides on crossbar pads, multiple kayaks can be easily positioned and strapped in place.

Yakima's Kayak Stackers

Ski Carriers. There are many types of standard ski racks on the market, but if you own a Thule or Yakima system you'll want one of the easy-to-use ski component options they offer. Skis can be carried inside roof top storage containers or in one of the mounts listed below.

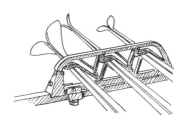

Thule's Angled Ski Carrier

• *Friction-Grip Ski Mounts.* These attachments allow skis of any type to be carried side by side running lengthwise with the vehicle. They consists of low-profile hinging brackets mounted directly to each crossbar. The top of the bracket swings up for loading, then closes tightly around the skis for transport. Protective foam pads top and bottom hold the skis firmly without harm. Store skis in pairs for maximum capacity, or one abreast with the bindings up to avoid scratching the car finish.

• *Sloping Ski Mounts.* Similar in use to friction-grip mounts, only with individual slots for ski pairs mounted at about a 30 degree angle for efficient storage. Each bracket holds three to four pairs of skis.

Fairings. Both Thule and Yakima offer plastic roof fairings that decrease the wind resistance of gear stored on the roof. Fairings typically attach to the front crossbar and angle toward the leading edge of the roof surface.

Construction and Operation - Roof Rack Systems

Roof rack crossbars are typically made from tough circular or rectangular galvanized steel bars with a protective plastic coating and end caps to seal the bars and protect accessories and gear. The mounting feet are made of either stamped steel or aluminum, or of high-strength nylon.

Crossbar Installation. Slide one end of each crossbar through the slot on the top of a mounting foot. Make sure the feet at each end are facing each other. Adjust the mounting feet so they are separated by roughly the distance across the vehicle roof. Place each crossbar in approximate position on the vehicle roof, then slide the mounting feet into place on the raingutter, door track, or artificial raingutter*, whatever the case may be. Make sure the feet are positioned correctly. Use the single adjustment screw on the foot to tighten the foot onto the crossbar while tightening the entire assembly to the roof. Place the security lock over the adjustment screw using the accompanying key. The crossbars are now ready to accept optional components.

Note: Artificial raingutters may be needed for some vehicles, and can be purchased from both Thule and Yakima. These are small metal brackets that are bolted to the side or top of the vehicle, providing a convenient attachment point for the mounting feet. The method of attachment may be through bolting when the roof's underside is accessible, or with Yakima's Plusnuts when installing above a headliner.

Installing Optional Components. Each component has a slightly different type of mechanism for attaching to the crossbar, but most either clip to or slide on the crossbar and are secured by hand-tightening several easy-to-grip handwheel screws. Locking mechanisms that provide extra security and prevent theft are available for most optional components.

Author's Recommendations - Roof Rack Systems

Thule and the Yakima both make high quality, long lasting roof rack systems. Chances are you won't be disappointed regardless of choice. The large outdoor retailers are split on their decision of which rack system to carry—EMS and L.L. Bean currently market Thule exclusively, while REI only handles only the Yakima line of products. The general construction and types of optional components offered by both companies are equivalent, although subtle differences in design are evident upon close inspection. At present it appears Yakima has the edge on innovative design, as evidenced by products such as their *Mighty Mounts*, small clips that allow most of their optional components to easily mount to factory roof racks or even Thule crossbar sets. Both systems work very well, however, and I feel it's more important to get the components best suited to your needs rather than worry about which manufacturer happens to supply them.

The optional components you select will depend on your vehicle and the type of sports you like to pursue. In general, I have the following recommendations:

General Gear. Use simple luggage baskets or racks and tie-down straps if carrying a few larger items that don't need additional protection from the elements. Storage containers are best when carrying a greater number of small items, or gear that does require extra protection.

Multiple Bicycles. You can easily carry up to four bicycles on one set of roof crossbars, making this system a great convenience for a family of four. You won't have to remove bikes to access the rear of the vehicle as you do with back racks. Choose a mounting style that is best for your needs. Upright carriers are most convenient if you carry a variety of bikes; they are especially nice for models without quick-release front hubs. Front fork carriers eliminate contact with the bike's finish, have a lower profile and are very stable. Use this mount if you repeatedly carry the same bikes.

Canoes or Kayaks. Canoes require the use of gunwale brackets that hold an upside down boat in position on the crossbars. Use some sort of foam guards to protect the canoe where it meets the bar. For carrying just one kayak I recommend the saddle mount. By nature it is easy to use and offers good protection for the boat. Two kayaks can be carried in adjacent saddle mounts if you have the room, or on their side with a stacking mount if space is at a premium.

Skis. Use any of the friction-grip or sloping mounts attached to the crossbars if only carrying skis on the roof. Storage containers are more practical when you also need room for boots, poles and other ski gear.

Kayak Stacker, 2 LockJaw/GT's   SpaceCadet, 2 SRL   3 LockJaw/GT's, BasketCase

Combination Loads. At times, you'll probably be carrying gear for more than one type of outdoor activity when you travel. Some possible load combinations are shown in the illustration above provided by Yakima.

Costs. A good roof rack system will probably be one of your biggest gear purchases, especially if you're a family outfitting for multiple sports. Try to view it as an investment in flexibility and convenience. A set of crossbars with appropriate mounting feet typically cost around $100 to $120. Bicycle carrier costs vary according to mount, with upright carriers and front fork models costing $60 to $100. Ski mounts cost around $75 to $125. Storage containers cost $200 and up, while storage racks and baskets cost under $100.

If you don't have the money for a complete set-up, just buy the crossbars and mounting feet to start with, then add options as you can afford them. For those on a really tight budget, simply buy the mounting feet and rig your own crossbars out of 2"x4"s. With a little creativity (and probably a little more work loading and unloading), this rig can carry almost any type of gear. Yakima sells *Tower Sets* just for this purpose, a system that allows you to convert to Yakima crossbars at any time.

The following are some currently available rack systems and optional components:

Author's Recommendations - Roof Rack Systems

Brand	Model	Type of Gear	Description
Allen	Univ'rs'l Bike Rack	bike, rear deck	fits all cars and trucks, 2 bikes
Allsop	Access Rack	bike, hitch type	receiver hitch, fold'ng, 4 bikes
Graber	Hitchhiker	bike, hitch type	ball or receiver type, 2 bikes
Packasport	System 60	storage cont'r	12"x24"x90", 13 cu. ft.
Packasport	System 90	storage cont'r	12"x36"x90", 17 cu. ft.
Packasport	System 115	storage cont'r	12"x48"x90", 25 cu. ft.
Performance	MaxRac Hitch	bike, hitch type	tubular steel, holds 3 bikes
Performance	MaxRac Sp're Tire	bike, spare tire	similar to ab've, up to 3 bikes
Rhode Gear	Ultra Shuttle	bike, rear deck	folding, holds up to 3 bikes
Rhode Gear	Super Cycle Sh'ttle	bike, rear deck	folding, holds up to 2 bikes

Rhode Gear	Cycle Shuttle	bike, rear deck	basic model, holds 2 bikes
Rhode Gear	Spare Tire Shuttle	bike, rear deck	center bike with vehicle, 2 bikes
Thule	Adventurer	storage cont'r	92"x28"x15", 16.2 cu. ft., 46 lbs.
Thule	Weekender	storage cont'r	55"x38"x14", 13.1 cu. ft., 33 lbs.
Thule	Luggage Basket	luggage rack	4 sizes, adjustable end bars
Thule	Premier Upright	bike, upright	wheel track, down tube clamp
Thule	Classic Fork M'nt	bike, fork m'nt	short rear wheel tray, locking fork
Thule	Tandem Carrier	bike, tandem	for 1 fork-mounted tandem bike
Thule	Canoe Carrier	canoe carrier	for 1 upside d'wn canoe/boat
Thule	Kayak Carrier	kayak carrier	for 1 upright kayak
Thule	Kayak Stacker	kayak carrier	for 2 white water kayaks on edge
Thule	Angled Ski Carrier	ski carrier	2 or 3 pairs of skis on angle
Thule	Horiz'nt'l Ski Carr'r	ski carrier	6 pairs, poles, and snowboards
Yakima	BasketCase	luggage rack	29"x41"x2", hangs between bars
Yakima	RocketBox	storage cont'r	92"x23"x13.5", 11 cu. ft., 42 lbs.
Yakima	SpaceCadet	storage cont'r	57"x38"x13.5", 11 cu. ft., 39 lbs.
Yakima	Lockjaw	bicycle carrier	wheel track, pivoting down tube
Yakima	2A Standard	bicycle carrier	short rear wheel tray, locking fork
Yakima	Tandem II	bicycle carrier	1 fork-mounted tandem bicycle
Yakima	Gunwale Br'ck'ts	canoe carrier	for 1 upside down canoe/boat
Yakima	TLC Saddles	kayak carrier	for 1 upright kayak or other boat
Yakima	Kayak Stackers	kayak carrier	1 pair stabilizes up to 5 kayaks
Yakima	SkiSlopes	ski carrier	4 p'rs on angle, push-butt'n cl's're
Yakima	ButtonDown 4 &d 6	ski carrier	4 or 6 pairs, push-button closure

Maintenance and Repair - Roof Rack Systems

With a little care you can extend the life of your roof rack system. Yakima recommends the following:

• Occasionally wash the components with soap and water to remove dirt and grit.

• Apply Armor-All™ to racks, mounts and accessories to restore original appearance.

• Remove your rack when not in use to reduce exposure to weather and Ultraviolet deterioration.

• Use a water-insoluble lubricant in key holes, on handwheel threads and other moving parts.

• Loosen mounts and accessories completely before moving them to protect the plastic crossbar sheathing.

You'll rarely experience the need for repair of these fine rack systems, but if you do, contact your supplier for factory service or replacement.

TRAILERS

Another load-carrying option for active travelers is to pull a small trailer behind your vehicle. This technique has its advantages and disadvantages. You can get by with a smaller vehicle since all recreational gear can go in the trailer. It's actually less of a strain for your car to pull an equivalent load than to carry it on the roof. This is the same principle that makes children much easier to pull in a bicycle trailer than carry on a bicycle seat. The profile of a trailer is also much lower, reducing wind resistance. Loading and unloading is easier from a trailer than from up on a roof, and you have the option of leaving the trailer at a base camp for short-term touring without hauling your additional gear. On the other hand, pulling a trailer increases toll costs, restricts the vehicles mobility in tight spaces, is another axle and set of wheels to service, and still doesn't necessarily eliminate the need to carry long canoes or kayaks on the vehicle's roof.

If you decide a trailer makes sense for the way you travel, look for a model that best suits your needs. The most practical option might be to buy an inexpensive flatbed trailer kit made of tubular steel, available through U-Haul and other trailer equipment dealers. You can modify the trailer to suit your individual requirements. One recommendation is to build a watertight box about 12 to 16 inches high on the open frame. Install a pivoting, watertight lid for easy access. Then mount a standard roof rack system on top of the box using artificial raingutters (discussed in the section on Roof Rack Systems). This allows you to carry provisions and other gear in the box, with bicycles, skis, boats, and other sports gear just above it.

Gear Upgrades

- Personal Gear
- Shelter
- Sleeping
- Food and Water
- Cooking
- Lighting
- Specialty Gear

Instead of attempting to list all of the additional things you can carry when traveling with a vehicle, I'll try to give you an idea of the types of gear upgrades you might consider when you have extra load-carrying capacity. I want to emphasize that if you intend to do some occasional self-propelled travel during your trip, it pays to stick with lightweight models when purchasing items such as tents, sleeping bags, cooking gear, lanterns and so on.

PERSONAL GEAR UPGRADES

A number of personal items can be upgraded when traveling with a vehicle, including items of clothing, health and hygiene gear, specialty travel gear and children's travel gear.

Clothing

There's no reason not to carry some additional clothing if you have the room for it. You'll have more variety and extra clothes can always be left behind when you want to travel light. One likely candidate for improved variety is shoes—a vehicle allows you to take several pairs to cover a larger variety of conditions.

Health and Hygiene

You can also pack a more complete selection of personal care, preventative and first-aid items. Pack larger containers of frequently-used items, restocking small containers in the lightweight kits as necessary.

Specialty Gear

A vehicle allows you to carry a better selection of repair gear, a larger camera or additional lenses, more powerful binoculars, more complete guide books and maps, and additional recreational items.

Children's Gear

Children will be able to bring a few more of their favorite stuffed friends and special things, making them feel a little more secure when traveling. There will be room for more entertainment items, which is just as well since vehicle travel is so much more boring than self-propelled adventuring. You'll also be able to take a better selection of baby items, but try to resist the temptation to throw in the crib and other bulky gear. It will only tie you down, create more work, and make you feel as though you never left home.

SHELTER UPGRADES

Some real comfort can be gained by upgrading your basic shelter when traveling with a vehicle. Not only does a vehicle give you somewhere protected to go during inclement weather, but you also have a choice of creating sleeping accommodations inside a converted van or mini-bus, or packing a larger tent or other shelter. I recommend you still consider packing a lightweight tent or two so you can go backpacking or bicycle touring if the opportunity arises. If you intend to stay at pensions, hostels or bed and breakfasts when traveling light, there's no need to bring additional gear.

Family Camping Tents

If you don't plan to strike off periodically on overnight backpacking or bicycling tours, you can also upgrade the size of your tent when camping. Most manufacturers offer what they call their "family camping" models. These tents usually have standing headroom and lots of interior space for four people and their gear. Some large camping tents I recommend are listed below.

Quest's Horizon

Costs. The cost of these types of tents varies with size and quality. In most instances, they are not much more expensive than lightweight four-man models offered from the same company. Expect to pay around $350 to $550 for a good quality family or camping tent, over $700 for a high quality model such as the Moss *Encore*.

Author's Recommendations - Family Camping Tents

Brand	Model	Style	Sleeps	Packed Size	Wgt. (lbs.)
Diamond Brand	Ultra Dome	mod	6	13"x30"	15.0
Eureka	Willow Creek	umb	5/6	10"/12"x36"	24.7/29.3
Eureka	Sunrise	do	5/6	9/8"x27/33"	14/21.6
Kelty	Castle Rock	umb	5/6	10"/12"x36"	13.5/15.5
Moss	Encore	mod	4	9"x24"	16.0
Quest	Conquest V	mod	5	8.5"x25"	19.0*
Quest	Horizon	mod	6/7	N/A	25.0
Remington	Umbrella Tents	umb	5/6	N/A	23/29.0
Sierra Designs	Camp 5	mod	5/6	N/A	12.7

These models come with a vestibule.

STYLE: do=dome, mod=modified dome, umb=umbrella.

Large Dining Fly

We found that in wet or buggy climates we really appreciated being able to carry in a dining fly or screen. A dining fly can always be improvised from any waterproof piece of material if you have some poles or sufficient tie-off points. If you'd rather have something a little more formalized and easy to use, try the elegantly designed *Sunshade* from Kelty. This three-poled, free-standing waterproof arch fits over a picnic table, the entrance to your tent, or between tents as a common area protected from the sun and rain. Shock-corded poles make setup quick and easy. Packed size of the *Sunshade* is 8"x27", weight is 9.1 pounds and cost is around $100.

Kelty's Sunshade

In addition to Moss Tents' compact 12' version described in Lightweight Camping, they offer a 19' *Parawing* that is more suitable for vehicle travel. It includes two steel poles for unlimited pitching flexibility, measures 19 feet diagonally and has a total weight of 8.5 pounds (2.5 pounds without poles). It packs down to 6"x36" and retails for around $200. Campmor sells a similar model called the *Parafly*. It measures just over 19 feet on the diagonal, weighs about eight pounds,

Moss' 19' Parawing

includes two collapsible poles and costs around $120. Eureka markets the *Chenango Fly*, a 12'x12' polyester dining fly that weighs only 13 pounds and costs $120. This model gives good protection, but relies on four perimeter poles, one center pole and multiple guy lines for support.

Large Dining Screen

Eureka Tent offers a high-quality polyester *Screen House* with a waterproof roof that erects easily over a picnic table. Floor size measures 10'x12', packed size is 9"x50", weight is 30 pounds and cost is around $350 (10'x14' size available). L.L. Bean offers a moderately-priced model called the *Summer Breeze Screen House*, also made of UV-resistant polyester fabric. The floor area measures 11.8'x12', weight is just under 24 pounds and cost is around $180. Many outdoor retailers also carry the *Economy Screen House*, a great bonus when camping in buggy climates. Set up over a picnic table, this floorless shelter gives protection from rain and insects. It has a

L.L. Bean's Summer Breeze

waterproof ripstop plastic roof and plastic mesh screen sidewalls for keeping out mosquitoes. Black flies can actually crawl through the mesh, but don't seem inclined to do so. The mesh is not effective against no-see-ums. Aluminum pole sections and stakes are provided. Floor size is 11.5'x11.5', weight is about 23 pounds and cost is around $70.

SLEEPING GEAR UPGRADES

You can sleep a bit more comfortably when traveling with a vehicle, either by converting interior space to bunks, or by packing larger sleeping pads for use in the tent.

Sleeping Pads. Cascade Designs has two models of self-inflating sleeping pads that allow you to pamper yourself when weight is less critical. The *Camp Rest* comes in either 3/4 or full length, is wider (25"), longer (56" and 77"), and thicker (2") than standard pads and costs around $60. The *Camp Rest Deluxe* has even more cushioning (2.5"), plus a high-friction, stain resistant, water-repellent nylon outer fabric. The deluxe version is 77" long, weighs about 4.5 pounds and costs around $90. To add to the comfort level, a vehicle also allows you to bring a nice big pillow from home.

Sleeping Bags. You can also find inexpensive sleeping bags at almost any outdoor retailer that will be adequate for car or van travel. Just keep in mind that bulky sleeping bags are impossible to pack on lightweight ventures.

FOOD AND WATER UPGRADES

A vehicle can make a huge difference in how you provision for a trip. When backpacking or bicycle touring, it seems you are always searching for food, and are often at the mercy of what is available locally. For many of us this only adds to the adventure, but others are relieved at being able to stock up on food and drink. On a cruising sailboat, we often provision for months at a time, and while you can't do that in a moderately-sized vehicle, you can pack a supply of foods not easily found or too pricey when purchased at small local shops. For our vehicle trips we typically buy in bulk from a food cooperative or discount grocery store, including such items as dried fruit, natural peanut butter, packaged soups and other staples.

Coolers

When traveling with a vehicle, you'll probably have room for some type of cooler or icebox for keeping food and drinks cold. There are many different sizes and types to choose from. Try to find a model that fits your space, has good insulation and proper seals around the lid, and is easy to carry. Coleman, Gott, Igloo and Camping Gaz all offer a variety of high-quality coolers.

For those who don't want to be dependent on finding and fussing with ice, try one of the thermoelectric coolers currently on the market. They operate on either household or 12-volt current, using a thermoelectric cooling process and a pair of small circulating fans instead of the vapor compression cycle that is employed in most house and boat refrigerators. A switch reverses the process and the unit becomes a food warmer. They can also be used as a conventional cooler away from a power source or when vehicle batteries are low. Even though thermoelectric coolers are convenient and inexpensive compared to other forms of refrigeration, they do have some operating limitations. They will run almost constantly in hot climates, potentially draining batteries when based in one place for a while. They also will not lower the cooler temperature even near the freezing point, and therefore it's not possible to make ice or keep foods frozen.

One of the best thermoelectric models available is the *Thermoelectric Cooler* from Coleman. It has two inches of urethane insulation between a high-impact polyethylene case and a one-piece liner. This electric cooler measures 21.3"x14.6"x16.6", has a 32 quart capacity, weighs 19 pounds and costs around $115.

COOKING GEAR UPGRADES

The big difference a vehicle makes to your cooking gear is it allows you to upgrade the size of your stove and the amount of fuel you carry. Coleman and Camping Gaz both have good two-burner propane stoves with lift-up lids that serve as a windscreen. They use the larger gas cannisters, are about 12"x22"x3" when closed, weigh about ten pounds and cost around $50 to $60. A *Bulk Tank Conversion Kit* is available for less than $20 for those who have the space to carry a small refillable propane cylinder. This kit allows any Coleman or Primus propane appliance to be converted, drastically reducing operating costs.

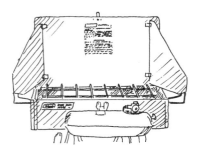

Coleman's Dual-Fuel Stove

Coleman now makes a *Dual-Fuel Two-Burner Compact Stove* that operates on either white gas or unleaded auto gas. It measures only 11.5"x18"x5", weighs about 11 pounds and costs around $81. When using auto gas it costs less than one-tenth as much to operate as stoves using disposable propane cannisters. Larger two- and three-burner models are also available.

Along with a larger stove, you'll be able to pack additional cooking gear, fuel, dishes, and cutlery. You can also upgrade your clean-up gear by packing a sturdy plastic tub for dishes and laundry.

LIGHTING GEAR UPGRADES

If you have the load-carrying ability, one of the best things you can do is upgrade your camp lighting.

Electric Lanterns

Any time our vehicle is parked near camp, we simply run a length of wire from the battery to a 12-volt fluorescent lantern used on the picnic table or in the tent. It's great for reading. Fluorescent lights use less than 25% of the electricity for the same light output as incandescent bulbs, and are therefore the lamp of choice when away from a household power source. There are many models to choose from, all capable of providing efficient lighting inside and outside of the vehicle. Coleman's *Deluxe Twin-Tube Fluorescent Lantern* operates directly from the vehicle's 12-volt battery, as well as on two 6-volt disposable batteries. Coleman also offers a rechargeable version described below. The solar lantern discussed under Lighting in the Lightweight Camping section is another excellent option for vehicle camping.

Innovation - Coleman's *Rechargeable Lantern*

Even better than our makeshift system described above is Coleman's *Rechargeable Lantern*, a compact twin-tube fluorescent that can recharge from either household current or any 12-volt source, including car or boat batteries. This eliminates the need for having your car near the table or tent, and you won't have a wire running through camp. Just use the lamp at night and plug it in for a recharge during the day. This lantern stands 12" high, weighs around 4.3 pounds and uses two four-watt tubes. It will last up to seven hours per charge on two tubes, up to nine hours when using only one. The weight precludes its use for lightweight travel, but for vehicle camping it offers tremendous flexibility. I applaud products such as this that help reduce our dependence on disposable batteries.

Rechargeable Lantern

High-Performance Lanterns

Larger high-performance lanterns using liquid or gaseous fuel, suitable when weight is less of a concern, are also possible for vehicle travel. Coleman's *Dual-Fuel Lanterns* operate equally well on white gas or auto unleaded gas. The *Powerhouse* has a bright 300-candle-power output, is 14" high with a base diameter of 6", holds two pints of fuel, weighs six pounds and costs around $60. The *Dual-Fuel* has a 220-candlepower output, is 12.3" high with a base diameter just over 5", holds 1.3 pints of fuel, weighs four pounds and costs around $50. Both models operate up to 14 hours on low setting, up to seven hours on high. Carrying cases are available.

Kerosene lanterns are available for traveling abroad where white gas and unleaded fuel are not available. Coleman offers a *One-Mantle Kerosene Lantern,* and Optimus has two models of kerosene lanterns (the *1200M* and the *1550G)* that are beautifully crafted of solid or nickel-plated brass.

Optimus' 1200M Lantern

Coleman and Camping Gaz offer larger models of lanterns that operate on propane or butane fuel. Coleman models include the *One- and Two-Mantle Propane Lanterns* (160/175 candlepower, $22-$28), as well the self-lighting *Electronic-Ignition One- and Two-Mantle Propane Lanterns* (160/200 candlepower, $30 to $38). If you have the carrying capacity, you'll be better off using refillable propane or butane cylinders. Conversion kits are available to run the Coleman Lanterns on refillable cylinders (see conversion kit listed under Cooking). Coleman's 30" *Distribution Tree* extends up from any refillable cylinder, allowing you to mount the lantern up high for general camp lighting. It has two additional outlets for connecting other appliances. Camping Gaz has several propane lanterns made to operate on their refillable butane cylinders (be aware that these cylinders can only be refilled at authorized Camping Gaz service outlets).

SPECIALTY GEAR UPGRADES

There are also a few specialty items that you may want to upgrade when traveling with a vehicle.

Fuel Bottles

A vehicle allows you to buy and carry larger quantities of cooking and lighting fuel, with a great savings in cost. White gas can be purchased in one gallon cans. Use the can to refill smaller bottles or integral fuel tanks on stoves and lanterns. Refillable propane cylinders are available in six-pound, 11-pound and 20-pound models. Bulk propane can be purchased worldwide, although you may need an adapter to fill tanks abroad.

Battery Chargers

If you intend to base yourself in one place from time to time, and have substantial electrical loads from lighting, an electric cooler or other appliances, you'd do well to investigate some method for recharging the vehicle's battery. The best solution is to invest in a photovoltaic (PV) solar panel or two. These amazing panels convert sunlight directly into electricity. They are rugged, have a 20-year life, operate with no noise or moving parts and pump electricity into your battery anytime the sun is out. Permanently mount them on the vehicle's roof, or better yet keep them mobile so you can face them into the sun for best performance.

Solar panels are rated by their peak electrical power output (watts), and by the peak current they produce to charge a 12-volt battery (amps). Typical PV panel sizes for boat or vehicle use are between 20 and 60 watts. Cost is currently around $7.50 to $8.50 per watt depending on panel size and type. Those of you who are waiting for solar electricity to become "perfected", consider this: solar panels sold today are more efficient at converting light to electricity (about 14%) than incandescent light bulbs are at converting electricity to light (about 10%). Brand names to look for include Siemans, Solarex, Kyocera, Hoxan, and Unisolar. You can buy PV panels from a number of marine or RV suppliers.

Table and Seating

Campgrounds do not always provide you with a picnic table. If you want to ensure good camp seating and a place to eat or work, it's advisable to bring your own. While fabric and foam seating is fine for lightweight travel, a vehicle allows you to also pack a table, as well as upgrade to seats that get you up off the ground. New collapsible camp tables and chairs now available are compact and easy to carry. Some of my favorite products are described below.

Folding Picnic Table. This rugged no-maintenance piece of gear folds out to provide a 34"x26" table with seating for four adults, then collapses to suitcase dimensions of 34"x14"x4" for carrying and storage. Table and seat tops are ABS plastic, legs and supports are aluminum. These units are sold at L.L. Bean and other outdoor equipment suppliers. Overall weight is 24 pounds. Cost is around $90.

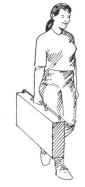

Folding Picnic Table

Roll-up Camping Table. A unique concept in camp tables, this unit is made of strong wood slats hinged inside an attractive royal blue waterproof fabric. Simply unroll it and screw on the four aluminum legs to create a 32"x32" table that is 28" high. Total weight is about 10 pounds and cost is around $35. Seating can be provided with the optional *Roll-A-Chair* . These collapsible camp stools come with a fabric seat and three aluminum legs. Total weight per stool is 1.5 pounds, costing around $13.

Roll-A-Table
and Roll-A-Chairs

Ultralight Folding Chairs. Lafuma produces a line of folding chairs that are strong and stable, yet remarkably lightweight and easy to pack. The most appropriate for active travel are the Sports/Travel chairs, available in either the *Regular* (36"x3.6" folded, 3.25 pounds) or the *Maxi* (46.3"x4.9" folded, 4.4 pounds). The frame provides four support points for a piece of durable fabric. They feature aluminum tube construction with patented joints for easy operation, removable fabric seat and a carry strap. Lafuma also makes two versions of a conventional-style folding seat—The *Folding Chair* (folds to approximately 25"x18.3"x2.9", weighs 4.2 pounds) and the *Junior Armchair* (with armrests, 24.3"x18.9"x2.9" folded, weighs about 5.3 pounds).

Lafuma's Regular Travel Chair

Axe and Saw

It's not a bad idea to include a small axe and some type of saw in your camping kit if you have the space and load-carrying ability, and will be camping where open fires are permitted. The Sven *Folding Saw* has a tempered steel blade that folds into the handle for storage. Folded dimensions are 24"x1.8", weight is about 14 ounces and cost is around $16. The Sven saw is a little too heavy for most lightweight campers, but quite popular among those traveling with a vehicle.

Solar Shower

Take along one of these portable units when traveling and you'll always be able to take a hot shower. A solar shower consists of a plastic bag that holds from one to five gallons of water. One side is clear to allow sunlight to penetrate, the other dark to absorb the light and convert it to heat. A few hours in the sun and you'll have enough sun-warmed water for several showers. If the weather won't cooperate, just boil some water on your campstove and mix it with cold to have a shower at a comfortable temperature. The most popular solar showers are the *H2O Sun Showers* from Basic Designs. They come in a three-liter size (for solo use) and 2.5-gallon, five-gallon and six-gallon capacity. For privacy or wind protection, try their plastic *Shower Enclosure*. This 30"x30"x65" unit has an inflatable frame, weighs less than four pounds and costs around $20. It also works well with portable toilets.

Portable Toilet

If you are setting up a van for extended travel, you might want to consider including a portable toilet in your equipment inventory. Don't bother with the folding type that use disposable bags. If you opt for a portable toilet, get one that has an adequate storage compartment to keep waste until you are near a permanent toilet facility. Thetford makes the *Porta Potti*, a high-quality unit with fresh water flush, waste holding tank, emptying spout and built-in deodorant storage compartment. There are two models to choose from, the *135* (approximately 27 uses, costs around $85)) and the *155* (approximately 45 uses, costs around $105). Reliance makes the *Hassock Portable Chemical Toilet*, a sturdy polyethylene pail that holds three gallons, cleans easily, is 14" high and 14" in diameter and costs around $40. Another good alternative is the *Luggable Loo*, a bucket-style, economy-priced toilet (around $30) with snap-on seat and tight fitting lift-lid.

Any portable toilet requires the use of a chemical deodorant. Many brands on the market use formaldehyde, harmful to the environment and poisonous to animals and humans. I strongly recommend the use of biodegradable deodorants such as the *Bio-Blue Sol-U-Pak*. This deodorant comes in 12 pre-measured, water soluble packets and is appropriate for the *Hassock* or *Luggable Loo*. Campa Chem products also offers a line of biodegradable products for portable toilets such as the Thetford models.

Stainless Steel Vacuum Bottle

We find this item a great convenience for providing hot drinks while traveling. An internal vacuum between two layers of unbreakable stainless steel keeps liquids piping hot all day long. Heat up some extra water in the morning before you break camp and pour it into the bottle. You'll be able to make tea, coffee or other drinks while on the road, or at the end of the day after a strenuous activity. Good quality vacuum bottles are manufactured by Gott, Nissan and Aladdin. Nissan vacuum bottles come in three sizes, the *One-Pint* (weighs 13 ounces, costs around $30), the *One-Quart* (weighs 22 ounces, costs around $30), and the *Two-Quart* (weighs around 43 ounces, costs around $40). L.L. Bean also markets their own line of vacuum bottles, the *One-Quart* (weighs 27 ounces, costs around $30) and the *Stowaway 12-Ounce* (weighs 14 ounces, costs around $24).

IV BACKPACKING

All of the personal and camping gear described thus far could be used on any adventure, regardless of your destination or what outdoor activities you intend to pursue. Now we're going to focus solely on the outdoor activities themselves. This is the first of three sections discussing equipment specific to individual sports for active travelers. I've placed backpacking first, since in many ways it is the purest, most universal form of self-propelled travel.

With little needed in the way of additional gear, backpacking is a great equalizer. It can be experienced by people of all ages and income levels, in all parts of the world and in a wide variety of ways. Whether hiking across America on a shoestring or trekking through Nepal with an outfitter, whether walking in the countryside in style or hiking deep into the backcountry in solitude, backpacking offers the opportunity to get back to basics when adventuring.

The popularity of backpacking is owed in part to its simplicity. What gear you bring is often determined by how much you can comfortably carry; where you go is limited only by how far you can walk. There are no boats to buy or bikes to maintain, no canoes to carry or vehicles to break down. The only necessities for a successful trip, other than lightweight personal and camping gear, are a good load carrier and appropriate footgear. These you will need to choose with care, basing selections on how, where and for how long you intend to travel.

To those used to traveling with a boat, bicycle or vehicle, the pace of backpacking may at first seem slow, the territory able to be covered too limiting, and the amount of gear you can carry too little. The pace is certainly slower, but you'll be amazed at how much more aware you are of the sights, sounds and smells that surround you when backpacking. The amount of territory you can reasonably cover is also reduced, yet how much is seen will seem less important than how you see it once you've discovered the joy of foot travel. And you'll find that while you may not be able to carry as much gear, you will be more than compensated by the unbridled mobility this mode of travel offers.

P acks

- Frameless Packs and Rucksacks
- Convertible Travel Packs
- Internal Frame Packs
- External Frame Packs

The obvious place to start when talking about equipment for backpacking is the pack itself. We are concerned only with your main load carrier here, packs used for hiking, trekking or general travel. Daypacks for short-term use, as well as child carriers, are covered under the appropriate sections of Personal Gear.

Backpacks come in all different shapes, sizes and styles. A trip to your local outdoor retailer may have you reeling at the sheer quantity of models available. While it may be overwhelming at first, you'll soon discover that there are only a few distinct categories of packs. The large variety in sizes and styles reflects the industry's commitment to the customer, allowing any potential traveler or outdoor enthusiast to find the perfect pack to suit their individual budget, body shape and destination. Packs are no longer designed with just the adult male physique in mind. Women and children are now equally catered to, making comfortable backpacking possible for everyone.

If you haven't shopped for a backpack in a while, you'll be pleasantly surprised at recent changes in pack design and construction. Don't be fooled by this seemingly straightforward piece of gear; there's a lot more to a good pack than meets the eye. Plan on spending some time choosing this item, since your decision could easily influence the success of your trip.

Review of Generic Types - Backpacks

Packs are categorized according to their intended use, whether for general travel, backcountry hiking and camping, or mountaineering and expedition use. The intended use of a pack helps influence other factors such as its load-carrying capacity, its type of frame or support system, as well as the specific method of loading.

By Intended Use. The term "backpacking" covers a wide range of activities, each requiring a pack with certain desirable attributes. Some people buy a pack with a specific trip or use in mind, while those on tighter budgets opt for one that can adapt to a variety of uses. The major pack classifications according to intended use are listed below:

• *Travel Packs.* These are good all-around load carriers, designed with the active traveler in mind. Despite being somewhat of a compromise between performance and style, comfort and convenience, travel packs work equally well in town or on the trail. A good travel pack can be used easily for camping and backcountry travel, although they are generally not as well suited for long hikes or treks due to their less sophisticated support systems. Travel packs have a clean appearance, anywhere from a small to large carrying capacity and no frills construction. They usually feature an internal frame for easy carrying and stowing in tight spaces, panel-loading for easy access to gear and lockable zippers that help prevent petty theft.

Many travel packs available today are classified as *convertibles*, meaning they easily convert from backpack to shoulder bag or hand luggage simply by changing the straps. This appeals to those who only occasionally use a backpack, or want more convenience or better appearance from their load carrier when on public transportation or once at their destination. Travel packs usually have another nice feature, a removable daypack that serves as an outer compartment when on the pack. This is especially handy for those who explore an area by taking day trips from a base.

• *Backcountry Hiking and Camping Packs.* Backcountry packs are made for those who intend to carry larger loads and do more extended camping, hiking or trekking. More emphasis is placed on the frame and support system than on appearance and ease of use, although you'll find some packs that excel in all categories. These packs have moderate to large carrying capacity, either internal or external frames, and are typically top-loading.

• *Skiing and Mountaineering Packs.* These packs fit close to the body and are made for ultimate durability, weather protection, convenience and comfort. They are typically made of rugged yet lightweight materials, are designed to accept and protect all the specialty gear you'd ever need to carry, and have highly technical frame and support systems that provide multiple levels of adjustment for achieving a close, comfortable fit. Skiing and mountaineering packs can range in size from modest to large, while expedition models can be truly gigantic. These packs invariably have internal frames and can be either top or panel-loading.

By Carrying Capacity. Packs are also categorized according to their carrying capacity, or internal volume, usually rated in cubic inches (English) or in liters (metric). While the specific categories listed below are a bit arbitrary, they give you a good idea of what you should be looking for.

• *Small Packs.* With a carrying capacity up to around 3,000 cubic inches, small packs are good for short-term travel or treks when weight should be kept to a minimum, and camping and other specialty gear is not needed.

• *Medium-Size Packs.* Good for general travel and backcountry use, these packs have a carrying capacity ranging from 3,000 to 5,000 cubic inches. They typically have adequate room for all of your personal and camping gear, as well as space for a moderate amount of provisions.

• *Large Packs.* Ranging from 5,000 to over 7,000 cubic inches of storage space, these packs are considered expedition models by most manufacturers. Large packs are necessary when carrying bulky cold weather gear, specialty items or long-term provisions.

By Frame Type. Backpacks are commonly categorized according to the type of frame employed, either external, internal or frameless.

• *External Frame Packs.* On these models, a metal frame and support system are on the outside of the pack. The pack itself is suspended on one side of the frame, the backrest, shoulder straps and hipbelt on the other. An external frame pack creates an airspace that provides ventilation for the user in hot, muggy climates. It also distributes the load well, and makes it easy to strap on additional gear such as sleeping bags, pads and tents. The weight is placed over your body's natural center of gravity, making it possible to walk normally in an upright position. External frame packs typically have a moderate to large capacity, lots of external pockets, and are often a combination of top and panel-loading.

• *Internal Frame Packs.* These packs feature an internal frame and support system integral with the pack fabric that comes in contact with your back. The absence of an external frame makes them maneuverable during active sports and in tight spaces, as well as more forgiving of the abuse universally bestowed by baggage handlers. Most current internal frames consist of some combination of flexible stays, plastic sheeting and foam padding, providing a comfortable support that conforms to your body. Type and complexity of the internal frame is determined by intended use and carrying capacity. Internal frame packs typically don't have external pockets as standard features, although optional pockets can be easily strapped on. They can range from small to large, can be top or panel-loading, and usually come with several sets of nylon straps for attaching ancillary gear.

  • *Frameless Packs.* Larger than daypacks, smaller than most frame packs, models in this category of load carrier have no frame at all, yet are still capable of hauling a reasonable travel load. Falling somewhere in the 2,000 to 3,000 cubic inch range, these packs usually have no external pockets and rely on heavy construction and a padded back for their stability and your comfort. Frameless packs are lightweight, portable and reasonably priced.

  By Method of Loading. Backpacks are loaded in one of two ways, from the top or from the front and sides through individually zippered panels.

  • *Top-Loading Packs* are typically the most weather resistant and least subject to zipper failure, although they make it more difficult to access items located near the bottom. For this reason most top-loading packs have a lower compartment with a zippered panel access.

  • *Panel-Loading Packs* make it much easier to locate stored items, particularly if there are multiple panels. A typical combination is to have access through one lower and one upper panel, with an internal divider separating the load.

Features and Options - Backpacks

The features and options on currently marketed main load carriers are numerous. Look for the following when shopping for a backpack:

Frame and Support System. This is the single most significant feature of a pack. The frame and support system are there to distribute the load and provide user comfort. Your intended use will steer you toward an internal frame, external frame or frameless model.

Ventilated Back Pad. Most internal and external frame packs have a foam back pad with a breathable mesh fabric (or just the mesh fabric on some externals) to allow for adequate ventilation in hot climates.

Lumbar Pad. This protects and supports the lumbar region of your back when carrying a heavy load.

Adjustable Shoulder Straps. Padded shoulder straps help transfer some of the load and keep the pack positioned correctly on your back. While all shoulder straps have some method of length adjustment, many packs now feature shoulder strap systems where the upper point of contact with the frame is fully adjustable for various torso lengths. This allows you to get a perfect fit for your body size and shape.

Sternum Strap. This short, adjustable strap connects the two shoulder straps in front of your body at the sternum, keeping them in position. Without this strap in place, the shoulder straps tend to creep toward the outer edge of your shoulders. At least one pack manufacturer prefers a scapula strap, one that connects the shoulder straps in back rather than on your front.

Hipbelt. Any pack, even small daypacks, should have some type of hipbelt that transfers most of the load to your hips and keeps the bottom of the pack close to your body. As a rule, the larger and more technical the pack, the more sophisticated the hipbelt and its method of attachment and adjustment.

Load Stabilizers. These are adjustable straps that allow you to fine tune the placement of the pack load with respect to your body and the frame. Typical placement of stabilizer straps is on the each of the shoulder straps and one on each side of the hipbelt.

Compression Straps. These are adjustable straps that allow you to compress the load around the girth of the pack so it rides in a compact, streamlined fashion. The less bulky the load, the more maneuverable the pack and the easier it is to carry. These straps can also serve to lash down all sorts of gear. Dana Design takes this concept a bit further to create an adjustable compression sheet of fabric they fondly call a *Shovit Pocket*. It wraps around the entire front of the pack and holds bulky gear firmly in place.

Top Weather Flap. All packs with a top-loading upper compartment have a top flap that covers the load, providing weather protection and compression to reduce bulk. The top flap is typically sewn to the back of the pack and connects to the pack front with adjustable compression straps. On many internal frame models, the top flap is incorporated into a removable lumbar pack, great for short explorations.

Storage Compartments. Packs have many types of compartments for storing gear, most for general use and a few for specific pieces of gear.

• *Inner Compartments.* The simplest arrangement is one large main compartment, accessible through either a top drawstring or a zippered panel on the pack front or sides. Some packs feature a divided main compartment to cope with diverse loads and to provide better access to gear, usually with a top-loading upper space and a panel-loading lower area for a sleeping bag or clothing. Panel access can be through a straight horizontal zipper, or through the more popular semi-circular style of zipper that, when open, allows you to really rummage around for stored items. Some packs have the ability to increase their main load capacity by means of a drop-out bottom compartment or fold-out top, great for allowing you to carry additional items acquired during your travels. These expandable compartments are generally tucked away and held in place by nylon straps or zippers until needed.

• *Outer Compartments.* In addition to the inner storage space, packs often have a variety of outer storage compartments for carrying smaller gear. These include thin map pockets in the top weather flap; front and side zippered pockets for an assortment of smaller items and fuel and water bottles; organizer pockets with divided slots for storing writing materials, or other small items you need good access to; mesh pockets for wet gear; and pole sleeves for skis, tent poles, camera tripods, fishing rods, and other long items.

Internal Load Divider. Larger packs usually divide the inner compartment in two with an internal piece of fabric. Access is provided to both upper and lower areas. On some packs, this divider is removable, allowing for greater flexibility in load configurations.

Lash Points. All packs provide various lash points for securing additional items such as bulky camping or mountaineering gear to the outside of the pack. Lash points come in the form of slots, rings or loops of fabric for attaching nylon straps or cord, or they come complete with a lashing line in place. Climbing and expedition packs often feature an entire row of nylon loops called a "daisy chain" for securing ice axes, caribiners and other gear.

Wrist Loops. These simple nylon straps attach to rings on the front portion of the shoulder straps, allowing you to rest your arms while hiking.

Add-on Pockets. One of the most popular features on currently available packs is add-on external pockets. By having the external pockets as optional equipment, you're able to streamline the outside of the pack when packing light or in tight spaces, or load additional gear as necessary. They come in a variety of sizes and styles for placement on the side, top or front of the pack. They are also available as shoulder pockets, small pouches that attach to the front of your shoulder straps for carrying sunglasses, a compact camera or other small items.

Add-on Packs. In addition to adding pockets, some pack manufacturers allow you to strap their smaller daypacks and lumbar packs right on to their larger packs, giving great flexibility in creating a load capacity that fits your changing needs. This concept is similar to removable daypacks found on travel packs, yet distinct in that it allows a number of packs to function as components of a system.

Raincover. This is a waterproof piece of fabric that slips over the pack's top, front, sides and bottom, leaving the back free for access to the shoulder straps and hipbelt. Raincovers usually have a drawstring to cinch the cover tightly around your pack. Some models, such as the Dana Design *PackFly*, have an integral hood that also covers the wearer's head.

Lockable Zipper Pulls. Some travel packs come with true lockable zipper pulls, not just ordinary pulls with holes in the end for slipping a lock on. I was once given a demonstration on how easy it was for someone who knew what they were doing to pry open a locked zipper with standard issue pulls, steal something, then close the zipper back again without any evidence of tampering. The owner would have no idea how they could have lost the missing items. With lockable pulls, it is impossible to pry open a zipper without cutting the pack and leaving glaring evidence of theft.

Optional Travel Locks. Some pack manufacturers offer small locks for securing zipper pulls on travel gear.

Construction and Operation - Backpacks

Pack construction differs widely depending on intended use and frame type, but all packs have certain elements of construction in common.

Pack Body. The pack's fabric body is constructed of heavy packcloth or other abrasion-resistant nylon fabric, and sewn into the desired shape using tough synthetic thread. Double stitching is commonplace on all seams, with multiple passes of stitching the norm on all stress points. Nylon tape is often used for extra strength on load-bearing seams. Coil zippers of varying sizes are used on pocket and panel openings, with most models utilizing durable zipper pulls and fabric pull tabs for easy grip and reduced noise. Fabric flaps are sewn in place to cover zippers and provide weather protection.

Shoulder Straps. The shoulder straps of simple daypacks are usually just straight padded straps sewn at the appropriate angle for comfortable carrying. More technical load carriers develop this concept into a science, anatomically contouring the shape of the straps to best fit your body. This is now true for both external and internal frame models. The idea is to give maximum support while reducing stress on neck and shoulders, and maximum freedom of upper body movement without chafing.

Another evolution in backpack shoulder strap construction is the integration of an adjustable attachment point system. This is typically a sliding mechanism on the frame (externals) or back pad (internals) that allows the user to secure a better fit by raising or lowering the shoulder strap attachment point in relation to the pack body. Load stabilizers on the shoulder pads allow you to adjust the set of the pack. The stitching on shoulder straps is typically not sewn through, thus avoiding a potential area of chafing.

Hipbelts. Hipbelts have also undergone major changes lately. They have better padding and are contoured for greater comfort. Many models have additional lateral stiffeners to provide more support and adjustable stabilizing straps to help direct the load. Some manufacturers offer women the option of a hipbelt with more flare to better suit the female shape.

Internal Frame Packs. Internal frame packs require the use of an extra-heavy layer of fabric on the bottom section since they have no external frame extension to protect this area from wear. They also incorporate an inner lining of nylon cloth that encloses the frame and takes the wear of loading and unloading gear. Better models use heavier grades of cloth. The frame typically consists of flexible stays that run from top to bottom along the back of the pack, and work alone or in conjunction with plastic sheeting and foam padding to provide the desired degree of strength and comfort. The flexible stays can often be removed, shaped by the user for a perfect fit, and reinserted into the pack. Make sure to follow the manufacturers recommendations when attempting to custom fit support stays.

External Frame Packs. External metal frames are typically constructed of Heli-arc welded aluminum, usually with an anodized finish (silver or black). One exception is the molded one-piece plastic frame employed by PEAK 1. The shape of the frame is specific to a manufacturers' design criteria or style. In most cases, the bottom of the frame extends beyond the pack body for added protection or a convenient place to strap on sleeping bags and other bulky gear. The attachment points for shoulder straps, hipbelts, back pads and the pack body itself, typically consist of brass grommets in the fabric resting on clevis pin connections along the frame.

Sizing a Pack. Proper sizing is mostly related to the pack's frame height. A pack should be sized according to the length of your torso, measured from the top of the shoulder to the hipbone; it has nothing to do with the length of your legs. You'll notice manufacturers usually specify a range of torso lengths suitable for each model and, if applicable, a length of travel for adjustable shoulder strap systems. If in doubt on an internal frame pack, check to see that the framesheet or stays rise several inches above the top of your shoulders. More than that may reduce mobility, less means you should probably go for the next larger size. Wearing a pack that is too big or too small will invariably result in discomfort, so take care that the model you choose is right for your shape.

Another frame-related consideration is correct positioning of the shoulder stabilizing straps, which help to divert some of the pack load to the front of your shoulders. These straps must meet the pack frame above shoulder level to function properly, preferably somewhere close to ear level.

Once you've found a pack with the proper frame size, check out the hipbelt and shoulder straps, preferably with the pack loaded. These can often be replaced if the ones that come with the pack don't fit. The hipbelt padding should sit comfortably on your hips and stop short of meeting in the front. Women are often given the option of a hipbelt with increased flare. There should be plenty of room on the belt to adjust for various layers of clothing and slight weight gain or loss. In most instances, if the pack frame and hipbelt are appropriate for your shape, the shoulder straps will be too. Just make sure they aren't too short (the padding ends too close to your armpit) or too long (you run out of adjustment on the strap).

Suggestion for Loading. There are a few simple rules for loading a pack that make it easier to carry. In general, external frame packs should be loaded with the heavy items up high and close to your back, the lightweight gear down low and toward the outside. This keeps the load's center of gravity at shoulder level, so with only a slight bend at the waist the weight is perfectly aligned over your hips. Heavy items to be placed up high include tents, which are often mistakenly strapped to the lower portion of an external frame. Sleeping bags should go down low, either in a sleeping bag compartment or strapped onto the frame below the pack body.

Internal frame and frameless packs can be loaded in a similar fashion if you are walking on good trails and the terrain is gentle. For off-trail travel, climbing or skiing, place the heavier items toward the center and close to your back. This increases your balance and aligns the weight properly during strenuous activities, although you may find it necessary to bend over a bit more to be comfortable when the activity is less demanding.

Women and children tend to have a lower center of gravity than men, and therefore may find that keeping the weight toward the center of the pack is best for all conditions. Try to place water and fuel bottles in the long external pockets (either integral or add-on), and items you'll need often or in a hurry in other pockets. Keep sharp objects away from the back of the pack, especially when loading internal frame or frameless packs.

Adjusting the Pack. Once you've loaded the pack, tighten the exterior compression straps to reduce the bulk. Place the pack on your back and adjust it as necessary. Tighten the hipbelt so the load rides comfortably on your hips. Adjust the shoulder straps to position the pack in proper relation to your back. Tighten the shoulder strap stabilizers to shift some of the load to your shoulders. A good rule of thumb is two-thirds of the weight on your hips, one-third on your shoulders, although you can vary the placement of the load as often as you like while hiking to prevent fatigue. Now tighten the other pack adjustments until they are snug yet comfortable, including the hipbelt stabilizing straps, to achieve the best fit.

Author's Recommendations - Backpacks

Shopping for a pack can be a confusing business. To help you sort things out and choose a pack that best suits your needs, I offer the following recommendations:

Price vs. Performance. You invariably pay more money for better performance when purchasing travel and outdoor gear. Only you can determine what that extra performance is worth. If your backpacking time is limited or your destinations tame, almost any reasonably-priced pack of sufficient size and level of comfort will serve the purpose. If you have more ambitious tendencies, don't hesitate to spend a little more on a good quality pack. You'll undoubtedly have more fun and less pain on your adventures, and your investment will last a long, long time.

First Choose Frame Type. Which style of frame to get is your first big decision when buying a pack, a choice that should be based on how and where you intend to use it, your equipment budget and your personal preference. In general, an external frame pack is better suited for carrying bulky or heavy loads while hiking trails in the backcountry. This type makes it easy to pack and carry long-term provisions, and as a result is the frame style of choice for most long distance hikers. External frame packs are usually less expensive than internal frame models with equivalent features and degree of support, so they are also the choice of many groups, organizations and outdoor enthusiasts on a budget.

Internal frame packs, on the other hand, are much better suited for traveling, trekking, climbing, skiing as well as a host of other active outdoor sports. Currently available internal frame packs are so popular because they allow you to carry a load in reasonable

Jansport's Yosemite

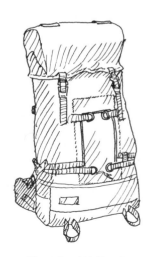

Mountainsmith's Frostfire

To The Best Outdoor & Recreation Equipment   259

comfort, don't restrict your mobility in tight places or during active sports, and stow more easily on public transportation or when not in use. This all adds up to a great deal of versatility.

Then Select Size. Get something in the 2,500 to 3,500 cubic inch range for weekend camping, summit assaults, or extended touring with minimal gear. A pack in the 3,500 to 5,500 cubic inch range is better suited for longer backcountry or general travel, when more gear is needed. Larger packs in the 5,000 to 6,500 range can handle the provisions and gear you'd need for hiking a long-distance trail, trekking with camping gear or participating in an expedition.

Get Versatility for Active Travel. Outdoor travelers should always look for the most versatile models they can find when shopping for packs and other costly gear. Versatility relates to how well a piece of equipment adapts to your changing needs. Since active travel transcends many outdoor sports, types of terrain and unusual situations, your needs can change quite drastically, even on a single trip. The equipment you choose should be able to meet those needs, and it doesn't have to cost you more in the long run. Most of us are on a tight budget when outfitting, yet it's usually less expensive to buy one high-quality item that works well over a range of conditions than have to purchase multiple pieces of gear.

If getting a main load carrier that offers the greatest flexibility appeals to you, I recommend purchasing a good quality, moderately-sized internal frame pack (around 4,500 to 5,000 cubic inches) that best fits your body shape, appeals to you aesthetically, and offers features that allow the pack to handle different types of loads. Features to look for include: expandable upper or lower compartments; removable daypacks, zip-out main compartment divider; add-on pockets and pouches that give you extra capacity when needed, yet stow away for a trim pack profile when not in use; and component systems that allow you to strap smaller packs to larger models, achieving a widely variable carrying capacity.

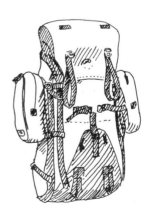

Lowe's Contour IV

Convertible Travel Packs. Relatively new to the market, convertibles offer one way for travelers to achieve flexibility in a pack. Their detachable daypack and expansive panel-loading compartments are among their strong points. Look for daypacks that have good suspension systems, padded shoulder straps and comfortable waist belts. Don't expect too much from these load carriers. Straddling the line between luggage and backpack, they are bound to have some compromises, and most models will perform more like one than the other. If general travel with the occasional trek is your style, choose a less technical version. If you are primarily looking for a comfortable backpack that can function as luggage on occasion, go for a more sophisticated model with a proper internal frame. What if you don't really need luggage at all, but like the removable daypack and panel-loading? Forget the convertibles and get a good panel-loading internal frame pack with proper support and some type of detachable pack.

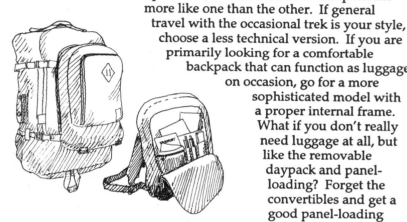

Eagle Creek's World Journey

When a Frameless Pack will do. As noted above, not everyone who travels needs the support of a frame pack. You may be venturing far yet traveling light, such as on an a short alpine climb, a walking tour of Britain, a hut-to-hut tour of the Alps or a group trek in Nepal. If you don't need to carry camping gear or much in the way of provisions, a comfortable, frameless rucksack in the 2,200 to 3,700 cubic inch range may be the best option.

Dana Designs' Blaze

Fitting the Female Form. Women will be glad to know that pack manufacturers have responded to requests that the anatomical differences between men and women no longer be ignored. Shorter, narrower frame sizes, specially designed shoulder straps and better fitting hipbelts head the list of features now available to women. You may find that standard models in smaller frame sizes fit you just fine, but if not, there's no need to settle for an uncomfortable pack. Almost all models listed on the comparison charts either come in women's frame sizes or have equivalents designed specifically for women.

Gregory's Petit Dru

Especially for Children. Manufacturers and outdoor retailers are finally coming around to the idea that not all children view Disneyland as their idea of adventure. While the variety could still be improved, there are a several good models of children's backpacks currently on the market. Recommended external frame models include the Camp Trails *Skipper*, the Jansport *Scout* and the Kelty *Junior Tioga*. Good internal frame packs just for children include the Tough Traveler *Camper* (ages six to ten, up to height of 5'2") and *Ranger* (ages nine to 14, height range of 4'6" to 5'6"). The nice thing about these packs is that they make excellent rucksacks for older hikers when the child outgrows them.

Camp Trails' Skipper

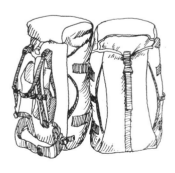

Tough Traveler's Camper and Ranger

Raincovers. If you are planning an expedition to a soggy climate, do yourself a favor and purchase a raincover for your pack. This low cost item will protect your pack and its contents whether on your back, at the campsite or just waiting for a train. Raincovers are available from most pack suppliers for around $15.

Pack Costs. Now it's time to place a price tag on these lovable load carriers. The cost usually reflects the level of sophistication and quality of workmanship and materials. Rucksacks and frameless packs can cost anywhere from $75 to $200 depending on quality and features. Convertible travel packs can be purchased for around $125 to $150. External frame packs generally range from $100 to $200, with children's models closer to $85 and a few expedition models going as high as $300. Internal frame packs also vary widely, with many good models in the $150 to $225 range. Climbing and mountaineering models can easily cost $250 to $350 or more.

With dozens of good pack manufacturers and close to a thousand pack models now available, it's definitely a buyer's market out there. Listed below are some of the most practical, high-quality packs currently on the market, categorized by activity. These are all considered main load carriers for travelers and outdoor enthusiasts. Daypacks and child carriers are covered under Personal Gear.

Author's Recommendations - Frameless/Intern'l Frame Packs (2200-3700 cu. in.)

Brand	Model	Cap'ty (cu. in.)	Features
Camp Trails	Trinity	2600, 3410	tl, pb, 5 ep, cs, lp
Caribou	Snopack	2200	pl, pb, 2 ep, cs, lp
Climb High	Alpinist	2700-3500	tl, pb, 1 ep, cs, lp
Dana Design	Blaze	2160	pl, ash, pb, 1 ep, cs, lp, apa
Eagle Creek	Solo Journey	3100	pl, 1 ep, cs, lp
Granite Gear	Precipice	2800	tl, pb, rdp, 1 ep, cs, lp
Gregory	Two Day	2255, 2450	pl, pb, cs, lp, apa
Jack Wolfskin	Beaver Creek	2684	tl and pl, pb, 2 ep, cs, lp,
Jansport	Tahoma	2583	tl, pb, cs, lp
Kelty	Brisbane	2940	tl, pb, 3 ep, cs, lp
Lafuma	Lady 55*	3000	tl and pl, ash, pb, 2 ep, cs, lp,
L.L. Bean	Mountain Trek	3700	tl, ash, pb, 4 ep, cs, lp
Lowe	Eclipse	2700	tl and pl, pb, 3 ep, cs, lp, apa
Madden	Penguin	2100, 2500	tl, pb, 1 ep, cs, lp, apa
McHale & Co.	Alpine Zero	3000	tl, ash, pb, 1 ep, cs, lp, apa
MEI	Citadel	2800	tl , pb, 1 ep, cs, lp, apa
Millet/Suunto	Delta 50	3051	tl, ash, pb, 2 ep, cs, lp
Mountainsmith	Classic R'cks'ck	2410, 3662	tl and pl, ash, pb, cs, lp, apa
Mountain Sys.	Cascade	3000	pl, ash, pb, 1 ep, cs, lp
Mountain T'ls	Ice Bash	3300	tl, pb, 3 ep, cs, lp
Osprey	Zephyr	2850	tl, ash, pb, 1 ep, cs, lp
Overland	Brokeoff	3054	tl, pb, 1 ep, cs, lp

Quest	Jupiter	2400, 2900	tl and pl, pb, 2 ep, cs, lp
REI	Toursac	2860	tl, pb, 4 ep, cs, lp
Remington	Mod. Daypack	2600	pl, rdp, pb, 1 ep, cs, lp
The North Face	Kinajou	2300	pl, pb, 2 ep, cs, lp
Ultimate Dirt'n	Shadow	3450	tl and pl, ash, pb, 2 ep, cs, lp
vauDe	Anatomic I	2800	pl, pb, zcd, 1 ep, cs, lp
Wildern'ss Exp.	Couloir	3200	tl, ash, pb, 1 ep, cs, lp

made specifically for women

FEATURES: tl=top loading; pl=panel loading; ash=adjustable shoulder harness system; rdp=removeable day pack; pb=padded back; zcd=zip-out compartment divider; ep=external pockets; cs=compression straps; lp=lash points; apa=add-on pockets available.

Author's Recommendations - Convertible Travel Packs (3000-5000 cu. in.)

Brand	Model	Cap'ty (cu. in.)	Features
Camp Trails	Vagabond	5000	pl, ash, rdp, acd, pb, 3 ep, cs, lp
Caribou	Gypsy Traveler	4650	pl, ash, rdp, pb, 1 ep, cs, lp
Eagle Creek	World Journey	5000	pl, ash, rdp, pb, 1 ep, cs, lp
EMS	Traventure	4300	pl, ash, rdp, pb, acd, 1 ep, cs, lp
Gregory	Wanderlust	4115-4700	pl, pb, acd, cs, lp
Jack Wolfskin	Columbus	2976-3720	pl, rdp, pb, 2 ep, cs, lp
Jansport	China Clipper	4250, 4600	pl, rdp, pb, acd, cs, lp
Kelty	Traveler	5000	pl, rdp, acd, cs, lp
L.L. Bean	2-in-1	3800, 4800	pl, rdp, pb, 1 ep, cs, lp
Lowe	Hitchhiker	4700	pl, rdp, pb, acd, 1 ep, cs, lp
Madden	Yankee Clipper	4000-5100	pl, ash, pb, acd, 1 ep, cs, lp
MEI	Trekker I and II	4400, 4900	pl, ash, rdp, pb, acd, 3 ep, cs, lp
Millet/Suunto	Titan	4270	pl, ash, pb, 1 ep, cs, lp
Outbound	Wanderer	5500	pl, ash, rdp, pb, 1 ep, cs, lp
Quest	Kiwi/Eurasia*	3850, 4750	pl, rdp, pb, 2 ep, cs, lp
REI	Tashkent	3940	pl, ash, rdp, pb, 3 ep, cs, lp
Tough Travel'r	Silver Streak	3200-4000	pl, ash, pb, 2 ep, cs, lp

Eurasia has a removeable day pack and fanny pack.

FEATURES: tl=top loading; pl=panel loading; ash=adjustable shoulder harness system; rdp=removeable day pack; pb=padded back; acd=adjustable compartment divider; ep=external pockets; cs=compression straps; lp=lash points; apa=add-on pockets available.

Author's Recommendations - Internal Frame Packs (4000-6000 cu. in.)

Brand	Model	Cap'ty (cu. in.)	Features
Camp Trails	Catskill	5195, 5695	tl & pl, ash, pb, zcd, 5 ep, cs, lp
Dana Designs	Glacier	5000	tl & pl, ash, rdp, pb, 3 ep, cs, lp, apa
Eagle Creek	Endless Journey	5700	pl, ash, 2 rdp, pb, 2 ep, cs, lp
EMS	Blackfoot	4750	tl & pl, ash, rdp, pb, acd, 3 ep, cs, lp
Gregory	Nova	5435, 5825	tl, ash, rdp, pb, 3 ep, cs, lp, apa
Jack Wolfskin	Yak II and III	5000, 5580	tl, ash, rdp, pb, 2 ep, cs, lp
Kelty	Redcloud	5640	tl & pl, ash, pb, 4 ep, cs, lp
Lafuma	Tassili	3600, 4800	tl & pl, ash, pb, acd, 3 ep, cs, lp
L.L. Bean	Mountain Star	4250-6000	tl, pl, ash, pb, acd, 3 ep, cs, lp, apa
Lowe	Contour IV	5400	tl & pl, ash, pb, acd, 1 ep, cs, lp, apa
Madden	Eagle	4800, 6000	tl & pl, pb, acd, 1 ep, cs, lp, apa
McHale & Co.	Standard Alpineer	3000-6000	tl & pl, ash, rdp, pb, 2 ep, cs, lp, apa
MEI	Starlite I and II	5242, 6325	tl & pl, ash, rdp, pb, acd, 3 ep, cs
Millet/Suunto	Nepal 80	4577	tl & pl, ash, pb, acd, 3 ep, cs, lp

Mountainsmith	Frostfire	4400-6037	tl & pl, ash, pb, 1 ep, cs, lp, apa
Mountain Sys.	Kailis	5000, 5500	tl & pl, ash, rdp, pb, acd, 1 ep, cs, lp
Mountain Tools	Hot Tamale	4650-5200	tl & pl, ash, pb, rdp, 2 ep, cs, lp, apa
Osprey	Highlander	4400, 5100	tl, ash, rdp, pb, 1 ep, cs, lp
Outbound	Rainier	4200	tl & pl, ash, pb, acd, 1 ep, cs, apa
Quest	Big Bang	4800, 5000	tl & pl, ash, pb, 1 ep, cs, lp
REI	Newstar	5419, 5743	tl & pl, ash, pb, 1 ep, cs, lp, apa
The North Face	Alpaca	4530, 5100	tl & pl, ash, pb, 3 ep, cs, lp
Tough Travel'r	Moonscape*	3120-3600	tl & pl, ash, pb, 1 ep, cs, lp
Tough Travel'r	Moonwalker	3900-4450	tl & pl, ash, pb, 1 ep, cs, lp
vauDe	Profile 65	4000	tl & pl, ash, pb, acd, 1 ep, cs, lp
Wildern'ss Exp.	Timberline	4000, 4800	tl & pl, ash, pb, 1 ep, cs, lp

*made specifically for women

FEATURES: tl=top loading; pl=panel loading; ash=adjustable shoulder harness system; rdp=removeable day pack; pb=padded back; acd=adjustable compartment divider; ep=external pockets; cs=compression straps; lp=lash points; apa=add-on pockets available.

Author's Recommendations - External Frame Packs (4000-6000 cu. In.)

Brand	Model	Cap'ty (cu. in.)	Features
Camp Trails	Omega	4980-5700	tl & pl, ash, rdp, pb, acd, 5 ep, cs, lp
EMS	Katahdin	4478	tl & pl, pb, 4 ep, cs, lp
Jansport	Bryce & Yosemite	4105, 4850	pl, ash, pb, 6 ep, cs, lp
Kelty	Radial Light XLT	3500-5000	tl and pl, ash, pb, 5 ep, cs, lp
Outbound	Matterhorn	4100	tl and pl, pb, 3 ep, cs, lp
PEAK 1	Passport	5402	tl and pl, ash, pb, 5 ep, cs, lp
REI	Wonderland	4093, 4918	tl and pl, ash, pb, 5 ep, cs, lp
Remington	Ext. Frame Pack	3600	tl, ash, pb, 5 ep, cs, lp
vauDe	Terkum*	4250	tl and pl, ash, pb, 2 ep, cs, lp
Wildern'ss Exp.	FXT	4400	tl and pl, ash, pb, 6 ep, cs, lp

This pack has the same type of frame as the Profile 65 internal frame pack. The difference is it is mounted on the outside of the pack.

FEATURES: tl=top loading; pl=panel loading; ash=adjustable shoulder harness system; rdp=removeable day pack; pb=padded back; acd=adjustable compartment divider; ep=external pockets; cs=compression straps; lp=lash points; apa=add-on pockets available.

Maintenance and Repair - Backpacks

While a well-made pack should last for many years, there are a few simple things you can do to extend its life.

Keep it Clean. Packcloth will last forever if it is treated kindly. Remove travel dirt and grime after each trip and before storing the pack. A little travel soap, some warm water and a soft laundry brush is best. Don't ever put a pack in the washing machine or dryer.

Keep it Dry. No, you don't have to find shelter every time it rains, but over the years a pack that is continually damp will become damaged. Dry it out as often as you can, especially before storage. Use a raincover in soggy climates.

Watch Sharp Items. Stow gear so that no sharp items press against the pack fabric. This includes items strapped onto the outside of the pack. Place protective padding over sharp points, or strap on a replaceable layer of fabric where sharp items are stowed.

Don't Overtighten Adjustment Straps. While the tendency is to give those straps a good pull, overtightening can deform pack components and cause damage. This is particularly common on compression straps and shoulder strap or hipbelt stabilizers. Go for a snug fit and leave it at that.

Repairs. Good quality packs are tough pieces of gear and have few things that go wrong with them. You may occasionally need to replace lost or damaged pieces of hardware, or repair the pack fabric if it becomes worn or accidentally torn. Damaged packs are usually returned to the factory for repair or replacement. Minor repairs can usually be handled by the equipment supplier. Before leaving for a trip, check out all pack components thoroughly. For extended travel, it's a good idea to stock your repair kit with a small piece of packcloth and a heavy-duty needle and thread.

Spare Parts. The need for spare parts is more often a result of something being lost or misplaced rather than damaged. Ask your pack supplier what common replacement parts, if any, they recommend.

Backpacking Boots

- Hiking and Light Trekking Boots
- Trekking and Backcountry Boots
- Mountaineering Boots

Suitable types of footgear for active travel are discussed in the Clothing section of Personal Gear. Specific shoe and boot models recommended there are great for general adventuring, and most are fine for backpacking when your load is light and the terrain is level. Larger loads and more difficult terrain, however, demand boots that give your feet additional support and protection. In this section, we'll concentrate on boots with a medium to high cut, specially made for the more rugged conditions encountered when backpacking.

Review of Generic Types - Backpacking Boots

Backpacking boots are typically classified according to their intended use. Determining intended use has as much to do with the loads to be carried as with the type of trail conditions to be encountered. Pack load and type of terrain are two major concerns of boot manufacturers. They must produce boots for a variety of backpacking conditions, and as a result they offer a range of models that fit into one of the following four categories:

Ambitious Hiking and Light Trekking. This type of boot gives lightweight support without sacrificing agility. It is for those who carry light loads on short, yet often demanding trips, and occasionally heavier loads into the backcountry. These boots are equally suitable for trail use or general adventure travel.

Serious Trekking. The term trekking is a bit nebulous, but usually denotes backpacking with moderate loads on mountain trails that feature rough terrain. Boots for this type of activity must offer more protection and support, and while fine for ambitious hiking and country rambling, are less suited to general travel comfort.

Extended Backcountry Travel. Trails in the backcountry can serve up almost any type of conditions, from level, dry, groomed paths to steep, rough, muddy tracks. Extended travel there inevitably means carrying a heavy load of provisions and camping gear. A boot for extended backcountry travel must have great support and durability, as well as a good level of traction, to perform when times are tough, yet be comfortable enough for long-distance hiking. True backpacking boots can certainly be worn while hiking and trekking, but are generally too stiff and heavy for general travel wear.

Mountaineering. Serious mountaineering is eloquently defined in the Vasque catalog as "expeditions at high altitudes under extreme weather conditions, carrying heavy gear over long periods of time." What could demand more from a boot? While many mountaineers take the sport less seriously, all mountaineering boot models must have a high level of support, stiffness and traction for coping with rugged terrain, ice and snow, and heavy loads. The features that make these specialty boots great for alpine work also cause them to be not suited for general trekking or backpacking. Some mountaineering boots for technical alpine work have two layers, a softer inner boot for warmth and some degree of support, and a stiff outer boot that provides weather protection, abrasion resistance, traction and the bulk of the required support. The outer layer often has incorporated a fabric gaiter into the boot upper.

Features and Options - Backpacking Boots

While materials and construction techniques used on boots for backpacking vary considerably with boot type, the basic components remain the same. Some of the features to look for when comparing boots are listed below.

Upper. This is the part of the boot that covers and protects the foot. It includes the outer layer, usually some combination of leather and densely-woven fabric mesh, plus any foam padding, waterproof membrane and inner lining employed. The cut of the upper helps determine the level of ankle support; the higher the cut, the more support it offers.

Collar. The collar is the part of the upper that surrounds your ankle. Point of contact depends on boot cut. The collar is typically padded with soft foam for comfort and protection.

Tongue. The part of the boot upper located underneath the laces that covers your instep. The tongue is usually padded for comfort and may have partial or full gusset construction (gussets connect the sides of the tongue to the upper, preventing moisture and debris from entering the boot). A fully-gusseted tongue is also termed a full-bellows closure.

Hardware. This refers to the metal hooks, D-rings or grommets that the laces attach to. D-rings are typically used for the first section of lacing, hooks and one or two sets of grommets for the rest.

Outsole. The outsole is what most people think of as the sole of the boot. It comes in contact with the ground and must be highly abrasion-resistant. Outsole tread patterns vary widely and are chosen for specific types of terrain. Some treads are labeled as self-cleaning, which means trail material tends not to get stuck between the lugs of the tread and be carried away. You'll notice that boots for more demanding terrain also have a pronounced heel built into the outsole, providing more traction when going downhill, while boots for relatively smooth terrain have no true heel at all.

External Counter. An external counter is employed to reinforce areas of high stress, typically around the boot heel and sides, just above the midsole. This adds stiffness and stabilizes the back part of the foot.

Rand. A rand is a flexible band around the perimeter of the upper, directly above the outsole. It provides some external support to stabilize the foot against lateral movement, as well as providing a protective barrier against abrasion and the elements. Waterproof boots almost always have a full rubber rand.

Midsole. Located between the outsole and the upper, the midsole serves to absorb shocks and provide cushioning, stability and dynamic support. Many boot manufacturers find innovative ways to include air cushioning in the midsole of some models, either through microporous materials or some type of honeycomb matrix that naturally creates air spaces.

Insole. This element links the boot upper to the midsole or sole, providing structural integrity and controlling torsional rigidity and flex at the ball of the foot.

Shank. Used solely as a stiffener, the shank is located between the midsole and insole. It supports the arch and gives the proper degree of flex.

Internal Counter. Similar to its external "counterpart," the internal counter reinforces high stress areas at the heel and toe from the inside. It centers and stabilizes these areas, and provides protection from impact.

Footbed. The footbed is what your foot actually rests on. It typically consists of several layers and is removable. Over time it conforms to the shape of your foot, yielding comfort and uniform support. Most manufacturers offer footbeds of varying thicknesses to achieve a perfect fit. Vasque has a complete system to vary boot fit or to accommodate a child's growing feet.

Weather Flap. Salomon has introduced a line of backpacking boots with slash-zippered weather flaps on the uppers, functioning vaguely along the same lines as mountaineering double boots. This integral flap encloses the boot like a well-fitting gaiter, preventing moisture and debris from penetrating as far as the tongue and laces.

Optional Insoles and Heel Pads. Various types of replacement insoles and heel pads are available to replace worn footbeds, to help achieve a perfect fit, or to provide extra cushioning for your feet.

Optional Gaiters. Gaiters are fabric weatherproof leg and boot coverings that prevent ice and snow from penetrating your boots or soaking your lower pant legs. They are discussed in the following section on Specialty Backpacking Gear.

Construction and Operation - Backpacking Boots

The materials and construction techniques used in backpacking boots must be able to withstand rugged conditions and hard use, although models for ambitious hiking or moderate trekking don't require the level of sophistication needed for serious trekking or extended backcountry use. Mountaineering boots are even more sophisticated, employing the ultimate in boot design, materials, and craftsmanship.

Materials. The materials commonly used on boots for backpacking are listed below:

• *Leather.* Leather is either used alone or in combination with a fabric mesh for boot uppers, tongues and collars. When leather and fabric are combined, the amount of each material depends on boot type. In general, less leather is used in lightweight hiking and trekking models these days, more leather in boots made for nostalgic hikers or for serious trekking, extended backcountry and mountaineering use. Salomon is breaking tradition with their new boot line that has minimal use of leather on all but their "Authentic" extended backcountry and mountaineering models. Various types of leathers are employed. You'll see labels sporting names like Nubuck, top grain, split grain, suede-out and waxed-down leather. Each has its own desirable characteristics.

• *Synthetic Fabrics.* A number of synthetic fabrics are used in boot construction. Boot uppers, collars and tongues are most often made of Cordura® nylon mesh for its abrasion resistance. This fabric mesh adds breathability and flexibility while reducing weight. Inner linings are typically made of some type of woven nylon or polyester that has the ability to wick moisture away from the foot. The upper portion of footbeds are also made of synthetic fabric.

• *Waterproof Membrane.* Some models employ waterproof membranes such as Gore-Tex® in the construction of the boot upper. This gives an added measure of protection from the elements in wet conditions.

• *Synthetic Foams.* Soft synthetic foams are found in the boot collar, in the inner lining of the upper and in the footbed. They protect the foot and provide comfort. Rigid foams are found in the midsole, the most common being a compound called EVA (ethylvinylacetate) and polyurethane. Rigid foams are designed to give the proper mix of support and cushioning for a given boot model, while reducing overall boot weight.

• *Rubber.* Natural and man-made rubber is used in the water-resistant perimeter rand and in the midsole of the boot. Molded high-carbon rubber is used in the outsole for its durability and abrasion resistance, the most widely known type being Vibram® soles.

• *Molded Plastics.* Plastics have been used in the counters and shanks of backpacking boots for many years. Now they are beginning to appear as hinged ankle cuffs on the exterior of boot uppers, giving them more of a technical climbing or ski boot appearance. Despite their unusual looks, they do provide a high level of flexible support.

• *Steel.* A thin layer of steel in the shank of the boot supports the arch and enhances proper flex.

• *Nylon or Polyester.* Nylon, polyester and other synthetic materials are commonly used for the boot stitching and laces.

Construction Techniques. Boot components are held together by a combination of gluing and stitching techniques.

• *Gluing.* Gluing with industrial strength adhesives is typically used to laminate outsoles, midsoles and insoles into a composite. Rubber rands, toe bumpers and external counters are typically bonded with adhesives. Many shoe and boot uppers are also permanently glued to the sole. This technique, while not as durable as stitching, is employed in most lightweight hiking footgear.

• *Stitching.* The various components of the upper are stitched together with single or double rows of synthetic thread. On boots designed for rugged use, the upper is double-stitched to the sole using waterproof thread. Two of the most common stitching techniques are the Norwegian Welt and the Inside Stitch. The Inside Stitch is performed from the inside of the boot, vertically through the insole and midsole. The Norwegian Welt is an exterior stitch, attached horizontally through the insole, then vertically through the midsole.

• *Waterproofing Techniques.* Various degrees of waterproofness can be attained by combining different boot materials and construction techniques. Boot models that claim good weather protection have highly water-resistant leathers and synthetic fabrics as the first line of defense. Further protection is found on models that have an inner layer of waterproof/breathable membrane such as Gore-Tex®. On some models, the perimeter area where the upper meets the midsole is also protected by a bonded rubber rand. Weather protection can be enhanced further by the conscientious use of applied waterproofing treatments.

Socks. Wearing two layers of socks is appropriate for almost all backpacking activities. The inner layer should be a lightweight liner sock of polypropylene or Hydrofil® nylon. The outer layer should be either a wool or some type of wool/synthetic blend. Recommended socks for active travel, including backpacking, are listed in the Clothing section of Personal Gear. Adjust the thickness of the socks to get a perfect fit in your boots. Too thick and your foot will be pinched, too thin and your foot will slide around, causing blisters.

Sizing. Boots should be sized while wearing the appropriate socks. Put the boot on and leave it unlaced. Push your toes forward against the end of the boot. There should be enough space at the heel to slip in a finger. If not, the boot is probably too small. Now bring your heel back against the heel cup and lace the boot. It should feel snug but not tight across the ball of the foot, at the heel and at the ankle. Your toes should be free to wiggle. Walking up an incline your heel should lift no more than half an inch. When walking downhill or tapping the toe of the boot against the floor your toes should just gently touch the end of the boot.

Adjusting the Fit. You may need to adjust the boot fit if you have the right size but the side of your foot still feels too tight or loose. Choosing a different thickness of footbed will often solve the problem. If your foot tends to slide toward the toe of the boot, either get a thicker footbed or try padding the boot tongue to keep your foot in place. Sorbothane's *Heel Insert* and *Ultra Sole,* or Hawks *HR200 Insoles,* give added cushioning and shock absorption, while helping you achieve the correct fit.

Break-in Period. Make sure to give your boots a proper break-in period before taking off on an adventure. They need time to conform to the shape of your foot, and until they do you'd be wise to take it easy. Most lightweight boots need only a minimal break-in period. The stiffer the boot, the longer it will take before they are comfortable for long-distance hiking. You might consider wearing a little protective tape on sensitive heel and toe areas during the break-in period. The best idea is to buy boots well in advance of your anticipated travels and wear them in gradually.

Author's Recommendations - Backpacking Boots

A properly chosen pair of backpacking boots will be as faithful as an old friend, serving you well for many years. Conversely, selecting the wrong type can be a costly mistake. To help you make the right choice when purchasing boots, I offer the following recommendations:

Overall Weight. Take the overall boot weight into account when selecting footgear for backpacking. Stiffer boots with more rugged materials tend to be quite heavy. If you need this level of protection, by all means get it. If you don't, you'll regret that extra weight on a long-distance hike or on a tour abroad.

Height of Cut. Try to select the proper boot cut for your intended activity. A higher cut offers more ankle support when hiking, trekking or mountaineering. Rougher terrain and heavier loads to carry mean selecting boots with a higher cut. Choosing a lower cut will give greater freedom of movement for long-distance hiking over less demanding terrain, and can also be used for occasional biking.

Degree of Stiffness. The same applies to the overall stiffness of the boot. Covering shorter distances on more rugged surfaces, as

Merrell's Wilderness　　　　　　**Hi-Tec's Yosemite**

when mountaineering, requires a stiffer boot. More flexible boots are the best option for long-distance travel over varying terrain.

Tread Pattern. The tread depth and pattern should also be chosen with care. Shallower, more passive tread patterns keep you light on your feet and are good for rambling and ambitious hiking. Deeper, more aggressive patterns supply extra grip on slippery tracks and trails, making them better suited to trekking and extended backcountry travel. Mountaineering boots require the most pronounced tread pattern.

Size of Heel. You'll notice that heel size varies widely on the boot models now on the market. Rugged walking and light hiking shoes hardly have a heel at all, making them more comfortable for general wear or for walking on relatively level terrain. Ambitious hiking boots have a slight heel, combining overall comfort with a moderate amount of traction. Boots for more ambitious activities such as serious trekking, extended backcountry travel and mountaineering have a very pronounced heel. This gives good downhill traction on the trail, yet makes them less comfortable for level walking and general wear. Choose a boot that gives you an appropriate type of heel for your intended use.

Level of Waterproofness. Decide how waterproof you need your boots to be. Waterproofing treatments applied to boot uppers can be quite effective, even on lower-priced models. If you need more protection, choose boots that use superior materials in the uppers, or have an integrated waterproof membrane. Other options include purchasing waterproof oversocks that protect your feet rather than the boot, or

Salomon's Adventure 7

using some type of gaiter or overboot that protects both feet and boots from the outside.

Rubber Rand or Extended Counter. I'm partial to boots that have a sturdy rubber rand, or a continuation of the external counter along both sides. Regardless of whether the upper is glued or stitched in place, the perimeter where upper meets sole is a vulnerable area to stress. This is where material failure most often occurs. A rand or external counter prevents water penetration and protects that part of the upper from wear.

Price vs. Performance. Try to determine how much you have to spend on boots based on your overall equipment budget and how

Raichle's Monte Rosa   Vasque's Super Hiker II

ambitious you feel your travels will be. If you are only an occasional, short-term backpacker, and carry light to moderate loads on relatively good terrain, any number of reasonably-priced lightweight boots will do. At the same time, don't skimp on price if you're going to be carrying a loaded pack over some rough territory, even for a relatively short period of time. Higher priced boots give added protection that your feet will thank you for, and will certainly influence the success of your adventure.

Costs. You'll be glad to know that there are many good boots appropriate for ambitious hiking and light trekking for under $100. Higher quality models can be as high as $150. Serious trekking boots can be found in the $125 to $170 price range. Sturdy, long-lasting boots for extended backcountry travel cost a bit more, typically anywhere from $125 to $225. Mountaineering boots, depending on their level of sophistication, usually run from $175 to $275, with specialty models and double boots priced as high as $500.

There are many specific models of boots to choose from. Some of the most practical, best-selling boots currently on the market are listed below.

Author's Recommendations - Boots for Ambitious Hiking and Light Trekking

Brand	Model	Sizes	Description
adidas	Adventure High	m, f	high-cut, leather uppers, moderate tread
adidas	Whistler	m, f	high-cut, leather/fabric uppers, mod. tread
Alico	Nomad	m, f	high-cut, leather uppers, moderate tread
Alpina Sports	Rambler	m, f	high-cut, leather/fabric uppers, mod. tread
Asolo	Voyageur	m, f	high-cut, leather/fabric uppers, mod. tread
Coleman	Base Camp	m, f	med-cut, leather/fabric uppers, mod. tread.
Danner	Mountain Spirit*	m, f	high-cut, leather/fabric uppers, mod. tread
Hi-Tec	Yosemite	m, f	med-cut, leather/fabric uppers, mod. tread
Hi-Tec	Gannett Peak	m, f	high-cut, leather/fabric uppers, mod. tread
K-Swiss	Siero-DH	m	med-cut, leather uppers, moderate tread
L.L. Bean	Knife Edge	m, f	high-cut, leather/fabric uppers, mod. tread
Lowa USA	Tahoe	m, f	med-cut, leather uppers, moderate tread
Merrell	Timberline	m, f	high-cut, leather/fabric uppers, mod. tread
Merrell	Westw'nd/Mariah*	m, f	high-cut, leather/fabric uppers, mod. tread
One Sport	Chapparal	m, f	high-cut, leather uppers, moderate tread
Raichle	Brava	m, f	high-cut, leather/fabric uppers, rubber rand
Raichle	Olympic	m, f	high-cut, leather uppers, rubber rand
Reebok	Telos High	m, f	med-cut, leather/fabric uppers, hiking tread
Reebok	Virazon	m, f	high-cut, leather/fabric uppers, rubber rand
Rockport Co.	Discovery Boot	m	high-cut, leather uppers, moderate tread
Rockport Co.	XCS*	m	med-cut, leather uppers, moderate tread
Salomon	Outdoor High	m, f	high-cut, leather uppers, moderate tread
Salomon	Adventure 5	m, f	high-cut, leather/fabric uppers, mod. tread
Salomon	Authentic 5	m, f	high-cut, leather uppers, moderate tread
Tecnica	Traveler	m, f	high-cut, leather/fabric upper, mod. tread
Tecnica	Mesa	m, f	med-cut, leather/fabric uppers, aggr. tread
Timberland	Eurohiker	m, f	high-cut, leather/fabric uppers, rubber rand
Vasque	Voyager*	m	high-cut, leather/fabric uppers, rubber rand
Vasque	Clarion II	m, f	high-cut, leather/fabric uppers, mod. tread

Gore-Tex is used, or equivalent models with Gore-Tex are available.

Author's Recommendations - Serious Trekking & Extended Backcountry Travel

Brand	Model	Sizes	Description
adidas	Trekker/Kitima	m, f	very high cut, leather uppers, aggr. tread
Alico	Tahoe	m, f	high-cut, leather uppers, aggressive tread
Alpina Sports	Ranger	m, f	high-cut, leather/fabric uppers, aggr. tread
Asolo	AFX 530*	m, f	high-cut, leather uppers, aggressive tread
Asolo	AFX 570	m, f	high-cut, leather uppers, rubber rand
Danner	Mountain Light*	m, f	high-cut, leather upper, aggressive tread
Dunham	Waffle Stomper	m, f	high-cut, leather/fabric upper, aggr tread
EMS	Traverse	m, f	high-cut, leather uppers, aggressive tread
Hi-Tec	50 Peaks Series	m, f	high-cut, leather uppers, various models
Hi-Tec	Twist Hiker*	m	high cut, leather uppers, leather rand
La Sportiva	Tibet	m	high-cut, leather uppers, aggressive tread
L.L. Bean	Cresta Hikers*	m, f	high-cut, leather & leather/fabric, rub. rand
Lowa USA	Appalachian	m, f	high-cut, leather uppers, rubber rand

Merrell	Cascade Boots	m, f	high-cut, leather/fabric uppers, trek'g tread
Merrell	BlazerGTX*	m, f	high-cut, leather/fabric uppers, trek'g tread
Merrell	Wilderness	m, f	high-cut, leather uppers, aggressive tread
Merrell	Leather	m, f	high-cut, leather uppers, aggressive tread
One Sport	Arete	m, f	high-cut, leather/fabric uppers, trek'g tread
One Sport	Talus	m, f	high-cut, leather uppers, aggressive tread
One Sport	Moraine	m, f	high-cut, leather uppers, aggressive tread
Raichle	Sierra/Verbier	m, f	high cut, leather uppers, rubber rand
Raichle	Burma*	m, f	high-cut, leather uppers, aggr. rubber rand
Reebok	Surazo*	m	high-cut, leather uppers, molded rand
Reebok	Zen	m	high-cut, leather uppers, aggressive tread
Reebok	Pump Massif	m	high-cut, leather/fabric uppers, pump act'n
REI/Raichle	Roland	m, f	high-cut, leather uppers, rubber rand
Salomon	Adventure 7	m, f	high-cut, leather/fabric uppers, rubber rand
Salomon	Authentic 7	m, f	high-cut, leather uppers, aggressive tread
Tecnica	Nevada	m, f	high-cut, leather uppers, rubber rand
Tecnica	Sasslong	m, f	high-cut, leather uppers, rubber rand
Timberland	Backcountry	m	high-cut, leather/plastic upper, rubber rand
Timberland	Backc't'y Trad'l	m	high-cut, leather uppers, rubber rand
Vasque	Trailwalk	m, f	high-cut, leather/fabric uppers, aggr. tread
Vasque	Super Hiker II	m	high-cut, leather uppers, rubber rand

Gore-Tex is used, or equivalent models with Gore-Tex are available.

Author's Recommendations - Boots for Mountaineering

Brand	Model	Sizes	Description
Alico Sport	Guide	m, f	high-cut, leather uppers, aggressive tread
Alpina Sports	Explorer	m, f	high-cut, leather/plastic upp'rs, v. ag. tread
Asolo	Yukon	m, f	high-cut, leather uppers, very aggr. tread
Asolo	Ridge	m	high-cut, leather uppers, rubber rand
Asolo	AFS 101	m	very high cut, plastic uppers, rubber rand
Climb High	Trezeta 8000	m	technical mountaineering double boot
Hi-Tec	McKinley	m	high cut, leather uppers, very aggr. tread
Hi-Tec	Katahdin*	m	high cut, leather uppers, leather rand
Lowa USA	Rainier GT	m, f	high cut, leather uppers, rubber rand
Lowa USA	Kodiak	m	very high cut, leather uppers, rubber rand
La Sportiva	Caucaso	m	high-cut, leather uppers, very aggr. tread
Merrell	Alpinist	m, f	high-cut, leather uppers, very aggr. tread
Merrell	Guide	m, f	high-cut, leather uppers, very aggr. tread
One Sport	Presles**	m	high-cut, nylon fabric uppers, wide rand
One Sport	Everest/Jannu	m	technical thermal double boot w/ gait'rs
Raichle	Monte Rosa	m, f	very high cut, leather uppers, rubb'r rand
Raichle	Avanti	m	very high cut, plastic/leather, d'ble boot
Salomon	Adventure 9	m, f	very high cut, leath'r/fabric/plastic, rand
Salomon	Authentic 9	m, f	very high cut, leather/plastic, rubb'r rand
Tecnica	CR7	m	very high-cut, leather upper, rubb'r rand
Tecnica	Sherpa GTX*	m	high-cut, leather uppers, rubber rand
Vasque	Montana	m	high-cut, leather uppers, aggres. tread
Vasque	Vagabond II	m	high-cut, leather uppers, aggres. tread

Gore-Tex is used, or equivalent models with Gore-Tex are available.
**See Innovative Product under Gaiters and Overboots.*

Maintenance and Repair - Backpacking Boots

You can extend the life of your backpacking footgear by performing a little routine maintenance. It's simple to do, costs little,
and you'll be rewarded with shoes and boots that last many seasons.
Most boot uppers are made of leather or a leather/fabric combination. The three types of routine care for this type of shoe are cleaning, conditioning and waterproofing.

Cleaning. This removes dirt and oils from leather or fabric that
cause stains and decrease material life. Select a good cleaner for
your type of shoe and use it as needed. One recommended cleaner
for fabric and leather uppers is Aquaseal's *Techniclean* (cleans and
deodorizes), sold separately with a small bristle brush or included in
the *Care-Kit* described below.

Conditioning. Leather tends to dry out with age, particularly if
it's not adequately waterproofed. Conditioning restores suppleness
to leather and increases its life. Most good leather sealers, such as
those listed below, also condition while they waterproof.

Waterproofing. This is necessary to protect the shoe or boot
from damage, and your socks and feet from frequent soakings.
Waterproofing materials for leather usually come in paste form and
are rubbed in and left to dry overnight. Recommended products
include *Biwell, Aquaseal, Mink Oil, Bee Seal Plus* and *Sno-Seal*. The
fabric mesh on shoe and boot uppers can be treated with any water
repellent product made for synthetic materials, such as *Camp Dry,
Zepel, Scotch Guard* or *Silicone Water Guard*. A complete kit for
cleaning, conditioning and waterproofing shoes and boots is the
Fabric/Leather Care Kit from Aquaseal. It contains a four-ounce bottle
of *Techniclean*, a four-ounce bottle of *Liquid Aquaseal* with dauber
applicator, a small bristle scrub brush and detailed instructions for
use. Gore-Tex® uppers should be treated the same as other fabrics.

Shoe Repair. The two most common repairs needed on trail
boots are replacing worn or split soles and restitching or regluing the
uppers where they meet the sole. You can restitch the seams of
shoes and boots with a *Speedy Stitching Awl* and waxed synthetic
thread. If the problem is more serious, any shoe repair shop will be
able to assess the damage and do a professional repair job. The most
annoying type of damage is a tear that occurs at the junction of the
sole and uppers. There's usually not enough material showing to do
an effective repair. That's why I recommend shoes and boots with a
wide rand of rubber or other material around the perimeter where
the sole meets the upper.

Specialty Backpacking Gear

- Gaiters
- Overboots
- Walking Staffs
- Trekking Poles

In addition to finding a comfortable pack and an appropriate pair of boots, you may want to consider some specialty backpacking items such as gaiters, overboots, walking staffs, and trekking poles.

GAITERS AND OVERBOOTS

Gaiters and overboots are simple, effective pieces of outdoor gear that give backpackers an extra layer of protection against scree, snow, ice and wet weather. Skiers also find them invaluable in their quest to keep their feet and lower legs warm and dry. Gaiters and overboots come in pairs, consisting of one or more layers of water-resistant or waterproof fabric sewn into an appropriate shape to cover your lower leg and boot. Some combination of elastic bands, zippers, Velcro® and nylon straps are employed to hold gaiters tightly in position when in use, yet also allow them to be easily removed.

Review of Generic Types - Gaiters and Overboots

There are several different types of gaiters and overboots to choose from, each well suited to a specific activity or set of conditions. They are generally categorized according to their shape and type of fit.

Low Gaiters. Low gaiters are a short version used for hiking on scree, hiking and ski touring on snow that isn't very deep, or for use as added protection with waterproof pants. This type of gaiter is only about eight to nine inches high, covering the area just below the calf to about mid-point on the boot upper.

High Gaiters. A higher cut version for deeper snow, high gaiters are approximately 16" to 18" in length. They generally cover from just below the knee to about mid-point on the boot upper. High gaiters give additional weather protection and warmth in deep snow.

Supergaiters. Supergaiters offer the best protection you can get for your feet and boots without wearing full overboots. They typically are full length, insulated gaiters for serious backcountry skiing or mountaineering that cover the entire boot upper while leaving the boot sole exposed (important for skiing).

Alpine Gaiters. This type of gaiter is simple and functional. It is primarily used for alpine skiing, since its purely cylindrical shape wraps neatly around the upper part of bulky alpine boots, protecting the lower leg and keeping snow from entering the boot tops. Alpine gaiters are around 14" high. They do not flare out at the bottom (as "spat" gaiters do) in an attempt to cover the lower part of the boot.

Overboots. Overboots are supergaiters with an integral sole, and are similar in concept to using a double boot. They have an outer covering that provides additional warmth and protection for cold weather climbing and mountaineering. Their main advantage over double boots is the flexibility of layering they offer. You can wear boots without them for fair weather conditions, with them for wet or cold weather, or even alone as mukluks around camp.

Innovation - *Presles* Overboot by One Sport

Originally designed to be worn over rock shoes for approaches to alpine rock climbs, the new version of Presles can also be worn over light trail shoes or boots for crossing snowfields and glaciers. This allows the freedom to travel into areas that would normally require another pair of heavy mountaineering boots. Presles are overboots with rigid Vibram® soles for traction and tough Cordura® nylon uppers with wide rubber rands for complete protection from mud, snow, water, and scree. They effectively convert light hiking boots into light mountaineering boots. Presles are lightweight and fold almost flat for easy packing. They weigh about two pounds and have a suggested retail price of around $70.

Features and Options - Gaiters and Overboots

Even though gaiters and overboots are relatively simple pieces of gear, they do have some technical features you should be aware of when comparison shopping.

Upper and Lower. Most gaiters, other than low models for hiking, are composed of two distinct parts, an upper and a lower. The upper part covers the calf and lower leg, the lower covers the ankle and flares out at the bottom to cover the boot. The upper is often a different color, and many times, a different type of material from the lower.

Lining. Some heavy-use gaiters incorporate an inner lining for comfort and weather protection. Cold weather supergaiters and overboots often have a layer of foam in the lining of the lower section for extra protection and warmth. This foam lining is usually removable during warmer conditions or for trimming to achieve a good fit when using crampons.

Rand. Most supergaiters have a perimeter rubber rand at the bottom that seals the gaiter to the boot. The rand is flexible to accommodate minor variations in boot design, but should be sized properly to ensure a good fit.

Sole. Overboots incorporate an integral sole that totally encloses the inner boot.

Method of Access. Gaiters need to open at least most of the way so they can be put on without removing your boots. Full length openings are the most popular, although there are a few "step in" models that maintain a small unopenable section of fabric at the bottom. The opening can be on the front, on the side, or in the back, depending on the model and method of closure. The most common methods of closure are full length zippers or hook and loop Velcro strips. A hook and loop closure creates its own weather flap. If a zipper is used, an additional weather flap of fabric, held in place with snaps, typically covers the closure.

Fastening System. Gaiters are held in place by one or more fastening methods. The most common method employs elastic or adjustable bands around the top and bottom of the gaiter, plus an adjustable stirrup that runs from a point on one side of the lower, under the instep of the boot, to a point of attachment on the other side. Some high gaiters also have a middle strap or elastic band where the upper meets the lower. The front part of the foot section typically attaches to the boot laces with a simple hook so it won't slide up during use.

Waterproof Models. Many manufacturers offer optional waterproof uppers in addition to standard fabrics for extreme wet conditions.

Thermal Models. You'll also find some models that offer optional insulated linings for extreme cold weather use.

Construction and Operation - Gaiters and Overboots

Gaiters are constructed using a variety of materials and techniques depending on intended use.

Materials. On simple gaiters for backpacking or ski touring in tracks, the uppers and lowers are constructed of single layer coated or uncoated nylon packcloth or Supplex®. More sophisticated gaiters intended for heavier use often have coated Cordura® nylon lowers for greater abrasion resistance, with uncoated packcloth or Gore-Tex® uppers for breathability. A few especially rugged models have Cordura® on both uppers and lowers, with an inner nylon lining for complete protection.

The lower part of the foot section varies according to gaiter style. Simple low and high gaiters require only an elastic or adjustable band at the bottom to provide a tight fit and help keep out snow and moisture. Supergaiters for mountaineering or ski touring typically have a tough rubber rand that secures the bottom of the gaiter and provides the weather seal. On Outdoor Research's *X-Gaiters,* the rubber rand is replaced by an innovative nylon-covered shock cord system. Overboots also employ some type of rand that separates the foot section from the sole, plus either a soft Cordura® nylon and foam sole, such as that found in Outdoor Research's Brooks Rangers, or a rigid Vibram® sole such as that incorporated into One Sport's *Presles.*

Fitting Gaiters. Gaiters are really easy to slip on and off without the need to remove your boots; even young children generally find them no problem to use. Simply wrap a gaiter around your lower leg and fasten the full length closure (either hook and loop or zipper). If you have a step-in model, unfasten it as far as you can, step into remaining opening, then fasten the closure. Fasten the snaps along the closure (just top and bottom on Velcro® models), then pull the stirrup under the instep and either tie or buckle it in place. Elastic band models can be pre-set and just pulled into position. Fasten the front hook over a convenient crossing of the laces, then adjust the band at the top of the upper (if available) so it is secure yet comfortable against your leg.

Author's Recommendations - Gaiters and Overboots

The first thing to determine is whether you even need gaiters for your type of backpacking. Keep in mind that while gaiters provide good protection from scree and wet weather, they are primarily intended for outdoor activities on snow. If most of your travels are below snowline or in moderate weather, you'll probably find you can get along just fine without them. Gaiters really come into their own for extremely wet conditions, high altitude climbing, backpacking on snowfields or ski touring away from set tracks.

OR's Rocky Mountain Low Gaiters

North by Northeast's Willoughby

General Backpacking. If you're just looking to keep occasional moisture, scree and shallow snow out of the top of your boots, any good pair of coated low gaiters will do. These are lightweight and easily stowed when not in use. High gaiters are for those who expect to encounter deeper snow or really wet conditions. Choose coated packcloth for moderate conditions, or Gore-Tex® versions for really wet conditions. If you travel frequently to alpine regions, you should consider a better quality high gaiter that will stand up to more rugged use. Models that use Cordura® or other tough fabrics for foot sections and uppers, and have sturdy fastening systems are recommended.

Mountaineering and Ski Touring. The better quality high gaiters described above will be fine for light mountaineering and ski touring use. For more strenuous expeditions or added protection in cold climates, thermal supergaiters are recommended. Mountaineers may opt for overboots or integrated double boots if conditions warrant.

Cost. You can find good low gaiters of coated packcloth for around $20 a pair, same quality high gaiters for about $25 to $30. High quality gaiters using Cordura® nylon run $30 to $40. Any models that use waterproof/breathable fabric on the uppers cost a bit more. Overboots and supergaiters with Cordura® lowers and rubber or shockcord rands cost $70 to $80.

Author's Recommendation - Gaiters and Overboots

Brand	Model	Description
Adventure 16	El Cheapo	high, coat'd packcl'th, back closure, elastic stirrup,
Black Diamond	Shortee	low gaiter, nylon
Campmor	Super Coated	high, coated oxford nylon, zipper w/ front storm flap
Climb High	Premium	high, Cordura low'rs, Gore-Tex upp'rs, front zipper
EMS	High Gaiters	high, packcloth uppers and lowers, rear zipper
Granite Gear	Telegaiters	high, Cordura lowers, Ultrex uppers, hook and loop
Granite Gear	Backcountry	high, packcloth lowers, Ultrex uppers, hook & loop
L.L. Bean	GT Gaiters	high, Gore-Tex lowers, Supplex uppers, elas. stirrup
L.L. Bean	Rand'd Telmrk.	supergaiters, Cordura lowers/uppers, rubber rand
N x NE	Easy Trail	high, ctd. packcl'th low'r, Supplex upp'r, zip. w/ flap
N x NE	Willoughby	high, Cordura upper/lower, nylon lining, zip. w/ flap
N x NE	Quick Fit	high, packcl'th uppers and lowers, step-in model
Outdoor Prod.	Combo	high, Cordura lowers, 60/40 uppers, zippered back
OR	Rocky Mtn.	low & high, packcl'th lowers, packcl'th or Gtx uppers
OR	Kids Gaiters	high, similar to Rocky Mountain gaiters
OR	Crocodiles	high, ctd. Cordura lowers, Gore-Tex uppers, 2" flap
OR	X-Gaiters	supergaiters, ctd. nylon or Cordura lowers, G-Tex
OR	Brooks Rang'rs	overboots, Cordura lower/rand/sole, G-Tex uppers
Powderline	Cross Country	high, ctd. Cordura lowers, poplin uppers, Velcro flap
Sequel	Greater Gait'rs	high, Cordura/nylon lowers, G-Tex/Supplex uppers.
vauDe	Scree	short, tough nylon fabric, fits any hiking boot, zipper
vauDe	Sympat'x	high, Sympatex fabric/Cordura, zipper & drawstring
vauDe	Sympat'x Kev.	high, triple layer Sympatex with Kevlar trim, Vel. flap
Wild Country	Tundra	supergaiters, Cordura lowrs., G-Tex uprs., rub. rand
Wild Country	Overboots	overboots, Propex ballistic lowrs, G-Tex uprs, foam

WALKING STAFFS AND TREKKING POLES

Walking staffs and trekking poles can be a great help when backpacking, allowing you to reduce the amount of your body weight resting on your legs. They are also a handy deterrent to unfriendly dogs and other unwelcome guests. You can always scrounge around for a suitable stick at your destination, but finding one that is strong, lightweight and sized for your build is often hard to do. If you want to guarantee that you'll always have the right size staff or pole when rambling, trekking or entering the backcountry, it's best to pack your own.

Walking staffs and trekking poles are roughly sized by measuring from armpit level to the ground, rounding up when in doubt. If your model is adjustable, you'll want to shorten it for uphill climbing, lengthen it when going downhill.

Walking Staffs

Walking staffs are typically used solo, and are good for country rambling, general hiking and backcountry travel. You can fashion

your own out of wood easily enough, or purchase one of the finely crafted wooden or telescoping aluminum models available from outdoor retailers. If you decide to buy one, there are several different models to choose from, many of which convert to camera monopods by having a hidden threaded mount on top of the handle. This is a convenient feature for steadying a full-size camera when shooting action photos, in reduced lighting, or when using heavy telephoto lenses. Other features to look for when choosing a walking staff include a durable wrist loop, a comfortable hand rest, a sturdy tip that will hold up to repeated use, and the ability to break down to a smaller size for travel.

Wooden staffs are a nice choice when weight and packing size are less of a concern. L.L. Bean markets their handsome, single-piece *Ash Walking Staff* ($23, various lengths) that has a simple thong wrist loop and tapered brass ferrule at the point. Wind River offers their distinctive *Hiking Staff* ($30; 48", 54", and 60" lengths) made of walnut with a sculptured twist. This staff has an optional camera mount, replaceable non-slip neoprene tip, and interchangeable stainless steel ice tip. Some models break down into two parts for travel. The telescoping Sherlock *Walking Staff* from Tracks ($50, weighs one pound, stows in 33 inches), made of lightweight aluminum, is an excellent hiking or trekking staff. It features a camera mount hidden under a wooden knob, a nonslip foam grip, a rubber or steel point for changing conditions, and the ability to adjust from 40 to 56 inches in two-inch increments.

Trekking Poles

Trekking poles are better suited to serious trekking over rough terrain or snow. Made of aluminum and similar in style to ski touring poles, they are used in pairs to reduce the amount of body weight carried by your legs by up to 30%. Trekking poles typically come with telescoping sections, making them well suited to travel. One of the best models available is the Climb High *Trekker Pole* (each pole costs around $35, weighs about 18 ounces), featuring three telescoping sections that extend from 24 to 56 inches, a molded hand grip, adjustable wrist loop, snowflake basket and break-away carbide tip. Another good trekking pole is the *Edelrid Vario* pole from Germany. This three-section pole is similar to the Climb High model and costs around $40.

V BICYCLING

Another exciting means of self-propelled travel is bicycling. As with backpacking, this broad outdoor category covers several different individual activities, each with its own set of conditions and specific gear requirements. In this section, we'll concentrate on the equipment available for those bicycling activities that are trip-related. These include short and long-distance touring on paved roads, mountain biking trips on tracks and trails, cross-terrain travel on a combination of roads and tracks, and local exploration on bicycles once at your destination. The types of gear to be discussed are the bicycles themselves, bicycle trailers, pack and pannier systems, and specialty bicycling equipment for travel.

Bicycling allows you to go where and when you want, to cover great distances when you must and sizeable distances even when the pace is more relaxed. It also allows you to always have a local means of transportation at your disposal for shopping, exploring or just having fun. Whether taking a short holiday or setting off on an extended adventure, touring the countryside or sightseeing in the city, bicycling is a wonderful way to travel.

Those traveling with children soon find out how enjoyable family bicycling can be. Unlike vehicle travel, bicycling provides children with a great way to burn up their inexhaustible supply of energy. Viewed from a child's perspective, bicycling is an ideal means of transportation. They like it because it's exciting and there's always something new to look at. They also pick up on the fact that their parents are doing this fun activity with them. This creates a family bond that carries over into other aspects of adventure travel. Children too young to cycle on their own have the option of riding in one of the many excellent bicycle trailers now on the market. This is a perfect way for young children to be comfortable and cozy on a bicycle tour.

While bicycling has many advantages, there are a few things you should prepare yourself for when considering this mode of travel. Having bicycles along can be more difficult at times. If you want to travel by air with your bicycle, you'll have to do some advance planning. Most airlines make you box your bicycle before it can be taken on board, and you may have to pay an additional fee if it puts you over the limit for weight or total pieces of luggage. Check with the airline ahead of time to see what they require. Boxes are often available at airports, but the price may be steep. It is often impossible to get a box from any airline other than the one you are ticketed with. The best bet when setting off from home is to get boxes for free from a local bicycle shop and pack your bicycle ahead of time. If traveling by air to several different destinations, it is often possible to store your bicycle box at the airport until you fly out again. In general, foreign airlines seem to have an easier time dealing with bicycles than domestic carriers. A permanent solution, although a fairly expensive one, is to buy a reusable carrying case that can be stowed at your destination until you need it for the return trip.

Another consideration is the logistics of dealing with your gear. Instead of one backpack to think about you'll have a bicycle and numerous individual pieces of gear to keep track of on your travels. It's no problem when the gear is on the bicycle; everything has its place and the load is well distributed. Carrying it off the bicycle or getting it on or off public transportation is another matter. At times this can be overwhelming. Picture yourself carrying two large rear panniers, a smaller set of front panniers and/or a handlebar pack, two water bottles, a pump, a tent, sleeping bag, pad and any other items you've strapped to your back rack. You can avoid some of the confusion by packing a large, lightweight cargo bag with shoulder straps that you can load everything into when necessary, or just use a duffel bag on the back rack for all of the loose gear. Another possibility is to use rear panniers that convert to backpacks, an ingenious solution discussed in detail under Pannier and Pack Systems.

Weight will be of major importance, so plan on investing in lightweight gear if you don't already own it. Camping equipment deserves special consideration. While it gives you a much greater degree of freedom and helps cut dining and lodging costs, it can also add substantially to your load. Just the food and water you consume when touring and cooking your own meals can be quite heavy. You often end up shopping several times a day to avoid carrying too much weight. This won't be of great consequence if your route allows you to pass through villages and small towns frequently. In addition to consumable provisions, a tent, sleeping bag and other camping equipment create additional weight. This can all be easily accommodated if you select compact, lightweight equipment, carefully control how much you pack, and frequently restock provisions. If you don't want to carry all that food and extra gear, forget about camping and tour in style by dining out and staying at bed and breakfasts, hostels or inexpensive pensions. You can set up your own itinerary and travel independently, or travel with one of the many packaged tour companies operating around the globe. Tour operators will transport the bulk of your gear by van from one accommodation to the next.

You'd be well advised to do some precipitous route planning when bicycling. Sometimes it's unavoidable, but stay away from highways and well-trafficked routes whenever possible, even if it means going out of your way to do so. Busy roads force you to concentrate on the passing cars and trucks instead of your surroundings. You'll infinitely prefer the more relaxed pace and the greater visual stimulation found when bicycling the backroads. Locating less traveled roads on the map when planning your trip is usually easy. Find the line size or color that indicates the smallest size paved road. Look for roads that are designated as scenic routes; they are usually paved and have light traffic and spectacular scenery. You can help the cause by bicycling off season when the number of vehicles on the road is drastically reduced.

When looking on a map, if you find a portion of the road has many twists and turns, it usually means it's a local road winding through hilly or mountainous terrain. Some maps even indicate direction of the incline with a series of small arrows. If a particular stretch of road is too steep for your liking, it's usually not too difficult to find someone willing to give you a lift on the uphill section. Someone may even provide this service on a regular basis in popular tourist areas. Try to plan your route so it favors the backroads and takes you through villages and towns at necessary intervals for provisions and accommodations. If you are uncertain about the terrain or your abilities in a certain region, try going with an organized group the first trip.

With the appropriate attitude and equipment, bicycling can be a highly rewarding experience, combining the best of what active travel has to offer—self-sufficiency and mobility, outdoor travel at a comfortable pace, the ability to cover sizeable distances, exercise, and the opportunity to interact easily and comfortably with local people.

Bicycles

- Touring Bicycles
- Hybrid Bicycles
- Mountain Bicycles
- Tandem Bicycles

The first order of business when equipping yourself for two-wheeled travel is to acquire an appropriate type of bicycle. This will probably be your most expensive equipment purchase and the one you should spend the most time researching. Selecting and outfitting a bicycle can be great fun, but before heading out to the stores you should determine how and where you intend to use the bicycle, what features you'd like to have, and how much you want to spend. There are an overwhelming number of bicycle models on the market. A little forethought allows you to focus quickly on those suitable for your needs.

You'll find a wide price range when shopping for bicycles. The higher prices usually reflect more sophisticated designs and materials, yielding lighter bicycles with a higher level of performance. You certainly want a bicycle that performs well for your needs, but don't feel you need a high-tech model that costs a fortune in order to have successful adventures. Any good quality bicycle will get you where you want to go, and besides, the experience is more important than how fast or how far you go. If you're on a budget, forget the high performance and high price tags and concentrate on reasonably-priced bicycles that will serve your needs.

Review of Generic Types - Bicycles

To create order out of the myriad models of bicycles currently on the market, they are typically categorized according to their intended use. The five major categories are racing, sport-touring, touring, hybrid, and mountain bicycles. They share common traits, but close inspection reveals a world of difference in design, materials, and construction techniques. Bicycles are also often labeled according to the number of speeds they have (such as a "10-speed" or an "18-speed"), the number of intended riders (there are many "tandem" models on the market built for two riders), or by the age and sex of the rider (as in men's, women's, or children's models).

By Intended Use. The five basic types are described below:

• *Racing Bicycles.* The thoroughbreds of the bicycle world, these high-performance machines are made for speed, excitement and competition on paved roads. The narrow tires, drop handlebars, close-ratio gearing and lightweight frames that make them so appropriate for racing also make them totally unsuitable for loaded touring or any type of off-road travel. Since this book has a recreational travel focus, racing bicycles will not be discussed in depth.

• *Sport-Touring Bicycles.* Sport-touring bicycles represent some middle ground between the thrill of a racing bike and the stamina of a touring model. They are lightweight and responsive, with many features incorporated strictly for speed, yet are loaded with features that also allow them to excel on a road tour. While they don't have the strength and load-carrying capacity or the wider-range gear ratios of a true touring bicycle, they are more versatile and represent a greater value to those who do more with their bike than just tour.

• *Touring Bicycles.* These are the classic workhorse bicycles made for long-distance adventure on paved roads. What they lack in excitement they more than make up for in long-term comfort. Touring bicycles are easily distinguished from hybrid or mountain bicycles by the sleek profile, long wheelbase and low ground clearance; drop handlebars; narrow, large diameter wheels; low-profile tire tread; and the multiple frame fittings they incorporate for water bottles, racks and fenders. They have stability for carrying heavy loads and comfort for long stretches in the saddle, yet their design and gearing allow for consistently good average speeds. This is the bicycle of choice when considering an extended road tour.

• *Hybrid Bicycles.* This is only one of the terms used to describe bicycles that have some characteristics of both touring and mountain bikes, yet are distinctly different from either one. Other labels include cross, cross-terrain, and fitness bikes, reflecting both their versatility and a certain amount of confusion that exists within the industry. Hybrids are increasingly popular since they perform reasonably well on extended road tours, yet continue to hold their own when the pavement ends, which it frequently does at many interesting destinations. There are many variations on the hybrid theme, but in general the features that allow this type of bike to straddle the line include straight handlebars with some type of alternative hand positions, a wider range of gearing than touring models, moderate wheelbase length and higher ground clearance, and wider tires with a more aggressive tread.

- *Mountain Bicycles.* Mountain or all-terrain bicycles are made for off-road travel. The more sophisticated the design, materials and construction of a mountain bike, the better it can provide both comfort and stability on truly rough terrain. The most distinguishing feature of a mountain bicycle is the wide, knobby tires mounted on 26" diameter wheels. In addition, these models typically have stronger, smaller frames, shorter wheelbases with higher ground clearance, wide-range gearing and straight handlebars for good control.

By Number of Speeds. This specifies the total number of individual gear combinations. It is helpful in selecting a model with enough combinations for your type of travel, but tells little about the gearing size or the bicycle itself. Two bicycles having the same number of speeds can be worlds apart in design and intended use. Bicycles suitable for travel typically have between 14 and 21 speeds.

By Number of Riders. The vast majority of bicycles are intended for one rider, but a popular touring configuration is the tandem bike, where two or more persons ride one behind the other. Capable of remarkably high speeds, this type of bicycle works well with a parent and child or any two riders of unequal strength and ability. It also keeps the speedster in the group from always riding ahead. There are several variations of tandem bicycle, the most popular being the two-person touring version. The front rider, called the captain, handles the steering, derailleurs and brakes, while the rear rider, or stoker, provides extra pedaling power and helps guide the bicycle while cornering. This is the bicycle of choice if you and your traveling companion work well as a team and you only want to take one bicycle on your travels.

By Age and Sex of Rider. The final classification of bicycles has to do with the intended user. Bicycles are available in men's, women's, and children's models. Variation between men's and women's models is achieved with a difference in frame size and the length and location of the top tube (or crossbar). Ladies' versions either have a shorter frame, a shorter top tube length, a step-through frame with an angled top tube, or some combination of these features. Children's bicycles have smaller frame sizes and smaller wheel diameters.

Features and Options - Bicycles

Though a seemingly simple piece of gear, there are a multitude of features and options you should be aware of when shopping for a bicycle. The features are organized below according to their location on the bike. The major groupings are the frame, the steering assembly, the wheel assembly, the seat assembly, and the component group which includes shifting package, front chainwheel assembly, rear freehub assembly, chain, brakes, and pedals.

The Frame. The frame itself is probably the feature that deserves the most attention when selecting a bicycle. Frames come in various shapes, sizes and materials, and should be selected according to your personal needs and your overall budget. A bicycle frame consists of metal tubing fabricated in a such a manner to provide strength, rigidity and a convenient place for the other components to attach to. Frame size is determined by the length of the seat tube (see Seat Tube below). Typical adult frame sizes run anywhere between 16" to 25", while a juvenile frame might be 13" to 15". The various parts of the frame are described as follows:

• *Top Tube.* Also called the crossbar, this tube extends from the top of the head tube to the top of the seat tube on men's models or lower down on the seat tube on lady's step-through models. Brake and derailleur cables are often led through cable guides on the top tube.

• *Down Tube.* This is the tube that connects the bottom of the head tube to the bottom bracket that houses the crank mechanism. Gearshift levers on touring bicycles are often located on the upper portion of the down tube.

• *Head Tube.* This is the short section of tubing at the front of the frame where the top tube and down tube end. The head tube houses the front fork stem and contains bearings to ensure smooth operation of the steering assembly.

• *Seat Tube.* This is the long vertical tube at the rear of the frame that usually runs from just above the top tube down to the bottom bracket. The seat post slides inside the top of this tube. Bicycle frame size is determined by the distance from the centerline of where the top tube meets the seat tube to the center of the bottom bracket (called center-to-center), or the top of the seat tube to the center of the bottom bracket (called center-to-top).

- *Bottom Bracket.* This is usually located at the junction of the seat tube and the down tube. The bottom bracket houses the crank assembly.

- *Chainstays and Seatstays.* Chainstays are the tubes that extend from the bottom bracket to the rear hub, while seatstays go from the top of the seat tube to the rear hub. Chainstays and seatstays run on either side of the rear wheel, joining together at the rear hub.

- *Dropouts.* These are the flat metal brackets that the front and rear wheel axles actually rest in. They are attached to the bottom of the fork legs in the front and chainstays in the rear. Dropouts on all the better models are precisely machined and welded in place, while inexpensive bicycles use bolt-on versions.

- *Cable Guides.* Brake and derailleur cables are led to the appropriate spots through cable guides on the frame. Guides are either incorporated into the frame tubing itself (high-end models), small metal pieces brazed onto the frame (most common), or separate metal or plastic mounts that rest on the frame.

- *Water Bottle Mounts.* These are typically metal threaded inserts that are brazed onto the frame in pairs for the attachment of water bottle racks. Two or three sets of water bottle mounts are common, with one set on the seat tube, one set on the upper surface of the down tube and another set on the lower surface on touring models.

- *Rack Attachment Points.* Most production bicycles capable of touring have rack attachment points on the frame on each side of the rear chainstay. Front rack attachment points are located on the front fork.

Steering Assembly. The steering assembly consists of the front fork, the handlebar stem and the handlebars. High-end mountain bicycles are beginning to sport front forks fabricated with integral shock absorbers similar to those found on motorcycles.

- *Steering Tube.* This is the single tube at the top of the front fork that projects up through the head tube. The handlebar stem slides into this tube and is tightened into the desired position. The steering tube (and thus the front fork) is held in position and able to pivot freely because of a durable bearing system located in the head tube. These items are called the "head set" and are technically part of the component group described below.

• *Fork Legs.* Below the steering tube, the front fork splits into two legs that go on either side of the front wheel and rest on the wheel's hub axle. Some fork legs are tapered, while others maintain a constant diameter along their length. You'll see some front forks that incorporate a suspension system similar to that found on motorcycles. While intriguing, suspension forks are expensive and continue to be better suited for mountain bike competition and serious off-road use.

• *Rack Attachment Points.* Bicycles set up for front racks have rack attachment points at the end of each fork leg near where the axle rests.

• *Handlebar Stem.* Handlebar stems come in a variety of configurations, but in all cases they consist of a two-legged piece of tubing with some mechanism for adjusting the height of the handlebars off the frame. One leg is straight and slides into the steering tube on the front fork. The other leg angles forward and upward to some favorable point where the handlebars attach. The distance forward and upward varies widely depending on overall bicycle design. An adjustable clinch ring holds the handlebars in place.

• *Handlebars.* The handlebars slide into a clinch ring in the handlebar stem and are secured in place on the centerline. Mountain bicycles usually have straight bars, touring bicycles have drop style, and hybrid bicycles have some variation of a straight bar, typically incorporating a gentle rise toward the bar ends to keep the rider in a more upright position. Custom versions of straight handlebars have additional twists and turns for more grip positions. Optional handlebar extensions are also available that offer additional hand positions.

• *Handgrips.* All handlebars have some type of padding to provide hand comfort and a sure grip. On drop handlebars, a roll of padded friction tape is used to accommodate the curve, wound from handlebar stem all the way to bar ends. It actually terminates inside the tubing and is held in place with end caps. All variations of straight handlebars employ sets of padded handgrips, some new models even incorporating shifters (see Shifters below).

Wheel Assembly. The wheel assembly consists of the spokes, rims, tires and tubes on both the front and rear wheels. The front and rear wheel hubs are technically part of the component group described below.

- *Spokes.* These are thin, flexible pieces of metal that run from the hub to the rim. There are typically 36 spokes per wheel. When properly adjusted spokes provide tension that keeps the hub perfectly in position, both concentrically with respect to the rim and from side to side. If the spokes are not tensioned correctly, or if they become damaged, the hub can become out of balance and the wheel will not run true. A bike shop can easily remedy the problem by balancing the wheel. Some high-end models eliminate flexible spokes by using composite wheels that incorporate the hub and the rim in one component connected by several wide, rigid spokes.

- *Rims.* This stiff circular piece of metal provides a place to attach the outer end of the spokes (at tiny holes along the perimeter of the rim), a bed for the tube to ride in, and a lip for the tire to seal against. A larger hole in the inner surface of the rim allows the tube stem to protrude and be accessible. Rim type and size determines the type and size of tires able to fit a particular bicycle.

- *Tubes.* Since the rim has lots of holes along the inner surface for spoke attachment, a sealed rubber tube is needed to maintain air pressure. Tubes are sized to fit specific tire diameters and widths, although you actually have some latitude on the width. The elasticity of rubber tubes allows them to function over a small range of widths. There are two types of tube valves currently in use. The Schrader valve is similar to those found on car tires. The Presta valve is a bit different, with an inner mechanism that must be unscrewed before pumping or releasing pressure. The Schrader valve stem is a bit larger. This means Presta tubes can fit a Schrader-style rim in a pinch (or for long-term use with the aid of a rubber grommet), but you must drill out a Presta rim slightly for a Schrader valve stem to fit. Make sure your tire pump is matched to your tube valve type. Simple adapters can be purchased that allow you to carry one pump for both types of valves.

- *Tires.* There are two basic types of tires—clincher and tubular. Clincher tires are shaped similar to car tires; they have an internal sidewall bead that clinches the wheel rim as the tire is inflated. Tubular tires are quite different; they consist of an outer covering that is sewn together around the inner tube, then glued to a special wheel rim. Tubulars have their advantages, but almost all bicycles on the market, other than a few road-racing models, come with clincher tires as standard equipment since they are inexpensive and make it easier to service a flat.

As with car tires, there's a host of different tread designs to suit any bicycling requirement, from low-profile touring treads to aggressive mountain bike treads. Tire diameter must match wheel diameter exactly, although tire width can vary over a specified range for each particular wheel type. Common tire diameters are 24" for juveniles, 26" for mountain bikes and some hybrids, and 27" or 700C (metric) for most hybrids and all touring bicycles. Typical tire widths range from 0.75" for racing bikes, 1.0" to 1.25" for road models, 1.25" to 1.38" for hybrids, and 1.38" to 2.5" for off-road bikes. Equivalent metric widths include 20, 25, 28, 32, 35, 38, 43 and 45 mm. Tires are specified by their diameter and width, such as a 700x28 (mm), 27x1.25 (inches), or 26x1.5 (inches). Narrow road tires are made to be inflated to higher pressures (90 psi or more). This allows for fast road riding, but since it places more weight on a smaller surface area of the tire it also increases your chances of getting a flat. Medium-width hybrid tires operate at a slightly reduced pressure (around 75 psi), while wide mountain bike tires cushion your ride with pressures in the 40 psi (off-road) to 60 psi (on-road) range.

Seat Assembly. The seat assembly consists of the seat itself, the seat post that fits inside the seat tube, and the seat post binder that clamps the seat post in position.

• *Seat.* Bicycle seats are designed to give you as much support and comfort as possible while allowing total freedom of movement for your upper legs. Seats come with various degrees of firmness and padding, but long-term comfort relates more to correct positioning of the seat than to the amount of padding provided. Adjustments allow the seat to tilt up or down, as well as slide back and forth in relation to the handlebars.

• *Seat Post.* The seat post is a long metal tube that slides into the seat tube on the frame. The post height above the frame can be adjusted to fit different leg and torso lengths. The seat post must be strong since it is cantilevered from the frame and has to take the considerable loads imposed by the weight of the rider.

• *Seat Post Binder.* The binder is simply a metal collar incorporated into the seat tube that, when tightened, holds the seat post in position. Seat post binders use either a bolt and nut arrangement or a pivoting quick-release mechanism that does not require tools.

The Component Group. This is where things get interesting. All the various mechanical items that help determine how a bicycle performs, including the shifting package, the chainwheel assembly, the wheel hubs and the brake assembly, are referred to as a unit called the Component Group. The items of the group that come as standard equipment are màtched to the frame, the intended use, and the price range of a particular model. As the component performance increases or the weight decreases, the cost of the bicycle increases. While standard components are perfectly adequate for almost all recreational needs, some bicyclists are compelled to do a certain amount of customizing. For an additional cost, the individual components of the group can be interchanged and tailored to suit your exact requirements.

Shifting Package. The shifting package is just what is sounds like, the components that allow you to change gears while riding. The package consists of a front derailleur, a rear derailleur, the hand-activated shifters and the cables that connect them.

• *Front Derailleur.* The front derailleur is mounted on the seat tube down near the chainrings. Changing the position of the front shifter changes the length of connecting cable, which in turn moves a metal guide that the chain passes through. Shifting with the front derailleur repositions the chain from one chainring to another. There are typically three chainrings on bicycles suitable for travel, and therefore three different positions for this derailleur.

• *Rear Derailleur.* This piece of gear is attached to the dropout on the chainstays. Function is similar to the front derailleur, although the design is quite different. The rear derailleur not only repositions the chain over a series of five to eight sprockets mounted on the rear hub, it also provides constant spring-loaded tension for the chain regardless of what gear you are in.

• *Shifters.* There has been a revolution in shifter design over the past decade, creating models for straight handlebars that allow you to shift rapidly while keeping your hands firmly on the bars. There are three basic types of shifters—simple lever shifters, thumb-activated shifters and new hand-grip shifters. The simple lever shifters found on touring bicycles are located either on the handlebar stem (on inexpensive bicycles), on the upper portion of the down tube, or even on the ends of drop handlebars (on many touring bikes). Thumb-activated shifters sit just above or just below the handgrips. You operate them with your thumb or thumb and index finger while maintaining your grip. The new handgrip shifters operate by twisting the inner portion of the handgrip with your thumb and index finger.

Most bicycles currently on the market have what is called indexed shifting, at least for the rear derailleur. Indexing means that there are pre-set stops (or clicks) on the shifter that relate to specific gear positions. This allows you to shift smoothly and rapidly without diverting your attention or spending time wondering if your derailleur is in the proper place.

• *Cables.* Thin metal cables transfer the shifter motion to the derailleurs. They run from the shifters, through guides in the frame, to an adjustment point on the derailleur. The shorter the cable is, the more rapid the shifting. The cable is encased in a flexible housing when it curves to span the distance between shifters to frame and frame to derailleur.

Front Chainwheel Assembly. The front chainwheel assembly, containing the crankset and the assorted chain rings (front sprockets), is the component mounted into the bottom bracket which provides attachment points for the pedals. Well-lubricated internal bearings allow for smooth, low-friction cranking motion.

• *Crankset.* The crankset consists of opposing lever arms mounted onto a center shaft. Lever arm length varies between 165-180 mm, depending on frame and body size as well as the amount of leverage desired. The ends of the lever arms have threaded holes for mounting pedals. Threads on the right side are right-handed, threads on the left are left-handed. This means both pedals tend to tighten as you pedal instead of loosening up.

• *Chain Rings.* What most of us blithely refer to as the front gears or sprockets are actually called chainrings, differentiating them from the cassette of sprockets on the rear hub. The number of chainrings depends on the type of bike—one, three, and six-speed bicycles have only one chainring; 12 and 14-speeds have two; and 15, 18, and 21-speed bicycles have a third small chainring especially for low gearing.

• *Pedals.* The free-spinning pedals are threaded tightly into the lever arms for use. As you are sitting on the bicycle, the right pedal has right-hand threads (that tighten clockwise) and the left pedal has left-hand threads (that tighten counter-clockwise). They can easily be unthreaded and removed for transport. Pedals must be able to spin freely so your foot can maintain its position as the crankset completes a full rotation. While the pedals have a rough surface that grips your shoe, toe clips and straps keep your feet positioned so they won't slide off as you pedal. Some models have integral clips that mate with the bottom of special bicycling shoes for even better performance.

Wheel Hubs. Both front and rear wheels contain center hubs. The hubs consist of an outer cylinder with spoke holes, an inner axle, the bearing assembly that allows the wheels to spin freely, some type of release mechanism for attachment to the frame, and in the case of the rear hub, a freewheel mechanism and a sprocket set.

• *Release Mechanism.* This is common to both hubs, allowing the wheel to be removed for service. Inexpensive bicycles usually just have a nut and lock washer threaded onto both ends of the axle, while better quality models sport quick-release skewers with a cam lever that allows you to remove the wheels quickly without tools.

• *Freehub.* The rear hub on a bicycle has a mechanism called a freehub that engages to transmit power from the sprockets to the rear wheel whenever you are pedaling forward, yet disengages at all other times. This allows you to stop pedaling and rest your legs, or even pedal backwards, even though the wheels are rapidly turning forward.

• *Sprocket Set.* All multi-speed bicycles have a rear set of sprockets mounted from smallest to largest on the rear hub. The smallest sprocket in front relates to your highest gear, used when zipping along at high speed. The largest sprocket in the rear next to the spokes relates to your lowest gear, used for slower speeds up steep inclines. Multiply the number of rear sprockets (anywhere from five to eight) by the number of chainrings on the crankset (one to three) to determine the total number of speeds.

Chain. A strong, flexible means of transferring power from the crankset to the rear wheel is mandatory on a bicycle. Multi-link metal chains have proved the most practical method over the years. They are relatively inexpensive to make, mate easily with sprocket teeth, work well with derailleur mechanisms, and are strong enough to take the punishing stress imposed by enthusiastic cyclists.

Brake Assembly. All multi-speed bicycles have hand-operated front and rear brakes. The brake assembly consists of hand levers mounted on the handlebars (one for each wheel), a connecting metal cable, the brake mechanism itself that translates cable movement into gripping action, and the brake pads that actually slow the bicycle by pressing against the wheel rims.

• *Brake Mechanism.* Gripping action is created in one of two ways, depending on type of mechanism. Standard side-pull caliper brakes have been around for many years, and are still seen on most road bicycles. They have a central pivot point on the centerline of the head tube and gently arc over the wheel. As the brake cable pulls, levers with brake pads on either side of the wheel move toward each other in unison until they engage the rim. Quick-release levers are often fitted to this type of brake for easy removal of the wheels.

Mountain and hybrid bicycles typically employ cantilever brakes because they offer greater clearance for wider tires. Instead of a single brake mounted on the centerline, these have two separate cantilever mechanisms mounted on brazed-on bosses on each side of the frame (or on the fork legs in front). The cable runs on the centerline, hooking up to a short bridle (separate metal cable) that runs between the brakes. As the cable pulls, the bridle operates both cantilevers smoothly and simultaneously. They pivot rapidly toward the wheel, eventually pressing the brake pads tightly against the wheel rim. Quick-release levers are not necessary on cantilever brakes since you can easily squeeze the cantilevers together and release one end of the bridle cable by hand.

Tandem bicycles typically have an additional drum brake on the rear hub to aid in slowing the bike. This is necessary since a loaded tandem can get up quite a head of steam, especially on long down-hill runs.

• *Levers.* Brake levers are conveniently located on the handlebars so you can operate the brakes without losing control of the bike. On drop handlebars, the brake levers are typically located facing forward on the tightest part of the curve so they can be accessed from a racing position. "Aero-levers" have the cable hidden inside, leading it under the handlebar tape for a clean appearance. Extension levers can be installed for touring so you can also activate the brakes when your hands are resting on top of the handlebars. On straight handlebars, they are located above the handgrip at each end.

• *Cables.* Metal cable runs between the levers and the brake mechanism. On some touring and all racing models, "aero-brake levers" are used so the cables can run under the handlebar tape, giving the bicycle a cleaner appearance while reducing wind resistance. As with shifting cables, these cables are typically fed through integral attachment points on the frame.

• *Pads.* Rubber brake pads are the only part of the brakes that actually make contact with the wheel, and they do so along the flat part of the rim just below the tire. Pads have an elongated shape that gives them maximum contact length for a given width.

Handle Bar Extensions. There are many types of attachments available that give additional hand positions for both touring and off-road cyclists. The shape of drop handlebars offers three distinct hand positions: resting on top, stretched out at the curve (where the brake levers are), or gripping down near the bar ends. This usually gives touring cyclists enough variety. Standard straight handlebars only offer one position, on the handgrips. This is reasonably comfortable, but alternative positions are easier on your back and prevent your hands from falling asleep. "Bar ends," short pieces of curved tubing that extend forward, give multiple hand positions and are inexpensive to buy and easy to install. A more sophisticated alternative is clip-on "aero-bars" that extend forward over the front wheel in an elongated U-shape. Aero-bars have padded forearm rests that allow you to place your weight forward in comfort.

Racks. There are a variety of front and rear racks that you can get for any style of bicycle. They allow you to carry additional gear with ease, including panniers, bulky items, and even child seats. See Bicycle Racks later in this section for more information.

Water Bottles and Holders. Almost all bicycles come with one or more braze-on mounts on the seatpost and down tube for attaching water bottle racks. These are simple cages of metal or composite material that provide a secure nesting place for standard bike water bottles. Braze-ons and bottle rack mounting holes are standardized throughout the industry. Better bikes typically have two bottle locations, one on the front of the seat tube and one on the top of the down tube. Touring bikes often have a third located on the bottom of the down tube. Water bottle racks are also available as clip-on models, if you want additional carrying capacity.

Fenders. Serious bike tourists often elect to arm their bicycles with fenders to prevent road muck from spattering rider and gear. Most touring enthusiasts do without them to save on weight, but a rear fender is a good idea when towing a child trailer.

Tool Kit. Every cyclist should carry a serviceable tool kit for making minor repairs and adjustments away from home. The type and sophistication of the kit depends on your bicycle and where, and for how long, you plan to ride. For tool kit recommendations, refer to the Specialty Gear section of Bicycling.

Toe Clips and Straps. Toe clips and straps are accessories that keep your feet properly positioned as you pedal. They allow for more efficient pedaling since your feet are always in position and tend to work together instead of separately. The foot is held securely yet can easily exit when necessary. On many bike models toe clips and straps are included as standard equipment, on others they are offered as optional components so you can choose your own style.

Mirror. Cyclists have a hard time seeing what is behind them. Constantly turning around when touring can be annoying and dangerous. Small mirrors that attach to the handlebar ends, brake levers or to the side of a helmet solve this problem for minimal cost.

Kickstand. Bicycles don't usually come with a kickstand, and most purists leave them off to save weight and clutter. Optional stands are widely available and easily installed.

Air Pump. All cyclists should have a compact air pump handy for maintaining adequate air pressure or fixing the inevitable flat. Touring models are longer and usually made to fit in brackets along the bike's top or seat tube. Mountain models are more compact, made to be strapped to the bike's tubing or to other gear. Good quality pumps are available from Blackburn, Rhode Gear and Zéfal. Make sure to select a pump that is compatible with your type of tube valve.

Tube Protection. You can get tough strips of material that run along the inside of the tires to protect the tube from a puncture. *Tuffy Tire* is a plastic strip available at most bike shops that is relatively inexpensive and easy to install. Kevlar models perform better but are more expensive.

Seat Cover. Some riders find conventional bike seats too hard on their own seat, and opt for a padded cover to ease the pain. The most popular type of seat cover consists of a fabric-covered gel that is particularly comfortable and stable to sit on.

Construction and Operation - Bicycles

Once you are familiar with the many different design features and options of a bicycle, the next step is to investigate the various materials and techniques used in construction, along with some basics on how to size and operate your bike. Having a basic understanding of how a bicycle is made helps to give you the confidence to make the right choice for your needs.

Bicycles having high strength, light weight and low cost are the three major goals manufacturers shoot for. They must try to incorporate materials that do the job at an affordable cost without adding excessive weight to the bike. As you can imagine, it's relatively easy to attain any two of these goals, much more difficult to achieve all three. On production models, a certain amount of compromise must be made. A brief review of bicycle material and construction specifications is given below.

Frame Construction. A good quality bicycle frame is a work of art. It is an amalgamation of the design, materials and craftsmanship that went into it. All recreational bicycle frames are made of tubing fabricated into the desired shape, and while they may all look alike, there are many differences between the various models. So you'll be up to speed when you hear terms and specifications bandied around the bike shop, here's a brief description of bicycle tubes and frames:

• *Straight Gage or Butted.* Tubing manufactured with a constant wall thickness is called straight gage, while tubing where the wall thickness varies is called butted. Butted frames are more costly to make, but they are lighter and more efficient since they place more material in areas of high stress, less material in areas of low stress. Double-butted, the most common type, describes tubing with two different wall thicknesses. Almost all models found in bike shops (as opposed to department stores) have butted frames.

• *Tapered or Non-Tapered.* Frame components can be either tapered, where the outside diameter gradually gets smaller toward the ends, or non-tapered with a constant outside diameter.

• *Seamed or Seamless.* Seamed tubing is made from metal sheets that are rolled into shape and welded along the seam. Seamless tubing takes raw material and extrudes it into the desired shape tube. Seamed tubing is the least expensive and by far the most commonly found. The level of craftsmanship is revealed by how well those seams are hidden in the finished bicycle.

• *Tube-and-Lug (Lugged) or Welded.* On many bike models the metal tubing has been cut at exact angles and welded together. This method is strong, yet it's hard to make it look finished. The more popular approach is to employ lugs at the junction points that the tubes slip into or over, then either braze or solder (metal tubes), or glue (metal or composite tubes) them in place.

• *Tubing Materials.* Bicycle frames are most often built from tubing made of steel, either standard high-tensile steel found on inexpensive models, or lighter steel alloys such as chrome-moly (a chromium and molybdenum alloy) found on more costly bikes. Another common material for lightweight frames is aluminum tubing. Although it's not always the case, in general the diameter of aluminum tubing must be greater to compensate for the reduced inherent strength of the material. For this reason, aluminum frame bicycles are fairly easy to spot in the showroom. Most aluminum-frame bicycles still have chrome-moly front forks to handle the repeated stress. Some combination frames even have aluminum top and down tubes and steel seat tube, chainstays and front fork. More exotic frame tubing materials include titanium and carbon fiber/epoxy or other composites, although for most recreational needs you'll be choosing between steel, steel alloys and aluminum.

• *Seat Angle.* This describes the angle of the seat tube from horizontal. The seat tube angle helps determine the leg/pedal relationship and the distance of reach to the handlebars.

• *Head Angle.* This is the angle of the head tube from horizontal. The head angle is very close to, and in many instances the same as, the seat angle.

• *Wheelbase Length.* This is the distance between the two wheel hubs. Touring and hybrid bicycles tend to have longer wheelbases than mountain bikes.

• *Bottom Bracket Height.* This is the height from ground level to the center of the bottom bracket. Touring bicycles need less ground clearance and therefore have lower bottom bracket heights. Serious off-road bikes have much larger bottom bracket heights.

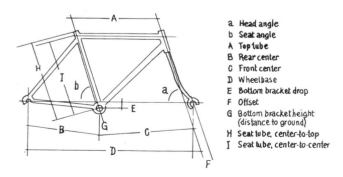

a. Head angle
b. Seat angle
A. Top tube
B. Rear center
C. Front center
D. Wheelbase
E. Bottom bracket drop
F. Offset
G. Bottom bracket height (distance to ground)
H. Seat tube, center-to-top
I. Seat tube, center-to-center

Common Bicycle Frame Measurements

• *Front Fork Rake or Offset.* This describes the distance the front fork legs (at the front wheel hub) are raked forward from the centerline of the head tube. If the front fork legs extended straight down, there would be no offset. Most bicycles have some offset, anywhere between 3.5" to 6.5", in an effort to provide a better ride. Mountain bicycles average around 4" to 4.5" of rake, hybrid and touring bicycles a bit more at around 5".

• *Handlebar Stem Rise.* Stem rise denotes the vertical distance, measured along the head tube angle, from the top of the head tube to the centerline of the stem's handlebar clinch ring. This dimension is determined by both the shape of the handlebar stem and the exact positioning of the stem with respect to the head tube. In general, the angle of the stem (from vertical) is less pronounced in mountain bikes and hybrids, allowing for a greater stem rise and a more upright riding position. Touring bicycles have a more severe stem angle, making the stem rise less and lowering the riding position. Rider position is also influenced by other factors, including the stem reach (described below).

• *Handlebar Stem Reach.* Reach describes how far forward the stem's handlebar clinch ring is from the centerline of the head tube. Touring bicycles have the longest stem reach, mountain bicycles have the shortest, and hybrids are somewhere in between.

Other Components. Most of the other components on the bicycle are made of either stainless steel, high-tensile or chrome-moly steel, lightweight alloys or aluminum. As always, you pay more for increased strength and reduced weight. Front forks are typically made of chrome-moly steel for strength. Handlebars and seat posts are coated steel on less expensive models, lightweight alloys or aluminum on better makes. The entire component group is typically a combination of stainless steel, alloys and aluminum. Wheels are most often aluminum or a lightweight alloy, with steel used only on low-end models. Pedals are either plastic, coated steel, alloy or aluminum depending on the model.

Sizing a Bicycle. The process of sizing a bicycle to fit your body shape and your style of riding can be as simple or sophisticated as you want to make it. While most riders get satisfactory results by following a few simple rules of thumb, others may need to take more care to ensure proper sizing. Bicycle shop personnel are usually more than willing to spend some time to work out minor sizing problems. A nominal fitting fee may be charged if they have to spend too much time, but if the service helps you make the right choice, then the money is well spent. If you can't seem to make it work on a particular model, it may be necessary to try other models or even other makes to find a suitable fit.

Selecting the frame size is the first step. Frame size is determined by seat tube length, but this dimension also affects other considerations such as top tube length and handlebar positioning. Manufacturers of moderately-priced production bicycles typically offer three or four different frame sizes per model. Standard touring bicycle frame sizes are 19, 21, 23 or 25 inches. Frames on mountain bicycles, which run a little smaller to give more clearance between the crotch and top tube, are usually 16, 18, 20 or 22 inches in height. In general, the more expensive the model, the broader the selection of frame sizes.

The first sizing rule of thumb is that if you straddle the top tube of a bicycle in your stocking feet, you should have about one to two inches of clearance below your crotch on a touring model or a hybrid model used for road work, two to three inches for a hybrid that splits time between on road and off, and three inches or more on an off-road mountain bicycle. If your frame size is 21" in a touring bike, try a mountain bike with a 19" frame. This rule of thumb relates leg inseam measurement to frame size, the theory being that if this condition is met then most riders can be accommodated by adjusting the seat angle, the seat fore-and-aft position, and the seat post and handlebar stem heights. This isn't always the case, especially for women who, in general, have longer legs and shorter torsos than men. Before deciding on a particular frame, check to see if the handlebars are within comfortable reach. If they are, then the top tube length and the placement of the handlebars are roughly correct.

Adjusting the Fit. Once you select a frame size that seems to work, you need to determine if there is enough room for adjustment to customize the fit.

• *Seat Height.* First adjust the seat height so that, with the balls of your feet on the pedals, your legs are almost, but not quite, fully extended at the bottom of each pedal stroke. By stopping just short of full extension you prevent hyper-extending your knees as you ride. As a rule of thumb, the angle of knee bend at the bottom of the stroke should be around 15 degrees.

• *Seat Fore-and-Aft Position.* Now check the fore-and-aft position of the seat. On a touring model, you should be able to adjust it so that when the crank arms are horizontal and your feet are on the pedals, the knee of your lead leg is in line with the pedal spindle. This places you in a comfortable position for touring. Mountain bike riders prefer to sit a little further back, so on a mountain bicycle the knee of the lead leg should be just behind the pedal spindle.

• *Handlebar Stem Length.* The handlebar stem shape and placement help to determine the reach, or the distance between the seat and the handlebars. The stem placement is the next adjustment to fine tune. On a touring bicycle, with your hands in the drop position, you should be stretched out over the frame with your back almost horizontal and your elbows comfortably bent. You have two alternative hand positions with drop handlebars (at the brakes and on top), so you can vary your reach while riding. On a mountain bicycle, your reach should be somewhat shorter, your back slightly inclined with a more pronounced bend in your elbows to counter a rough ride. If everything else is fine, but you can't get a comfortable reach, a different stem may need to be fitted.

• *Handlebar Width.* Most stock handlebars are sized to suit the largest number of people for a given model and frame size. The drop handlebar width on touring models is fairly standardized. On hybrids and mountain bicycles, you can adjust the standard width by adding extensions or replacing the stock bar with something that feels more comfortable for the way you ride.

• *Other Considerations.* Most travelers stop the adjustment process here, while purists continue seeking perfection, even altering things such as crank arm length to suit. Unless you have the money for a custom bicycle, the best advice is to select a model that feels comfortable and has plenty of room for adjustment, then slowly fine tune it for your needs. Your concept of what feels right may well change as you get used to the bike or you change riding habits, necessitating further adjustment.

Shifting Operation. There is a great deal of confusion among new riders regarding the operation and proper shifting techniques on multi-speed bicycles. It's not like a car; just because you have an 18-speed bicycle doesn't mean you shift 17 times as you gather speed. Say you have an 18-speed bike, with three front chainrings and a rear hub with six sprockets. Your lowest speed is when the chain is on the smallest chainring and the largest rear sprocket. Conversely, the highest gear is on the largest chainring and the smallest rear sprocket. The exact order of gearing depends on the chainring and sprocket sizing. Front chainrings and rear sprockets are meant to be used together in small groups so that the chain doesn't become angled too sharply from side to side. This means that each chainring has a range of three to four rear sprockets that are most comfortable to work with. As a rule of thumb, don't match a large chainring to large rear sprockets or a small chainring to small rear sprockets.

For example, you'll most often start off somewhere in the middle of your gearing order, perhaps with the chain on the middle front chainring and the second or third largest of your rear gears. As you increase speed on a straight or downhill run, you can go to higher gears by shifting your rear derailleur to progressively smaller rear sprockets. After several shifts it makes sense to shift your front derailleur to the larger front chainring before going to even smaller rear sprockets. Once in the larger chainring, you can go all the way to the smallest sprocket (your highest gear) if it becomes necessary. If you start off in your middle gears and are faced with an uphill climb, you can begin downshifting by changing to larger rear gears. After a few shifts, it makes sense to shift to the smallest chainring. In some cases, this is too drastic a change, so you shift your rear derailleur up to a smaller rear sprocket and gradually increase to the largest sprocket (your lowest gear) if necessary.

Mountain bike cyclists on steep terrain may be constantly shifting gears, while road touring cyclists on relatively flat terrain may only change gears occasionally. One practical gear combination for general touring is to set your rear derailleur so the chain is on your second or third largest sprocket, then only use your front derailleur to shift back and forth between your two largest chainrings as needed. This seems to work well when pedaling at a relaxed pace on gently rolling terrain.

Here are a few final comments on proper shifting techniques: Always shift while pedaling; you need some motion for smooth shifting. This is important when climbing a hill. Don't wait to downshift until the pedaling is hard and you are practically stopped. Changing gears when there's little chain motion and a lot of torque is bad for the bike, not to mention for your knees. Try to downshift to your smallest chainring firmly yet smoothly. Shifting too quickly may send the chain sliding off the chainring, a definite pain on an uphill climb. If you are in too high a gear to start pedaling on an uphill, face your bike across the hill and do a few switchbacks as you get proper gearing. After shifting with your rear derailleur, and angling the chain one way or the other, you'll often also have to adjust your front derailleur slightly to eliminate any chain noise.

Boxing for Air Travel. Sooner or later, you'll get the urge to take your bicycle to some adventurous destination, making boxing up for air travel necessary. It is very easy to do, but you should practice a few times beforehand. That way you'll know what you're doing, you'll be sure to have the correct tools, and you'll loosen up any parts that may give you trouble when you're in a hurry. The first thing to do is to let most of the air out of the tires, lower the seat post all the way, and remove the pedals. I usually tie the pedals onto the frame so there's no chance of them slipping out of a damaged box (which happens occasionally).

Drop handlebars should be removed from the head tube and tucked sideways inside the frame triangle. For most boxes, straight bars need only be lowered and turned sideways in line with the frame. If they don't fit this way go ahead and remove them and tie them to the frame. Handlebar stems are always loosened by the bolt at the top of the stem, either with an allen or hex wrench (never loosen the nut at the top of the head tube as that is only for securing the front fork). There is a sliding wedge at the other end of the bolt inside the head tube. As you tighten the bolt, the wedge is drawn up and tightens; as you loosen the bolt, the wedge slides down and becomes loose. The wedge is threaded onto the bolt, so make sure you don't unscrew it too far or it will come off and drop down inside the fork.

The last thing to do is remove the front wheel if necessary. Some airport bike boxes are quite large and the front wheel can remain on. If you have a quick-release mechanism, simply pull the lever and the wheel becomes loose. Otherwise loosen the lock-nuts on each side of the wheel. You may have to release the tension on the front brake to slide the wheel off. Store the front wheel next to the frame in the box. It's not a bad idea to wedge something inside the box (perhaps some of your other gear) to keep the bike from bouncing around.

Author's Recommendations - Bicycles

There are so many good bicycles on the market that you may have trouble making a decision. In the low to moderate price range, it doesn't matter so much which manufacturer you choose, since in most cases only the frame itself, if even that, is actually made at their facility. All of the other components are typically purchased from major vendors such as Shimano, SunTour, SR Sakae, Ritchey and

Avocet. This makes for a certain similarity between bicycles in a given price range. As the price increases, subtle differences of design and construction become more apparent.

It is most important to select a bicycle shop that you feel comfortable with and has a good selection of bicycles in your price range, for your style of riding. Then start trying out various models and frame sizes. Currently, mountain-style bicycles outsell all others combined, but popularity is greatly influenced by fashion rather than function. A large number of mountain bikes never leave the road. I recommend you give it some thought before narrowing your selection down to one style of bike. Once you decide on models that suit you, don't hesitate to give them a good test ride. Make sure that you get the features and options that you want, and that everything feels comfortable before you buy. You'll know immediately when you find the right one. Just sitting on it in the showroom you'll feel as though you've found an old friend. Taken for a ride it will seem as though the bicycle has come to life, awakened by your presence, and that together there's no limit to where you can go.

Sport-Touring Style. The bicycles in this category are surprisingly inexpensive considering the thrills they can give you, whether they are loaded with touring gear or not. While not as agile as racing bikes nor as rugged as straight touring models, they may well be the best option for those who want a responsive touring bike that you can really have some fun with when the panniers are removed. These are a good choice when most of your time is spent riding on roads of good quality. If you decide a sport-touring model is most appropriate for your needs, make sure it has a chrome-moly or aluminum frame, a third chainring and a sufficiently wide range of gearing in the rear cluster for general-purpose touring. You may want to exchange the rear cluster for a more suitable gear range, although in some cases you also have to change the rear derailleur to accommodate the larger sprockets. Sport-touring bicycles typically have 700C x 1.125" wide tires. Slightly wider tires (1.25") with a deeper tread pattern should be fitted for general touring. Rack attachments on the dropouts and multiple water bottle mounts are desirable features as well.

Touring Style. Be honest with yourself about how and where you intend to ride. If you plan on covering large distances on paved roads, this is the bike for you. Find a model in your price range that has the features you want. Try to get a good quality bike with a chrome-moly or aluminum frame to reduce the weight. If you know

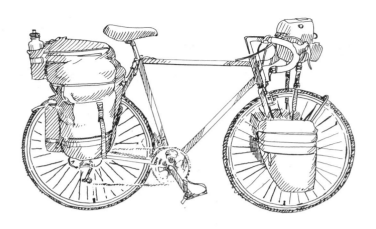

Novara's Randonee, shown with full touring gear.

you'll be strictly touring in flat to moderate terrain, then a 14-speed will be sufficient, although I recommend you make sure the rear sprockets have a wide gearing range. You can easily tell by checking the size of the largest sprocket (it should be quite large) and comparing the relative difference in size between largest and smallest sprockets. A small difference (indicating a smaller gear range) is more suitable for speed-riding than touring. A third chainring (which means an 18- or 21-speed model) is a better long-term choice since you never know where your adventures may lead you. Make sure to select a touring model that has adequate provisions for water bottles, front and rear racks, and optional fenders. Toe clips and straps, as well as a good touring pedal/shoe combination are desirable for efficient pedaling when touring.

Try to get quick-release wheel hubs and seat post for easy maintenance and breakdown when traveling. Take care with quick-release components in areas where theft is a concern. Handlebars and tires can be exchanged to meet the needs of a particular trip. The 27" or 700C wheel sizes are both available for touring. Drop handlebars and relatively narrow (1.25"), high-pressure tires (90-100 psi) with a passive tread pattern are best for making time on good paved roads. A set of straight handlebars and wider (1.38"), lower-pressure tires (75 psi) with a more aggressive tread are recommended for greater handling and braking control on rough, unpaved roads. In essence, they turn your touring bicycle into a modified hybrid style that is more versatile. When changing from drop handlebars to straight, you have several choices. If your shifters are on the down tube, you can leave them there and just mount brake levers and handgrips on the new bars. This is fine since most of your riding will be on roads anyway. If the shifters are on the handlebar ends or on the stem, then it's just as easy to mount new shifters on the replacement handlebars. The other option is to set up another set of handlebars complete with stem, handgrips or tape, shifters, brake levers and cables. This way you can swap easily whenever you like.

Hybrid Style. This has to be the best choice of bicycle for adventure travelers. When the focus is on travel instead of simply working up a good sweat, you're more concerned with versatility than performance. Hybrids offer that versatility in a practical, moderately-priced package. Travelers who are road cyclists at heart enjoy the ability to have larger diameter 700C wheels (vs. 26" for off-road use) and drop handlebars. Travelers who are mountain bikers at heart find the ability to have low-pressure knobbies and ride on rough terrain irresistible. I feel the key to enjoying a hybrid is to find a responsive, lightweight model that has good touring characteristics, since most of your travel is likely to be on pavement. The balance of your riding will probably be on unpaved roads (as opposed to extended off-road exploration) so it should also have moderate ground clearance and good stability.

I recommend 18- or 21-speed models with a third chainring and wide gearing range. Straight handlebars with handgrips and bar-end brakes are the best choice for mixed paved and unpaved road riding. You can easily switch to drop handlebars, or mount a clip-on handlebar extension, either of which allows you to stretch out and

Specialized's Crossroads

assume a more efficient touring posture. You'll be thankful for the variety of hand positions when touring long distance. Toe clips are essential on a hybrid, too, when touring. A versatile tire width and tread design are also desirable. Hybrids typically allow for every-thing between a narrow road tire with a smooth tread to a narrow knobby tire for off-road work. For general travel and the best of both worlds, I recommend a 1.38" wide tire with a combination tread pattern.

Mountain Style. Mountain bikes are fun to ride and can go places hikers can hardly get to, but take some time to consider whether your needs are oriented more toward travel or pursuing an outdoor sport. Despite their vast popularity, this should only be your choice if most of your riding is done off-road, and if you have the money to invest in a good quality model. Inexpensive mountain bikes (under $400) are heavy and not very efficient for road travel, yet aren't of sufficient quality to stand up to really hard use off-road. In this price range, you'd be better off with a hybrid style that you can use for road and light off-road use.

A mountain bicycle should be chosen for the most comfort, strength, and the lightest weight you can afford. A butted chrome-moly or an aluminum frame is desirable. If you plan to use your bicycle for traveling long distances off-road, make sure it has ad-equate provisions for alternative hand positions, water bottles and racks for carrying gear. You'll have a wide choice in type of shifters, from above and below bar thumb-activated shifters to the new handgrip versions. Try to select a style that is comfortable for the way you ride. The same applies to shape and size of handlebar and

Cannondale's M500

stem. These are personal choices that should be selected with an eye toward comfort. All mountain bicycles use lightweight cantilever type brakes, so there won't be much of a choice there. Check out the bikes that have a suspension system integrated into the front fork. They are becoming increasingly popular, although you'll still pay a premium price for this feature. Tires can vary between 1.5" and 2.5" in width, and tread type ranges from hard-gripping knobbies to slicks for road use.

Mountain Bicycling Etiquette. Mountain bicycles now allow enthusiasts to ride off-road trails and tracks that were traditionally the domain of hikers, causing several concerns to those who also enjoy the slow pace and solitude of foot travel. The first issue is one of safety. I personally have had multiple encounters with mountain bikes while hiking with my children. In each case, we were almost run over by bike riders totally engrossed in their sport and oblivious to others using the trail. After forcing us off the trail, they didn't even bother to stop. Only once was I able to confront the riders when one of them mangled his bike on a rock around the next bend. Concentrating on speed and really pushing yourself on a deserted road is one thing, doing it on a hiking trail where you are likely to encounter and possibly injure pedestrians is another.

The second issue concerns the problem of determining where it's suitable to ride a bicycle. In the hiking world, there are ongoing debates about the damage done by hiking boot treads to fragile environments, yet you'll often see cyclists tearing up the turf in those same locations. Then there is the consideration of the effect trail cycling has on wildlife. In an effort to control this problem, for both hikers and the environment, mountain bicycles have been banned from many hiking trails, and bikers have been encouraged to ride on other, less fragile tracks of land. This seems to be an ineffective solution since several of my near misses with cyclists have occurred on trails that were posted as closed to bicycling.

These potential problems, perpetuated by a minority of thoughtless riders, can be eliminated if we all take time to reflect on proper riding etiquette, maintain respect for the natural world, and become more respectful as we explore the world on the seat of a bicycle.

Tandem Style. Those of you who travel in pairs may well want to consider a tandem bicycle for traveling. There are a host of obvious advantages that make tandems unique. You don't have to worry about staying together, with the stronger cyclist always miles ahead. On a tandem, you are never more than a few feet away from each other. This means you can communicate easily without risking riding two abreast down the road, or always turning around to locate your partner. There is only one cycle to maintain and repair. You also have the same great feelings of teamwork similar to those generated by good canoeists. And besides, you can really move on a tandem, usually much faster than on two separate bicycles. This can be great fun when touring long distances.

A good touring rig for a family with one or two young children is a tandem bicycle towing a child trailer. Tandems can also accommodate child riders very easily in the stoker (rear) position. Older children can use the existing set-up, while *Child Stoker Kits* (around $250 total cost) are available for younger children. This kit extends the handlebars and raises the pedals for smaller riders.

The disadvantages are also obvious—while you only have one bike to maintain, if something happens to it you're both going to walk for help. There are bound to be many places on your travels where the length of a tandem just won't fit, especially on some forms of public transportation. And despite the inherent coziness of a tandem, you might find there are times when a little solitude is nice.

Try to determine if riding a bicycle built for two is for you before investing in one. Cost is a factor, since decent tandems aren't inexpensive, and you undoubtedly already own a single bicycle or two. On the other hand, the cost of a good tandem isn't much more than two moderately priced single bikes, or even one high-performance model. If you choose to cycle tandem, select a model that is best suited for your needs. Touring tandems can be outfitted with racks, panniers, water bottles and anything else you might need for

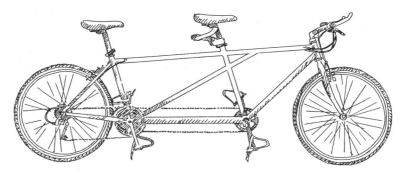

Yokota's Twin Peaks

road travel. For versatility, try exchanging your narrow road tires for wider slicks. They perform almost as well, and allow you to use lighter wheels with 36 spokes instead of 48. If the packing size of a tandem is a concern, investigate the new folding tandem from Montague (detailed in the Innovative Product section that follows). You can even pull a trailer with a tandem and transport the entire family in one touring machine.

Children's Bicycles. Children grow up riding a variety of bicycles. Most start with an inexpensive, single speed BMX style with 20" wheels at around age six. This serves them well until around age eight to nine when they are ready for a multi-speed bicycle. Relatively inexpensive juvenile models are available with 24" wheels, either in 12-speed touring style or 18-speed all-terrain models. Either one is fine for touring since your pace with children of that age should be relaxed. Most children enjoy an all-terrain bike for general use. Even on a road tour, they have fun exploring locally on this type of bike. There are some great models to choose from at this level. Giant offers the *Diversion* and *Awesome*, all-terrain bicycles with 18-speeds and 24" wheels. L.L. Bean's *Pathfinder* is a great children's all-terrain bicycle with 18-speeds, 24" wheels and a 13.5" frame. Novara (REI) offers the 10-speed *Scrambler* in both 20" and 24" wheel versions for kids. The 12-speed *Rockhopper* from Special-ized is a good all-terrain model for children, as are similar models from Jazz, Norco and Mongoose. Schwinn offers the *Caliente* 12-speed road bike in juvenile frame sizes with 24" wheels. Ross also has several juvenile road/touring models. Expect to pay around $150 to $300 for one of these good quality child's bicycles.

L.L. Bean's Pathfinder

Many parents prefer to skip the bike with 24" wheels due to its limited usefulness, unless there is a brother or sister to hand it down to. At most a child will get two to three years out of it before they are ready for a larger model. By age 12, they are ready for an adult bike with 26" wheels. It all depends on the age and size of the child, and how and where you plan to travel, but one solution is to choose an adult mountain or hybrid bike with a small frame when children are ready for their first good bike. They will eventually grow out of this bike, too, but this option typically covers a longer age span than a bike with 24" wheels.

Costs. You probably already know that you can spend anywhere from a hundred dollars to several thousand dollars for a bicycle. The hundred dollar model from the local department store will get you around, and if you work at it a bit, it may even take you on an adventure or two, but rest assured that you won't get lasting quality or reliable service from a department store. That only comes from selecting a quality model from a professional bicycle shop. This doesn't mean you have to cash in your savings bonds to buy one. Affordable bicycles of reasonable quality are on the market. Higher-priced bicycles give better performance in a lighter package. Pay less and you'll get heavier, less responsive frames and forks, as well as a less sophisticated component group. Pay more and you'll get lighter, more durable frames and higher quality components. Only you can determine how much those things are worth to you.

Decent quality touring bicycles start around $400, and from there climb to $1,100 or more for lightweight, high-performance models, and much more for custom cycles. Most touring cyclists try to find something suitable with either a butted chrome-moly or an aluminum frame in the $400 to $900 range. Appropriate hybrid bicycles are less expensive, with many good models under $350. Of course, you can easily pay up to $1,000 for a hybrid if you're seeking light weight and high levels of performance. A chrome-moly or aluminum frame model in the $300 to $800 range is best suited for general travel use. Mountain bicycles cover the widest range of prices. There is a good selection of mountain bicycles for under $500, although for rugged use you'd be well advised to steer clear of models costing much less than $350 to $400. A sizeable group of mountain bikes with better overall characteristics are in the range of $500 to $900, and an equally large number of high performance or competition models exist costing between $1,000 to $3,000.

Used Bicycles. If the price of a new bicycle is in danger of blowing your travel budget, take a close look at the used market. Unlike most other outdoor gear, there are lots of good quality, previously-owned bicycles available. You'd be surprised what might turn up for sale if you make the rounds of the bicycle shops just after the summer season. Persistence and a little patience may reap great rewards for those on a budget.

Listed below are some of the most practical bicycles currently available for active travelers. They are arranged in four separate categories according to intended use: touring, hybrid, mountain and tandem.

Author's Recommendations - Touring and Sport Touring Bicycles ($400-$900)

Brand	Model	Type	Speeds	Frame	Brakes
Bianchi	Eros	ST	21	CM	caliper
Bianchi	Europa	ST	21	CM	caliper
Bike Friday	World Tourist*	T	21	CM	cantilever
Bike Nashbar	4000R	ST	14	CM/HT	caliper
Bike Nashbar	6000T Toure	T	21	CM	caliper
Bridgestone	RB-T	T	21	CM	cantilever
Cannondale	T600	T	21	AL	cantilever
Cannondale	R500	ST	21	AL	caliper
Diamond Back	Expert TG	T	21	CM	caliper
Giant	Alondra	T	21	CM	cantilever
L.L. Bean	Eclipse	T/ST	21	AL	caliper
Miyata	700 GT	T	21	CM	cantilever
Miyata	721	T	21	AL	caliper
Novara (REI)	Randonee	T	21	CM	cantilever
Novara (REI)	Strada	ST	21	CM	caliper
Performance	Vitesse	T	21	CM	caliper
Peugeot	Cross Country	T	21	CM	caliper
Quantum	Q-745	T	21	CM	caliper
Raleigh	CT400	T/H	21	AL	cantilever
Specialized	Allez Sport	ST	21	CM	caliper
Trek	1100	ST	21	AL	caliper
Trek	520	T	21	CM	cantilever
Wheeler	1300	T	21	CM	caliper

See Innovative Product in this section.
TYPE: T=touring, ST=sport-touring, H=hybrid.
FRAME: HT=high tensile steel, CM=chrome-moly, AL=aluminum.

Author's Recommendations - Hybrid Bicycles ($300-$800)

Brand	Model	Speeds	Frame	Brakes
Alpinestars	Alpine XRoss	21	CM	cantilever
Bianchi	Advantage	21	CM	cantilever
Bianchi	Volpe	21	CM	cantilever
Bridgestone	XO-1	14	CM	caliper
Bridgestone	XO-2	21	CM	cantilever
Cignal	Kokomo	18	HT	cantilever
Cignal	Montauk	21	CM/HT	cantilever
Cannondale	H400	21	AL	cantilever
Cannondale	H600	21	Al	cantilever

Diamond Back	Approach	21	CM/HT	cantilever
Diamond Back	Avail	21	CM	cantilever
Eclipse	200CX	21	CM/HT	cantilever
Fuji	Palisade	21	CM/HT	caliper
Fuji	Del Ray	21	CM	caliper
Giant	Innova	21	CM	cantilever
Giant	Prodigy	21	CM	cantilever
GT	Cirque	21	CM	cantilever/caliper
GT	Virage	21	AL	cantilever/caliper
Iron Horse	XT 3000	21	CM	cantilever
Iron Horse	XT 5000	21	CM	cantilever
Jamis	Quest	21	CM	cantilever
Jamis	Coda	21	CM	cantilever
KHS	Cross Comp	21	CM	cantilever
L.L. Bean	Acadia	21	CM	cantilever
L.L. Bean	Evolution	21	CM	cantilever
Marin	Stinson	21	CM/HT	cantilever
Miyata	Sportcross	21	CM	cantilever
Miyata	Quickcross	21	AL	cantilever
Mongoose	Dynametric 735	21	CM	cantilever
Montague*	MX-7	21	CM/HT	cantilever
Nishiki	Meridian	21	CM	cantilever
Nishiki	Katmandu	21	CM	cantilever
Norco	Monterey Cross	21	CM/HT	cantilever
Novara (REI)	Corsa	21	CM/HT	cantilever
Novara (REI)	X-R	21	CM	cantilever
Offroad	252 Pro Flex	21	CM	cantilever
Performance	Transit	21	CM/HT	cantilever
Quantum	DPX-700	21	AL	caliper
Quantum	CMX-500	21	CM	cantilever
Raleigh	C50	21	CM/HT	cantilever
Raleigh	CT200	21	AL/CM	cantilever
Ross	Centaur Signature	21	CM	cantilever
Schwinn	Crisscross	21	CM	cantilever
Schwinn	Cross Point	21	CM	cantilever
Shogun	Metro CX	21	CM	cantilever
Specialized	Crossroads	21	CM/HT	cantilever
Specialized	Crossroads Trail	21	CM	cantilever
Trek	720	21	CM/HT	cantilever
Trek	750	21	CM	cantilever
Univega	Activa Trail	21	CM	cantilever
Univega	Via Montega	21	CM	cantilever
Wheeler	Cross Line 3000	21	CM/HT	cantilever
Wheeler	Cross Line 5000	21	CM	cantilever
Yokota	Ahwahnee Cross	21	CM/HT	cantilever
Yokota	Mariposa	21	CM	cantilever

See Innovative Product in this section.
FRAME: HT=high tensile steel, CM=chrome-moly, AL=aluminum.

Author's Recommendations - Mountain Bicycles ($375-$900)

Brand	Model	Speeds	Frame	Fork
Alpinestars	Cro-Mega LX	21	CM	CM
Alpinestars	Cro-Mega DX	21	CM	CM

Bianchi	Ibex	21	CM	CM
Bianchi	Osprey	21	CM	CM
Bike Nashbar	7000X	21	AL	CM
Bridgestone	MB-6	21	CM	CM
Cannondale	M500	21	AL	CM
Cannondale	M700	21	AL	AL
Cignal	Zanzibar	21	CM	CM/HT
Cignal	Silverado	21	CM	CM/HT
Diamond Back	Ascent	21	CM	CM
Diamond Back	Apex	21	CM	CM
Eclipse	300 MB	21	CM/HT	CM
Eclipse	550 MB	21	AL	CM
Gary Fisher	Aquila	21	CM	CM
Fuji	Tahoe	21	CM	CM
Fuji	Nevada	21	CM	CM
Giant	Iguana	21	CM	CM
Giant	Sedona ATX	21	CM	CM
GT	Timberline	21	CM/HT	CM/HT
GT	Tequesta	21	CM	CM/HT
Iron Horse	MT 400R	21	CM/HT	CM
Iron Horse	MT 600R	21	CM/HT	CM/HT
Jamis	Durango	21	CM	CM/HT
Jamis	Dakota	21	CM	CM
KHS	Montana Summit	21	CM	CM
KHS	Montana Pro	21	CM	CM
L.L. Bean	Approach	21	CM/HT	CM
L.L. Bean	Pathfinder	21	AL/CM	CM
Marin	Muir Woods	21	CM	CM
Marin	Palisades Trail	21	CM	CM
Miyata	Elevation 300	21	CM	CM
Miyata	Elevation 400	21	CM	CM
Mongoose	Rockadile	21	CM	CM
Mongoose	Iboc Comp	21	CM	CM
Montague*	939, M1000	21	CM/HT	HT
Nishiki	Backroads	21	CM	CM
Nishiki	Cascade	21	CM	CM
Norco	Bigfoot	21	CM	CM
Norco	Pinnacle	21	CM	CM
Novara (REI)	Arriba	21	CM	CM
Novara (REI)	Ponderosa	21	CM	CM
Offroad	550 Pro Flex	21	CM	CM
Performance	Pulse	21	CM	CM
Quantum	ES 300	21	CM	CM
Quantum	BT 400	21	AL	CM
Paramount	Series 20	21	CM	CM
Paramount	Series 30	21	CM	CM
Raleigh	M50	21	CM/HT	CM
Raleigh	MT200	21	AL/CM	CM
Research Dyn.	Coyote 2	21	CM/HT	CM
Research Dyn.	Coyote 3	21	CM	CM
Rocky Mt.	Fusion	21	CM	CM
Ross	Mount Hood	21	CM	CM/HT

Ross	Mount Rainier	21	CM	CM
Schwinn	Impact Pro	21	CM	CM
Scott	Sawtooth	21	CM	CM
Scott	Boulder	21	CM	CM
Shogun	Trail Breaker	21	CM/HT	CM
Shogun	Prairie Breaker	21	CM	CM
Specialized	Hardrock Sport	21	CM/HT	CM
Specialized	Rockhopper	21	CM	CM
Tech	Badlands	21	CM/HT	CM/HT
Tech	Nova	21	CM	CM
Trek	830	21	CM/HT	CM
Trek	7000	21	AL	CM
Univega	Alpina Uno-LX	21	CM	CM
Univega	Alpina Sport	21	CM	CM
Wheeler	Pro Line 2000	21	CM	CM
Wheeler	CompLine 5500	21	CM	CM
Yokota	Ahwahnee	21	CM	CM/HT
Yokota	Quick Silver	21	CM	CM

*See Innovative Product in this section. **All mountain bikes listed have cantilever brakes.*
FRAME and FORK: HT=high tensile steel, CM=chrome-moly, AL=aluminum.

Author's Recommendations - Tandem Bicycles ($1,000-$3,000)

Brand	Model	Speeds	Wheels	Frame	Fork
Bike Nashbar	10000 AT	21	700C	CM	CM
Burley	Rock 'n Roll	21	26 in.	CM	CM
Burley	Bossa Nova	21	700C	CM	CM
Cannondale	MT3000	21	26 in.	AL	CM
Cannondale	RT3000	21	700C	AL	CM
GT	Quatrefoil	21	26 in.	CM/HT	CM
Ibis	Uncle Fester Rd	21	26 in.	CM	CM
Ibis	Uncle Fester Mtn	21	26 in.	CM	CM
Ibis	Cousin It Road	21	26 in.	CM	CM
Ibis	Cousin It Mtn	21	26 in.	CM	CM
Miyata	Duplicross	21	26 in.	CM	CM
Montague	Triframe Tandem	21	26 in.	CM	CM
Nashbar	1000AT	21	26 in.	CM	HT
Rodriguez	Trillium Cross	21	700C	CM	CM
Rodriguez	Trillium Sport	21	700C	CM	CM
Rodriguez	AL26	21	26 in.	CM	CM
Santana	Visa	21	700C	CM	CM
Santana	Vision	21	26 in.	CM	CM
Santana	Arriva	21	700C	CM	CM
Santana	Cilantro	21	26 in.	CM	CM
Trek	T50	21	700C	CM	CM
Trek	T100	21	700C	CM	CM
Trek	T200	21	700C	CM	CM
Yokota	Twin Peaks	21	26 in.	CM	CM
Yokota	Grizzly Peak	21	26 in.	CM	HT

FRAME and FORK: HT=high tensile steel, CM=chrome-moly, AL=aluminum.

Innovation - Folding Bicycles For Travelers

Montague's *Folding Mountain Bike* is well known for its quality and ease of use. It was the first folding bicycle to perform like a standard mountain bike, and the first to provide collapsibility to the serious traveling cyclist. Now Montague has added a hybrid and a tandem bicycle to their line. The secret to the Montague's success is a rear assembly, including seatstays, chainstays, and rear wheel, that pivots 180 degrees to the front of the bicycle for transport. The tandem folds in the same way, only with a double pivoting assembly which Montague calls a "triframe." The pivoting action allows everything else

about the bicycle to be the same as on a standard model, with a good quality component group, 18 or 21-speed indexed shifting, standard-size 26"wheels and tires, lightweight alloy rims and a quick-release front hub. The Montague solo folding bicycles weigh about 30 pounds and are reasonably priced at around $400 (hybrid) to $500 (mountain). A flexible, sturdy carrying case is available from Montague as well.

Montague's Folding Bicycle

Another innovative bicycle for travelers is Bike Friday's *World Tourist*. This bike has 20" wheels and a small frame that folds easily into its own carrying case and checks through as standard luggage on an airplane. The amazing thing is that the case becomes a small bicycle trailer once the bike is unfolded, capable of carrying all of your travel gear! An extended seat tube and handlebar stem allow the rider to assume a normal touring position. Bike Friday offers three models, a 7-speed commuter, a 14-speed sport/racer, and a 21-speed touring bike. The complete travel system costs about $875.

Maintenance and Repair - Bicycles

Your bicycle represents a large investment, and with proper maintenance and care will serve you well, adventure after adventure. Many people are intimidated by the prospect of maintaining their own bike, preferring a professional cycle shop to do all the work. It's true that some things are best left to a qualified shop, but if you plan on touring to distant places, or very far off the beaten track, you'd do well to learn the basics of bike maintenance for yourself. There's bound to be lots of times when you won't have anyone else to turn to.

There really isn't much to bicycle maintenance once you get the hang of it. I recommend you get a good book, then supplement your reading with practice and some helpful advice from the shop where you purchased the bike. Shop employees are usually happy to assist you, although there may be a charge for their time answering technical questions. A good, lightweight tool kit and an assortment of spare parts are musts for touring. In general, you should regularly lube the chain, derailleurs and cables with a good teflon or silicon spray lube that won't attract dirt and road grit. In addition, regularly check the tire pressure and the tightness of all nuts and bolts. Special considerations for individual components are discussed below.

Bearings. Wheel, bottom bracket and pedal bearings should all be serviced yearly, or as needed, to ensure long life. Make sure to service bearings if you start to hear a clacking or grating sound caused by insufficient grease or intrusion of road grit past the outer seal.

Brakes. Keep the cables lubed for smooth operation and long cable life. Pads should be checked regularly for wear. Adjust the brakes so the wheel spins freely, yet there is minimal clearance so the brakes engage quickly.

Cables. All shifting and brake cables should be regularly lubed and checked for wear. Spare cables should be packed for long-distance touring.

Chain. Keep the chain lubed with a greaseless product that won't attract abrasive dirt and road grit. Carry a chain link tool on longer tours. This allows you to repair a broken chain, an infrequent yet potentially disastrous occurrence.

Derailleurs. Once set, derailleurs rarely get out of alignment. The biggest problem you'll encounter is keeping indexed gearing working smoothly over the entire range. Derailleurs typically have three adjustments, a side-to-side adjustment at the cable end that positions the chain with respect to the sprockets, and two screw adjustments that set the length of travel at each end. The side-to-side adjustment is matched to the indexed gearing, and occasionally it slips out of alignment with hard use. If the problem persists, you may have to use something to lock the adjustment screw in position. With a little practice, you'll be able to expertly make the necessary adjustments.

Frame. The most you'll need to do with your frame is to touch up the paint occasionally. If you take a bad fall and bend or break one of the tubes, only a bike or machine shop can repair it for you. Proponents of steel-frame bicycles point to the ease of repair as one of their best features. Aluminum frames are not as easy to repair, and not as many shops have aluminum welding capability.

Tubes and Tires. Touring cyclists can do themselves a big favor by investing in some type of tough tire liner to prevent flats. Several options are available, the most practical being a roll of plastic called *Tuffy Tire*. Repairing a flat isn't difficult. The first thing to do is locate the hole. Sometimes it is immediately apparent, other times it requires submersing the pressurized tube in some water until you find air bubbles coming from the hole.

Release the brakes and take the wheel off the frame. Release the pressure from the tube. Using a set of tire levers, gently pry the tire off one side of the rim. Take off the valve stem cap and remove the tube from the tire. Patch kits come with an abrasive paper or metal plate, bonding glue and a variety of patches. Rough up the area around the hole, place a thin layer of bonding glue on the tube equal to the size of the patch. When the glue becomes tacky, place the patch on and rub firmly on the patch with a smooth, hard surface. Allow the patched tube to set for 20 minutes or so before use. If you're in a hurry, use another tube and patch the damaged one at the end of the day.

Wheels. Wheel spokes and rims are quite tough, but they can become damaged or out of alignment if you have an unfortunate encounter with a rock or pothole. The most common occurrence is that the spoke tension is not uniform and the wheel becomes out of balance (also called "out of true"). This is easy to spot since you'll notice a slight wobble in the wheel at each rotation. You can adjust your own spokes with a small spoke wrench, but be forewarned that balancing a wheel is an art that takes practice. Beginners often do more harm than good with a spoke wrench, so you may want to leave this up to a bike shop. If you can find someone willing to show you the procedure, it might come in handy on a tour. Dealing with a bent or damaged rim is almost impossible on your own. You can attempt to straighten it, but most likely you'll end up having it repaired or replaced at a bike shop.

Bicycle Trailers

- Trailers For Carrying Children
- Trailers For Carrying Gear
- Trailers For Both Children and Gear

Bicycle trailers have opened up a whole new world for families with small children. There are many good models currently on the market that carry one or two children, extra gear, shopping bags, and most anything else you'd like to haul with your bicycle. Their main advantage is the ability to get children off the bicycle's back rack, where the weight rides high and the motion of the child causes instability, and into a trailer where the weight is pulled near ground level and the motion of the child cause little concern. Trailers also provide the only way of carrying more than one child per bicycle. There used to be a large span of years for traveling families that were hard to cope with, between the time when children were too big for a bicycle seat yet too young to ride their own bike over any distance. Trailers have solved the problem by allowing children of any age to ride comfortably and to be safely towed behind a bicycle.

Not only are trailers great child carriers, but they are also very useful for hauling touring and camping gear, as well as performing a multitude of other tasks. Many touring cyclists prefer to take the weight of panniers and other gear off the bicycle. They would rather pull it in a trailer where the low center of gravity doesn't have as much affect on bike balance and motion. In addition to hauling gear, accessories are now available to transform bike trailers from child carriers into utility carts for the garden, yard or woods; boat or board carts; stroller or baby joggers; cartop carriers; and even ski touring pulks.

Review of Generic Types - Bicycle Trailers

There are several different types of bicycle trailers on the market. They are differentiated by their intended use, whether or not they collapse easily for transport, the method of attachment to the bicycle, and by the seating positions they offer children.

By Intended Use. Most trailers on the market are primarily child carriers, with optional accessories for performing other tasks. The number of optional modes of use, along with the ease of conversion from one mode to another, allows consumers to help distinguish one trailer from another.

Collapsibility. Most trailers on the market break down easily for transport on airplanes or in the trunk of your car. This may not be important to those who stick close to home, but it is a very convenient feature for those who travel. Each trailer has its own distinct design and method of disassembly.

Method of Attachment. Bike trailer tongues either arch up and connect to the seat post, as in the Cannondale *Bugger*, CycleTote, Bike Burro, Blue Sky, and L.L. Bean models, or curve around and connect to the left hand chainstay on the opposite side from the rear sprockets, as in the Cannondale *Stowaway*, Burley, Equinox, and Winchester Original models.

Seating Positions. Trailers are also distinguished by the type of seating options they offer. This includes the number of riders comfortably seated and the direction of seating, either front-facing or rear-facing. Most models offer seating for two children and some additional gear, up to a manufacturers recommended weight limit. Front-facing seating is regarded as the more popular configuration, although several models allow for seating in either direction, as with the Bike Burro, Equinox, and Winchester Original child carriers, and two, the Cannondale *Bugger* and the L.L. Bean *Kiddie Kart*, face the riders toward the rear.

Features and Options - Bicycle Trailers

There are several prominent features, as well as a host of options, that you should be familiar with and carefully compare when shopping for a bicycle trailer.

Frame. A trailer frame is similar to the frame of a bicycle in that it provides rigid support and safety, plus a convenient place to attach the various other components. Since a good strength/weight ratio is as much of a concern for trailers as it is for bicycles, trailer frames are all made of either aluminum or steel tubing. Collapsible models are designed so the frame, wheels and enclosure nest together in a low-profile package for transport. Some trailer manufacturers offer a no-frills version of their trailer with just a bare frame and wheels (no enclosure) so you can use it to haul small boats, surfboards and other bulky items, or outfit it to suit your own needs.

Enclosure. This is the feature which, when attached to the frame, provides comfort and security for children or a convenient place to stow gear and other items. It is available with front-facing or rear-facing seating configurations, in either rigid plastic or heavy-duty fabric. Some models have internal pockets for storing books and other favorite children's items. Sun and rain hoods that attach to the enclosure are usually available as options.

Children's Seating. If the enclosure is made of fabric, chances are the seat is fabric as well. A rigid enclosure allows for rigid seats to be incorporated. Seating can be either front- or rear-facing. A safety harness is provided for each child.

Trailer Tongue and Hitch. The tongue of the trailer is the part that extends from cart frame to your bicycle, the hitch is the mechanism that actually attaches it in place. Each brand has its own distinctive style of tongue and hitch arrangement. Some attach to the chainstay, while others attach to the seat post. Most allow the bicycle to turn, lean or even lay down independent of the trailer. A safety strap is usually employed as a precaution against the unlikely event of a hitch coming apart while in operation.

Wheels. Trailer wheels are usually nothing more than converted bicycle front wheels with either road or all-terrain tires mounted. Most trailers come with steel-rim wheels as standard equipment, with lightweight aluminum rims offered as an option. Quick-release hubs are available on some models. Trailers are available with 16", 20", 24" or 26" diameter wheels depending on the brand.

Safety Features. In addition to safety harnesses, bicycle trailers usually come with several types of high-visibility markings, including reflectors on the wheels and enclosure, a safety flag (or provisions for one), and a brightly colored enclosure. Enclosures also feature some means of protecting children's hands from coming into contact with the wheel spokes, either through solid wheel covers (a few models), molded fender guards (models with a rigid plastic enclosure), lexan side panels (CycleTote's *Family* model), or fabric side panels (all other fabric enclosure models). Trailers should also have some provision for keeping wheel spray and road debris from coming into contact with the riders, either through splash guards, front netting, or facing the riders toward the rear.

Optional Brake. One of the currently marketed bicycle trailers has an optional brake available to help reduce bicycle brake overheating due to trailer and cargo loads. CycleTote's *Family* model uses an inertia-activated alloy drum brake in one of the trailer wheels. When the bicycle brakes are applied, the forward inertia of the trailer activates the trailer brake for a safe, uniform reduction of speed.

Infant Seats and Slings. Infants that are too young to be strapped into a regular trailer seat can be accommodated with an optional infant sling or harness. It holds the infant comfortably yet securely as you ride. Another option is to strap a regular infants' car seat into position on the trailer, an easy operation on a trailer such as Bike Burro's *Classic*.

Netting. A few models offer an optional netted screen to allow air flow yet protect front-facing riders from flying insects and other road debris.

Sun/Rain Hood. All brands offer some type of sun and rain protection, from simple canopies to sophisticated removable rain covers. Most full covers incorporate flexible plastic windows so the passengers can view the outdoors.

Stroller or Jogger Kit. These are available for several trailers with tongues that attach to the bicycles chainstay (see the Innovative Product that follows for details).

Cartop Carrier Kit. A few models can even be converted for use as cartop carriers. The Bike Burro *Classic* has a rigid plastic enclosure that can be strapped to the trunk or roof of any size car with the use of their optional *Car-Go* kit. With the optional kit from Equinox, their *Tourlite* can be used as a cartop carrier for gear (full enclosure in place) or as a roof carrier for two bicycles.

Ski Pulk Kit. Seeing this optional kit offered by Equinox makes me think that the additional uses for a bicycle trailer are almost unlimited. In this case, the frame and enclosure are mounted on skis instead of wheels, and the tongue is replaced by a metal extension that attaches pulk-style to the skier's waist. The full enclosure keeps kids warm and dry. Of course, gear can be carried in place of passengers.

The Equinox Tourlite

Innovation - Stroller/Baby Jogger Conversion Kits

It's widely accepted that trailers are incredibly useful when it comes to hauling young children, gear, or anything else you'd like to pull behind your bicycle. What is less well known is that they also make wonderful people-drawn carts, ideal for a variety of tasks. Perhaps the best option for harnessing pedestrian power is to convert the trailer to a stroller or baby jogger. Conventional strollers are notoriously poor for active travel or long-term use on all but the best pavement, and the expense of a baby jogger on its own is hard to justify. Collapsible bicycle trailers, on the other hand, are lightweight and rugged, able to go on almost any terrain, and, with simple conversion kits, they can be as easily pushed or pulled by hand as with a bicycle. The nicest part of the conversion kits is that, once mounted, you don't have to limit your load to children. They make the trailer just as suitable as a utility push-cart for hauling travel gear, boat equipment, and home and garden items. This versatility justifies the initial cost.

Burley now offers the optional *Walk 'n Roller* kit that transforms their *Burley-Roo* or *Burly d'Lite* into a high-quality stroller or baby jogger. This conversion kit includes a third wheel that remains on the trailer tongue, making the transition from trailer to stroller only a one-minute operation. The Equinox and CycleTote models can also be adapted for walking or running use with convenient extension handles that replace the tongue. Almost any collapsible trailer could be modified to this type of service. All you have to do is replace the tongue and hitch with a handle that attaches securely to the trailer frame and extends up to a convenient height for pushing or pulling. You can even design the handle so it could attach to either the front or the back of the trailer frame depending on the intended use.

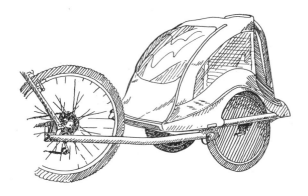

The Cannondale Stowaway

Construction and Operation - Bicycle Trailers

Construction. Manufacturers' individual designs vary considerably, although the basic method of construction is similar throughout the industry. All bicycle trailer frames are made from lightweight metal tubing that is either bolted or welded together into the appropriate configuration. The main goal is to provide a rigid base that the wheels, tongue and enclosure can attach to. On models having flexible fabric enclosures, the frame tubing is extended over the base into the desired shape. Enclosures consist either entirely of panels of durable fabric, suspended from or stretched over the frame tubing, or of a combination of a one-piece molded rigid plastic lower part and a fabric canopy for weather protection. Fabric or plastic side panels protect the child from road debris and from coming into contact with the wheels.

All current models use standard bicycle wheels and tires since they perform well, are reasonably priced and readily available. The wheels attach to metal flanges on the trailer frame in much the same way they would on bicycle frame dropouts. Quick-release wheels are an option on some models. Wheel diameter varies between 16" and 26", depending on brand and model, with 20" and 24" being the most popular. Tire width and type of tread can often be altered to suit your riding conditions.

The trailer tongue design and method of attachment, both to the frame and to the bicycle, are key factors to a trailer's success. Whether the tongue arches up to the seat post or around to the chainstay, the method of attachment should allow the bicycle to pivot independent of the trailer when cornering and leaning into curves. Some models go even further and allow the bicycle to lay down without tipping the trailer. For a bicycle to corner and lean independently there must be at least two degrees of freedom in the tongue and hitch arrangement. This is accomplished in one of several ways. A ball and socket joint, similar to yet smaller and more sophisticated than a car trailer hitch, is used on many models. It is located on the hitch where it attaches to the bicycle frame or seat post. A few models use a flexible neoprene rubber hitch around the seat post, favoring its simplicity and low cost over a more sophisticated ball and socket. Some trailer tongues also pivot at the frame itself, allowing additional freedom of movement.

Operation. It is really easy to use a bicycle trailer. Simply attach the tongue and wheels to the frame (if the trailer is disassembled) and install child seats if carrying passengers or load your gear as desired. Install the sun/rain canopy according to the manufacturers instructions during inclement weather. Then attach the tongue and hitch to the bicycle and latch the safety strap, if available. Children should always wear a helmet and be strapped into the safety harness when moving.

It takes a little while to get comfortable with pulling a trailer, especially if you are used to carrying your child in a seat on the back rack or your touring gear loaded onto the bicycle. You'll notice the slight drag of the trailer at first, but won't believe how responsive your bicycle is without all that weight on it. Overall, trailers offer greater comfort and carrying capacity with less effort.

There are a few things you'll have to be aware of when pulling a trailer. Most models are capable of carrying 100 pounds or more, a much greater load than you would normally carry on the bicycle. The more weight you pull, the harder you're going to have to work, especially on uphill climbs, and the harder your brakes are going to have to work on downhill descents and when stopping. Try to adjust for this by checking your brakes and pads regularly, braking smoothly and consistently, and allowing more distance for braking (especially in wet conditions). Standard bicycle brakes perform adequately for use with all trailers. For additional security check out CycleTote's automatic braking system, an expensive yet functional option for their trailers. The second consideration is that your turning radius may be increased slightly by pulling a trailer, so it's best to take it a little easier when cornering in tight spaces. The last point you should be aware of is that a trailer will undoubtedly increase your overall width, so you'll have to take this into consideration when choosing where to ride. In most touring applications this is no problem, but you might have trouble negotiating some trails, bike paths and doorways.

Author's Recommendations - Bicycle Trailers

There are currently some great bicycle trailers to choose from, each with a slightly different approach to carrying riders and gear. It's best to find one that is comfortable for the way you ride and has the features and options you want, although your choice may ultimately come down to price, aesthetic preference, or which one is recommended and carried by your local bicycle shop. My advice is to narrow down the selection, then try out a trailer or two before buying. Your bike shop can arrange a short test "pull" for the models they carry. For an even better trial, try renting one for a tour to see how it performs in a variety of conditions. If you select a model that is only sold by direct mail, ask if there is a money-back trial period so you can make sure you agree that it performs as advertised. Bike Burro and CycleTote both offer free trial periods on their direct mail sales.

In general, both the chainstay and seat post hitches work well and adjust to any size bicycle. Trailer operation appears to be similar regardless of wheel diameter, although the small 16" wheels found on Burley's *Burley-Roo* and L.L. Bean's *Kiddie Kart* are probably more appropriate for shorter tours than long-distance explorations. In theory maximum carrying capacity typically varies from 100 to 150 pounds, the one exception being the Blue Sky models that claim a staggering 300-pound maximum capacity. In reality, a 100-pound load is about all you'd want to pull or brake for on any long-distance tour. Most models make some provision for handling the spray from the bicycle's rear wheel, but I'd recommend mounting a small fender (even a makeshift one) on the bike for any long-distance tour.

Go for Versatility. As stated throughout this book active travelers need gear that is versatile, so I recommend that you look for models that offer the most versatility for the money. This means models that collapse into a compact package for transport; offer several seating positions for multiple riders; are able to carry riders, gear, or both; and are able to perform other tasks with easy-to-use conversion kits. If you're looking for a model for transporting children, consider that you'll probably want to continue using the trailer for hauling gear after your children are grown. If you are buying one to transport gear, consider that you might want to make provisions for hauling children from time to time.

Most of the current models collapse for transport and adapt from child carrier to gear carrier easily. Many provide room for extra gear when carrying children. A particularly versatile bike trailer is the Equinox *Tourlite*. This one basic collapsible model can be used for carrying children and an ample amount of gear (with the optional child's seat in place it forms two separate compartments) or just gear for straight touring. The riders are well protected by the rain cover option and the trailer tongue can be positioned so the enclosure and riders face either forward or toward the rear. A variety of conversion kits are available for performing other tasks.

Trailers as Child Carriers. A trailer in the child-carrier mode should offer little wind resistance and adequate weather protection.

Low wind resistance and good protection from sun, rain and road debris are important on a tour. You'll find both these features on most trailers now on the market. Even though facing the riders toward the rear offers more protection from wind and rain, it tends to isolate the child from the parent. There are some exceptions, but the most popular arrangement is currently side-by-side seating facing forward. Children should also be comfortable while riding since they could end up spending long hours in the trailer. Younger children, lulled by the gentle motion of cycling, will probably spend a large part of their time sleeping. Rigid plastic used on the lower part of the enclosure offers more comfortable seating for long-distance travel than the flexible slings found on most fabric-enclosed models. The rigid plastic does, however, make it harder to collapse and transport the trailer. Burley has solved this problem on their *Burley-Roo*, as did Cannondale on their *Stowaway* model, by incorporating a pivoting rollbar and flexible seatback.

I find the most practical trailers for active traveler's with kids to be the Burley *d'Lite* and *Burley-Roo*, the Cannondale *Stowaway*, Equinox *Tourlite*, and the Winchester Originals *WT-3A* (aluminum frame and rims). Bike Burro's *Classic* is interesting, with its large barrel-shaped plastic enclosure that allows two children to sit comfortably facing each other, one toward the rear and one facing forward. Its suitability for travel, however, is a mixed bag. There's much more interior room and the padded rigid seats are easier on the riders over long distances, but the enclosure places a wide flat surface forward into the airstream, the rigid enclosure is heavy and bulky to carry on public transportation, and the sun canopy offers little protection from driving rain or road spray. The *Classic* works well for car travel if you get their conversion kit that transforms the frame and enclosure into a cartop carrier.

Trailers as Gear Carriers. This variation on the trailer theme concentrates on providing a sleek, weatherproof package for touring. In all cases, the gear carrier uses the same basic frameset as the child carrier version, often with the same enclosure. You can use any existing child-carrier model to carry gear. Sometimes a separate, lower-profile enclosure is used, as with the Burley *d'Lite Cargo* and the CycleTote *Touring* model. Bike Burrow markets their basic trailer frame and wheels without an enclosure at a bargain price so you can customize your own touring rig. They also offer their low-profile *Cooler* model that utilizes a 96-quart insulated cooler as the enclosure that serves as a sealed gear compartment. That's not a bad idea since the cooler is completely waterproof and capable of being sectioned off to store food. Extra gear can be strapped on top. Blue Sky Cycle Carts has a basic touring version that is the foundation for their child-carrying models, only without an upper enclosure. This basket-type trailer can fit lots of bulky gear or be modified to suit your own needs.

Costs. Bike trailers vary considerably in cost, although the price difference is minor compared to the long-term use you'll get out of this piece of equipment, especially if you can use it for a variety of tasks. As a rule, you'll pay more for greater strength and lighter weight, added versatility, and the ability to collapse for transport. If most of your riding is near home or on short tours, select an inexpensive model that does the job. For extended tours or more ambitious riding, spend the extra money and get a trailer with the features you need. Prices for trailers set up as child carriers range from $150 for the *Kiddie Kart* to $250 to $300 for the *Classic, Burley-Roo* and *Stowaway*, up to $325 to $400 for the high-end models such as the *d'Lite, Family, Tourlite* and *WT-3A*. Basic framesets and models strictly for carrying gear are less expensive, ranging from $175 to $350.

Author's Recommendations - Bicycle Trailers For Children and Gear

Brand	Model	Type	Encl.	Wheels	Weight	Options
Bike Burro	Basic	G	N/A	24", steel	16 lbs.	aw, ah
Bike Burro	Coolier	G	RP	24", steel	26 lbs.	aw, ah
Bike Burro	Classic	C(2)	RP	20", steel	38 lbs.	aw, ah, sh
Blue Sky	BA2	G	F	24", steel	22 lbs.	aw, ah
Blue Sky	BS2	C(2-4)	F	24", steel	31 lbs.	aw, ah, sh, rc, is
Burley	Burley-Roo	C	F	16", plastic	21 lbs.	ah, rc, sj, gp
Burley	d'Lite	C/G	F	20", alum.	19 lbs.	ah, rc, sj
Burley	d'Lite Cargo	G	F	20", alum.	18 lbs.	ah
Cannondale	Bugger	C	RP	20", alum.	23 lbs.	sh, rc, wg
Cannondale	Stowaway	C	RP	20", alum.	23 lbs.	sh, rc, wg
CycleTote	Family	C(2)	F/RP	700C, alum	23 lbs.	ah, rc, br, sj
CycleTote	Touring	G	F	700C, alum	18 lbs.	ah, br
Equinox	Tourlite	C/G	F	20", alum	19 lbs.	rc, gp, is, sj, cc, sp
L.L. Bean	Kiddie Kart	C/G	RP	16", steel	23 lbs.	sh, rc, wg
Winchester	WT-3A*	C/G	F	20", alum.	21 lbs.	ah, sh, rc (st'nd'rd)

* This model has aluminum frame and rims; other models available.

TYPE: C=child (seating capacity), G=gear. ENCLOSURE: F=fabric, RP=rigid plastic.

OPTIONS: aw=alloy wheels, ah=additional hitch, sh=sun hood, rc=rain cover, gp=gear pouch, is=infant sling, wg=wheel gaurds, fb=floor board, br=brake, sj=stroller/jogger, cc=cartop carrier, sp=ski pulk.

Load Carriers

After you find the perfect bicycle, and bike trailer if you choose to pull one, you'll want to take a close look at the equipment available to carry gear and children directly on the bike. This gear includes bicycle racks, child seats, and pannier and pack systems.

BICYCLE RACKS

Metal or composite racks are available for carrying a set of front panniers on either side of the front wheel, a set of rear panniers on either side of the rear wheel, or a variety of other gear on top of the rack, including child seats above the rear wheel. A back rack is one of the first options riders choose for their new bike. Without it, carrying capacity is severely limited. Back racks are simple metal frames with a flat top surface (open-frame or solid) for storing gear, long extension struts that connect to screws on the rear dropouts, and front connectors that secure to the seatpost or rear brake bolt or to points on the seatstays (either bolt-on or braze-on options are available).

Open-frame tops offer the most flexibility, solid tops also serve (roughly) as fenders. One end of the rack's top surface is usually curved up to hold gear in place. A reflector is typically mounted on the back end. Front racks come in two basic styles, one that is similar to a rear rack with a flat top carrying surface (although a little shorter), the other a low-riding frame strictly for carrying front panniers. The low-riding frame actually consists of two separate frames, connected to the fork legs on each side of the front wheel (either bolt-on or braze-on options available). On some models, the two frames are connected with a U-shaped piece of metal for additional support.

Inexpensive racks made of coated steel are available for around $15. Better models constructed of lightweight alloys cost $30 to $40. When shopping for a rack, make sure to select one that provides adequate strength for your type of riding, adequate tire clearance if you use wide tires, and sufficient strut length, a consideration for touring bikes with large diameter wheels. Good quality bicycle racks are made by Blackburn, Cannondale, Performance, Rhode Gear, and Specialized.

Blackburn. The Blackburn racks, hand-welded of aircraft alloy, have a reputation for superior strength and performance. Popular rear rack models include the *MTN-1 Mountain*, the *XR-1 Crossrack* and the *SX-1 Expedition* with heavy duty bars and three-strut design for serious touring. Blackburn front racks with a flat top surface include the *MTF-1 MTN Front* for mountain bikes, and the *AF-1 Front* for hybrid and touring models. Front pannier racks from Blackburn include the *FL-1 Lowriders* that bolt on, and the *CL-1 Custom Lowriders*, strong front racks made for bikes with *CL-1* braze-ons on the front forks.

Blackburn's CL-1 (top) and MTN-1 bike racks.

Cannondale. Cannondale, a leading manufacturer of aluminum-frame bicycles, also makes great racks. Their sturdy aluminum *Mountain Rack* has a wide, non-skid deck that provides a stable platform for rack packs or cargo, while also serving as a fender. This rack is available in a more basic version without the solid top. Cannondale's aluminum *Low-Riding Front Pannier Racks* sandwich the front fork blades, attaching from both sides for solid, sway-free mounting of loaded panniers.

Performance. The Performance *XCZ* is a sturdy rear rack of aluminum alloy with a solid top surface, three-strut design and four-point attachment system that allows it to fit any bike.

Rhode Gear. Rhode Gear models include the *VR1000* rear rack, a three-strut design made of aircraft-quality aluminum that is compatible with Rhode Gear's *Child Seat II* and *Kid Seat*, and the *Composite Rack*, a unique rear rack constructed of glass-reinforced nylon and stainless steel, compatible with Rhode Gear's *Kit Seat*.

Specialized. Their racks include the *Rock Rack Front* and the *Rock Rack Rear*. These racks are made of aluminum tubing instead of solid rod for increased strength and reduced weight. They feature a detachable titanium top plate.

CHILD SEATS

For those who have only one child to transport and limit their bicycle explorations to day riding near home or a base-camp, a child seat is probably the most practical option. Its strong points are light weight, portability and low cost. A number of inexpensive models are available from department stores and bike shops, but there's really no reason to compromise the safety and comfort of your child with a mediocre model when you can get a high-quality version for just a little more.

Rhode Gear is currently the leading name in child seats, and for good reason. Their child seats, made of high-density polypropylene and reinforced nylon, are versatile, strong and made to last. They are compatible with Rhode Gear back racks that allow them to be installed and removed in seconds with no tools. There are two models available, both with weight limits of 40 pounds. The *Child Seat II* (around $95) has a three-position tilting back, padded grab bar, removable padded seat lining, and leg straps. The more basic *Kid Seat* (around $65) is a single position seat with removable padded seat lining and leg straps.

Troxel also markets good child seats for bicycles, including their *Luxury Child Seat* model (around $50) that features leg rests, wheel guards, removable seat lining, and a grab bar.

PANNIER AND PACK SYSTEMS

Once you have the bicycle of your dreams, it's time to turn your attention to the various types of pack and pannier systems available for carrying personal, travel and outdoor gear. If your only experience with carrying things on a bike has been wearing a daypack or strapping things on the back rack, you'll be pleasantly surprised at the other options on the market. Whether for commuting, short trips or long-distance tours, it's nice to have additional load-carrying capacity that keeps the weight down low and off the rider. Packs and panniers specifically designed for bicycles allow you to load gear with ease, much more, in fact, than you can comfortably carry when backpacking. Minimalists scoff at the idea of a loaded bicycle, but there is no feeling quite like cruising down the road on a well-tuned bicycle, carrying everything you need to be a self-sufficient traveler.

Review of Generic Types - Panniers and Packs

The key to success for packs and panniers lies in placing most of the weight down low and close to the centerline of the bicycle. This gives maximum stability to both the bike and the rider. There are several basic types of load carriers for bicycles, categorized by their location on the bike or the type of gear they carry. These include front and rear panniers, handlebar packs, frame packs, seat packs, rack packs, and compact duffel bags. Since a balanced bicycle is the goal, choosing a combination of carriers to distribute the load makes the most sense.

Panniers. Panniers are sets of packs that hang from either side of a front or rear rack. Rear panniers are the foundation for any well conceived load-carrying system. They come in a variety of sizes, from small commuting models to large expedition panniers. Front panniers are generally smaller versions of those on the rear. They are used when additional carrying space is needed, always in combination with rear panniers. They help place some of the weight forward, although you want to be careful when loading the front fork so that bicycle steering and control aren't adversely affected.

Handlebar Packs. Handlebars also provide a convenient spot to place a small load carrier. Handlebar packs for touring typically clip on to the bars with a small metal adapter that hangs the pack out forward over the front wheel. Smaller versions that rest on top of the handlebars and stem are available for mountain and cross bikes. A new type of small bar pack is now available that attaches to clip-on aero-bars.

Frame Packs. This type of pack is a low-profile, triangular-shaped load carrier located inside the bicycle frame area, either where the top tube and seat tube intersect or where the top tube and down tube intersect. Some frame packs that fit at the top tube/seat tube junction also serve as padded support for carrying your mountain bike over obstacles. These are also called portage packs. While frame pack capacity is limited, it provides a handy place for a tool kit, a spare tube and a few personal items.

Seat Packs. Similar in concept to the frame model described above, this small wedge-shaped pack hangs just below the seat to provide an alternative location for gear you need easy access to. Most seat packs are expandable for carrying a few additional items from time to time.

Rack Packs and Duffel Bags. Rack packs are also available so you can carry additional personal gear on the rear rack. Similar in concept to small duffels, these specialty packs are made to sit lengthwise on the back rack. They work well alone or with a rear pannier system. Some models are insulated for storing food or drinks. Compact duffel bags can also be used as a companion piece to a pannier system. While not as compact and easy to use as a rack pack, they are generally less expensive and are capable of holding more gear. Most panniers mount so their top is flush with the top of the back rack. This creates a large flat surface ideal for strapping a duffel crosswise for hauling camping gear and other large bulky items.

Shopping Bags. With the growing popularity of bicycle transportation, heavy-duty detachable shopping bags, mounted in the same manner as rear panniers, are now widely available. You can use them separately or in pairs. These convenient carriers clip on to a back rack and maintain a rectangular shape capable of holding a loaded grocery bag. They typically have a compression strap to stabilize the load.

Hip Packs. Even though it is usually best to get the weight off the rider and on to the bicycle, there are times on day tours when a low-profile hip pack comes in handy. Any type of fanny or lumbar pack will do, although some models cater more to the needs of cyclists.

Features and Options - Panniers and Packs

Here are several features and options you should be familiar with when comparing pack and pannier systems for your bicycle.

Attachment Device. This is the mechanism that holds the packs or panniers in place while riding. Panniers that are not held firmly may bounce off the rack and become damaged, or even cause damage by slipping into the spokes. There are several different methods employed, from simple hooks and elastic straps to Velcro® fasteners and more sophisticated locking devices. Look for carriers featuring quick-release attachment systems that hold the load securely in all riding conditions.

Internal Frame or Stiffeners. Most packs and panniers have some type of stiffener so they maintain their shape when mounted. Stiffeners consist of rigid plastic sheets or lightweight metal rods placed in strategic locations such as the back, sides and bottom of the carrier.

Exterior Pockets. Rear panniers, rack packs and handlebar packs typically have some combination of exterior pockets for stowing gear that you need quick access to. Front panniers, if they have pockets at all, have only low-profile zippered slots or a mesh pouch for carrying wet gear.

Zippers. The zippers on packs and panniers for bicycles are similar to those found on backpacks. Look for sturdy zippers that give good access to stowed gear, have convenient zipper pulls, and feature protective weather flaps to seal out moisture.

Internal Dividers. Some packs and panniers have internal dividers to aid in organizing your touring gear. On a few models, these dividers are removeable or adjustable.

Compression Straps. As with backpacks, these adjustable nylon straps help to stabilize the load as the amount of gear you carry changes.

Reflective Tape. Strips of reflective tape are always included on packs and panniers to make the cycle and rider more visible at night. Occasionally, you'll find rear panniers and back racks with plastic reflectors bolted through to the fabric on the back surface.

Map Holder. Some handlebar packs come with provisions for an optional weatherproof, clear plastic map holder that sits on top facing the rider. A sealed pouch holds the map of your choice in good view while riding, always a convenience for those touring in unfamiliar territory.

Raincovers. Panniers are water-resistant, but will eventually soak through during extended periods of rain. Many manufacturers offer waterproof raincovers for their front or rear panniers to protect your gear in these conditions.

Construction and Operation - Panniers and Packs

The materials and methods of construction for bicycle packs and panniers is similar to the actual bag part of backpacks and daypacks. Most models are constructed of Cordura® nylon for its durability and abrasion resistance. The framework of panniers is much less sophisticated than backpacks since they are generally much smaller individual load carriers and are not trying to conform to something as demanding as the human back. The framework usually consists of thin, rigid plastic panels that slip into pockets in the back, sides and bottom of the bag. Some models also use thin metal rods or stiff

PVC welting around the perimeter. Stiffness in the back is essential since the pannier must not be able to curve around the rack struts and risk getting caught in the spokes. Excessive use can cause this to happen on lesser quality models.

Bicycle load carriers must be designed so they have low wind resistance, don't interfere with the pedals or motion of the rider, and can be packed so the weight rides low and as near the centerline of the frame and wheels as possible. That's why most front panniers are small, sleek and have no large external pockets, and why rear panniers are relatively thin, ride low on the frame, and are sloped away from the rider's leg to give maximum carrying capacity while maintaining adequate heel clearance.

The method of attachment is another important design criteria. Panniers typically have a three-point attachment system on the back surface. Two points at the top hang the pannier from the top of a rack, the third point toward the bottom holds the pannier firmly in position by attaching to a special clip mounted on one of the rack braze-ons on the frame. Panniers are held away from the chain and wheels by the vertical struts of the front and rear racks. The ability to adequately support panniers should be considered when selecting bicycle racks. On less expensive models, the top attachment points are nothing more than plastic-coated metal hooks, and the bottom attachment point is simply an elastic bungee strap with a ring at the end. More elaborate attachment methods are used on better quality models, including cinch straps, positive locks and quick-release mechanisms.

Author's Recommendations - Panniers and Packs

The type and size of load carriers you choose depends on how, where, and for how long you plan to travel. Smaller, less sophisticated gear is fine for near home or on short tours. High-quality, high-capacity packs and panniers are called for on long-distance adventures. Since the goal is to balance your total load, it's best to choose a combination of carriers that distributes the weight evenly and makes sense for the way you travel. Since increased durability and performance always cost more, you'll need to look at your total equipment budget and see how much those things are worth to you. Don't sacrifice getting a good bicycle just so you can afford top of the line panniers. Conversely, don't spend so much on your bike that there's no money left over for adequate load carriers. Try to keep things in proper perspective when outfitting.

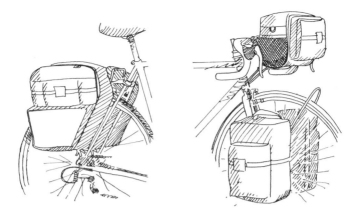

Madden's Gran Tour rear panniers, Simplex front panniers, and Superlite handlebar pack.

Road Touring Gear. Panniers are the first thing to select when outfitting for a bicycle tour. You'll always have a set of rear panniers as the foundation of your system, while front panniers are more a matter of personal preference. There are several possible gear combinations to choose from. Most serious tourists with equally serious loads choose a set of moderate-to-large rear panniers, a set of small-to-moderate front panniers, a small handlebar pack, and a rear rack pack or duffel to carry bulky items. This makes the most sense from the viewpoint of weight distribution and balance, but it means you have multiple racks and panniers to buy, and lots of gear to lug around and keep track of anytime it's off the bike (unless you can load most of it in your rack duffel).

An alternative solution is to skip the front panniers and buy slightly larger rear panniers and a larger handlebar pack. While not as good in terms of load distribution, this setup is less expensive to outfit for and more convenient to carry off the bike. A rack pack or duffel can be included as needed. The obvious disadvantage to this arrangement is that it places more weight on the back of the bike and often too much weight on the handlebars for good steering control. You can get away with it, however, if your total load is moderate and your riding is limited to paved roads. Our family has covered thousands of miles by bicycle with only rear panniers, a handlebar pack and miscellaneous camping gear strapped to the back rack.

A handlebar pack is nice for carrying items you want to get to in a hurry. Just make certain not to over pack and place too much weight on the handlebars. Look for models that have a shoulder strap (good for carrying off the bike) and an optional map holder on top. Rack packs and duffels are great for stowing all your individual pieces of gear, both on and off the bicycle. Rack packs are compact and easily secured to the back rack. They are the best choice for carrying a limited amount of bulky travel gear, as well as water bottles, a bike pump and other loose items when you are off the bike. Since most rack packs are too short to carry sleeping pads and tents, duffels strapped across the panniers make more sense for bicycle camping. Seat and frame packs are useful load carriers, but are not a necessity for touring. If they appeal to you, and you have specific gear in mind that you'd like to place in those areas for quick access, by all means include them in your inventory.

Off-Road Load Carriers. Load carriers for off-road travel are slightly different. These packs and panniers must be more durable and compact, and more securely fastened to the bike for travel over rough terrain. Weight distribution is also much more important. Carrying too much weight on the back of a bike can have disastrous results when climbing hills, just as too much weight up front can be harmful on steep descents. Steering control must be maintained at all times off the road, so even more care must be taken when loading handlebar packs and front panniers. A good set-up for off-road travel is a moderate-sized set of rear panniers, a small set of front panniers, a small handlebar pack, a frame pack, and a rack pack or duffel. The frame pack is optional, and the front panniers can be eliminated if your total load is modest.

Panniers for Children. You obviously have to keep the load light for young cyclists, yet allowing them to carry their own gear gives them a great sense of freedom and accomplishment. By carrying their own personal items, they don't have to go to a parent every time they want something. One way to satisfy them while easing their load and controlling costs is to mount smaller front panniers as rear panniers on their bicycle. These work just fine, even for longer tours, until they reach age 12 or 13 and are able to carry a larger load. Most kids enjoy having a handlebar pack for sleeping toys, a snack and other personal items. You can also fill up their handlebar pack with lightweight, bulky items such as the toiletries kit, the first aid kit or toilet paper.

Include a Daypack. No matter how committed you are to bicycle travel, there's always room for explorations on foot along the way to, or once you've arrived at, your destination. Walking and day-hiking are perfect complementary forms of exercise for cyclists, and many points of interest can only be reached on foot, so make sure to include a comfortable daypack in your inventory. The trend among quality pannier manufacturers is to offer a models that convert to daypacks, eliminating the need to carry an additional piece of gear (see the Innovative Product in this section).

Costs. Pack and pannier systems range from $50 to $120 for a set of front panniers, $75 to $175 for a set of rear panniers, $15 to $35 for handlebar packs, $35 to $55 for rack packs and duffels, and $12 to $30 for seat and frame packs. Reasonably priced packs and panniers are available from Novara, Kangaroo Baggs, Outbound and Performance. As with backpacks, higher prices indicate lighter weight, higher performance and greater durability. High performance gear is available from Blackburn, Cannondale, Cyclesmith, Lone Peak, Madden, and Overland.

Listed below are some of the best bicycle packs and panniers currently on the market. Only front and rear panniers, handlebar packs and rack packs are covered. Many seat and frame pack models are also offered by these and other manufacturers.

Author's Recommendations - Pannier and Pack Systems

Brand	Model	Type	Style	Capacity (cu. in.)
Avenir	Rear Panniers	rear panniers	T/M	1600
Blackburn	BRP 1850	rear panniers	T	1850
Blackburn	BFP 1600	front panniers	T	1600
Blackburn	MTN R 1800	rear panniers	M	1850
Blackburn	MTN F 1600	front panniers	M	1600
Blackburn	RB 500	rack pack	T/M	500
Blackburn	UF 300	handlebar pack	T/M	300
Cannondale	Overland*	rear panniers	T/M	2500
Cannondale	Expander	front or rear panniers	T/M	800-1600
Cannondale	Caboose	rack pack	T/M	N/A
Cannondale	Crossroads	handlebar pack	T/M	560
Cannondale	Trestle	handlebar pack	T/M	560
Cyclesmith	Apex*	front or rear pannier	T/M	2195
Cyclesmith	Mountain*	front or rear pannier	T/M	1254
Cyclesmith	Summit*	rack pack	T/M	1020
Cyclesmith	Quatro*	handlebar/frame pack	T/M	353
Kangaroo Baggs	Explorer	rear panniers	T	3600
Kangaroo Baggs	Ridge Runner	front or rear panniers	T/M	1900
Kangaroo Baggs	Bikemor**	front or rear panniers	T/M	1750
L.L. Bean	Bike Duffel	rack duffel	T/M	800
Lone Peak	P-300	rear panniers	T/M	2000
Lone Peak	P-400	rear panniers	T/M	2500
Lone Peak	P-099	front panniers	T/M	1500
Lone Peak	P-100	front panniers	T/M	2000

Lone Peak	PD-200*	pannier and daypack	T/M	1230
Lone Peak	RD-330	rack duffel	T/M	1420
Lone Peak	RP-600	rack pack	T/M	760
Lone Peak	H-050	handlebar pack	M	330
Lone Peak	H-100	handlebar pack	T	660
Madden	Gran Tour	rear panniers	T	2350
Madden	Trans Am	rear panniers	T	2550
Madden	Simplex	front panniers	T	1350
Madden	Buzzard	rear panniers	T/M	3000
Madden	Baby Buzzard	front or rear panniers	T/M	2250
Madden	Badger	front panniers	T/M	1350
Madden	Lizard	front panniers	T/M	1650
Madden	Rough Rider	front or rear panniers	M	1900 and 2150
Madden	Rough Rider*	rack pack and daypack	M	1250
Madden	Superlite	handlebar pack	T	600
Madden	Mountain Lite	handlebar pack	M	600
Mountain Mind'd	Meridian	rear panniers	M	2300
Mountain Mind'd	Paragon	rear panniers	T/M	2200
Mountain Mind'd	Abominable Exp.	rear panniers	T/M	3050
Mountain Mind'd	Solitaire	front panniers	T/M	1650
Novara	Explorer	rear panniers	T	3200
Novara	Nomad	front panniers	T	1500
Novara	Rack Trunk	rack pack	T/M	909
Novara	Deluxe	handlebar pack	T	463
Novara	Mountain	handlebar pack	M	360
Outbound	Hightour	rear panniers	T	2120
Outbound	Malahat	rear panniers	M	2100
Outbound	Rally	rack pack	T/M	680
Outbound	Quest	handlebar pack	T/M	200
Overland	Chaos Crag	rear panniers	T/M	2630
Overland	Little Butte	front or rear panniers	T/M	1568
Overland	Doe Mill	front or rear panniers	T/M	1697
Overland	Rack Trunk	rack pack	T/M	758
Performance	Deluxe	rear panniers	T	2400
Performance	Standard	front or rear panniers	T/M	1300
Performance	Deluxe	rack duffel	T/M	432
Performance	Deluxe	handlebar pack	T	750
Performance	ATB	handlebar pack	M	130
Specialized	Sandbag	front or rear panniers	T/M	1017-1342
Specialized	Windbag	front or rear pannier	T/M	808
Specialized	Velotrunk II	rack pack	T/M	580
Trek	Backpack*	pannier and backpack	T/M	N/A
vauDe	Pannier Central	rear panniers	T	2320
vauDe	Pannier Lot	rear panniers	T/M	2320-3172
vauDe	Pannier	front panniers	T/M	976
vauDe	MB Rucksack*	pannier and backpack	M	732
vauDe	Rucksack Cicle*	pannier and backpack	T/M	915
vauDe	Rucksack Loire*	rack pack and rucksack	T/M	1038
vauDe	Bag Vigan	handlebar pack	T	336

*These models convert to a daypack for use off the bicycle.
**Made exclusively for Campmor. STYLE: Touring=T, Mountain=M

Innovation - Panniers that Convert to Backpacks

I've always been fascinated by products capable of serving more than one purpose. Active travelers engage in multiple outdoor activities, yet their carrying capacity is limited, so they appreciate versatile products allowing them to do more with less. Bicycling packs and panniers have traditionally been strictly for use on the bike, forcing travelers to improvise or include an additional pack for carrying gear comfortably off the bike. Fortunately, this trend is changing rapidly with the introduction of convertible bike packs and panniers. Lone Peak, Madden, Trek and a few others have taken the approach of modifying one of their rear pannier or rack pack models so it converts to a comfortable daypack. These solid performers are sold individually so the rider can carry one convertible pannier and one less expensive regular model.

Cyclesmith has taken a completely different tack, opting to produce an entire line of bicycle packs and panniers that not only work equally well on or off the bike, but also have the ability to attach to each other. This modular approach with a multitude of possible load-carrying combinations is similar to Mountainsmith's pack systems. It gives the active traveler a chance to get serious about other modes of exploration, or to simply have better control of his gear anytime it's off the bike. Cyclesmith's convertible panniers are well conceived backpacks, capable of carrying a sizeable load comfortably. They are all sold individually so you can customize your own system. The large *Apex* pannier/backpack could be the foundation of a total touring package. The *Mountain* lumbar pack, the *Summit* rack pack, and the *Quatro* and *Cinco* handlebar packs can be mounted to the *Apex* to expand the load capacity. Many other combinations are possible. Chances are you'll pay a good bit more for a complete pack and pannier set-up than you would from other manufacturers, but for those who require versatility on the road, this gear warrants investigation.

Cyclesmith's Apex, shown as a bike pannier, as a single backpack and as a base pack for attaching smaller load carriers.

Specialty Bicycling Gear

- Tool and Repair Kits
- Bicycle Helmets
- Bicycling Footgear
- Bicycling Apparel

There are a few other specialty items you'll probably want to consider for bicycling. These include a proper tool and repair kit, a safety helmet, and bicycling apparel and footgear. This gear helps make the sport safer and more fun.

TOOL AND REPAIR KITS

A well-stocked tool and repair kit is essential for your cycling peace of mind. Most of the time you'll only be concerned with performing proper maintenance and fixing the occasional flat. For these situations, a basic tool kit, spare tube and patch kit tucked in a seat, frame or handlebar pack is adequate. Those who ride off the beaten track or on long-distance tours will want a more extensive kit for a greater level of self-sufficiency.

I recommend you include the following in your tool and repair kit inventory:

	Short Tours and Day Trips	Add For Longer Tours
Allen wrenches	4, 5, and 6mm	--
Sockets	8, 9, and 10mm	11, 13, and 14mm
Small crescent wrench	1	--
Flat and Phillips screwdriver	1 each	--
Lightweight tire levers	2-3	--
Patch kits	1-2	4 or more
Spare tubes	1-2	2 or more
Chain lube	1 small container	optional 2nd tube
Multi-purpose knife	1	--
Small cloth rag	1	--
Spoke wrench	--	1
Chain rivet tool	--	1
Small pliers	1	--
Metal wire	--	1 small roll
Thin nylon cord	--	10-20 feet
Duct tape	1 small roll	--
Spare fasteners	--	assortment
Spare cables	--	1 brake, 1 derailleur
Spare spokes	--	2
Teflon grease	--	1 small tube

To The Best Outdoor & Recreation Equipment   **349**

You have the choice of putting together your own kit or buying one of the pre-assembled tool kits on the market. Buying a pre-assembled kit and customizing it to suit your needs is probably the best option. Great compact tool kits are available from Cannondale, Performance, Rhode Gear, Specialized, and many other bicycle equipment suppliers.

Cannondale. Cannondale offers the compact *Ripple Grip Folding Tool* with integral allen bits, screwdrivers and a spoke wrench.

Eldi. This company offers the *Deluxe Tool Kit* which contains four open-end wrenches (8-15mm), allen bits, screwdrivers, cone and spoke wrenches, tire levers and pliers.

Eldi's Deluxe Tool Kit

L.L. Bean. L.L. Bean offers the *Wedge Seat Bag* complete with a basic tool kit that includes a T-handle, socket set, allen and screwdriver bits, tire levers, and a patch kit. They also offer the *Bike Tool Kit*, a more comprehensive kit in a convenient, zippered carrying case.

Performance. Their tool kits include the *Pocket Mate*, a folding assortment of allen bits and screwdrivers; the *Versa-T* tool set, a combination of allen bits, sockets, and screwdrivers that stow in a compact T-shaped handle; the *Tool Box*, similar to the *Versa-T* but with integral spoke wrench and chain rivet tool; the *Standard* tool kit containing a good assortment of tools in a handy zippered carrying case; and the *Deluxe* tool kit that has most everything you'd need for a long tour stored in a folding fabric tool pouch.

Rhode Gear. Rhode Gear offers the *Tool Pod II*, a clever light-weight package containing allen bits, screwdrivers, socket wrenches, a tire lever, and a spoke wrench.

Specialized. Their *Gear Pak* tool kit fits under the seat with a quick-release mechanism that allows it to be removed and clipped to your belt for use off the bike. Included are sockets, allen bits, screwdrivers, tire levers, and a foam tool holder.

Costs. Expect to pay $10 to $15 for a small, folding tool kit, $20 to $25 for a moderate-size kit, and up to $35 for an all-inclusive tool and repair kit for longer bicycle tours.

BICYCLE HELMETS

Everyone acknowledges the safety benefit of wearing a helmet while riding. Even close to home, at relatively slow speeds, an unprotected fall can lead to severe head injuries. Ultimately the choice is yours, but using a helmet on a bicycle as conscientiously as a seat belt in a car gives you a fighting chance against serious injury. There are some additional benefits that help make the idea of wearing a helmet more palatable. Their aerodynamic shape increases your speed and they actually keep your head cooler by forcing air to move faster as it travels through carefully designed cooling slots in the top surface, drawing off heat from your head. Once you make the decision that a helmet is a necessity, not an accessory, all you need to do is select a model that has the right combination of function, fashion and price.

Review of Generic Types - Bicycle Helmets

Bicycling helmets are typically categorized by the type of outer shell material, by their intended use (touring, mountain biking or competition), and by the intended user (adult, child or infant). All helmets use virtually the same type of expanded foam for the inner liner, but there are various outer shell materials used, either soft shell, hard shell, or the more recently developed thin shell models. Soft shell models use only a stretch fabric cover over the inner foam shell; the hard shell models have a hard plastic cover that completely surrounds the helmet exterior; and the thin shell models bond a very thin layer of rigid material to the foam.

Author's Recommendations - Bicycle Helmets

Certification. The first thing to look for are models with ANSI (American National Standards Institute) and the more stringent SNELL (Memorial Foundation) certifications that should be placed on the inside of the helmet. These certifications assure you that the helmet offers adequate protection. Don't think you have to pay big money for big protection. There are many reasonably-priced children's and adult models that have ANSI and SNELL approval. Price is much more likely to be influenced by style and weight.

Rhode Gear's Airlight

Function. The next decision is whether to go with a helmet that has a hard shell or soft shell. Both types have an inner lining of EPS (expanded polystyrene foam) that actually does the job of absorbing shock upon impact. The lightweight soft shell models put a smooth finish on the exterior surface of the foam and leave it at that. An optional Lycra® fabric cover can be added to improve the appearance and protect the foam from UV radiation and road debris. Hard shell models weigh a bit more, but in general are more durable and will last longer. The hard plastic shell not only protects the foam from UV and flying objects, it also protects it from all the small dents and dings resulting from normal use. The recent introduction of a very thin, yet hard, shell coating has made a third choice called thin shells available to cyclists. Thin shells have the advantages of the hard shell helmets with the reduced weight of soft shell models.

Fashion. So much for the function, now you can concentrate on fashion and the price you can afford. Manufacturers make a big deal about their individual style. In reality, although there are some subtle differences, all helmets for general use are shaped pretty much the same. Truly different aerodynamic, lightweight designs become evident in the upper end of the market, which caters primarily to competitive cyclists.

Fabric Covers. On soft shell helmets the biggest difference in style isn't from helmet shape, but from the design of the fabric cover. Covers come standard with many models or are available as an option. Choose one that appeals to your sense of aesthetics, and if you get tired of that color or style, you can replace it for under $10.

Children. Helmets for infants and young children typically have added protection for the sides and back of the head. They must also be lightweight, have adequate cooling, and have multiple-size internal fit pads for a growing child. A good example of a well-designed child's helmet is the *Rhodester III* from Rhode Gear. Other good, reasonably-priced child models are available from Advent Air, Avenir, Bell, Giro, L.L. Bean, Specialized, and Troxel.

Adjusting the Fit. Most helmets come with a variety of foam sizing pads so you can get a good fit for your head. This is especially important for growing children; pads can be simply exchanged as needed. A helmet won't do its job if it isn't secured properly. The helmet should fit comfortably, yet snugly against your head. Snap the strap and give your head a shake; if the helmet stays in place the fit is pretty good. Now level the helmet so it covers your forehead.

Adjust the straps so the fore and aft straps join just below and a bit forward of the ear. Pull the straps until the helmet feels secure. When you have it correctly adjusted, the helmet should slide no more than an inch or so in any direction.

Costs. Approved helmets for young children range from around $30-$50. Equivalent models for adults cost around $35-$65. You should be able to find a certified helmet that is right for your needs in this price range. Higher priced helmets cater to those seeking high performance. Listed below are some of the most practical helmets currently on the market.

Innovation - Helmet Cover with Visor

Helmets are great for protecting your head, but as a hat they leave something to be desired. Cycling exposes your face to the sun's rays for hours on end, yet with standard helmets you have no way of shading it properly. This must be because helmets are designed more for competition than touring, and the needs of travelers are often ignored. Performance has at least improved the situation with their *Helmet Visor Cover*. This fabric cover incorporates a neoprene visor to shield your eyes from glare and protect your nose and face from sunburn. It comes in blue and white, or red and white, with a black visor, costs around $7 and fits over most thin shell and standard EPS helmets.

Author's Recommendations - ANSI and SNELL Approved Helmets

Brand	Model	Type	Fabric Cover	Wgt. (oz.)
Advent Air	Air	soft shell	standard	8.0
Advent Air	Aero	thin shell	no	11.0
Advent Air	Child	thin shell, infant	no	8.0
Avenir	Event	thin shell	no	10.0
Avenir	Youth	thin shell	no	8.0
Avenir	Infant	thin shell	no	10.0
Bell	Quest	soft shell	standard	N/A
Bell	V-1	thin shell	no	8.8
Bell	Streetrider	thin shell, child	no	9.7
Giro	Hardtop	hard shell	no	9.0
L.L. Bean	Super-Lite	soft shell	standard	8.0
L.L. Bean	Air-Lite	thin shell	no	8.0
L.L. Bean	Air-Lite Child	thin shell	no	9.0
Performance	Micro Tec	thin shell	no	9.0
Performance	Aero II	soft shell	standard	8.5
Rhode Gear	Airlight	thin shell	no	8.5

Rhode Gear	Ultralight III	soft shell	standard	8.5
Rhode Gear	Rhode Runner	soft shell	optional	6.0
Rhode Gear	Rhodester III	soft shell	no	6.5
Specialized	Air Force II	hard shell	no	8.5
Specialized	Mega Force	hard shell	· no	8.5
Trek	Micro	thin shell	no	8.0
Trek	Child	hard shell	no	N/A
Troxel	Coronado	hard shell	no	10.0
Troxel	Elan CX II	soft shell	standard	8.5
Troxel	Niño	hard shell	no	10.0
Vetta	Testarossa	thin shell	no	8.0
Vetta	Testarossa SL	soft shell	optional	7.0

BICYCLING FOOTGEAR

Having proper cycling shoes can make a big difference to performance and comfort when riding. Unlike standard walking, running or hiking shoes, these models are specially made for the sport of bicycling. In general, this type of footgear has a sleek, lightweight design, a lower profile for easy entry and exit from toe clips, a stiffer sole for transmitting more power to the pedal, and some means of gripping the pedal integrated into the sole to prevent slipping.

Review of Generic Types - Bicycling Footgear

Bicycling footgear is categorized according to intended use, either racing, touring or mountain bicycling, as well as by the type of sole employed and the type of pedal used.

By Intended Use. Different shoes are available for the three major cycling sports of racing, touring and mountain biking.

• *Racing.* Racing shoes are the lightest and have a sleek profile for smooth pedaling. They also have either external cleats for grabbing the pedal cage or mating with the relatively new clipless pedals, or the newer recessed cleats for mating with special clipless pedals. External cleats make most racing shoes only appropriate for use while on the bike.

• *Touring.* Touring shoes focus less on all-out performance and more on versatility both on and off the bike. Touring shoes are designed more like low-top trail shoes. They still have low profiles for use with toe clips and stiff, pedal-gripping soles, but usually lack the external cleats of a racing shoe. Shimano's *SPD* recessed cleat system, however, has been very popular with touring cyclists (see the Innovative Product in this section).

• *Mountain.* Shoes for the sport of mountain biking are similar to touring shoes only with higher uppers for added protection, stiffer soles and more aggressive treads. They also are designed to be compatible with toe clips.

By Sole Type. There are two different types of soles used on cycling shoes.

• *Cleated.* Racing shoes employ tiny cleats on the sole for grabbing the pedal firmly and efficiently, or for slipping into one of the clipless pedal system. Cleated shoes are mostly for racers seeking high-performance.

• *Non-cleated.* This is a more versatile type for general touring, traveling and adventuring. They have no external cleats to make off-bike walking a nightmare.

By Pedal Type. Cycling shoes also can be used with one of two types of pedal systems: standard pedals that employ toe clips, and those with locking cleats that don't require toe clips for efficient pedaling.

• *Clip Type.* This describes any standard type of pedal that accommodates toe clips and straps.

• *Clipless.* These types of pedals incorporate a locking system to mate with specially designed cycling shoes. This system holds the foot firmly in place without the use of toe clips, yet allows the foot to exit easily with a simple twisting motion. Clipless pedals are matched to shoe soles, either the external cleat variety or the more versatile new type with a recessed cleat that allows for comfortable walking (see the Innovative Product in this section). These pedals are smaller than regular pedals since they don't rely on a large surface area for gripping, making them less suitable for use with standard shoes.

Author's Recommendations - Bicycling Footgear

There is no doubt about the advantages of a good cycling shoe for increased comfort and performance. The questions that arise are how much performance do you really need, and how much are you willing to spend for it. Since this book focuses on outdoor recreation, it seems appropriate to recommend sacrificing some performance in favor of increased versatility. In doing this, we can immediately eliminate the cycling shoes with external cleats made for clipless pedals, and the standard models made for toe clips that perform poorly when walking. If you do wish to investigate these types of cycling shoes, go to your local cycling shop for more information. Good standard cycling shoes that give some extra pedaling efficiency, yet are comfortable enough for walking and light hiking are a good choice when pursuing multiple sports. Choose from the various models made for use with standard toe clips, or any shoe with a recessed cleat that is compatible with Shimano's *SPD* clipless pedal system.

Keep in mind that the clipless pedals are great for increasing pedaling efficiency, but are totally unsuitable for use without the cleated shoes. This might be a consideration on a long-distance tour where replacement shoes might not be available. The pedals can always be replaced with a standard type if necessary.

If you can't find a cycling shoe that suits your needs for general travel, chances are a standard rugged walker or lightweight trail shoe such will do the job admirably. Check out the models offered by manufacturers listed under Footgear in the Personal Gear section.

Costs. While there are high-performance competition cycling shoes on the market approaching $200 a pair, you should be able to find something suitable for touring or mountain use for the same price as a good trail or cross-training shoe. That places them in the $50 to $100 range, including all of the standard and Shimano *SPD* models listed below, except for the Shimano *SH-M200* ($140), and the Time *Action* ($140), which offer a higher level of performance. Added to this is the cost of the special pedals ($100 to $150) if you choose a clipless system. The shoe models below are considered among the most practical specialty cycling shoes on the market for active travelers.

Author's Recommendations - Bicycling Shoes For Active Travelers

Brand	Model	Type	Sizes	Description
Avocet	Cross 40	T	m, f	leather/mesh, non-cleated, tc type
Avocet	Cross 50	M	m, f	leather/mesh, non-cleated, tc type
Diadora	Cross Terrain	T	m, f	leather/mesh, non-cleated, tc type
Diadora	ATX All Trax	M	m, f	leather/mesh, Shim. SPD compatible
Diadora	Poggio	M	m, f	leather/mesh, non-cleated, tc type
Nike	Terramac ATB	M	m, f	leather/mesh, non-cleated, tc type
Nike	Cross Terrain	M	m, f	leather/mesh, non-cleated, tc type
Performance	Pacer Plus	T	m, f	leather/mesh, non-cleated, tc type
Performance	Durango	M	m, f	leather/mesh, Shim. SPD compatible
Shimano	SH-M050	T	m, f	leather/mesh, recess'd cleat, clipless
Shimano	SH-M030	T	m, f	leather/mesh, recess'd cleat, clipless
Shimano	SH-M100	M	m, f	leather/mesh, recess'd cleat, clipless
Shimano	SH-M100	M	m, f	leather/mesh, recess'd cleat, clipless

Specialized	Wild Dog	T	m, f	leather/mesh, non-cleated, tc type
Specialized	Trail Force	M	m, f	leather/mesh, non-cleated, tc type
Time	Start	T	m, f	leather/mesh, recess'd cleat, clipless
Time	Action	T	m, f	leather/mesh, recess'd cleat, clipless

DESCRIPTION: tc=toe clip type

Innovation - Recessed-Cleat Cycling Shoes

Every once in a while an innovative idea comes along that changes an industry forever. The new recessed-cleat cycling shoes and pedal systems may have done just that for cycling shoes. With the introduction of these systems, clipless pedals have become practical for all cyclists, especially for active travelers who want one pair of shoes to serve both cycling and walking/light hiking needs. There are two systems of clipless pedals and recessed-cleat shoes, Shimano's *SPD* system and Time's *TWT* system. Some other cycling shoe manufacturers offer models compatible with the *SPD* pedals.

Shimano's *SPD* system is currently more affordable and their shoes are more suitable for rugged walking and hiking. The system incorporates two-sided pedals for easy access and shoes with a recessed cleat hidden beneath a plastic cover plate. The plate is removed when cycling and secured in place for cleat protection when walking. The shoes and pedals come in several styles to choose from, either racing, touring or mountain use.

Shimano's SH-M050

BICYCLING APPAREL

Even if you're a casual rider there are also some specialty clothing items you may want to consider for use when bicycling. Bicycling clothing is generally close-fitting and comfortable, offering little wind resistance while transporting moisture and protecting critical areas of your body from chafing. Serious cyclists are aware of, and take full advantage of, the benefits of this specialty apparel. Active travelers less concerned with performance can decide for themselves whether the unique style and additional costs of specialty clothing are for them. The three items I recommend you consider are bicycling shorts, shirts and gloves.

Bicycling Shorts

Bicycling shorts have a distinctive look about them—long legs and a clingy, close fit. Developed for competition, these shorts are now widely used by all types of cyclists. While their fashion takes some getting used to, their function is instantly agreeable. Bicycling shorts have little resistance to the air stream or comfortable leg motion, but more importantly they typically incorporate a padded chamois section in the crotch to protect against chafing on the bicycle seat. Even if you've never considered bicycling shorts for your type of riding, this feature alone is worth investigation. Other nice features found in many cycling shorts include an angled waistline for full coverage in the back and no bunching of material in the front when you're in a cycling position, as well as elastic thigh bands to prevent the legs from riding up.

Don't feel you have to switch to cycling shorts to ride a bicycle. Regular shorts are fine for short tours and casual riding. If you do decide to try them out, great bicycling shorts are available for between $20 to $50, including models offered by Cannondale, Descente, Hind, L.L. Bean, Nike, Novara (REI), Schnaubelt, and Trek. Performance also offers their *Cotton Duck Cycling Shorts* for cyclists who want padded comfort in a more conventional style short.

Bicycling Shirts

In my opinion, bicycling shirts are less of a priority for active travelers. They do have some distinct advantages, and you'll probably want to include one in your inventory for serious cycling, but, for most recreational riders, any comfortable shirt without an irritating collar will be just fine.

The design features of cycling shirts are the close-fitting, pullover style for low wind resistance and comfort, and the stretch material with moisture wicking properties for freedom of movement and the ability to stay warm and dry. If you do choose to try out a bicycling shirt, my advice to travelers carrying a limited selection of clothing is to find a reasonably-priced model in a style you feel comfortable with either on or off the bike. Good models are offered by many manufacturers, including those listed above under bicycling shorts.

Bicycling Gloves

The last apparel item for consideration is bicycling gloves. Long hours in the saddle can have your hands feeling numb and sore, particularly if you travel on rough roads and trails. Cycling gloves provide just the right amount of protection. They come in a variety of styles, from fingerless models for most types of riding to full-fingered versions for serious off-road use.

Gloves aren't a necessity by any means. In fact, they've become more of a fashion item than a necessity. For short tours and casual riding, you can get along just fine without them. If your bicycle takes you further afield, or if you just want additional hand protection, I recommend you check out cycling gloves at your local equipment supplier. Good models are available in the $12 to $24 range.

VI CANOEING & KAYAKING

The outdoor activities of canoeing and kayaking are worlds apart from their land-based counterparts of backpacking and bicycling. They offer adventurers a unique opportunity to experience the freedom and excitement of self-propelled boat travel. There are so many waterways waiting to be explored; once on them you are free to travel where you wish, unrestricted by man-made roads, tracks and trails. Canoes and kayaks allow for an additional degree of independence by their shallow draft, portability and relatively low cost. You are able to explore places where larger, deeper draft vessels can't go, usually for a fraction of the cost.

Excitement is another component of water travel. Part of it comes from being subject to the forces of nature in an alien environment, one that can be gentle and forgiving or unpredictable and demanding. On the water, your perspective is vastly different from being on land. Even at rest you are in motion, suspended on the surface of a moving fluid. Perceptions of your surroundings are invariably altered for the better. Wildlife flourishes in and on the water, keeping you in touch with nature. Remote areas become larger than life, simultaneously vast and accessible. Congested urban areas show only their good side as you engage in the rhythms of life in a busy harbor or waterway. Almost anywhere looks inviting when viewed from the confines of a boat's cockpit.

As canoeing and kayaking have many similarities, it seems appropriate to include them in the same section of this book. Both sports use narrow, low-profile watercraft, powered by one or two paddlers, for various types of water sports and explorations. In fact, some of the recent designs of decked canoes and open cockpit kayaks look noticeably alike. All canoes and kayaks are relatively lightweight and portable, allowing them to be easily carried on the tops of cars or by hand over short distances from one waterway to another. Many of the major features, options and specialty equipment are also very similar, if not exactly the same. Becoming proficient at one of these activities develops skills that will help you master the other.

On close inspection, however, the boats, equipment and paddling techniques of canoeing and kayaking are quite distinct. Each type of craft has its strengths and weaknesses, just as each sport has its proponents and loyal followers. Most water sports enthusiasts find themselves developing an affinity for one over the other based on where they travel, what type of gear they want to take, and how they prefer to paddle.

Canoes and kayaks allow you to get away from it all for a few hours, a few days or for weeks at a time. They can be used for sport, for fun and recreation, and as a satisfyingly self-sufficient mode of travel. They are wonderful adventure travel vehicles for families. Children love the pace of travel, the gentle motion, and water as an ever-present source of entertainment. Parents are enamored with the increased carrying capacity and the ease with which children can participate in a fun, outdoor activity.

There are a few things you'll have to adapt to when switching from hiking or backpacking to water travel. First of all the expense of outfitting can be much greater, although the cost to outfit a group for canoeing or kayaking is probably less than for long-distance bicycle travel. Another consideration is that while canoes and kayaks allow you to move through the water with ease, your mobility out of the water is limited. Kayaks and canoes can be carried short distances by hand, but a car with a good set of roof racks is necessary for covering longer stretches. With a canoe or kayak in tow, you may feel a bit tied down at times, but this is usually more than compensated for by the wonderful places you can explore and the copious amounts of gear you can comfortably carry with these crafts.

The first equipment to investigate for these sports are the boats themselves. There are hundreds of different canoes and kayaks currently on the market, each with slightly different elements of design, construction and performance. Taking the time to select the right model for your needs can be fun and also yield high dividends.

Canoes

- Recreational Canoes
- Tripping Canoes
- Cruising Canoes
- Whitewater Canoes

Canoes are the more familiar of these two types of watercraft. Many of us grew up with canoes at camp, lakeside resorts, or available for use from someone in the family. There are good reasons for their popularity. In general, canoes are affordable, good load carriers, forgiving and relatively easy to use. Most models are well suited for use in ponds, lakes, rivers, and other protected bodies of water, while some are capable of handling whitewater rivers or open bodies of water. With their open-deck design and good initial stability, everyone can have a fun time on the water. One of the differences between canoes and kayaks is the paddling technique. Canoes typically use single-bladed paddles for stroking on one side of the boat at a time, while kayaks use double-bladed paddles for alternating sides with each stroke.

Review of Generic Types - Canoes

There are quite a few different types of canoes, differentiated by their intended use, the intended number of paddlers, and the various hull materials employed.

By Intended Number of Paddlers. Canoes for recreation normally have one or two paddlers. "Solo" canoes have characteristics such as a centrally-located seat so they can easily (with a little practice) be handled by one person, while "tandem" canoes are intended for use by two paddlers. In addition to the actual paddlers, most canoes can accommodate a passenger or two depending on their size and weight. In the past, some Native American and French Voyageur expedition canoes were meant to be propelled by large groups of paddlers. These models exist today only in the form of large competition canoes.

By Hull Material. Another way canoes are categorized is by the material used to make the hull. One of the most interesting aspects of canoes is the amazing diversity of construction materials used, everything from traditional wood and canvas to rotomolded polypropylene and Kevlar-reinforced plastic.

By Intended Use. This carries the most weight when describing canoe type since the intended use greatly influences the design and construction of a particular model. In general, canoes currently marketed fall into one or more of the following categories: recreational, tripping, cruising, whitewater, utility, or competition. These classifications and their interpretations described below are somewhat subjective and not meant as hard and fast distinctions. Subtle variations exist, and many models are purposefully designed to have characteristics from several different categories. If the designer is clever, he'll achieve this without compromising too much.

• *Recreational.* Recreational canoes are intended for having a good time on the water, in a variety of conditions and at a relaxed pace. They have only a moderate load capacity and level of performance, can be fairly heavy, but score high in stability, safety, low cost and low maintenance. Many of the models found in scout camps, rental places and backyards are recreational canoes.

• *Tripping.* Tripping canoes are ruggedly built for varied conditions, capable of transporting a large load over long distances. Their design and construction inspire the confidence to face the challenges of traveling to remote areas. This broad category covers everything from moderate-sized touring models to larger expedition canoes.

• *Cruising.* In a cruising canoe, roughly equivalent to a sport touring bicycle, you'll experience the pure joy of paddling as you cover large distances with minimal effort. While longer tours and rougher waters are not out of the question, in general this type of craft's streamlined form and reduced weight are best suited for traveling light and fast on relatively protected waters.

• *Whitewater.* Whitewater conditions place quite different demands on the design and construction of a canoe. These specialty models must be dry, responsive and highly maneuverable. The attributes that allow them to perform well down turbulent rivers also make them less suited for long tours over flat waters. There are whitewater designs available for all types of river conditions.

• *Utility.* If your idea of canoeing is a means of getting you and your gear to the best hunting or fishing grounds, a utility canoe is for you. Also called a sport canoe, these models sacrifice performance for durability and load-carrying capacity. With their inherent stability, even the family dog will feel at home in one of these canoes.

• *Competition.* Every recreational activity seems to have a competitive element, and canoeing is no exception. There are many classes of competitive canoeing, for both flat and whitewater. Light weight and maximum performance are revered above all else, regardless of intended water conditions.

Features and Options - Canoes

Once you understand the basic differences between canoe types you should get familiar with the myriad features and options you'll find when researching and comparing individual models.

Hull Configurations. As with generic types, there are general hull configurations that are useful for discussion, but which don't always hold fast when describing a particular model. Subtle nuances of design mean there can be a great deal of variation between models labeled as having the same hull type. With this in mind, here are a few terms you'll hear floating around the canoe showroom:

• *Hull Length.* Straightforward as it seems, hull length can be crucial in design. Length is described in one of two ways, as LOA (length overall) or LWL (length at water line). In general, longer hulls are faster, track better, handle more load, and give more glide with less effort, while shorter hulls are easier for smaller or solo travelers, or when paddling in tight spaces.

• *Hull Width.* Since a streamlined shape is usually desirable, canoe hull widths are kept to a minimum while maintaining the desired degree of stability and load capacity. Canoe width can be defined as the "beam" (dimension at the widest point) or the width at the gunwale (dimension at the widest point across the gunwales). Only on straight-sided craft are the beam and distance across the gunwales the same. Equally important as width are the hull's fullness (how quickly the hull widens from bow and stern) and its symmetry (where the widest point is located).

• *Keel Line.* This describes the shape of a canoe's hull bottom as it runs from bow to stern. The amount of "rocker" in a keel line describes the keel line's curvature toward the ends. A straight keel line with little or no rocker is used when the emphasis is on speed and tracking ability, as in tripping and cruising designs. In general, as rocker increases so does maneuverability, usually at the expense of speed and tracking. Maneuverability is also highly dependent on overall length.

• *Shear Line.* The shear line describes the upper line of a canoe's hull. This is influenced by a variety of design factors, including design load capacity and bow and stern profiles.

• *Stem Profile.* A double-ended boat such as a canoe has a bow stem and a stern stem, the actual structural pieces at the extreme ends. The profile of these stems varies considerably. They can be raked forward (bow) or aft (stern), recurved (so they come in on themselves at the top), or relatively straight up and down.

• *Entry Line.* The sharpness of the bow is called the entry line. The sharper the entry line the better the paddling efficiency and tracking ability.

• *Symmetry.* As viewed from above, a hull can be symmetrical (the same shape either side of the midpoint) or asymmetrical (the widest part is aft of the midpoint). Symmetrical hulls are predictable and balance the smoothness of bow and stern movement. Asymmetrical hulls place the widest point (and therefore the hull's fullness) slightly aft, gaining efficiency while favoring the bow's smoothness over the stern.

• *Cross Section.* If you imagine cutting a canoe anywhere along its length and viewing it end on, you would be looking at its cross section. The shape of the cross section determines things such as hull width and fullness, and greatly influences freeboard, performance and stability of the canoe. Below waterline, the shape of the hull's cross section can be flat bottom, shallow V, shallow arch or round bottom. The shallow V and shallow arch configurations offer the best mix of stability and performance. Above waterline, the cross section can have flare (increase in dimension toward the gunwales) or tumblehome (curve inboard slightly toward the gunwales). Flare helps deflect waves and resist capsizing, while tumblehome allows for easier and more efficient paddling.

Gunwales. These are protective trims of wood, aluminum or synthetic material on the upper portion of the hull. Gunwales add strength and rigidity, and provide some protection from bumping into docks and other immovable objects.

Deck. The deck provides some type of solid covering over the canoe cockpit. Most recreational canoes have only small token deck areas at the bow and stern for added strength and to provide a hand hold for carrying.

Tie-Down Loops. These consist of small yet strong loops of line at the bow and stern for securing the canoe to the shore or a cartop.

Carry Handles. Convenient handles are typically located at the bow and stern decks for carrying the canoe right side up. Carry handles can be incorporated into molded plastic decks or separate bars on wooden deck models.

Thwarts. Thwarts are thin braces of metal or wood connecting the gunwales that provide necessary support and rigidity away from the bow and stern. Thwarts can be supplanted by seat and kneeling braces, a portage yoke, carry handles or larger fore and aft decks.

Portage Yoke. Located at the balance point midway along the canoe, this specialty thwart is sculpted to fit on your shoulders when carrying a canoe upside down single-handedly. These come standard on some models, as an option on others.

Seats. Most canoes have a seat for each paddler. The exact seat location and height varies slightly with the canoe design and manufacturer's preference. They are typically either suspended from the gunwales (hanging) or mounted to the hull sides (riveted) at the desired depth and locations for each specific model. Some manufacturers offer sliding seats so you can adjust the boat's trim for specific water conditions (level for flatwater, bow up for waves). Solo canoes usually have one seat just aft of center, while tandems have one at each end with an additional center seat on some models for solo paddling. If you'd rather kneel when paddling, the seat height should be a little higher so your legs fit under the seat more easily.

Braces. Some canoes come equipped with foot braces, either small foot rests or a single bar extending across the canoe at foot level, similar to a thwart. Thighbraces are similar in function, only for bracing your thighs when kneeling in a canoe. Footbraces and thighbraces allow you to transfer more of your paddling energy into canoe motion.

Paddles. Paddles for canoes come in all shapes and sizes. They vary by material (traditional wood or aluminum/plastic), length (sized for your height and arm length), blade size and shape (determined by intended paddling conditions and individual preference), and shaft type (either straight or bent).

Canoe Pole. Some manufacturers offer long canoe poles for poling rather than paddling your canoe in shallow water.

Spray Cover. Spray covers supply a flexible fabric deck material for keeping water out of the canoe cockpit. These can be partial covers used only in the bow for flying spray or more complete covers for use in less protected waters.

Skid Plates. Skid plates for protecting plastic hulls are available from some manufacturers. They typically come two to a kit, one for the bow and one for the stern.

Flotation. Air-filled flotation bags are available for whitewater canoeists or for serious expeditions in open water. These bags are designed for use in the bow, stern and midship. They protect the canoe and gear by providing flotation in the event of a capsize.

Sail Kit. Simple sail rigs are offered by many manufacturers. This is a great option for fun on a lake or for canoeists traveling long distances in relatively open water.

Rowing Kit. You can also turn your canoe into a rowing craft with the addition of an optional rowing kit. For just puttering around, inexpensive clamp-on oarlocks, a set of oars and an impro-vised seat are all you need. A kit for serious rowers, such as the model offered by Old Town, consists of a foot brace and a one-piece molded seat and outriggers with oarlocks that extend out over the gunwales.

Anchor Outrigger. A small bow outrigger for handling a light anchor is offered for some sport canoes. Anchoring is convenient for fishing or other activities where you want to stay in one place for a while. The outrigger protects the sides of the canoe and provides a convenient place to store the anchor.

Motor Mount. Some canoeists want to occasionally use a small motor to power their craft. A motor mount bolts to the canoe and allows for easy mounting of small electric or gasoline-fueled engines.

Construction and Operation - Canoes

In this section we'll take a closer look at canoe design, the materials and construction methods used, as well as a brief look at the proper operating techniques.

Design Criteria. Every canoe has its own unique set of charac-teristics given to it by the designer. In the previous section, we discussed some of the hull configurations that are considered features of the canoe. Now we can investigate the actual design criteria used to determine those features along with the generic type of the canoe.

Designers start with a broad generic category of canoe in mind and a list of desirable characteristics they'd like to incorporate, things such as speed, tracking ability, paddling efficiency, stability and maneuverability. They realize that every design is a compromise, and that in favoring some characteristics they'll be sacrificing others to some degree. The goal for each model is to choose the right combination of characteristics, then build and market it for the right price.

Potential buyers can benefit from a basic understanding of what the designer was attempting to do when creating a particular model. Some important design characteristics, and how they relate to each other and the final product, are described below.

• *Cost.* This is the bottom line for every product a company hopes to market, but not necessarily the controlling factor in design. A given price range determines the type of design and the potential materials and construction methods used. This, in turn, often limits a designer's ability to incorporate some characteristics.

• *Strength and Durability vs. Weight and Cost.* This is the classic designer's struggle with any outdoor product, to get the right combination of these factors. Adding strength and durability inevitably adds either weight, cost, or both. The strength of a given model depends on the overall design, as well as the materials and construction methods used. There are several different types of strength, such as long-term durability, stiffness and resistance to bending, or resistance to puncture, cracking, denting or buckling. The required strength varies with each generic type of canoe and each individual model.

Recreational canoes represent a compromise, a balance of moderate strength, weight and cost. Tripping canoes must be stronger to withstand more extreme paddling conditions, hard use and sizeable loads. For most tripping canoes this results in additional weight and cost over the recreational canoe. Higher-priced models using more sophisticated materials and construction techniques provide additional strength and durability without increasing weight. Reasonably-priced cruising and whitewater canoes sacrifice some strength for lighter weight and better maneuverability. Again, higher-priced models have light weight and maneuverability without sacrificing strength.

• *Stability vs. Efficiency and Performance.* This is another classic struggle, one that is unique to designers of boats and other vehicles. No one would deny that stability is a desirable characteristic in a boat, but it should be carefully weighed with considerations of speed, glide (distance the canoe travels with one paddle stroke), paddling efficiency (how well the canoe translates paddle motion into motion through the water) and maneuverability (how quickly the canoe can be turned) for each model.

There are two distinct types of stability for boats: initial (or primary) and final (or secondary). Initial stability can be thought of as the steadiness when the canoe is upright in flat water. Final stability is the ultimate resistance to capsizing when the canoe is tipped or riding in waves. A hull with a flat bottom has great initial stability but poor final stability and performance. Hulls with shallow arch or shallow V hulls have less initial stability but have better final stability and much better performance.

Designers of recreational and utility canoes need to favor stability, the former to allow for all levels of paddlers and the latter to provide a stable platform for photography, fishing and hunting. On tripping canoes, the emphasis is a little less on stability and a little more on speed, glide, tracking ability, and paddling efficiency. Cruising canoes should have even better speed and paddling efficiency, while whitewater canoes should ultimately be maneuverable.

• *Load Capacity vs. Performance and Windage.* The designer of a canoe must also wrestle with the desired load capacity and how that affects the boat's performance and tendency to be driven off course by the wind. Load capacity (also called "burden") has no true industry standard, but is commonly defined as the total weight (including paddlers and passengers) a canoe can carry while maintaining 6" of freeboard. Freeboard is generally accepted as the height from the water to the top of the gunwales at the canoe's center. Load capacity is relative to the cross section of the hull. It increases with the draft (maximum depth below waterline), width, fullness (how quickly the hull widens from the bow and stern), and height of the hull sides. Unfortunately, these things also increase windage and tend to decrease performance. The designer must reconcile these considerations for each particular model.

Designers of recreational canoes try to strike a balance, usually by compromising the three in equal measure. For tripping canoes, they favor load capacity, while trying to maintain moderately good performance and low windage. Cruising and whitewater canoes generally sacrifice load capacity for performance and low windage, while utility canoes favor load capacity over performance.

- *Maneuverability vs. Speed and Tracking Ability.* A good canoe designer tries to get the best combination of maneuverability, speed and tracking ability for any given model. A longer, more straight keel line and more streamlined hull, found on tripping and touring canoes, increases speed and tracking ability. A shorter waterline with increased rocker in the keel line, found in whitewater and some cruising canoes, increases maneuverability.

Hull Materials and Methods of Construction. You'll find there are many different materials and their associated methods of construction used in modern canoe hulls. They all have their strengths and weaknesses. Manufacturers usually choose one or two that work well for them and the market they are catering to.

- *Aluminum.* These canoes are made by stretch-forming sheets of aluminum, then stiffening the assembly with a series of ribs and a small keel. The small keel has little to do with tracking ability, which is mostly influenced by hull design. In general, aluminum canoes are inexpensive, durable, forgiving, and require little maintenance. Their weaknesses include being noisy, cold, heavy, and relatively poor performers due to construction limitations.

- *FRP (Fiber-Reinforced Plastic).* These composite canoes are made from multiple layers of fiberglass, Kevlar, or other woven synthetic fabrics bonded with plastic resins. FRP canoes are strong and lend themselves to more sophisticated shapes. Higher-priced models can be very lightweight when Kevlar or other exotic materials are used.

- *Royalex®.* This proprietary material from Uniroyal is actually a laminate of ABS plastic sheets with vinyl skins on the outside and an ABS core material in the middle. In an oven, the foam core expands, forming closed-cell flotation. The laminate is removed from the oven and vacuum-drawn into the desired hull shape. The advantages of this type of canoe are its positive flotation, low noise and maintenance, warmth and its ability to distort in shape temporarily without permanent damage.

- *RPF (Rotomolded Polyethylene and Foam).* In this process a structural mold is placed in a heated oven. Polyethylene powder is added, melted by the heat, then distributed by the motion of the mold being rotated and rocked. Several more powder dumpings create a buoyant center core and an abrasion-resistant outer layer. In this process, the polyethylene can be either linear or cross-linked. Linear polyethylene can be recycled easily and is easier to repair, yet is less stiff and abrasion resistant. Cross-linked polyethylene is difficult to repair and recycle, yet is stiffer and more durable. Canoes constructed by the RPF method are quiet, easy to repair, inherently buoyant, easy to maintain and can be temporarily distorted without permanent damage.

• *Wood.* This type of hull construction requires a high level of craftsmanship and creates a beautiful hull. Wood planks are attached to wood ribs bent over a hull form in either a smooth skin or lapstrake fashion. The craftsmanship comes from the fact that the wood planks are expected to fit perfectly to create a watertight seal. This type of construction gets high marks for its ease of repair, long life and ability to be recycled, yet the increased cost and maintenance make this type of canoe easier to admire than own.

• *Wood and Canvas.* This traditional method of construction creates an equally handsome and easy-to-repair canoe hull. It consists of bending wood ribs over the desired hull form, then attaching wood planks to complete the structural hull. Canvas is stretched over the hull and sealed with filler and paint to add protection and make it watertight. Aesthetic appeal, ecologically sound construction techniques and long life are in its favor; increased cost, weight and maintenance are its weaknesses.

• *Wood Strip.* An extremely versatile, efficient, and popular method of wood construction, the wood strip combines the beauty of wood and the strength and ease of construction of FRP laminates. Wood strips are laid over appropriately-shaped hull forms, then covered with a protective layer of fiberglass and resin. When dry, the rigid unfinished hull is removed from the form and another layer of glass and resin is placed on the inside. The main advantages are its ease of construction, strength, light weight and less maintenance than other wood canoes.

Loading Techniques. You can enhance your canoe's inherent stability and performance by using proper techniques when loading paddlers, passengers and gear. Everything that goes into a canoe, as well as where is goes and how much it weighs, affects how a canoe performs.

• *Load Capacity.* You should first take into account the suggested maximum load capacity for a given canoe. Since this actually varies with water and weather conditions, experience of the paddlers, and handling characteristics of the canoe, most manufacturers prefer to give a roughly equivalent rating in terms of the amount of stationary weight a canoe can hold and still maintain 6" of freeboard. This rating is best used only as a comparison between models. Under most conditions, your total load should be substantially less. A canoe supplier can help determine safe loads for you, your canoe and where you intend to travel.

• *Paddlers.* You and your paddling companion will most often represent the largest load, and as such your placement greatly influences stability and handling. Paddler location, fore and aft, affects boat trim (how the boat sits with respect to the waterline), while paddler location up and down influences stability (the canoe's steadiness). In most canoes, the location of the seats and their height off the bilge are fixed by the manufacturer for best general performance. Lowering the paddlers weight increases stability, so many canoes are fitted with lowered seats and footbraces. Kneeling down with your legs under a slightly higher seat accomplishes the same thing. Some manufacturers offer to set the seat height to your specifications, while others provide sliding seats that can be adjusted fore and aft to compensate for varying passenger weight and gear loads.

• *Passengers.* Passengers should sit low in the canoe with their weight centered on the keel line. Standing, sudden movements or exaggerated leaning over the side is definitely to be avoided. Passenger fore and aft placement should be determined by the desired trim, although it's more often a function of where there's a comfortable thwart to lean against. A portable canoe seat with a backrest solves that problem. The boat should be trimmed level for good speed and tracking in flat water, with a higher bow for turbulent water, and with a pronounced bow rise for waves and open water.

• *Gear.* Gear can be stowed after the paddler and passenger locations are set. Keep the heavy items down low and evenly distributed fore and aft and from side to side. Lash your gear down securely so it doesn't shift or go overboard in rough conditions. A sudden shift in weight can upset the balance of the canoe before the paddlers can compensate. Special canoe packs and waterproof bags are available to make loading easier and keep your gear dry.

Choosing Paddles. Proper paddle selection and use have as much to do with how well your canoe performs as how it is designed. Paddles come in a variety of materials, shapes and sizes. Choosing the right one can be confusing to the novice paddler, but it becomes easier once you understand what to look for.

- *Parts of the Paddle.* The major parts of a canoe paddle are the "top grip" (at the upper end), the "shaft" (in the middle), and the "blade" (at the lower end). The shaft has an "upper" and "lower" part, as well as a "lower grip" position (this varies slightly with each paddler). The blade is the part that enters the water, providing the thrust to move the canoe. Blade "shoulders" slope away from the paddle throat, the "edges" are located on the sides, and the blade "tip" is the part at the bottom end. A paddle's "throat" is where the shaft and blade meet, while the "spine" is a continuation of the shaft that provides strength and a point of attachment for the blade.

- *Paddle Material.* Paddles for recreation and travel are most often made of wood because of its strength, flexibility and appearance. Common woods used are Sitka spruce, western red cedar and ash. Some wood paddles have a clear fiberglass coating for additional strength. Less expensive paddles have aluminum handles and plastic blades, serviceable and low in maintenance yet lacking in general appeal.

- *Paddle Length.* Experts agree that shaft length, not overall length, is the more important dimension when sizing a paddle. You can envision why when you consider that when paddling properly the entire paddle blade should be in the water and the entire shaft should be out. This means the length of shaft determines arm placement and comfort of stroke, while blade length determines the ease and generated thrust of each stroke. A good rule of thumb is to select a shaft as long as the distance from your shoulder to the waterline when sitting in the canoe. Your equipment supplier can help you determine this measurement.

- *Blade Shape.* Blades have different shapes for specific uses. Flat, medium-length, medium-width blades offer more long-term comfort for cruising, touring and tripping. Wider, longer blades, or ones with a spooned surface, allow you to get more power with each stroke, but can wear you out quickly. Wide blades are especially useful when paddling in aerated whitewater. Longer blades require more effort to raise them out of the water. In general, a spooned blade increases paddling efficiency.

• *Straight or Bent-Shaft.* Paddles come in straight or bent-shaft versions. Straight paddles have been around since canoeing began, and serve novices and recreational canoeists well. Bent-shaft paddles are mostly intended for those seeking greater performance on flat water (as opposed to whitewater rivers). A 10- to 12-degree bend where the shaft meets the blade increases efficiency by allowing the blade to remain vertical through the stroke.

Brief Review of Paddling Techniques. There's enough to say about paddling techniques to fill an entire book. Learning to paddle correctly takes time and patience, and you'll undoubtedly continue to perfect your style for as long as you canoe. My advice to novices is to read what you can find on the subject, take a few lessons from someone who knows what they are doing, then get out in your canoe and practice. With time, the awkwardness of the motion will turn into smooth, efficient strokes, and you'll gain proficiency in controlling the canoe. To get a good start, select the proper paddle and find a comfortable paddling position.

• *Sitting vs. Kneeling.* It's best to be in a comfortable position for paddling. Most people prefer sitting, and canoe seats are located to best serve a variety of paddlers. If you have adjustable seats then position them for your needs. Some canoeists feel the traditional kneeling posture is better for them. A kneel-sit position allows you to kneel while resting your bottom on the edge of the seat. This is a stable, comfortable stance.

• *Using Braces and Kneeling Pads.* Regardless of whether you sit or kneel, braces can steady you and help to transmit your full paddling effort into canoe motion. They help you to relax, reducing fatigue on long journeys. Foot braces are used with the sitting position, thigh braces are used for the kneel-sit position. Kneeling pads in the bottom of the boat are designed to offer comfort when using the latter paddling position. For even more control when paddling solo in an open boat, try the *Saddle* from Perception. Made of rugged polypropylene, this one-piece unit provides a comfortable seat as well as terrific knee, thigh and foot bracing. The *Saddle* is easy to install and marketed wherever Perception equipment is sold.

Author's Recommendations - Canoes

The canoe is such a versatile craft, it's almost a shame to limit it to one type of activity. For most of us, there is a temptation to take full advantage of what a canoe offers by using it for many things—relaxing on a quiet river or pond, working out to stay in shape, photographing wildlife, family recreation at the lake, weekend camping, or longer expeditions. Most people only buy one or two canoes in a lifetime. Unless you need a single-purpose design for a specific trip or type of activity, I recommend choosing a canoe that is versatile.

Choose a Primary and Secondary Activity. Versatility should not mean mediocrity. Find a canoe that performs best for one chosen activity, yet also performs well for at least one other area. It should be clear that I'm not recommending a boat that does a lot of things moderately well, yet doesn't excel at any of them. Buy that type and you might end up with a mediocre boat that's a constant disappointment. I feel your selection should really shine when pursuing your primary activity, and be well suited for at least one other activity. Admittedly, it's still somewhat of a compromise, but in the end you'll get the most enjoyment out of your investment.

The first thing to do is decide which activity has priority. It can be your favorite activity or the one that you do most often. If you're lucky, these will be the same. Many canoeists choose touring/tripping as their primary activity, since that represents a good middle ground in canoe design requiring high levels of speed, performance, handling, and safety. Once the primary activity has been decided, choose a secondary activity that suits you, such as general recreation, cruising, whitewater river running or utility and sport. Now all you have to do is find a canoe that satisfies these demands.

Old Town's Canadienne

Choose a Tandem or Solo Model. This should be your next decision, whether to get a tandem or solo canoe. Tandems are by far the most popular. My advice to single paddlers is to try to find a responsive, slightly shorter tandem canoe that also performs well as a solo, possibly one that has a third seat for that use. This gives you the most versatility. True solo canoes have only one seat in the center. They are very easy for one person to handle, and you can always take a passenger along, but you may find it limiting if another paddler comes into your life.

Choose Length and Load Capacity. Length and load capacity will be strongly influenced by your choice of a primary and secondary activity. If touring/tripping is your primary activity, look for models with a 16'6" to 18'6" length and a 6" freeboard capacity of around 1,000 to 1,200 pounds. If cruising is your secondary activity, choose a tripping model that tends to be more streamlined and fun to paddle. If your second activity is going on extended expeditions, look for a model that favors strength and load capacity. If you occasionally want to paddle your canoe solo, look for slightly shorter models with a similar reduction in load capacity. Canoes that are strictly solo models for cruising, touring and tripping can be anywhere from 14' to 16'6" in length with a 6" freeboard capacity of around 700 to 900 pounds.

Choose a Hull Material and Price Range. As with the basic canoe type, choose a hull material that best suits your primary, then secondary, choice of activity. Your choice of material will affect the cost, so make sure it's within your budget. If the primary activity is touring or tripping the best materials are probably FRP (either fiberglass cloth or Kevlar), Royalex® or wood. These score the highest if you average their ratings of strength, stiffness, weight savings, ease of paddling, cost, impact and abrasion resistance, flexibility and repairability. Wood strip is potentially the lightest type of wood construction, as well as the best suited for home builders. RPF and aluminum have some good characteristics and can also be considered as long as the design, construction, and cost of the model you purchase compensates

Navarro's Otter

for the lower overall performance ratings of this material. Old Town's *Discovery* canoes, using cross-linked polyethylene in the RPF method, are a good example. They are well designed and constructed and sell for a fair price. The cross-linked RPF gives these boats good abrasion resistance and allows them to float even when filled with water. RPF is used more extensively in kayak hulls since their closed-deck design is better suited to the material.

Weight should be a controlling factor in your decision. Paddling, portaging or just lifting the canoe onto the cartop is so much easier with a light canoe. Wood strip canoes can be very light, as can FRP models that incorporate Kevlar and other exotic materials, especially when you skip the optional Gel-coat. On one popular touring/tripping canoe currently on the market the weight varies between 40 and 68 pounds depending on materials used. As reduced weight is often reflected in higher prices, you'll have to limit the selection to models you can afford.

A Touch of Wood. It's hard to deny the fact that wooden canoes are beautiful. Their appeal goes beyond aesthetics; they represent a simplicity and level of craftsmanship missing in many aspects of modern life. The initial cost and yearly maintenance on wooden boats, however, can be prohibitive to many canoeists. Don't despair, as there's an alternative to a completely wooden boat. Many manufacturers of FRP or plastic boats offer wood trim packages including gunwales, decks, thwarts, and seats. If this doesn't satisfy you, try one of the wood finish canoes from Stowe Canoe and Snowshoe Company (Mansfield Canoes) or Navarro (all models). Both manufacturers make reasonably-priced canoes that combine the beauty and strength of wood with the practicality of fiberglass. On these boats, in addition to a standard wood trim package, thin strips of wood are fitted crosswise on the inside of the hull in an alternating pattern—one piece that goes from gunwale to gunwale, one piece that just spans the bilge. The result is an attractive canoe with solid wood floor and alternating strips of wood running up the sides like ribs. The wood is then glassed over to protect it and add strength. Mid-Canada Fiberglass offers a similar wood finish boat (the *Mirage*) with cedar-reinforcing ribs bonded on the inside of an FRP hull.

For Traveling Abroad. If you have the desire to canoe abroad you have two choices, either carry a portable canoe with you or rent one at your destination. Portable canoes can be great fun and allow you to get out on the water when and where you like. Just make certain this is what you want before purchasing. These models can be more expensive, inevitably sacrifice some performance for portability, and can create quite a load if you're trying to travel light (for more information on portable boats, see the Innovative Product in the section on Kayaks).

Renting is a good option for occasional use at various chosen destinations. It also allows you to try out various designs before buying, whether abroad or near home. Rentals are usually available at good canoeing spots, allowing you the freedom to travel as you wish without being burdened with the extra bulk and weight. The cost of renting can add up quickly, so bringing your own canoe is usually better for extended use.

Costs. Canoes cost anywhere from $400 to over $3,000. If you simply want a versatile recreational model, you'll be able to find something suitable at the lower end of the spectrum. For a good quality touring, tripping, or cruising canoe you should expect to spend $600 to $1,200. Manufacturers of FRP canoes often have fiberglass models in the upper end of the $500 to $1,000 range and their equivalents in Kevlar or other lightweight materials somewhere in the $1,000 to $2,000 range. There are some good wooden canoes in the $1,000 to $2,000 range, although many canoes handcrafted from wood are over $2,000.

There are literally hundreds of canoe models to choose from. Listed on the following pages are some of the most versatile, reasonably-priced canoes suitable for day use, weekend camping or extended tripping in water conditions that vary from lakes and open water to river running and non-technical whitewater.

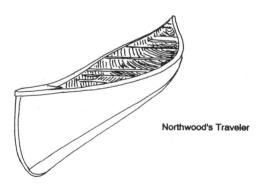

Northwood's Traveler

Author's Recommendations - Tripping/Touring Canoes ($500-$1000)

Brand	Model	Length	Type	Hull	Wgt. (lbs)
Allagash	Lite	16'6"	T	FRP	55-57
Allagash	Endurance*	16'	S/T	FRP	65
Bluewater	Saugeen	15'	S/T	FRP	65
Dagger	Reflection	15', 16'	S/T	RX	56-66
Dagger	Venture	17'	T	RX	67-80
Gillies	Scotian	17'	T	FRP	64
Hoefgen	Sport	17'	T	FRP	70
Hoefgen	Cargo	18'	T	FRP	68
Mansfield	Champlain	16', 17'	S/T	FRP/WO	66-78
Mansfield	Prospector	16'	S/T	FRP/WO	70
Mad River	Liberty*	14'8"	S	FRP	42
Mad River	Malecite*	16'6"	S/T	FRP	62
Mid-Canada	Elite*	14', 16'	S/T	FRP	40-50
Mid-Canada	Tripper*	16'	S/T	FRP	75
Mid-Canada	Adventurer*	17'	T	FRP	89
Mohawk	Nova	16'	S/T	FRP or RX	66-73
Mohawk	Nova	17'	T	FRP or RX	46-69
Mohawk	Blazer	17'4"	T	FRP	75
Nature Bound	Whisper II	16'	S/T	FRP	55
Nature Bound	St. Croix	17'3"	T	FRP	75
Nova Craft	Haida*	17'	T	FRP	72
Nova Craft	Prospector*	16', 17'	S/T, T	FRP	68-72
Navarro	Otter	14'6", 16'	S, S/T	FRP/WO	58, 64
Navarro	Loon	16', 17'	T	FRP/WO	63, 66
Old Town	Discovery 169	16'9"	T	RPF	74, 83
Old Town	Penobscot	15, 17'	S,S/T, T	RX	49-75
Old Town	Tripper	17'2"	T	RX	80
Quicksilver Mfrg.	Whitew't'r Expr's	17'2"	T	FRP	78
Quicksilver Mfrg.	Nahanni River	18'	T	FRP	82
Sawyer	X-17*	17'	T	FRP	72
Sawyer	Family 17	17'	T	FRP	74
Swift	Quetico*	16'	S	FRP	58
Swift	Madawaska	16'4"	S/T	FRP, RX	66
Swift	Keewaydin*	17'	T	FRP	66
Vermont Canoe	Northeaster	16'4"	S/T	FRP	70
Wenonah	Rendezvous*	15'6"	S	FRP	35-53
Wenonah	Spirit II*	17'	T	FRP	69
Wenonah	Sundowner*	17', 18'	T	FRP	65, 68
Wenonah	Itasca*	19'	T	FRP	71
Western Canoeing	Prospector*	14', 16'	S, S/T	FRP	54-76
Western Canoeing	Ranger 17*	17'	T	FRP	74
Western Canoeing	Tripper*	17'6"	T	FRP	72
Western Canoeing	Sea Clipper*	18'6"	T	FRP	74

These canoes are offered in Kevlar or other lightweight materials.
TYPE: S=solo, T=tandem. HULL: FRP=fiber-reinforced plastic, RX=Royalex, WO=wood.

Author's Recommendations - Tripping/Touring Canoes ($1000-$2000)

Brand	Model	Length	Type	Hull	Wgt. (lbs)
Bell	North Bay	17'11"	T	FRP	60
Bell	Fusion	16'6"	S/T	FRP	45

Bluewater	Saugeen	16'6", 17'	T	FRP	50-80
Bluewater	Jensen Tripper	17'	T	FRP	56-62
Curtis	Dragonfly Ruby	14'6"	S	FRP	49
Curtis	Northstar Ruby	16'	S	FRP	69
Easy Rider	Ouzel Series	15'8"-17'	S/T	RX, FRP	58-78
Easy Rider	Heron 17*	17'	T	FRP	68
Kruger	Kruger Cruiser	18'6"	T	FRP	80
Lincoln Paddle-Lite	5.3 Meter*	17'5"	T	FRP	54
Mad River	Eclipse	16'2"	S/T	RX	65
Mad River	Revelation	17'	T	RX	75
Mad River	Explorer Series*	16'4"	S/T	FRP, RX	50-72
Mad River	Lamoille*	18'4"	T	FRP	60-75
Mid-Canada	Mirage*	15'2"	S/T	FRP/WO	55
Navarro	Otter	14'6", 16'	S, S/T	FRP/WO	58, 64
Navarro	Loon	16', 17'	T	FRP/WO	63, 66
Old Town	Canadienne*	16', 17'2"	S/T, T	FRP	59, 69
Trailhead	Prospector	16', 17'	S/T, T	FRP,WC,RX	50-65
Wenonah	Odyssey	18'6"	T	FRP	45-57
Wenonah	Ithasca	19'	T	FRP	52-71
Wenonah	Encounter	17'	S	FRP	38
Western Canoeing	Whitewater II	18'6"	T	FRP	52-74
Whitesell	Long Haul	17'4"	T	RX	72
Voyageur	Tripper	16'	S/T	FRP	66
Voyageur	Norwester	17'	T	FRP	78

*These canoes are offered in Kevlar or other lightweight materials.
TYPE: S=solo, T=tandem. HULL: FRP=fiber-reinforced plastic, RX=Royalex, WO=wood, WC=wood/canvas.

Author's Recommendations - Wooden Touring Canoes ($1500-$3000)

Brand	Model	Length	Type	Hull	Wgt. (lbs)
Alder Creek	Champlain	16'	S/T	WC	60
Carrying Place	Stringer Classic	15'	S/T	WC	62
Carrying Place	Wilderness Exp.	16'	S/T	WC	65
Feather	Decked Canoe	18'	T	WO/FRP	40
Heritage	Red Bird	17'6"	T	WC	54
Island Falls	Guide	16', 18'	S/T, T	WC	62, 80
Kathadin	Atkinson Trav.	17'6"	T	WO	75
Middle Path	Belle Riviere	17'	T	WO	70
Morley Cedar	Guide Series	15'-18'	S/T	WO	60-80
Northwoods	Cheemaun	15'	S/T	WC	55
Northwoods	Traveler	17'6"	T	WC	75
Old Town	OTCA	17'	S/T, T	WC	76
Old Town	Guide	20'	T	WC	104
Rheaume	Huron	18'	T	WO/FRP	82
Spencer	Algonquin	15'5"	S/T	WC	55
Spencer	Champlain	16'4"	S/T	WC	65
Stewart River	Prospector	16'	S/T	WC	65
Stewart River	Quetico	18'	T	WC	70
Woodstrip Wat'rcr'ft	Goldeneye	15'	S	WO	45
Woodstrip Wat'rcr'ft	Brant	17'	T	WO	55

Note: Many of these wooden canoes are carried by American Traders of Greenfield, MA; they claim to have the largest selection of wooden canoes in the world.
TYPE: S=solo, T=tandem. HULL: FRP=fiber-reinforced plastic, WO=wood, WC=wood/canvas.

Maintenance and Repair - Canoes

Canoes are very durable, low-maintenance pieces of equipment with little to go wrong under normal use. In fact, the folks at Western Canoeing claim that most of their repairs over the years have been due to canoes falling off of cars, having been stored improperly or damaged in whitewater. An interesting note is that hull materials requiring the highest maintenance are among the easiest to repair in the event of damage, and those requiring the least maintenance are usually more difficult to repair.

Wood. Wooden canoes with all their brightwork require a fair amount of loving care to keep them in top shape. You'll occasionally have to repair or replace the canvas on wood/canvas models. The maintenance is reduced on models that use a skin of FRP to cover the wood. Wooden boats are quite easy to repair should damage occur.

FRP. Canoes made from FRP need only an occasional touching up and refinishing of the gel-coat (the outer layer). Gel-coat patch kits are widely available. Small cracks and holes can be easily repaired. Clean the damaged area thoroughly to remove dirt, wax or grease, then sand lightly to rough the surface. New cloth and resin are then built up in layers and feathered out smoothly. Boats made with fiberglass cloth require a bit less effort to repair than those made with Kevlar® or other lightweight fabrics

Royalex®. Royalex® canoes are very durable and require almost no maintenance, yet are surprisingly easy to repair. They can be patched in similar fashion to boats constructed of FRP. Mad River Canoes offers the handy *Royalex Repair Kit*, which includes packages of repair resin, one square foot of Kevlar® cloth, sandpaper, gloves, and instructions.

Aluminum. Aluminum hulls don't take much maintenance to keep them in good condition. Minor damage can be repaired, although not easily, through the use of patches and epoxy adhesives or by welding.

RPF. Hulls made of polyethylene (either cross-linked or linear) are also extremely durable and need no real maintenance. They can lose their shape under repeated stress, however, so care should be taken during storage and transporting in hot weather. The cross-linked versions have more resistance to impact but are also much more difficult to repair. Linear polyethylene hulls can be repaired with simple plastic welding techniques.

Kayaks

- Leisure Kayaks
- Touring Kayaks
- Whitewater Kayaks

In a canoe you feel as though you are riding up high on the water. In a kayak you feel as though you are almost in the water. Canoes are most often used in protected waters; kayaks most often in open coastal conditions or whitewater. Conditions that give cause for concern in an open-decked canoe are often easily handled by a skilled paddler in a closed-deck kayak. Sitting at or near water level in a low-profile kayak makes you feel more vulnerable, yet also more aware of and in touch with your surroundings. This is both the intimidation and the appeal of kayaking.

Kayaks traditionally have been less well known than canoes, and for good reason. Most kayaks are solo models, with no room for a passenger and a limited capacity for gear. Even most tandems can't take additional passengers, so kayak use is fairly limited in a recreational setting. Kayaks also require a higher level of skill than a canoe since they often have less stability, and the possibility of rolling over in a closed-deck kayak is understandably unappealing to novices. While kayaks were first used for exploration and coastal travel, their major role in modern times has been for running rivers. The fact that relatively few people have access to good kayaking rivers has further limited kayak acceptance by the general public.

Recently, however, the sport of kayaking has enjoyed an unprecedented rise in popularity. This is mainly due to the overwhelming enthusiasm for sea kayaking and the introduction of open-deck kayaks for use in warm climates. Sea kayaks are really nothing more than stable touring models with a few modifications for open water conditions, but the concept of coastal travel in a small, highly maneuverable boat has been successfully marketed to create an entirely new sport. Open-deck kayaks, on the other hand, are a radical departure from the traditional designs. With no deck or spray skirt to crawl into, they combine the easy use of a canoe with the maneuverability and paddling technique of a kayak. These designs have raised the general awareness of kayaking tremendously, and this exciting type of watercraft now represents a growing part of the small boat market.

Many of the same design criteria, hull materials and construction methods used for canoes also apply to kayaks. To avoid repetition, some of the descriptions for kayaking make reference to the section on canoes.

Review of Generic Types - Kayaks

There are several different types of kayaks on the market, which are easily distinguished by the intended number of paddlers, the design of the deck and their intended use.

By Intended Number of Paddlers. As with canoes, kayaks come in solo and tandem models for one or more paddlers. Most tandems are set up for two paddlers, although a few, such as Baldwin Boat's *Atlantic III*, can accommodate three paddlers by incorporating a third cockpit. Kayaks are different from canoes in that they generally have less room or weight capacity for gear, rarely have extra space for passengers, and, in the case of whitewater models, are almost exclusively designed for solo paddling.

By Deck Design. There are two major types of kayaks, the traditional closed-deck designs and the newer open-deck models.

• *Closed-Deck Designs.* The notion of a closed-deck kayak with a protective waterproof skirt around the paddler was conceived in the arctic, where water temperatures and weather conditions are extreme. This type of boat works well in colder climates and in technical whitewater since it stays buoyant and keeps the paddlers dry and warm, even if temporarily capsized.

• *Open-Deck Designs.* There is really no need for a closed deck and protective skirt in warm weather and less-demanding water conditions, especially when your gear load is light. This fact has lead to the production of many "sit-on-top" models that have become popular for sport, utility, touring and recreational use.

By Intended Use. This constitutes the largest distinction between types on the market. The various categories are similar to some of those used for canoes, including recreation, touring, whitewater, and competition.

• *Whitewater.* Whitewater kayaks are intended for running rivers, where paddling for control in a moving river is very different than paddling for speed on flat water. Models are available for every conceivable type of river and water condition, from narrow and winding to broad and straight, from flat and mildly turbulent to steep and highly technical. Whitewater kayaks typically have closed decks to keep out water and rounded ends for the inevitable collisions with boulders and other river hazards. As they must be easy to control, they are generally shorter and have more rocker in the keel line than touring versions. The more technical the whitewater, the shorter and more maneuverable the kayak must be. Some whitewater kayaks are also good load carriers for extended river trips, although most kayakers prefer to have the heavy gear hauled downriver on a raft when traveling in a group.

• *Touring.* This broad category of kayak is for trip-oriented activities, covering everything from day trips to extended expeditions, from flat water and non-technical whitewater to the varied conditions of coastal tripping. As touring kayaks favor speed, tracking ability and load capacity over maneuverability, they are longer, have a flatter keel, are more streamlined, and have finer bow and stern sections for smooth entry and exit from the water. Some models have low bow and stern profiles for less sensitivity to crosswinds, while others have higher topsides and raised prows, in the traditional West Greenland style, to handle rougher sea conditions. Touring and sea kayaks are basically the same thing, varying according to the different types of paddling conditions each model is intended for. Some touring kayaks such as Aquaterra's *Spectrum*, Hydra's *Horizon* and Prijon's *Yukon Tour* also have the ability to handle moderate whitewater.

• *Leisure.* While all kayaks can be used for recreation of some type, this category represents boats intended for fun, leisure and gentle touring. As this type of craft is more stable and easier to paddle, they are widely used by outfitters for novices and local exploration. Many of the open-deck or sit-on-top models are labeled as recreation boats.

• *Competition and Specialty Use.* Boats in this category are intended for downriver and slalom racing or for specialty and competition use in whitewater. You'll often hear specialty boats referred to as play boats. Entire whitewater rodeos are held in celebration of the amazing feats these boats and their paddlers can accomplish. They are designed for specific water conditions, some favoring speed and some favoring ultimate maneuverability, but all with little regard for carrying gear.

Innovation - Portable Kayaks

Necessity is said to be the mother of invention, and the traveler's need for boats that can be taken on airplanes or in the trunks of cars has motivated several companies to invent and manufacture unique types of portable kayaks. To be portable the boats must be either folding, take-apart or inflatable. Folding boats come mostly in the form of kayaks, with packable canoes such as Pakboats' fine whitewater and touring models the exception. These craft use a folding frame of tubular metal or wood to provide the basic structure, and a flexible rubber and fabric skin/deck assembly to create a waterproof craft. They are very light and perform well on the water. Take-apart kayaks are rigid boats manufactured in sections that can be easily disassembled for transport. While not as portable as folding or inflatable boats, they do offer portability in a rigid hull. Inflatable canoes and kayaks offer an alternative to folding boats. They consist of a durable rubber skin material that has been fabricated into boat shape with sealed air chambers (typically floor and two pontoons). Inflatable canoes and kayaks can be great fun for whitewater or coastal cruising.

Folding Kayaks. One of the most well known names in folding boats is Folbot, a company that has produced folding kayaks since 1933. Their frame-and-skin models are superbly crafted of polycarbonate frame plates, anodized aluminum tubing, brass frame fittings, Hypalon® rubber skin and durable fabric decks. Folbot has one solo model, the *Aleut* (48 pounds, 12', costs around $1,100), and one tandem, the Greenland II (62 pounds, 17', costs around $1,600). Boat and paddles fold neatly into two packages for easy transport. Georgian Bay Kayak offers half a dozen good quality folding frame-and-skin kayaks in the $900 to $1,600 price range, as well as sail kits and clip-on safety sponsons. Feathercraft, Klepper, and Seavivor all offer great boats that fall somewhere in the $2,500 to $4,500 range, many with sailing and rowing options for added versatility.

Folbot's Greenland II

Take-apart Boats. Easy Rider offers several take-apart versions of their standard kayaks, including the *Beluga* and the *Eskimo 15, 17* and *22*. These boats are manufactured in two, three or four sections. The end plates where the sections fasten together take the place of what would normally be integral bulkheads. The take-apart feature adds significantly to the price of the boat, but you may find the ease of transport and storage well worth the extra money.

Inflatable Kayaks. Many manufacturers of inflatable river rafts also offer inflatable canoes and kayaks. Popular models from Aire include their self-bailing whitewater kayaks, the *Lynx I and II* (28 and 38 pounds, 10′3″ and 12′6″, foam or air floor, costs around $750 to $1,050), the new *Super Lynx* canoe/kayak (39 pounds, 14′6″, air floor, costs around $1,250), and their seaworthy touring kayaks, the *Sea Tiger I and II* (39 and 45 pounds, 16′9″ and 19′9″, costs around $1,500). Hyside manufactures a line of whitewater play boats using a state-of-the-art rockered self-bailing floor for increased maneuverability, including the *One-Person and Two-Person* kayaks (9′11″ and 12′, costs around $850 and $1,050). Other good inflatable canoes and kayaks are offered by B & A Distributing Company, Sevylor USA, and WaterWolf Products.

Aire's Seatiger

Features and Options - Kayaks

Kayaks have a host of different features and options you should be familiar with before comparing models. Many of them are similar to those found on canoes.

Hull Configurations. Kayak hulls, though similar in some ways, are quite different from canoe hulls in most aspects. They are long and streamlined like canoes, yet in general they are much narrower with lower profiles that place the paddler closer to the water. A covered deck, if used, helps to keep the paddler dry. When the paddler's weight is down low, the displacement of the boat (the volume) can be reduced yet still maintain adequate buoyancy and stability. Specific similarities and differences between kayaks and canoes are discussed below:

• *Hull Length.* You'll notice hull lengths vary considerably as with canoes. Look for shorter hulls (10 to 13 feet) on agile, whitewater boats and quite long hulls (16 to 21 feet) on long-distance, tandem touring models.

• *Hull Width.* Kayak hulls are generally much narrower than canoes. The overall width (or beam) of a kayak hull varies slightly with intended use, and is influenced by whether it is a solo or tandem model. You'll find that most hulls average around 24 to 25 inches in width, with some sporty solos as narrow as 22 inches and a few high-volume tandems with a beam of 32 inches or more. Remember, it's not just the beam that determines buoyancy and performance, it's also how quickly the hull widens (the fullness) and the overall shape.

• *Slenderness Ratio.* You'll sometimes hear this quantity used to describe a kayak hull. It represents the length at the water line divided by the width at the waterline. A typical touring kayak might have a slenderness ratio of eight to one, while a sporty whitewater model might have one closer to six to one.

• *Keel Line.* As with canoes the keel line is shaped according to the water conditions expected—straight keel line for long-distance touring boats, exaggerated rocker for technical whitewater, and somewhere in between for a combination of touring and moderate whitewater use.

• *Shear Line.* The shear line for kayaks with closed decks and single-piece construction is bound to be very different from an open-deck canoe. In many designs the shear line is flat and the decks arched with the high points along the centerline and at the cockpit for proper drainage.

• *Symmetry.* You'll find both symmetrical and asymmetrical hull shapes on kayaks. Symmetrical hulls offer the predictable and responsive handling favored by whitewater enthusiasts. Asymmetrical shapes, with the beam aft of center, allow for a smoother bow entry, desirable when touring on flat or open water.

• *Cross Section.* You'll hear references to hull cross sections that sound similar to canoes—they can have flat or shallow V bottoms, sharp (hard) or gently rounded "chines" (where the bottom meets the sides), as well as sides that are straight or have outward flare. In general, look for flat or slightly rounded bottoms and soft chines on whitewater boats requiring maneuverability, and shallow V bottoms and hard, well-defined "chines" on touring kayaks.

• *Deck Type.* Most closed-deck kayaks have either arched or peaked decks for shedding water quickly. The low deck profile of many technical whitewater models precludes the pronounced arch or peak found on most touring kayaks.

Ramcap. Sometimes available on whitewater kayaks, this tough cap is fitted to the bow to protect against damage inflicted by boulders and other obstacles.

Grab Loop. This is a small loop of nylon line at the bow and stern for carrying the kayak. It is more common on touring kayaks than shorter whitewater models.

Deck. This is the entire top surface of the kayak. Exactly where it begins and ends is sometimes difficult to discern on single-piece, molded plastic boats with rounded edges.

Deck Cleats. Found only on certain touring models, these cleats are used to secure lines and gear on the deck.

Bulkheads. Bulkheads are thin "walls" placed periodically across the boat to give it structural rigidity. Some bulkheads have cut-outs so they can provide rigidity without reducing the usable interior space of the craft. If the bulkhead has no cut-out and is sealed, the area behind it becomes a watertight compartment used for positive flotation.

Cockpit and Coaming. The cockpit is the part of the kayak where the paddlers sit. It consists of an opening in the deck surface (the size dependent on the number of paddlers) and the interior space underneath the opening. The coaming is a raised lip around the cockpit that serves to prevent water from entering the cockpit and as a point of attachment for the sprayskirt.

Seats. All kayaks have seats (one or two, depending on model), located at or near floor level so that the paddler's weight rides low.

Foot and Knee Braces. Foot and knee braces allow you to efficiently transfer your paddling energy into kayak motion or maneuverability. Without them you may be wasting energy trying to keep yourself properly positioned. Most boats come with adjustable foot braces and either standard or optional knee braces/pads. Kayak knee braces/pads are different than those for canoes. Instead of providing padding for the kneeling posture, they are positioned to give the knees a place to push against when the paddler is sitting. Touring kayaks with rudders have foot pedals that serve both as braces and as controls for steering the craft.

Foot-Operated Rudder. Only found on long-distance touring kayaks, rudders ease the paddling effort by helping to keep the kayak on course. Foot pedals are used in a push-pull motion, operating a wire linkage connected to a rudder off the stern. Some models provide a convenient mount so the rudder can rotate up and lock onto the aft deck when not in use.

Hatches. Hatches are the large (usually elliptical) openings fore and/or aft that provide access to larger stored gear. To maintain watertight integrity, hatches need to be fitted with rigid or flexible covers when paddling. These come as standard or optional equipment. Hatch covers are often held in place by elastic bungee cords.

Access Ports. Similar to hatches, only smaller, access ports are typically round holes in the deck providing easy access to smaller stored gear and provisions. They are often covered with a screw-on lid that seals tightly.

Bungee Cords. What would kayakers do without bungee cords? These useful elastic lines serve many purposes, including securing hatches, paddles and other external gear to the kayak deck.

Bilge Pumps and Self-Bailing Valves. Some method of bailing out water from the inside of the kayak is desirable. With their closed-deck design, water removal can be difficult on land, let alone on the water. A hand-operated portable or deck-mounted bilge pump is one answer. These are reliable and easy to use. Another solution is the self-bailing valves featured on some kayaks. Self-bailing valves automatically open to allow water to escape, even when underway.

Drain Plugs. Some Kayaks have removable drain plugs at the bow or stern that make draining a kayak on land a much easier proposition.

Paddles. Kayak paddles are quite different from canoe paddles. Instead of having just one blade they have two, one at each end. The blades are often angled 90 degrees from each other so the recovering blade slices through the air edge first, lowering the wind resistance and minimizing the paddling effort required.

Flotation. Some kayaks, including models with sealed bulkheads or inflated air chambers, come with positive flotation incorporated as standard equipment. For others you must purchase flotation bags as optional pieces of gear. If you're worried that the flotation bags will take up all your usable storage space, consider using combination bags that provide both dry storage and positive flotation when they are sealed and secured in place.

Compass Mount. Some touring kayaks have a special mounting place for a compass on the deck forward of the cockpit. Manufacturers can usually supply the compass as an optional piece of gear. If your kayak doesn't have a formal compass mount, one can easily be improvised.

Sprayskirt. This is a flexible fabric covering that totally covers and encloses the cockpit, making it watertight in whitewater or rough conditions. Sprayskirts have adjustable openings that fit tightly to the waist of the paddlers (one or two, depending on the model).

Cockpit Cover. Cockpit covers are convenient for paddlers who like to keep the inside of their kayak clean and dry during storage or travel. These fabric covers attach securely around the cockpit coaming.

Backstrap. Adjustable padded backstraps or backrests add control and a great deal of comfort during long stretches in a kayak. These come as standard equipment on many kayaks, and as optional equipment on others.

Fishing Rod Holder. Since fishing is a favorite activity with kayakers, fishing rod holders are readily available as optional equipment. They mount to the deck and hold a rod and reel securely in position. This allows you to fish in one location or troll while underway.

Construction and Operation - Kayaks

Once you've had a chance to familiarize yourself with the various kayak types, features and options, it's helpful to take a closer look at the design criteria, the hull materials and construction methods used for the various models currently on the market.

Design Criteria. As with canoes, every kayak has its own unique set of characteristics given to it by the designer. Earlier we discussed the hull configuration of a kayak as one of its major features. Now we can examine the actual design criteria used to determine the hull design and other features, including those for the generic type of the kayak. Since most of the material on canoe design criteria is also applicable to kayaks, only the differences will be discussed here.

• *Strength and Durability vs. Weight and Cost.* Everything said about strength, weight and cost for canoes also holds true for kayaks. One of the differences, however, is that kayaks have closed decks, cockpit coamings and sometimes internal bulkheads that automatically add stiffness to the design. This allows kayak designers to use hull materials and construction techniques a little differently. You'll find that all kayaks tend to be similar in weight per foot of boat length (around three to four pounds per foot), regardless of their generic type or overall length.

Leisure or recreational kayaks represent a compromise, a balance of moderate strength, weight and cost. Whitewater kayaks must be strong to hold up to repeated abrasion and impact loads, but they must also be light for good maneuvering, buoyancy and easy transport. Their weight is controlled somewhat by their shorter length. Touring kayaks are longer and so must be sufficiently stronger in terms of stiffness, load capacity and ability to cope with rough water conditions. As with canoes, some of the higher-priced FRP models use more sophisticated materials and construction techniques to provide additional strength and durability without increasing weight.

• *Stability vs. Efficiency and Performance.* Kayak hulls are vaguely similar in cross-section shape to canoe hulls, and as such are also judged according to their initial and final stability, their efficiency, and their maneuverability. Flat bottom, high volume hulls with rounded chines are seen mostly on whitewater kayaks since this allows for good levels of stability, maneuverability, and buoyancy when running rivers. Buoyancy is important when paddling in big, boisterous water or small, steep runs. Shallow V hulls with sharper chines are typically found on touring kayaks since they give a nice balance of initial and final stability and paddling efficiency.

• *Load Capacity vs. Performance and Windage.* The designer of a touring kayak for whitewater or open sea conditions must also wrestle with the desired load capacity and how this can affect the boat's performance and tendency to be driven off course by the wind. Load capacity increases with the boat's total displacement (volume), which is influenced by hull draft (maximum depth below waterline), width, fullness (how quickly the hull widens from the bow and stern), and height of the hull sides. Unfortunately, these things also increase windage or tend to decrease performance. The designer must reconcile these considerations for each particular model.

Designers of leisure kayaks try to strike a balance, usually by compromising the three in equal measure. For touring kayaks they favor load capacity, while trying to maintain relatively good paddling performance and low windage. Some touring models such as those in the West Greenland style have upswept ends that slice through waves, yet are more influenced by wind. Boats with lower bows don't have much windage, but also fail to protect the paddler as well in rough seas. Designers of whitewater kayaks for river running don't worry as much about load capacity and windage as they do about buoyancy and the ability to maneuver well in a variety of water conditions.

• *Maneuverability vs. Speed and Tracking Ability.* A good kayak designer tries to get the best combination of maneuverability, speed and tracking ability for any given model. The longer, more straight keel line and more streamlined hull, found on touring kayaks, increases speed and tracking ability. A shorter waterline with increased rocker in the keel line, found on whitewater models, increases maneuverability. Some models designed for touring and moderate whitewater have a nice balance of these characteristics.

Hull Materials and Methods of Construction. You'll find that the selection of kayak hull materials and their associated methods of construction differ slightly from canoes. Aluminum and Royalex are not used at all, and wood is only used in the wood strip method. The two most popular hull materials are FRP and RPF.

• *FRP (Fiber-Reinforced Plastic).* These composite kayaks are made from multiple layers of fiberglass, Kevlar or other woven synthetic fabrics bonded with plastic resins. FRP kayaks are strong and lend themselves to sophisticated shapes. Higher-priced models can be very lightweight when Kevlar or other lightweight materials are used. While a great many touring models are made of FRP, most currently available whitewater kayaks are made of either RPF or HTP due to the lack of maintenance required. The ability to recycle FRP is questionable, but the long life expectancy helps justify its use.

• *RPF (Rotomolded Polyethylene and Foam).* RPF is more commonly used for kayaks than canoes since this material lends itself well to kayak design. Closed-decks, cockpit coamings and internal bulkheads can all compensate for RPF's inherent lack of stiffness. Kayaks constructed by the RPF method use either cross-linked or linear polyethylene. Cross-linked material has better ratings in terms of strength, durability, resilience, and memory. Linear polyethylene costs less, can easily be repaired and recycled, and is reasonably durable. Recycled linear polyethylene, if used at all, is found only in secondary boat components. Virgin material is used on the hull and other parts where maximum strength is needed. The RPF process uses a heated oven to mold plastic into boats. This has environmental implications in terms of energy used and pollutants emitted into the air. Some manufacturers, such as Aquaterra with their Zylex 2 linear resins, claim their molding process emits no airborne pollutants.

• **HTP (High Performance Thermoplast).** Polyethylene is used in Prijon's proprietary blowmolding process.

Innovation - Prijon's *HTP*

HTP is the result of Prijon's unique polyethylene blowmolding process. This procedure applies pressure rather than heat to simultaneously extrude and blowmold polyethylene plastic into tough, rigid boats. The environmental implications of using HTP are impressive. Since no heat is used in the blowmolding process, the molecular structure of the plastic goes unchanged other than to become tightened. Not only are HTP materials recyclable, they can also be reused to make completely new boats. Prijon claims the material has a very long service life, and that the HTP process uses less energy, while emitting no fumes into the atmosphere, than most rotomolding operations. Prijon's U.S. distributor, Wildwasser Sport, is going one step further environmentally. They now pack their boats in reusable packing bags that can either be kept and used for transport and storage, or returned by their dealers for a full credit.

• *Wood Strip.* An extremely versatile, efficient and popular method of wood construction, this technique combines the beauty of wood with the strength and ease of construction of FRP laminates. Wood strips are laid over appropriately-shaped hull forms, then covered with a protecting layer of fiberglass and resin. When dry, the rigid unfinished hull is removed from the form and another layer of glass and resin is placed on the inside. The main advantages are ease of construction, strength, light weight and less maintenance than other wood canoes.

It should be noted that portable kayaks, described as an Innovative Product at the beginning of this section, use either frame-and-skin construction (wood, metal, or polycarbonate frames with rubber and fabric skins) or inflatable compartments made of some combination of Hypalon® rubber, PVC, nylon, polyester or urethane.

Loading Techniques. Most of the same information on loading techniques found in the canoe section also applies to kayaks, although there are several important differences. First of all, the load capacity is typically much less in a kayak for a given boat length. Kayaks are usually narrower and have a lower profile than canoes, reducing their volume and ability to carry gear. Load capacity is further reduced (although stability is increased) by placing the paddler's weight down low in the boat, sitting at or near water level with legs fully extended.

The second major difference is where the gear is carried. In a kayak the paddlers are in the middle of the boat, resulting in the static loads being carried toward the ends instead of toward the middle. Gear should be stowed fore and aft and the boat trim adjusted according to the techniques previously discussed for canoes. Since gear is accessed through the hatches it should be loaded in order of use. To compensate for the lack of storage space, most touring kayaks are equipped with bungee cords on the deck surface where waterproof gear can be lashed. It's fine to store gear on the deck, but make certain that stability is not compromised by placing too much weight up high.

There is usually not much additional room for passengers in a kayak, only set positions for paddlers. This eliminates the concern of distributing passenger loads. You also won't have to worry as much about the possibility of someone leaning out over the side since the cockpit does a nice job of confining children and other paddlers to the centerline of the boat.

Choosing Paddles. Kayaks are narrower and lower on the water than canoes, allowing for the use of a two-bladed paddle and a continuous, alternating stroke. Proper paddle selection and use have as much to do with how well your kayak performs as how it is designed. Paddles come in a variety of materials, shapes and sizes. Choosing the right one can be confusing to the novice paddler, but becomes easier once you understand what you should be looking for.

• *Parts of the Paddle.* The parts of the kayak paddle are similar to a canoe paddle, only kayak paddles are longer and have two blades, one at each end. This allows for a continuous stroke that alternates between the left and right side of the boat.

• *One-piece or Take-apart.* Kayak paddles come in either one-piece or take-apart styles. The one-piece designs are favored for whitewater use since they are stronger and more reliable (no joint to break or jam). The take-apart models are easier to stow and more versatile (they usually can be feathered or unfeathered, right- or left-hand control), and so are favored by many touring kayakers, especially as back-up paddles. Some take-apart models can accept optional canoe handle adapters (12 to 18 inches long) which allow one kayak paddle to convert to two separate canoe paddles.

• *Feathered or Unfeathered.* This describes the relationship between the two paddle blades. Unfeathered paddles have the blades mounted in the same plane. Feathered blades are set 70 to 90 degrees apart from each other. Feathering can increase paddling efficiency since the blade out of the water (the recovering blade) has less wind resistance when it travels through the air edge-first. Most paddlers use feathered blades and must therefore learn the basic twisting motion that places each blade perfectly in position with each stroke.

• *Right-Hand or Left-Hand Control.* If you opt for a feathered blade, you must also choose whether it will have right- or left-hand control. The handedness of a paddle is determined by the direction of blade feathering (which way one is twisted from the other) and describes which hand remains firm on the shaft while the other rotates to accommodate the feathered blade. The majority of kayakers, even those who are left-handed, begin with a right-hand paddle since they are most readily available. Later on this can be an important consideration should you need to replace a paddle while touring. The handedness of take-apart paddles can usually be easily changed.

• *Paddle Material.* Kayak paddles come in a variety of materials. Those with a plain or plastic-coated aluminum shaft and plastic blades are reasonably-priced and adequate for most needs, although they can vary widely in quality. Look for models such as Harmony's *RIM* (Reaction Injection Molding) whitewater or touring paddles. Those with wood shaft and blades feel good, look great and are very strong, but tend to be expensive and require more maintenance. Even higher in price are the fiberglass and graphite paddles, known for their strength and durability.

• *Paddle Length.* In general whitewater kayakers tend to favor shorter paddles, while touring enthusiasts favor longer ones. Length can roughly be determined by the user's height and arm reach (paddle tip should fall somewhere between wrist and fingertips when arm is extended overhead), but must also be adjusted for the type of kayaking you plan to do. Whitewater paddles are available in the 196 to 210 centimeter range, touring paddles in the 210 to 230 centimeter range. To get the most long-term comfort you should get advice from your supplier, then try out a few different models before buying.

• *Blade Shape.* Blades have different shapes for specific uses. They come as simple flat rectangles or in shapes that are more sophisticated and efficient. Long, narrow, asymmetrical (one side cut differently than the other) blades that are relatively flat are more popular for long-distance touring. Wide, symmetrical, relatively short blades are especially useful when paddling in aerated whitewater. In general, a flat blade is less expensive than a spooned blade. The spooned version increases paddling efficiency, but can also be more tiring on a long trip.

Brief Review of Paddling Techniques. There's as much to say about kayak paddling techniques as there is about canoe paddling—enough to fill an entire book. My advice to novice paddlers is to get some basic instruction from their equipment supplier, supplement that with reading on the subject, then get out in a kayak and practice. Taking formal lessons from a qualified instructor can help perfect your style safely and quickly. Most paddling courses start in a swimming pool or other protected water, and include fundamental maneuvers and safety techniques. Most kayakers continue to improve their technique for as long as they pursue the sport. A few of the basics are described below.

• *Hand Positions.* Start by holding the kayak paddle out in front of you with both hands on the shaft, a comfortable distance apart and in a top-grip position (fingers over and thumbs under the shaft).

• *Basic Stroke Cycle.* The basic stroke cycle consists of a right-hand stroke and a left-hand stroke. As the right blade enters the water the left blade is just beginning its recovery motion to be in position for the left-hand stroke. Assuming that you're using a feathered blade with right-hand control, you must roll your right hand in a twisting motion while letting the shaft rotate in your left hand. This adjusts the angle of the left blade so it enters the water properly. As the left blade enters the water, the right blade is recovering for the beginning of the next full cycle, and so on. The idea is to connect a series of smooth stroke cycles together to create a fluid, efficient paddling motion.

• *Bracing.* Bracing for better control and paddling efficiency is equally important for kayaks. By bracing yourself against the kayak you form a direct link with it. You have better control over yourself and the boat, and almost all of your paddling energy is transformed into boat motion. Most boat models come with adjustable foot braces, and many have either standard or optional knee braces (see Features and Options).

Author's Recommendations - Kayaks

There are hundreds of kayaks specifically made for play, sport and competition. My recommendations are limited to trip-oriented touring and whitewater models.

In the previous section I suggested looking for versatility when choosing a canoe. That's harder to do when selecting a kayak, for kayaking is more specialized and the differences between the various types are much more pronounced. True, there are a few models available that claim to perform well for both long distance touring and up to class II whitewater, including Aquaterra's *Spectrum*, Hydra's *Horizon* and Prijon's *Yukon Tour*. These are good boats that might be perfect for your needs. But potential buyers should bear in mind that whitewater river running and flat-water touring are vastly different activities. In trying to improve versatility you may end up compromising performance, especially as you gain expertise, and loss of performance is nothing to take lightly when kayaking. You should also note that in choosing a craft suited for whitewater you are, with few exceptions, limiting yourself to a solo model.

Touring or Whitewater? Assuming you want a single-purpose kayak, first decide whether it is to be a maneuverable whitewater boat or an efficient touring craft. Then try to match a model as closely as possible with the exact type of water conditions you are most likely to experience. If whitewater travel is your choice, ask yourself if you'll be on large rivers or small winding creeks; will the whitewater be relatively gentle or steep and technical; and will you be carrying your own gear or have the load carried by an accompanying raft? If touring is your choice, ask yourself if you'll be mostly in protected fresh water or in open coastal waters; will you be coping with surf, and if so, how large and how often; and how much gear do you need to carry? Answer these questions first and you'll be well on your way to selecting a boat that has the hull configuration, handling characteristics and features that are right for you.

• *Touring on Top.* Just because you might want to do some serious touring doesn't mean you should completely write off a sit-on-top model. There are some great boats on the market that combine the features of a long-distance touring kayak with the ease of use and comfort of a sit-on-top model, including Aquaterra's *Prism* and Prijon's *T-Yukon* for shorter tours, and Hydra's *Adventurer* for longer tours.

Hydra's Adventurer, a sit-on-top kayak.

• *Touring Under Sail.* You can add a secondary means of propulsion by equipping your kayak with an optional sail kit. Sailing is great fun, but more importantly it allows you to take a temporary break from paddling. Most of the compact, easy-to-use sail kits are intended only for downwind sailing, although a few suppliers such as Easy Rider and Eddyline offer more sophisticated rigs (with accompanying pivoting leeboards to keep the boat on course) that are also capable of windward work.

Easy Rider's Eskimo, shown with bat-wing sail rig.

Choose Tandem or Solo Model. This should be your next decision, whether to get a tandem or solo kayak. You'll find that almost all whitewater kayaks on the market are solo models, with the exception of a few boats such as Hydra's *Duet*. Most touring models are also solo, but manufacturers of touring kayaks typically offer one or two good tandems to choose from. Paddling with a companion can be great fun, whether traveling or just exploring locally. A tandem touring model can usually be paddled solo from the aft cockpit. All it takes is some practice, and perhaps some additional weight placed up forward to maintain proper trim. You may be interested to know that there are a few large tandems on the market that can be fitted with three cockpits, while others, such as Eddyline's *San Juan* and Pacific Water

Current Designs' Libra, a tandem touring kayak.

Sports' *Skookumchuck,* can accommodate two paddlers in fore and aft cockpits as well as one or two small passengers in the center hatch area.

Choose Length and Volume. Length is chosen for degree of maneuverability desired, especially for whitewater models, while volume is most often chosen for degree of buoyancy and load capacity desired. If you are planning to tour with your kayak, make sure to get one with adequate dry-storage capacity for the type of trips you intend. Don't buy a sleek, low volume model only to find out it can't hold enough gear for your needs. On the other hand, if month-long wilderness expeditions aren't in your future, don't waste money and paddling effort on a heavy, high-volume expedition kayak.

Length and volume should also be chosen according to your body size and weight. Most models are designed for adult males of average height. Those who are shorter or weigh less, including women and older children, may be more comfortable in a kayak that is slightly scaled down. Good touring models for smaller people include the *Esprit* from Northwest Kayak, the *Spectrum S* from Aquaterra, and the *Sea Otter Series 500 LP* and *Widgeon* from Pacific Water Sports.

Choose a Hull Material and Price Range. Now you can select a hull material and price range for your kayak. Polyethylene is by far the most popular material for whitewater kayaks, although there are some FRP models available as well. Kayaks made from FRP are strong and lightweight, but don't score as well on resilience, impact resistance or maintenance as polyethylene. If you tend to punish your kayak and come into close proximity to immovable objects, RPF (or HTP) is probably for you. If your style of whitewater kayaking keeps you relatively free from contact with boulders and river bottoms then there's no reason not to consider FRP.

For touring models the choice is wide open. Since you are less concerned about impact resistance and more con-cerned with stiffness and resistance to stress, models made from wood, FRP or polyethylene are all good options. Wood and FRP, while a little more expensive, tend to be the material of choice for long-distance

Aquaterra's Chinook

and expedition touring models. Polyethylene is usually more affordable and tends to be found mostly on models for general touring and leisure.

Weight should be a controlling factor in your decision. Paddling, portaging or just lifting the kayak onto the cartop is much easier when it's lightweight. Wood strip kayaks can be very light, as can FRP models that incorporate Kevlar and other exotic materials. As reduced weight is often reflected in higher prices, you'll have to limit the selection to models you can afford.

Just for Fun. Leisure kayaks are good for beginners and well-suited for car travel and recreation in relatively protected water. Choose this type when performance can be waived in favor of affordability and ease of use. The popular sit-on-top models such as Aquaterra's *Kahuna* and *Prism* (12 and 14 feet), Ocean Kayak's *Frenzy, Scrambler,* and *Scupper Pro* (9, 11 and 15 feet), and Old Town's *Dimension Solo* (13 feet) are great for warm weather/warm water use. Models with large cockpits such as Aquaterra's *Keowee* (a solo model with removable child seat) and *Keowee II* (tandem/solo model with adjustable seats), Folbot's polyethylene *Otter* (solo, 9 feet) and *Sprint* (tandem, 16 feet), and Kiwi Kayak's *Kopapa, Lobo,* and *Q Star* (solo models), are ideal for families and gentle explorations.

For Children. The interesting thing about kayaking is that it can be a demanding solo sport or an adventurous activity for a whole group. Children can easily enjoy kayaking as passengers or secondary paddlers in tandem kayaks. Traveling in this manner allows them to gain kayaking proficiency while having the security of an older, more experienced paddler.

Children can also learn to solo from an early age if they have access to an appropriate kayak. One of the best models for this purpose is the Englehart *Epitike 1000* (9'0", 22 pounds, costs around $450), an affordable child-size kayak best suited for paddlers in the 70- to 100-pound range. This kayak made of linear polyethylene is not just shorter;

Englehart's Epitike 1000

every aspect of the design is proportioned for a child's needs. This kayak is part of Englehart's *Primer* concept, a complete system for teaching kayaking skills to youngsters. West Side Boat Shop offers their *Baby Otter* for children (9'8", 19 pounds, costs around $525).

Another quality training kayak well-suited to a child's needs is the Betsie Bay *Miko* (13'0", 25 pounds, costs around $900), an adaptation of one of their larger wooden touring kayaks. Many of the sit-on-top models are also great for youngsters, as is Prijon's closed-deck *Topolino* (it means "Little Mouse"; 7'2", 33 pounds).

For Traveling Abroad. If you have the desire to kayak abroad you have two choices, either carry a portable kayak with you or rent one at your destination. Portable kayaks can be great fun and allow you to get out on the water when and where you like. They are just as convenient for car travel as for public transportation. Just make certain this is what you want before purchasing. These models can be more expensive, inevitably sacrifice some performance for portability, and can create quite a load if you're trying to travel light. Some recommended portable boats are described in the Innovative Product description at the beginning of this section.

Renting is a good option for occasional use at various chosen destinations. It also allows you to try out various designs before buying, whether abroad or near home. Rentals are usually available at good kayaking locations, allowing you the freedom to travel as you wish without being burdened with extra bulk and weight. The cost of renting can add up quickly, so bringing your own kayak is usually better for extended use.

Costs. Kayaks cost anywhere from $400 to over $3,000. If you simply want a versatile recreational model such as Aquaterra's *Keowee* or *Keowee II*, or Kiwi Kayak's *Kopapa, Lobo,* or *Tadpole II*, you'll be able to find something suitable for $400 to $500. Whitewater kayaks are typically made of polyethylene, and are shorter and have less volume than touring models. This usually keeps their price down in the $500 to $1,000 range for playboats, closer to $1,500 for touring models. You'll find many good quality closed-deck sea touring kayaks in the $600 to $1,400 range for solo models, somewhat more for tandems. You can also spend up to twice this amount on models that incorporate Kevlar or other lightweight materials, exhibit high levels of craftsmanship, or incorporate special features such as sail kits or the ability to pack up for travel.

Author's Recommendations - Whitewater/River Touring Kayaks ($500-$1400)

Brand	Model	Length	Type	Hull	Wgt. (lbs)
Baldwin Boat	Downriver K-1*	13'2"	solo	FRP	35
Hydra	Horizon**	13'1"	solo	PO	50
Kiwi	Lobo	9'2"	solo	PO	38
Loki	Mischief*	13'2"	solo	FRP	26
Loki	Gremlin Duo*	17'3"	tandem	FRP	44

Perception	Spirit	12'10"	solo	PO	41
Phoenix Prod'cts	Cascade*	13'2"	solo	FRP	39
Phoenix Prod'cts	Appalachain*	13'9"	solo	FRP	39
Prijon	Taifun	12'9"	solo	PO	48
Prijon	Yukon Tour**	14'5"	solo	PO	44
Seda Products	River Runner	13'0"	solo	PO	35

These kayak models are offered in fiberglass and/or Kevlar cloth construction.
**These kayaks are suitable for whitewater and sea touring.*
HULL: FRP=fiber-reinforced plastic, PO=polyethylene, WO=wood or wood strip.

Author's Recommendations - Sea Touring Kayaks ($600-$1400)

Brand	Model	Length	Type	Hull	Wgt. (lbs)
Aquaterra	Scimitar	15'	solo	PO	52
Aquaterra	Chinook	16'	solo	PO	53
Aquaterra	Sea Lion	17'2"	solo	PO	59
Baldwin Boat	Atlantic*	17'	solo	FRP	55
Cal-Tek Eng.	Harbor Seal	16'6"	solo	FRP	44
Dagger	Seeker	16'	solo	PO	N/A
Dunn's Custom	Narwhal Tracker*	16'10"	solo	FRP	43
Fobot	Osprey	14'6"	solo	PO	57
Hydra	Sea Runner	17'1"	solo	PO	60
Hydra	Sea Twin	18'	tandem	PO	92
Kiwi	Mark Twain	13'4"	tandem	PO	58
Loki	Sprite	14'9"	solo	FRP	30
Necky	Kyook	15'	solo	PO	60
Pacific W't'r Sp.	Widgeon	14'3"	solo	FRP	42
Phoenix Prdts.	Isere*	14'9"	solo	FRP	29
Phoenix Prdts.	Vagabond K2*	16'5"	tandem	FRP	46
Prijon	Seayak Exped.	16'	solo	PO	57
Rainforest Des.	Puffin	16'3"	solo	PO	63
Seda Products	Viking*	16'6"	solo	FRP	44
Seda Products	Swift*	17'	solo	FRP	44
Seda Products	Glider*	19'	solo	FRP	48
West Side Boat	Delta*	13'10"	solo	FRP	28
West Side Boat	Seafarer Series*	16'8"-20'	solo	FRP	42-75
Woodstrip W'c'ft.	DD 17	15'9"	solo	WO	35

These kayak models are offered in fiberglass and/or Kevlar cloth construction.
**These kayaks are suitable for whitewater and sea touring.*
HULL: FRP=fiber-reinforced plastic, PO=polyethylene, WO=wood or wood strip.

Author's Recommendations - Sea Touring Kayaks ($1500-$2500)

Brand	Model	Length	Type	Hull	Wgt. (lbs)
Baldwin	Atlantic III*	17'	tandem	FRP	56
Betsie Bay	Manitou	17'10"	solo	WO, FRP	45, 52
Current Designs	Solstice*	17'6"	solo	FRP	52
Current Designs	Libra*	21'8"	tandem	FRP	84
Dragonworks	Islander*	17'	solo	FRP	49
Easy Rider	Beluga*	16'8"	tandem	FRP	65
Easy Rider	Sea Hawk*	17'	solo	FRP	47-56
Easy Rider	Eskimo 16E, 17E*	16', 17'	solo	FRP	39, 45
Eddyline	Raven*	16'9"	solo	FRP	52
Eddyline	Whisper*	18'6"	tandem	FRP	70
Eddyline	San Juan*	20'	tandem	FRP	88

Mad River	Monarch*	17'3"	solo	FRP	50
Mariner	Express*	16'	solo	FRP	46
Morley Cedar	TK1 and TK2	16', 18'	solo	WO	35, 40
Mariner	Mariner II*	17'11"	solo	FRP	50
Necky	Arluk I-IV*	16'-19'	solo	FRP	varies
Necky	Tofino*	20'3"	tandem	FRP	95
New Wave	Sea Break*	16'10"	solo	FRP	65
New Wave	Sea Tripper	17"	solo	FRP	65
Northwest	Esprit*	16'4"	solo	FRP	51
Northwest	Seascape Pt. 5*	18'4"	tandem	FRP	75
Northwest	Seascape 2*	21'	tandem	FRP	95
Pacific Canoe B.	Nordkapp*	17'1	solo	FRP	56
Pacific W't'r Sp.	Sea Otter Series*	16'4"	solo	FRP	54
Pacific W't'r Sp.	Skookumchuck*	21'	tandem	FRP	95
Rainforest Des.	Nimbus Horizon*	16'3"	solo	FRP	53
Seaward Kay'ks	Baidarka Expl'r	16'10"	solo	FRP	52
Seaward Kay'ks	Icefloe	16'8"	solo	FRP	56
Seda Products	Tango*	21'	tandem	FRP	55
Superior Kay'ks	Sea Hawk	17'6"	solo	WO/FRP	46
Superior Kay'ks	Arctic Hawk	18'	solo	WO/FRP	50
Valley Canoe	Skerray*	17'	solo	FRP, PO	56, 66
Valley Canoe	Nordkapp*	17'10"	solo	FRP	55
Valley Canoe	Aleut Sea*	22'	tandem	FRP	88
Wilderness Sys.	Sealution*	16'6"	solo	FRP	44
Wilkinson Boat	Sitka*	16'	solo	FRP	50
Wilkinson Boat	Enetai*	17'	solo	FRP	60
Woodstrip W'c'ft	DK 21	17'10"	solo	WO	35
Woodstrip W'c'ft	Tursy II	19'	tandem	WO	65

*These kayak models are offered in fiberglass and/or Kevlar cloth construction.
**These kayaks are suitable for whitewater and sea touring.
HULL: FRP=fiber-reinforced plastic, PO=polyethylene, WO=wood or wood strip.

Maintenance and Repair - Kayaks

In general, kayaks are durable, low maintenance pieces of equipment. How much maintenance and repair work your particular kayak will need depends largely on how you care for it. One of the best things you can do is to have proper flotation installed. This is not only a safety feature, it keeps the boat on the surface and away from most immovable objects, in case of a whitewater capsize. Other helpful hints are to handle your boat properly, both in and out of the water, and keep your boat well-supported, shaded and dry during long periods of storage.

Wood. Wooden kayaks require a fair amount of loving care to keep them in top shape. Maintenance is reduced somewhat on models that use a skin of FRP to cover the wood. Wooden boats are quite easy to repair should damage occur.

FRP. Kayaks made from FRP need only occasional touching up and refinishing. They can also be easily repaired, with fiberglass cloth requiring less effort than Kevlar or other lightweight FRP fabrics. Holes and large cracks are sanded smooth, covered with a screen mesh, then filled with fiberglass bonding material. New cloth and resin is built up in layers and feathered out smoothly beyond the damaged area.

RPF and HTP. Hulls made of polyethylene (either cross-linked or linear) are also extremely durable and need no real maintenance. They can lose their shape under repeated stress, however, so care should be taken during storage and transport in hot weather. Their exposure to direct sunlight should also be minimized to ensure long life. The cross-linked versions generally have more resistance to impact but are also much more difficult to repair. Linear polyethylene hulls can be repaired with simple plastic welding techniques.

Specialty Boat Gear

- Boat Carts
- Load Carriers
- Watertight Map Cases
- Safety Gear
- Watersports Apparel

BOAT CARTS

A boat cart can simplify the job of carrying a loaded canoe or kayak down to the shore, especially if it's a sizeable distance and you're on your own. These handy carts consist of two large diameter wheels mounted on a small tubular frame with a flat section to hold the boat. Most models come with fastening straps that hold the boat securely in place on the frame. You simply place the balance point of the boat on top of the frame (usually right side up), tighten the straps, then grab one end of the boat and push or pull it to your destination.

There are several good models to choose from, including the Canadian Folding Boat Walker found at many watersports equipment suppliers. This model folds flat for transport and has large-diameter wheels, similar to those found on bicycle trailers, allowing it to roll smoothly over rough terrain. It weighs only 16 pounds, adjusts to a variety of hull shapes, carries up to 250 pounds, and costs around $160.

LOAD CARRIERS

Carrying gear in a boat is quite different than on a bicycle or on your back. Since the load is mostly resting in the bottom of a boat, designers of this equipment are less concerned with aerodynamics and ergonomics than they are about simply keeping your gear safe and dry. Load carriers for canoes and kayaks must be durable, dependable, easy to access, and above all resistant to water penetration. Of course, you can use standard backpacks and inexpensive waterproof bags to store your gear, but if you're looking for something better suited to the job at hand, try one of the specially made load carriers now available.

There are several basic types to choose from, including dry boxes and barrels, waterproof dry bags, portage packs, and miscellaneous load carriers such as seat and thwart packs. The larger versions of this gear are mainly for use in an open canoe, while the dry bags are primarily used for kayaking.

Dry Boxes and Barrels

These load carriers may not be pretty to look at, but most models keep out the elements, hold tons of gear, and are made to stand up to repeated punishment. They can be constructed of aluminum or plastic and come in all shapes and sizes. The larger aluminum dry boxes are used mostly on rafting expeditions. The plastic boxes and barrels work well for canoes and kayaks. Northwest River Supplies carries several good versions, including their plastic barrels (the *Papa* has a 50 gallon capacity, costs around $37; the *Baby* has a five-gallon capacity, costs around $13) that have a two-piece lid (like a mason jar) and an O-ring seal to keep your provisions dry. NRS also offers their rectangular plastic *Dry Box* (4.5 cubic foot capacity, 31"L x 25"W x17"H, costs around $135) that doubles as a cartop carrier and comes with a three-year guarantee against tears and cracks.

Voyageur offers their *York Pack 200*, a molded polyethylene waterproof storage box built to withstand the rigors of outdoor expeditions. This box features tie-down points, hand grips, a neoprene gasket, quick-release straps, an optional nylon internal organizer, and optional shoulder straps to turn it into a portage pack.

Dry Storage for Valuables. For cameras, instruments and other expensive equipment that must be protected, try the *Pelican Case* (also carried by Northwest River Supplies). This tough ABS plastic box comes with a foam lining that can be customized to suit your needs. It is available in six sizes, is waterproof, and has a lifetime warranty.

Waterproof Dry Bags

Watersports enthusiasts who need to protect their gear without the bulk or weight of a rigid box have the option of using heavy-duty waterproof dry bags. Constructed of nylon or dacron fabric that has been coated with thick layers of PVC or urethane, these amazing flexible containers aren't just waterproof, they're practically indestructible. They are available in a host of sizes, as either duffel bags or top-loading sacks, and in either opaque or see-through models. The sacks have roll-down tops with clips that secure them tightly. Heavy-duty waterproof duffels cost $65 to $150 depending on model, and the sacks cost from $15 to $45 depending on size. Some of the best dry bags on the market are described below.

Cascade Designs. They make the *Seal Line* dry sacks and duffels, including their *Baja Bags, Kodiak Sacs* and *Great Barrier Bags*.

Northwest River Supplies. NRS offers various waterproof bags, including their *Dri-Stow, Ripsack* and *Sea Stow* lines. If you need a larger watertight bag for bulky camping equipment, try the NRS *Kitchen Bag* (21"L x19"W x14"H, costs around $72). If you want a conical dry storage bag that fits almost anywhere in a kayak, try their *Payette Pack*.

NRS' Dri-Stow Bags

Seattle Sports. Seattle Sports offers two great lines of dry storage bags, their *Super Sacks* (four sizes available) and their *Dry Sacks* (five sizes available).

Stohlquist. This well known supplier of watersports equipment offers the *CKS Bruneau Bags*. These conical-shaped bags are made to be used in pairs and fit neatly in the bow or stern of a kayak. Whitewater kayaks can use both bow and stern pairs (cost around $53 and $85 respectively), while touring models can use an additional single-end bag behind the stern set (costs around $53).

Voyageur. Some of the best dry bags you'll ever find are in Voyageur's line of *H2O-Proof Stuff Sacks*, available in three convenient sizes. These incredible bags of urethane-coated nylon combine the best features of a waterproof dry bag with those of a compression stuff sack. The result is essential protection for your gear and a big savings in bulk when packing, thanks to Voyageur's exclusive *Dry Cinch Seal* system.

Innovation - Combination Flotation/Dry Bags

If you're worried that your gear will take up precious flotation space in your kayak, you might consider using combination *Storage Flotation Bags* from Northwest River Supplies. These cone-shaped watertight bags feature an inner nylon storage bag and an outer airtight shell. Simply pack your gear, then inflate the middle air chamber for flotation. They come in stern only or bow and stern models for around $60 to $65. Voyageur also offers their *Slide Closure* dry storage bags, the *Caboose* and the *Yukon*. These are inflatable duffel-style waterproof bags that serve as a gear-carrying alternative to flotation bags. Made of 400-denier nylon, they come with a slide closure, corner grommets, inflation hose, and repair kit.

Portage Packs

Duffels and sacks are fine for storing gear on or off the boat, but for frequent or long-distance portaging you'll need a load carrier that functions equally well as a backpack. Portage packs do just that, with many good models currently on the market. You'll find several different types of portage packs, including the traditional wooden "pack-basket", nylon fabric portage packs that are similar to regular backpacks, and heavy-duty waterproof bags that have been modified for portage use. Some of the best models available are described below.

Camp Trails. The Camp Trails *Canoe Pack* (6,000 to 7,400 cubic inches, costs around $100) has to be one of the most practical portage packs available. Made of heavy-duty Kodra® nylon, this top-loading pack features a foam back panel; oversized padded shoulder straps; a removable hip belt (to keep it from catching in canoe or car); compression, sternum and side stabilizing straps; a large mesh map pocket; and lash points. Watertight integrity is maintained by the coated nylon fabric, a dry bag style roll-and-clip closure, and a full-cut storm flap.

Cascade Designs. This company offers two different portage pack versions of their *Seal Line* dry bags, both constructed of heavy-duty 20-ounce PVC-coated fabric. Their *Pro Pack* comes in two sizes (3,938 and 6,938 cubic inches, costs $60 to $90) and features an oval bottom, removable padded shoulder straps and hip belt, tough buckles and extra tie-down hardware. Cascade Designs' *Boundary Packs* are similar in size and construction, with a few less features and lower cost.

Granite Gear. This company offers outstanding fabric portage packs, with six different models to choose from. They have three *Traditional Packs* (3,300, 3,500 and 6,000 cubic inch, costs $100 to $115) refined in the age-old portage pack design, and three *Expedition Packs*

(2,600, 5,000 and 7,400 cubic inches, costs $180 to $195) that combine some innovations with the best features of traditional portage packs and state-of-the-art mountaineering packs. The rugged *Expedition Packs* are similar in design to the Camp Trails *Canoe Pack*. Granite Gear offers models specifically made for women.

Granite Gear's Expedition Packs

L.L. Bean. L.L. Bean still offers their traditional wooden *Pack-Basket*, available in four sizes and ranging in cost from $20 to $40. This is the original hard canoe pack. The basket is crafted of ash strips, the backstraps are unpadded nylon. There are more comfortable portage packs available, and you'll still need to waterproof your gear, but you won't find a more attractive portage pack that provides this kind of protection inside the boat. *Pack-Basket* options include shoulder pads, nylon liners, and nylon weather caps.

Northwest River Supplies. NRS offers three different models of portage packs in their dry-bag style. The original *Bill's Bag* comes in two different sizes (3,800 and 6,560 cubic inches, costs around $55) and features a serviceable set of shoulder straps and a carry handle. A heavy-duty version of the larger bag is available for about $20 more. For more demanding paddlers NRS offers their *Paragon Portage Pack*, a true internal frame backpack made in the dry-bag style. It consists of a pack similar in size and style to the *Heavy Duty Bill's Bag* that has been modified to include a high-grade suspension system, a padded back, fully adjustable shoulder straps and hip belt, sternum and compression straps, and one inch tie-down straps.

Seattle Sports. Seattle Sports offers their *River Pack*, the perfect dry-bag portage pack for canoe trips and extended raft trips. This durable pack has padded shoulder straps, roll-and-clip top closure, cross-over cinch straps and a round bottom.

Seat and Thwart Canoe Packs

Granite Gear makes several specialty load carriers for canoes in addition to their regular portage packs. Their *Stowaway* (700 cubic inches, costs $32) attaches under your canoe seat, the perfect place to store items you want to be accessible and kept clear of the bilge water. They also offer two sizes of thwart bags, the *Navigator* and the *Mariner* (550 and 950 cubic inches, costs $25 and $40). They easily attach to the thwart of a canoe and feature snap hooks that allow them to attach to a portage pack or be worn as chest packs, daypacks or shoulder bags. Voyageur offers two different models that convert to fanny packs, the *Standard Thwart Pack* (400 cubic inches, costs around $38), and the *Deluxe Thwart Pack* (810 cubic inches, costs around $60).

WATERTIGHT MAP CASES

Anyone who's traveled on the water knows how convenient it is to have a waterproof map case. These clear vinyl pouches allow any map to be used while underway and remain protected and dry. You can fabricate your own map case from a heavy-duty zip-lock bag, or try one of the sturdy Granite Gear map cases. They come in two sizes, the *Thunderhead* and the *Storm* (cost around $17). One of them is certain to suit your needs. They feature a heavy-duty vinyl window, packcloth fabric for strength and snap hooks at the corners that attach to a variety of gear. Aquaterra makes an all-vinyl *Watertight Map Case* that is large enough for nautical charts (14"x12"), and Seattle Sports offers the waterproof *Chart Case* (18"x12") that has a nylon backing, perimeter tape and lash points on the four corners.

SAFETY GEAR

Anytime you're out on the water in a small craft you should be accompanied by some basic safety equipment. It will give you peace of mind and protect you and your passengers in case of an emergency. The following are some recommended safety items to pack along for canoeing and kayaking.

Personal Flotation Devices

Whether you call them PFDs, lifejackets or buoyant vests, this gear can save your life and should be used any time you go out on the water. You'll be doing yourself a favor while also satisfying a Coast Guard requirement. The U.S. Coast Guard states that all boats must have approved personal flotation devices, even canoes and kayaks. The specific type of PFD you should have varies with boat length and the water conditions you'll be boating in. There are five basic types of PFDs.

Type I. This type is an off-shore lifejacket, recommended for open, rough or remote water where rescue may be slow coming. It provides the best flotation, turns most unconscious wearers face-up in the water, has a highly visible color, but is bulky to wear.

Type II. This near-shore buoyant vest is recommended for calm inland water or open water when there is a good chance of fast rescue. It turns some unconscious wearers face-up in the water and is less bulky and more comfortable than Type I.

Type III. This flotation aid is the type preferred by most canoeists and kayakers who travel in protected waters. It is generally the most comfortable for continuous wear, but is not designed for rough water, and the wearer may have to tilt his or her head back to avoid being positioned face-down.

Type IV. Type IV PFDs are throwable devices, either buoyant life rings or seat cushions. They can easily be thrown to someone in trouble and serve as a good back-up to other PFDs. They are not for unconscious people, non-swimmers, children, or for long use in rough water.

Type V Hybrid. This type is a hybrid inflatable device that, as with Types I, II, and III must be worn to be counted as a regulation PFD. It combines the comfort and buoyancy of either a Type I, II, or III with an inflatable chamber for extra flotation in emergency conditions. Most canoeists and kayakers choose this type for technical whitewater conditions.

Coast Guard Regulations. The U.S. Coast Guard requires that all recreational craft 16 feet or longer, except all canoes and kayaks, must have a wearable PFD for every person on board (Type I, II, III, or V), and at least one throwable device (Type IV). If your boat is less than 16 feet, or is a canoe or kayak of any length, you may choose either wearable or throwable PFDs, one for each person on board.

Style and Cost. I highly recommended that every canoeist and kayaker wear a comfortable PFD suited to the existing water conditions. It's also a good idea to have a boat cushion or two on board to toss to swimmers in trouble. Paddlers and passengers alike need sufficient buoyancy and freedom of movement in a PFD. Those in boats with a closed-deck design need the most freedom, so they usually wear models that are short-waisted and loose around the arms. Most freshwater boaters prefer Type III models for general use, a higher buoyancy Type III for rougher water or coastal travel, and Type III/V hybrids for more demanding conditions. Child or

youth models often come with leg straps for security and should fit snugly for proper performance. Infant models have flotation collars, but parents should always exercise extra care with young children in a boat. There are many good models to choose from. PFD costs vary according to type, buoyancy, size and quality, and can range from $30 to $90. Some of the best models currently on the market are described below.

Extrasport's Buddy

Author's Recommendations - Personal Flotation Devices

Brand	Model	Type	Sizes	Description
America's Cup	Challenger	III	A	economical jacket, 17 lbs. floatation
America's Cup	III/V	III/V	A, Y	generous flotation, inflatable
America's Cup	Ultra Float	III/V	A	high flotation, inflatable
Extrasport	Children's	III, II	Y, I	with or without flotation collar
Extrasport	Rogue	III	A	shorty jacket, up to 21 lbs. flotation
Extrasport	Hi-Float	III	A	high buoyancy, best jckt. for "big water"
Extrasport	Buddy	III/V	A, Y	comfortable, adjustable, segm't'd collar
L.L. Bean	Freedom	III	A, Y	vest, economic'l, comfort'ble, 2 models
Mad River	PFDs	III	A, C	regular or low profile vests, adjustable
Old Town	PFDs	III	A	custom designed for extra comfort
Perception	River Vest	III	A	high flotation shorty vest for kayak'g
Perception	Touring	III	A	close fitting, ample shoulder rotation
Safeguard	Lifejackets	III/V	A, Y	commercial grade jackets, comfortable
Stearns	Heads-Up	II	I, C	adjust. belt, leg straps, floatation collar
Stearns	Children's	III	C, Y	adjustable belt, leg straps
Stearns	First Mate	III	A	economical vest, fast-dry'g mesh lining
Stohlquist	Max Vest	III	A	high buoyancy, loops for rescue gear

SIZES: A=adult, Y=youth, C=child, I=infant.

Paddle Floats and Sponsons

An inflatable paddle float is a basic self-rescue device for deep-water touring kayakers. It consists of a urethane-coated nylon bag which, when fitted over the blade of a kayak paddle and inflated, serves as an outrigger float for deep water entries into the kayak. These simple, lightweight bags cost only $20 to $30.

An alternative to using a paddle float is to purchase and install an inflatable sponson (float) system. The concept is simple—sponsons work in pairs, mounted amidships and partially immersed on each side of the boat. Georgian Bay Kayak markets their *Sea Wing* self-rescue safety sponsons for touring kayakers. A nylon harness for the sponsons mounts permanently to the kayak deck. In the event of a capsize, or anytime you'd like a more stable platform, simply clip on the sponsons and inflate. They serve as an aid during re-entry and add stability to the boat in rough sea conditions. After re-entry the sponsons can be removed or left in position as you paddle.

Rescue Throw Bags

Rescue throw bags are handy devices intended for rescuing stranded paddlers or swimmers in the water. They consist of 50 to 75 feet of 0.25" to 0.375" diameter buoyant rope (so it stays on the surface of the water) packed inside a highly visible nylon bag. One end of the rope is attached to the boat or shore, then bag is thrown toward the victim. The balance of the rope deploys as it passes through the air. Intended more for whitewater or rough, open conditions, throw bags are much more accurate and easier to throw than a ring or a coiled line. The rope should be repacked carefully after use for proper operation. Rescue throw bags are durable, only weigh a pound or two, and cost between $30 to $70 depending on rope diameter, length and test strength. Some great models currently on the market are listed below.

L.L. Bean. L.L. Bean markets their reasonably-priced *Emergency Throw Line* (60 feet, polypropylene).

Northwest River Supplies. NRS offers several good quality models, including their *Pro Rescue Bag* (75 feet, Spectra® rope), the *Kayaker's Rescue Bag* (60 feet, Spectra® rope, compact version just for kayaks), and the NRS *Rescue Bag* (65 feet, polypropylene).

Perception. Perception has two good models, including their *Throwbags* (50 or 75 feet) and the *Spectra Throwbag* (60 feet, buoyant, Spectra® rope that is stronger than Kevlar®).

Stohlquist. Stohlquist offers the *Kayaker's Lifeline* (lightweight, 50 feet, polypropylene) and the *CKS Standard Lifeline* (large diameter rope, 65 feet, polypropylene).

Emergency Kit

Everyone who travels off the beaten path should be prepared for emergency situations. Traveling in a boat only increases the need for a well stocked emergency kit.

First Aid Kit. The first thing to consider is a good quality first aid kit, such as those described in the Health and Hygiene section of Personal Travel Gear. In addition to the first aid kits listed there, some suppliers offer models specifically made for whitewater paddlers. Adventure Medical Kits markets their *Comprehensive Whitewater*, which comes in a waterproof, see-through dry bag, and their *Paddler* for watersports.

Survival Kit. If you travel by boat into the backcountry, you should also pack some basic survival items that can help keep you warm, dry and well fed in an emergency. For recommendations look in the Health and Hygiene section of Personal Gear. One additional item for boaters is a good signal kit, which should include some combination of the following: a whistle for each person, to be worn when paddling; an air horn; marking dye for locating position in the water or snow; signal flares; and a battery-operated strobe light. These components can be purchased separately from Aquaterra or from a watersports or marine equipment supplier.

Bilge Pump

A small hand-operated bilge pump is another desirable safety item, especially for kayak paddlers who venture off-shore. A bilge pump can be used to keep you afloat in an emergency, or for just removing water from your boat without having to flip it. Portable bilge pumps consisting of a rigid plastic intake line and a flexible plastic outfall line, such as the *Thirsty Mate* (10 gallons per minute, 24" long intake, 24" long outfall hose, costs around $15 to $20) are available from any marine supplier. Bilge pumps that are mounted to the hull or deck and can be operated from the cockpit while underway are also offered by several watersports suppliers. One popular model is the *Guzzler* (15 gallons per minute, 1.5" diameter hose not included, costs around $50).

Watersports Helmets

Whitewater canoeists and kayakers are advised to wear head protection when paddling in whitewater. The most well known name in affordable whitewater helmets is Pro-tec. Their helmets are lightweight, fit securely, and have a high density polyethylene shell with a removable and replaceable foam liner for protection and comfort. These helmets have generous ventila-

Pro-tec's Watersports Helmet

tion holes to drain water rapidly and ear openings for unimpaired hearing. Sizes run according to hat size or by measuring the circumference of your head (in inches) just above the brow. Helmet liners of synthetic fleece can be purchased for use in cold water and climates. Pro-tec helmets cost around $38, replacement foam liners around $15, and fleece liners around $10.

Seda is another American whitewater helmet manufacturer with a good reputation for quality. Their helmets come in either fiberglass or Kevlar®, with solid construction (no ear or drain holes) that provides extra strength, but may impair hearing or be slow to drain. Seda helmets cost around $45 for the fiberglass version and $70 for the Kevlar®.

Navigational Aids

Paddlers heading on coastal expeditions should also have proper navigational aids on board.

Compass. A hand-held or deck-mounted compass is highly recommended for safe navigation. Hand-held versions are recommended under Specialty Gear in the Personal Travel Gear section. The most popular deck-mounted compass for coastal kayaking is the *Sailor II* from Aquameter. This liquid-filled marine compass comes with bull's-eye level markings to indicate boat trim and a snap-off mounting plate.

Charts, Tide Tables and Cruising Guides. Marine charts are the boater's road map. Available in different scales covering all coastal and deepwater cruising grounds in the world, they show depths of water, navigational buoys and markers, and prominent coastal navigational aids. Tide tables help you determine the time and strength of local tides and currents, making them an indispensable aid to coastal navigation. A good cruising guide can help you find hidden waterways and good overnight stops, as well as provide some local knowledge about your cruising area. Check at any marine bookstore for appropriate guides for the area you intend to explore.

WATERSPORTS APPAREL

There is no end to the specialty apparel you can wear when paddling, assuming your budget is large enough. My advice is to determine what is really suitable for your needs. Canoeists don't really require much that is different from normal outdoor wear, with the possible exception of better raingear and footgear, but kayakers certainly need additional protection from the wet and cold, especially when paddling in whitewater. Your apparel will depend mostly on the weather conditions and water temperature in the area you'll be paddling in. The primary items to consider are a good paddling jacket and pants, a wetsuit or drysuit, paddling gloves or mitts, and appropriate footgear.

Paddling Jackets

Also called spray jackets or drytops, this outerwear is unlike any other type of jacket. Paddling jackets are made of coated nylon in a loose-fitting pullover style for maximum freedom of movement and water protection. The high neck and snug wrist areas typically have comfortable neoprene closures to seal out spray. The waist area usually has an elastic drawstring. Matching pants are offered by most suppliers. Some of the most well know paddling jacket suppliers are Kokatat, Patagonia and Stohlquist.

Kokatat. This company offers a wide range of paddling jackets. Their most practical models for general travel are the *Super Breeze* (their toughest model, costs around $75) and their full-cut multi-use paddling outfit, the *Splash* jacket and pants (jacket costs around $40, pants around $32). For more demanding conditions try their *Whirlpool Drytop* (with built-in sprayskirt apron, costs around $145).

Patagonia. Patagonia is a recognized name in outdoor wear, and the *Paddling Jacket* (costs around $90, adult and child sizes) lives up to their reputation for quality. This jacket has a Velcro neck closure, an elastic drawstring waist and a zippered mesh pocket.

Stohlquist. While Stohlquist offers an entire line of quality paddling jackets and other apparel, the *Shredder* jacket and pants (cost around $89 and $75 respectively) and the *Nude-X* drytop (with built-in sprayskirt apron, costs around $115) are among their best. For those on a tighter budget, try their *Basic* jacket and pants (costs around $46 and $29 respectively).

Stohlquist's Shredder Jacket

Wetsuits and Drysuits

Staying warm and dry is critical to enjoying any watersport. Cold-water kayakers who tend to spend as much time in the water as on it need to consider the use of either a wetsuit or drysuit. A wetsuit keeps you warm by allowing a thin layer of water to get between you and the suit. The water is heated by your body and acts as a thermal layer of insulation. A dry suit takes the opposite approach, using considerable measures to prevent water from reaching you in the first place.

Wetsuits are typically made of neoprene and come in various styles, including "full-length" with long arms and legs, "farmer" with long legs and a sleeveless top, "shortie" with short arms and legs, and vests or jackets. Wetsuits are available in either front- or shoulder-entry styles and are usually more economical than drysuits, costing around $75 to $150 depending on the style and model. Wetsuits keep you warm, but chances are you'll be wet when you leave the boat.

Drysuits can be thought of as full-length versions of high quality paddling jackets, made of waterproof fabrics and available in either front- or rear-entry styles. They have replaceable, water-resistant "gaskets" around the neck and wrists for maximum water protection. Gaskets can be trimmed by the user for an exact fit. Drysuits do cause you to perspire (Gore-Tex® models are more comfortable), but generally you'll be much drier when you leave the boat than in a wetsuit.

Some of the most popular wetsuits and drysuits currently on the market are described below.

Dry Fashion. Dry Fashion offers several models of drysuits, including their *Avilastic* with latex gaskets (front- or rear-entry, costs around $275), the less expensive *Texlon* model (front- or rear-entry, costs around $230), and the *Gore-Tex®* waterproof/breathable model (front-entry, costs around $460).

L.L. Bean. This company offers a complete line of wetsuits, including their *Full Wet Suit* (rear-entry, costs around $125), *Shortie Wet Suit* (rear-entry, costs around $90), and the *Farmer John* and *Farmer Jane* (front-entry, costs around $105).

Kokatat. Recommended drysuits from this fine company include the *Meridian* (front-entry, costs around $330), and the less expensive *Front Entry* (front-entry, costs around $280).

Northwest River Supplies. NRS offers their own line of wetsuits, including the *Farmer Bill* (farmer-style, shoulder-entry, costs around $80), the *Farmer John* and the *Aqua-Tux* (farmer-style, front-entry, costs around $90), and the NRS *Wetsuit Jacket* (costs around $70). NRS also carries drysuits by Dry Fashion, Kokatat and Stohlquist.

REI. REI markets a good line of wetsuits, including their *Long Johns* (farmer-style, front-entry, costs around $105), the *Spring Suit* (shortie, front-entry, costs around $90), and the 3/2 *Full Wetsuit* (full-length, front-entry, costs around $140).

Stohlquist. A leader in watersports apparel for many years,

Stohlquist's most practical drysuits include the *Paragon* (front-entry, costs around $280) and the *Ultralight* (two-piece suit, built-in sprayskirt apron, costs around $300).

Watersports Footgear

Watersports often call for more appropriate footgear than regular shoes and boots. The wetter the activity, the more special protection you need. There are several different types of watersports footgear available, including sport sandals, reef shoes and wet shoes. All have the ability to provide adequate foot protection in a wet environment.

Sport Sandals. This type of footgear is great for the active traveler. Unlike standard sandals, sport sandals have rugged bottom soles for good traction and long life, comfortable top soles, and high quality nylon webbing designed to secure and stabilize the feet in position. You can actually run and climb comfortably with these sandals, making them equally suited for both watersports and land-based activities. They dry quickly, are not harmed by total immersion in water, and can also serve as general-purpose travel shoes or camp footwear. Sport sandals come in a variety of sole and webbing styles for different levels of traction and support. Open-toe designs allow the use of socks. Costs range from $35 to $55.

Teva's All Terrain Sport Sandal

Reef Shoes. Reef shoes are lightweight slip-on footgear that provides more protection than sandals around rocks and pavement. These low shoes, typically constructed of neoprene with nylon mesh uppers, cover the foot completely. They are extremely comfortable for beachcombing, stream crossings, watersports, and as secondary shoes for active travel. Costs range from $30 to $50.

Wetshoes. Also called cold water shoes or boots, wetshoes work on the same principle as wetsuits. They are constructed of neoprene and allow a thin layer of water to penetrate and provide thermal protection. Wetshoes come in soft- and hard-sole versions, in either shoe or bootie styles. Costs range from $25 to $45.

Author's Recommendations - Watersports Footgear

Brand	Model	Type	Description
Alp	Pro River Guide	SS	suction cup sole, tubul'r webb'ng w/ buckles
Alp	Sport	SS	similar to above with laces
Alpina	Wet Shoe	WS	high-cut neoprene boot, laces and side zipper
Fibus	Whitewater	SS	thong-toe, all-terrain or high-traction tread
Fibus	Summit Pro	SS	open-toe, all terrain or high-traction tread
HiTrax	Sierra I and II	SS	high-friction lugged sole, Velcro webbing
L.L. Bean	Booties	WS	high-cut, neoprene, slip-on booties
Merrell	Belize	SS	open-toe, all-terrain sole, cross'v'r fr'nt strap
Merrell	Baja	SS	open-toe, all-terrain sole, cross'v'r fr'nt strap
Nike	Air Deschütz	SS	synthetic leather strapping system
Nike	Aqua Sock	RS	low-cut, slip-on shoe for gen'l watersports
Nike	Aqua Turf	RS	low-cut, sturdier sole with aggressive tread
NRS	Zippered	WS	high-cut, flexible, buckle and side zipper
NRS	Paddler's Pull-On	WS	high-cut, neoprene, slip-on bootie
Omega	Reef Runner	RS	low-cut, lightweight, instep strap with buckle
Omega	Reef Warrior	RS	low-cut, heavy-duty sole with aggr. tread
Reebok	Amazon	SS	open-toe, all-terrain sole, double front strap
Reef	Convertible	SS	open-toe, adjust. & removable back straps
Reef	Crossover	SS	open-toe, cross'v'r web'g, remov'ble straps
Scott	Sport Sandal	SS	open-toe, durable sole, instep support strap
Scott	Scott "AT"	SS	open-toe, aggr. tread, quick-release strap
Speedo	Surf Walkers	RS	low-cut, elastic instep, padd'd coll'r uppers
Teva	All Terrain	SS	open-toe, moderate tread, multi-purpose
Teva	Contour	SS	open-toe, aggressive tread, g'd for walking
Thunderwear	Water Shoe	WS	high-top, buckle over instep, rubber sole

TYPE: SS=sport sandal, RS=reef shoe, WS=water shoe.

Innovation - Acorn's *SandalSox*

With the surge in sport sandal popularity, it's no wonder an innovative company like Acorn came out with a comfortable, quick-drying line of socks to go with them. Designed to go with all-terrain, sport, or casual sandals, the synthetic fleece *SandalSox* are made for durability and high performance. They function well in harsh environments where standard socks would fail, cushioning your feet while wicking away moisture. *SandalSox* are available in a variety of colors and sizes, ranging in price from $10 to $14.

Paddling Gloves and Mitts

Canoeists and kayakers may also want to consider paddling gloves or mitts for warmth, gripping power and protection from chafing when on the water. There are several different styles to choose from, including fingerless boat gloves, neoprene water gloves and water-resistant paddle mitts.

Boat Gloves. These gloves, primarily used to protect hands from blisters, rope burns and chafing, have leather palms for gripping and open fingertips that enable full freedom of movement. They also provide moderate warmth and are great for paddlesports and other activities that require good gripping power under wet conditions. Boat gloves cost around $15 to $30. Good models currently available are Northwest River Supplies' *Boaters Gloves*, Patagonia's *Bunting Fingerless Gloves*, Thunderwear's *Fingerless Watersports Gloves*, and West Marine's *Catamaran, Explorer* and *Sailing Gloves*.

Water Gloves. Water gloves provide some gripping power, but are mainly intended to keep hands warm during wet activities. They are typically worn with a wetsuit and are made of neoprene with a textured or rubberized neoprene palm for better gripping. Water gloves cost around $20 to $30. Good models to choose from are L.L. Bean's *Neoprene Gloves*, Northwest River Supplies' *Paddlers Gloves* and Thunderwear's *Neoprene Gloves*.

Paddle Mitts. Similar to outer mitts for cold weather climbers and backpackers, paddle mitts are intended for serious canoeists and kayakers paddling in cold conditions. These warm mitts combine an insulating inner layer of synthetic fleece with a rugged water-resistant nylon outer layer. They have large "gauntlets" that extend over the arm for additional water protection. One good model is Lochsa's *Polar Paws*, available from NRS and other watersports retailers for around $25 to $30. Stohlquist also offers several good models, including their *Yellow Jacket/Seamitts*.

Index

Q

R

Appendix

EQUIPMENT MANUFACTURERS
A-Z

Accuventure
9915 Southwest Arctic Drive, Beaverton, OR 97002
Water purifiers

Acorn Products
2 Cedar Street, P.O. Box 7780, Lewiston, ME 04243-7780
Footwear, slippers, socks

Adidas U.S.A.
15 Independence Boulevard, Warren, NJ 07060
Footwear, apparel

Adventure Foods
Rt.2, Box 276, Whittier, NC 28789
Camping food, baking gear

Adventure Medical Kits
6812 Phinney Avenue North, Seattle, WA 98103
First aid kits

Adventure 16
4620 Alvarado Canyon Road, Bay 3, San Diego, CA 92120
General outdoor gear

After the Stork
1501 12th Street NW, Albuquerque, NM 87104
Children's clothing

Aire
110 W. 33rd, Boise ID 83703
Inflatable boats

Allagash/Stowe Canoe & Snowshoe
P.O. Box 207, Stowe, VT 05672
Canoes, snowshoes

Alico Sport
471 Victoria Ave., Westmount, Quebec, Canada H3Y 2R3
Hiking/telemark boots

Aloe Up
P.O. Box 2913, Harlingen, TX 78551
Sun/skincare products

Alpina Sports
P.O. Box 23, Etna Road, Hanover, NH 03755
Hiking boots

Alpine Aire Foods
13321 Grass Valley Avenue, Grass Valley, CA 95945
Camping foods

Alpine Designs
6400 Lookout Road, Boulder, CO 80304
Outerwear

Alpinestars USA
4145 Santa Fe Road No. 2, San Luis Obispo, CA 93401
Bicycles

Alp Sport Sandals
10565 Sunshine Hill Road, Sonora, CA 95370
Sport sandals

American Traders
627 Barton Road, Greenfield, MA 01301
Canoes

Aquaseal/Trondak
5629 208th Southwest, Lynnwood, WA 98036
Waterproof sealants

Aquaterra
P.O. Box 8002, Easley, SC 29641
Kayaks

Asolo/Kenko International
8141 W. 1-70, Frontage Road North, Arvada, CO 80002
Hiking boots

Atwater Carey Ltd.
218 Gold Run Road, Boulder, CO 80302
First aid kits

Avocet
P.O. Box 120, Palo Alto, CA 94302
Sports instruments

Backpacker's Pantry
1540 Charles Drive, Redding, CA 96003
Freeze-dried food

Baldwin Boat Co.
RFD 2, Box 268, Dept C, Orrington, ME 04474
Kayaks

Basic Designs
5815 Bennett Valley Road, Santa Rosa, CA 95404
Camping accessories

Bear Creek Canoe Inc./Arrow Canoes
RR#1, Box 126B, Limerick, ME 04048
Canoes

Bell Canoe Works, Inc.
28312 144th Street, Zimmerman, MN 55398
Canoes

Betsie Bay Kayak
P.O. Box 1706, Frankfort, MI 49635
Kayaks

Bianchi USA, Inc.
270 Littlefield, Suite C, South San Francisco, CA 98080
Bicycles

Bibler Tents
5441 Western Avenue, Boulder, CO 80301
Tents, sleeping bags, accessories

Bike Burro
P.O. Box 2594, Carson City, NV 89702
Bicycle trailers

Bike Friday
4065 W. 11th Ave. No. 14, Eugene, OR 97402
Bicycles

Blackburn
1510 Dell Avenue, Campbell, CA 95008
Bicycle panniers, racks, pumps

Black Diamond Equipment
2084 E. 3900 South, Salt Lake City, UT 84124
Tents

Blue Sky Cycle Carts
P.O. Box 704, Redmond, OR 97756
Bicycle trailers

Bluewater Canoes
699 Speedvale Avenue West, Guelph, ON N1K 1E6, Canada
Canoes, kayaks

Bolle
3890 Elm Street, Denver, CO 80207
Sunglasses, accessories

Bridgestone Cycle, Inc.
15021 Wicks Blvd., San Leandro, CA 94577
Bicycles

Brunton/Lakota
620 E. Monroe, Riverton, WY 82501
Compasses, knives

Bucci Sunglasses
1 Camp Evers Lane, Scotts Valley, CA 95066
Sunglasses

Buck Knives
1900 Weld Boulevard, El Cajon, CA 92020
Knives

BullFrog/Chattem
1840 South Elena, Suite 107, Redondo Beach, CA 90277
Suncare products

Burley Design Cooperative
4080 Stewart Road, Eugene, OR 97402
Bicycles

Buzz Away/Quantum
754 Washington Street, Eugene, OR 97402
Insect repellents, suncare products

Cal-Tek Engineering
36 Riverside Drive, Kingston, MA 02364
Canoes, kayaks

Camping Gaz/Suunto 21
51-F Las Palmas Drive, Carlsbad, CA 92009
Fuel, stoves, lanterns

Campmor Inc
810 Rt. 17 North, P.O. Box 999, Paramus, NJ 07653
General outdoor gear

Camp Trails/Johnson Camping
P.O. Box 966, Binghamton, MY 13902-0966
Packs, bags

Cannondale Corporation
9 Brookside Pl., Georgetown, CT 06829
Bicycles

Canoes by Whitesell Ltd.
2362 Dresden Drive NE, Atlanta, GA 30341
Canoes

Caribou Mountaineering
46 Loren Ave., Chico, CA 95928
Packs, sleeping bags

Cascade Designs
4000 1st Ave. South, Seattle, WA 98134
Sleeping pads, dry bags

Cebe/Suunto
2151 Las Palmas Drive, Carlsbad, CA 92009
Sunglasses

Cherry Tree
166 Valley Street, Providence RI 02909
Children's outerwear

Chestnut Canoe Company
RR 1, Baltimore, ON K0K 1C0, Canada
Canoes

Chums Ltd.
130 S. Main Street, Hurricane, UT 84737
Eyeglass retainers

Climb High
1861 Shelburne, Shelburne, VT 05482
Climbing products, sleeping bags

Coghlans' Ltd.
121 Irene Street, Winnipeg, Manitoba, R3T 4C7 Canada
Outdoor accessories

Coleman Footgear/Wolverine
9341 Courtland Drive, Rockford, MI 49351
Footwear

Coleman/Peak 1
250 Street Francis Street, Wichita, KS 67202
Outdoor products, canoes

Columbia Sportswear
6600 North Baltimore, Portland, OR 97203
Sportswear

Crazy Creek Products
1401 S. Broadway, Red Lodge, MT 59068
Camping chair

Croakies
1240 Huff Lane, Jackson, WY 83001
Headwear, sandals, accessories

Current Designs
10124 MacDonald Park Road, Sidney, BC V8L 3X9 Canada
Kayaks

Curtis Canoe
P.O. Box 188, Hemlock, NY 14466
Canoes

Cyclesmith
Heritage Square Building P, Golden, CO 80401
Bicycle packs, panniers

CycleTote
517 North Link Lane, Fort Collins, CO 80524
Bicycle trailers

Dagger Canoe
P.O. Box 1500, Harriman, TN 37748
Canoes, kayaks, accessories

Dana Design
1950 North 19th Street, Bozeman MT 59715
Backpacks

Danner Shoe
12722 Northeast Airport Way, Portland, OR 97230
Hiking/hunting boots

Delorme Mapping
P.O. Box 298, Lower Main Street, Freeport, ME 04032
Maps, gazettes

Denali International
Box 466, Williston, VT 05495
Alcohol stoves, gaiters

Diamond Back
403 Via Pescador, Camarillo, CA 93012
Bicycles

Diamond Brand Canvas
Hwy 25, Naples, NC 28760
Tents, packs, accessories

Dragonworks Inc.
RFD 1, Box 1186, Bowdoinham, ME 04008
Kayaks

Drive Outdoors
6908 West Expressway 83, Harlingen TX 78551
Skincare, apparel

Dunn's Custom-Built Kayaks
8991 Gowanda State Road, Eden, NY 14057
Kayaks

Duofold
120 West 45th Street, 15th Floor, New York, NY 10036
Thermalwear, T-shirts

Eagle Creek
1740 La Costa Meadows Road, San Marcos, CA 92069
Travel gear, accessories

Early Winter
P.O. Box 4333, Portland, OR 97208-4333
Clothing, general outdoor gear

Earthly Concerns
100 Nubble Road, York Beach, ME 03910
T-shirts

Eastern Mountain Sports
One Vose Farm Road, Peterborough, NH 03458
General outdoor gear

Eastpak, Inc.
50 Rogers Road, Ward Hill, MA 01835
Packs

Easy Rider Canoe & Kayak Co.
P.O. Box 88108, Seattle, WA 98138
Canoes, kayaks

Ecosport
28 James Street, South Hackensack, NJ 07606
Cotton clothing

Edko Alpine Design
P.O. Box 17005, Boulder, CO 80308
Backpacks

Eddyline Kayak Works
1344 Ashten Road, Burlington, WA 98233
Touring kayaks, paddles

Englehart Products Inc.
18008 Owen Road, Middlefield, OH 44062
Canoes

Epigas/Taymar
2755 South 160th Street, New Berlin, WI 53151-3601
Stoves, lanterns

Equinox
1142 Chestnut Avenue, Cottage Grove, OR 97424
Bicycle trailers

Eureka!/Johnson Camping, Inc.
P.O. Box 966, Binghamton, NY 13902
Tents

Extrasport
5305 NorthWest 35th Court, Miami, FL 33142
PFDs, fleecewear

Feather Canoes Inc.
1705 Andrea Pl., Sarasota, FL
Canoes

Feathered Friends
2013 Fourth Avenue, Seattle, WA 98121
Sleeping bags

Fibus Sport Sandals
25935 Frampton Avenue, Harbor City, CA 90710
Sandals

Flexo-Line Company
Box 162, Dunbridge, OH 43414
Traveler's clothesline

Folbot Inc.
P.O. Box 70877, Charleston, SC 29415
Kayaks

Fox River
P.O. Box 298, Osage, IA 50461
Socks, handwear

Fuji America, Inc.
118 Bauer Drive, Oakland, NJ 07436
Bicycles

Gary Fisher Bicycle Co.
45 Mitchell Boulevard, Suite 17, San Rafael, CA 94903
Bicycles

Gemini/Earth Pads
35 Balch Street, Beverly, MA 01915
Earth pads

General Ecology
151 Sheree Boulevard, Exton, PA 19341
Water treatment gear

Gerry Baby Products
12520 Grant Drive, Denver, CO 80241
Infant carrier frame

Giant Bicycle, Inc.
475 Apra Street, Rancho Dominguez, CA 90220
Bicycles

Gillies Canoes & Kayaks
General Delivery, Margaretville, NS B0S 1N0, Canada
Canoes

Gramicci
1050 S. "A" Street, Oxnard, CA 93030
Sportswear

Granite Gear
P.O. Box 278, Two Harbors, MN 55616
Packs, bags, accessories

Great Canadian Canoe Co.
240 Washington Street, Auburn,MA 01501
Canoes

Gregory Mountain Products
100 Calle Cortez, Temecula, CA 92390
Packs

Grumman Boats/OMC
2900 Industrial Drive, Lebanon, MO 65536
Canoes

GT Shasta
17800 Gothard Street, Huntington Beach, CA 92647
Bicycles

Gymwell
2531 237th Street, Ste. 118, Torrance, CA 90505
Sleeping pads

Harvest Foodworks
66 Victoria Avenue, Smith Falls, Ontario, Canada K7A 2P4
Freeze-dried foods

Helly-Hansen
P.O. Box 97031, Redmond, WA 98073
Sportswear, outerwear

Hi-Tec Sports
4801 Stoddard Ave., Modesto, CA 95356
Footwear

High Sierra
880 Corporate Woods Parkway, Vernon Hills, IL 60061
Apparel

Hind Performance
3765 S. Higuera, San Luis Obispo, CA 93401
Activewear

Hoefgen Canoes
N1927/Hwy. M-35, Menominee, MI 49858
Canoes

Hydra Kayaks and Canoes
5061 S. National Drive, Knoxville, TN 37914
Kayaks

Hyside
P.O. Box Z, Kernville, CA 93238
Inflatable river boats

Hytek Helmets
124 Belvedere, Suite 5, San Rafael, CA 95910
Helmets

Ibis Cycles
Box 275, Sebastopol, CA 95473
Bicycles

Integral Designs,
Inc. 5516 Third Street S.E., Calgary, Alberta, Canada T2H 1J9
Tents, sleeping bags

Iron Horse
11 Constance Court, Hauppauge, NY 11788
Bicycles

Island Falls Canoe
RFD 3, Box 76, Dover-Foxcroft, ME 04426
Canoes

Island Sandal Hawaii
1733 Dillingham Boulevard, Honolulu, HI 96819
Sport sandals

Jack Wolfskin
P.O. Box 966, Binghamton, NY 13902
Tents, sleeping bags, apparel

Jamis, Cignal
151 Ludlow Avenue, Northvale, NJ 07647
Bicycles

Jansport
10411 Airport Road S.W., Everett WA 98204
Backpacks, daypacks

Jolly-Tundra
5012 Washburn Avenue South, Minneapolis, MN
Outerwear

K-Swiss
12300 Montague Street, Pacoima CA 91331
Footwear

Kanga Company
P.O. Box 26038, Phoenix, AZ 85068-6038
Cartop carriers

Katadyn
3020 North Scottsdale Road, Scottsdale, AZ 85251
Water treatment gear

Katahdin Canoe
999 Roosevelt Trail #19, Windham, ME 04062
Canoes

Kelty Pack (Kellwood)
P.O. Box 7048-A, Street Louis, MO 63177
Packs, tents, sleeping bags

Kenyon Consumer Products
P.O. box 3715, Peace Dale, RI 02883
Sportswear, underwear

KHS, Inc.
1264 E. Walnut Street, Carson, CA 90746
Bicycles

Kiwi Kayak
P.O. Box 1140, Windsor, CA 95492
Kayaks, accessories

Kokatat
5350 Ericson Way, Arcata, Ca 95521
Watersports apparel

Kruger Ventures
2906 Meister Lane, Lansing, MI 48906
Canoes

La Fuma U.S.A.
P.O. Box 812, Farmington, GA 30638
Packs, tents, camp chairs

La Sportiva U.S.A.
3235 Prairie Avenue, Boulder, CO 80301
Climbing footwear

Lincoln Paddle-Lite Canoes, Div. Martin Tooling
RR 2, Box 106, Freeport, ME 04032
Canoes

L.L. Bean, Inc.
Casco Street, Freeport, ME 04033
General outdoor gear

Log House Designs
HCR 68 Box 248, Center Conway, NH 03813
Outerwear

Loki Kayaks
P.O. Box 8004, Cherwood Postal Station, London, N6G 2B0, Canada
Kayaks

Long Road
111 Avendida Drive, Berkeley, CA 94708
Bed insect netting for travelers

Lowa USA
P.O. Box 152-B1, Hudson, NY 12534
Footwear

Lowe Alpine Systems
P.O. Box 1449, Broomfield, CO 80038
Packs, daypacks

Mad River Canoe
P.O. Box 610, Waitsfield VT 05673
Canoes, kayaks

Madden U.S.A.
2400 Central Avenue, Boulder, CO 80301
Backpacks, bike equipment

Mansfield/Stowe Canoe & Snowshoe
P.O. Box 207, Stowe, VT 05672
Canoes, snowshoes

Manzella Productions
5684 Main Street, Buffalo, MY 14221
Gloves

Marin Mountain Bikes
2066 4th Street, San Rafael, CA 94901
Bicycles

Mariner Kayaks, Inc.
2134 Westlake Avenue North, Seattle, WA 98109
Kayaks

Markill/Apex
P.O. Box 325, Middlefield, CT 06422
Cooking gear

Marmot Mountain International
2321 Circadian Way, Santa Rosa, CA 95407
Outerwear, sleeping bags

McHale & Company Backpacks
29 Dravus, Seattle, WA 98109
Backpacks

Merrell Footwear
55 Green Mountain Drive, South Burlington, VT 05406
Hiking boots

Mid-Canada Fiberglass Ltd.
Box 1599, New Liskeard, ON P0J 1P0, Canada
Canoes

Middle Path Canoes
Box 8881, Pittsburgh, PA 15221
Canoes

Miyata Bicycle of America
2526 W. Pratt, Elk Grove, IL 60007
Bicycles

Mohawk Canoes
963 N Hwy 427, Longwood, FL 32750
Canoes

Mongoose
23879 Madison Street, Torrance, CA 90505
Bicycles

Montague Corporation
432 Columbia Street, Cambridge, MA 02140
Bicycles

Montbell America
940 41st Avenue, Santa Cruz, CA 95062
Outerwear, backpacks, sleeping bags

Moonstone Mountaineering
5350 Ericson Way, Arcata, CA 95521
Outerwear, sleeping bags

Morley Cedar Canoes
P.O. Box 147, Swan Lake, MT 59911
Canoes

Moss
P.O. Box 309, Camden, ME 04843
Camping tents

Mountain Equipment
4776 East Jensen, Fresno, CA 93725
Backpacks, daypacks, frame packs

Mountain Minded
P.O. Box 114, Lopez Island, WA 98261
Bicycle packs, panniers

Mountain Safety Research
4225 Second Avenue South, Seattle, WA 98134
Water treatment gear, stoves

Mountainsmith
Heritage Square, Building P, Golden, CO 80401
Packs

Mountain Tools
P.O. Box 222295, Carmel, CA 93922
Packs

MZH Sleeping Bags
230 Fifth Avenue, Suite 400, New York, NY 10001
Sleeping bags, camp mats

Appendix

Nalge/Nalgene Trail Products
P.O. Box 20365, Rochester, NY 14602
Bottles, containers

Nature Bound Canoe
Route 140, 93 Gardner Road, Winchendon, MA 01475
Canoes

Nashbar
4111 Simon Road, Youngstown, OH 44512
Bicycles

Navarro Canoe
17901 Van Arsdale Road, Potter Valley, CA 95469
Canoes, accessories

Necky Kayaks
1100 Riverside Road, Abbotsford, BC, Canada V2S 4N2
Kayaks

New Wave Kayak Products
2535 Roundtop Road, Middletown, PA 17057
Kayaks

Nike
Nike World Campus, Beaverton, OR 97005-6453
Activewear, footwear

Nikon
1300 Walt Whittman Road, Melville, NY 11747
Optics

Nishiki Bicycle Company
22710 72nd Avenue South, Kent, WA 98032
Bicycles

Noall Tents
26 Garner Valley, Mountain Center, CA 92561
Tents

Norco Products Limited
7950 Enterprise Street, Burnaby, British Columbia, Canada V5A 1V7
Bicycles

North by Northeast
181 Conant Street, Pawtucket, RI 02862
Rainwear, apparel

Northern Lights
P.O. Box 3413, Mammoth Lakes, CA 93546
Candle and oil camping lanterns

Northlake/Georgia Boot, Inc.
P.O. Box 10, Franklin, TN 37068-0010
Footwear

Northwest Kayaks
15145 Northeast 90th, Redmond, WA 98052
Kayaks, accessories

Northwest River Supplies
2009 South Main Street, Moscow, ID 83843
Kayaking and rafting gear

Nova Craft Canoes
4389 Exeter Road, London, Ontario N6L 1A4, Canada
Canoes

Novara (REI)
6750 South 228th Street, Kent, WA 98032
Bicycles

Ocean Designs
P.O. Box 5338, Santa Barbara, CA 93150
Canvas hats

Ocean Kayak Inc.
1920 Main Street, Ferndale, WA 98248
Kayaks

Old Town Canoe
58 Middle Street, Old Town, ME 04468
Canoes, accessories

Omega
1638 Parker Avenue, Fort Lee, NJ 07024
Activewear

One Sport/Brenco
7877 South180th Street, Kent, WA 98032
Footwear

Open Country
1710 Monroe Street, Two Rivers, WI 54241
Cookware, accessories

Optimus/Suunto U.S.A.
2151-F Las Palmas Drive, Carlsbad, CA 92009
Stoves, lanterns

Osprey Packs
504 Central Avenue, Dolores, CO 81323
Backpacks

Outbound/Taymor
1580 Zephyr Avenue, Hayward, CA 94545-6148
Tents, packs, sleeping gear, accessories

Outdoor Research
1000 First Avenue South, Seattle, WA 98134-1206
Accessories

Overland Equipment
2145 Park Avenue, Suite 4, Chico, CA 95928
Fannypacks, bike packs, backpacks

Pacific Canoe Base
562 David Street, Victoria, British Columbia, V8T 1C8, Canada
Kayaks

Pacific Dry Goods/Hudco
26010 Eden Landing Road, Suite 1A, Hayward, CA 94545
Packtowl, talktowl

Pacific Water Sports
16055 Pacific Hwy S, Seattle, WA 98188
Kayaks

Packasport Systems
P.O. Box 1630, Bend, OR 97709
Cartop carriers

Patagonia
239 West Santa Clara Street, Ventura, CA 93001
Apparel

Peak 1/The Coleman Company, Inc.
250 North Street Francis Street, Wichita, KS 67201
Backpacks, sleeping bags

Perception
1110 Powdersville, Easley, SC 29640
Kayaks, paddling accessories

Performance, Inc.
1 Performance Way, Chapel Hill, NC 27514
Bicycles, bicycling gear

Peugeot, Look
9095 25th Avenue, Street Georges, Quebec, G6A 1A1, Canada
Bicycles

Phoenix Products
P.O. Box 109, 207 North Broadway, Berea, KY 40403
Kayaks

Prijon/Wildwasser Sport
P.O. Box 4617, Boulder, CO 80306
Kayaks

Protec/Perception
1110 Powdersville, Easley, SC 29640
Helmets, paddling accessories

Pur/Recovery Engineering
2229 Edgewood Avenue South, Minneapolis, MN 55426
Water treatment gear

Quantum Bicycle & Fitness, Inc.
1142 Woodlake Drive, Carol Stream, IL 60188
Bicycles

Quest/JWI
254 East Hacienda Avenue, Campbell, CA 95008
Tents, backpacks

Quicksilver Manufacturing Limited
1 Main Street, Strome, Alberta, T0B 4H0, Canada
Canoes

Raichle
Geneva Road, Brewster, NY 10509
Hiking boots

Rainforest Designs Limited
6-9903 240th Street, Albion, British Columbia, V0M 1B0, Canada
Kayaks

Raleigh Cycle Corporation
22710 72nd Avenue South, Kent, WA 98032
Bicycles

Real Goods Trading Company
966 Mazzoni Street, Ukiah, CA 95482
Solar lanterns, flashlights

Reebok
100 Technology Center Drive, Stoughton, MA 02072
Footwear, apparel

Reef Brazil
155 West 35th Street, Suite C, San Diego, CA 92050
Sandals

REI/Recreational Equipment, Inc.
P.O. Box 88125, Seattle, WA 98138-2125
General outdoor gear

Remington Camping Products
14760 Santa Fe Trail Drive, Lenexa, KS 66215
Camping products

Research Dynamics
P.O. Box 303, Ketchum, ID 83340
Bicycles

Rhode Gear
765 Allens Avenue, Providence, RI 02905
Bicycle child seats, helmets, tool kits

Richmoor
6923 Woodley Avenue, Van Nuys, CA 91406
Camping foods

Ritchey Design
1326 Hancock Avenue, Redwood City, CA 94061
Bicycles

The Rockport Company
220 Donald J. Lynch Boulevard, Marlboro, MA 01752
Footwear

Rodriguez Tandems
798 Auburn Way North, Auburn, WA 98002
Bicycles

Ross Bicycles USA
51 Executive Boulevard, Farmingdale, NY 11735-4710
Bicycles

Royal Robbins
1314 Coldwell Avenue, Modesto, CA 95350
Sportswear

Safesport
1100 West 45th Avenue, Denver, CO 80211
Accessories

Salomon North America
400 East Main Street, Georgetown, MA 01833
Hiking boots, accessories

Santana Cycles
P.O. Box 1205, Claremont, CA 91711
Bicycles

Saranac Glove
P.O. Box 1477, Green Bay, WI 54301
Gloves, mittens, accessories

Sawyer Canoe Company
234 South State Street, Oscoda, MI 48750
Canoes

Schwinn Bicycle Company
217 North Jefferson Street, Chicago, IL 60661-1111
Bicycles

Scott Hawaii
1212 Kona Street, Honolulu, HI 96814
Sandals

Scott USA
P.O. Box 2030, Sun Valley, ID 83353
Bicycles

Seattle Sports
12604 Interurban Avenue, South Tukwila, WA 98168
Watersports accessories

Seaward Kayaks Manufacturing
Rural Route 1, Site 16 C-1, Summerland, BC, V0H 1Z0, Canada
Kayaks

Sebago, Inc.
72 Bridge Street, Westbrook, ME 04092
Footwear

Seda Products
926 Coolidge Avenue, National City, CA 91950
Canoes, kayaks

Sequel
P.O. Box 3185, Durango, CO 81302
Outerwear

Seventh Generation
North Colchester, VT 05446-1672
Clothing, general ecology items

Shimano
P.O. Box 19615, Irvine, CA 92713-9615
Bicycle components, shoes

Shogun
7620 South 192nd Street, Kent, WA 98032
Bicycles

Sierra Designs
2039 Fourth Street, Berkeley, CA 94710
Tents, outerwear, sleeping bags

Skaggs & Ingalls
P.O. Box 707, Juneau, AK 99802
Stroller packs

Slumberjack
1224 Fern Ridge Parkway, Street Louis, MO 63141
Sleeping bags

Specialized
15130 Concord Circle, Morgan Hill, CA 95037
Bicycles, custom waterbottles

Sportif
445 East Glendale, Sparks, NV 89431
Activewear

Stewart River Boatworks
Route 1, P.O. Box 203B, Two Harbors, MN 55616
Canoes

Stohlquist
22495 US Highway 285, South Buena Vista, CO 81211
Watersports accessories

Stowe Canoe & Snowshoe
P.O. Box 207, Stowe, VT 05672
Canoes, snowshoes

Superior Kayaks Inc.
213A Dartmouth Court, Bloomingdale, IL 60108
Kayaks

Suunto U.S.A.
2151-F Las Palmas Drive, Carlsbad, CA 92009
Camping products

Swift Canoe Company
Rural Route 1, Oxtongue Lake, Dwight, Ontario, P0A 1H0, Canada
Canoes

Swiss Army Brands
151 Long Hill Crossroads, Shelton, CT 06484
Knives, compasses

Tech
123 3016-10th Avenue Northeast, Calgary, Alberta, T2A 6A3, Canada
Bicycles

Tecnica
19 Technology Drive, West Lebanon, NH 03784
Footwear

Tekna
601 Rayovac Drive, Madison, WI 53711
Flashlights, batteries, sunglasses

Tender
P.O. Box 290, Littleton, NH 03561
Insect repellent

Terramar Sports
10 Midland Avenue, Port Chester, NY 10573
Thermal underwear

Teva/Deckers
1140 Mark Avenue, Carpinteria, CA 93013
Sport sandals

The North Face
999 Harrison Street, Berkeley, CA 94710
Tents, packs, sleeping bags, apparel

Thermos Nissan
300 North Martingale, Schaumburg, IL 60173
Vacuumware, insulated containers

Thor-Lo
2210 Newton Drive, Statesville, NC 28677
Socks

Thule-Eldon Group America
175 Clearbrook Road, Elmsford, NY 10523
Roofrack systems

Tilley Endurables
900 Don Mills Road, Don Mills, Ontario, M3C 1Z8, Canada
Activewear, hats

The Timberland Company
11 Merrill Drive, Hampton, NH 03842-5050
Footwear

Timex
P.O. Box 2126, Waterbury, CT 06722
Watches

T-Mos
P.O. Box 75, Redwood City, CA 94064
Coffee Products

Tough Traveler
1012 State Street, Schenectady, NY 12307
Child carriers, sleeping bags

Tragar
90 South Dearborn Street, Seattle, WA 98134
Backpacks

Trailhead
1341 Wellington Street, Ottawa, Ontario, K1Y 3B8, Canada
Canoes

Trails Illustrated
P.O. Box 3610, Evergreen, CO 80439
Maps

Traveling Light
836 Santa Fe Avenue, Albany, CA 94706
Camping oven

Trek Bicycle Corporation
P.O. Box 183, Waterloo, WI 53594
Bicycles

Ultimate Direction
1488 North Salem Road, Rexburg, ID 83440
Water packs

Ultimate Products
8310 North Saulray Street, Tampa, FL 33604
Hats

Univega/Sterling
3030 Walnut Avenue, Long Beach, CA 90808
Bicycles

Valley Canoe Products/Great River Outfitters
3721 Shallow Brook, Bloomfield Hills, MI 48302
Kayaks

Vasque Shoes
314 Main Street, Red Wing, MN 55066
Boots, footwear

vauDe U.S.A.
5311 Western Avenue, Suite D, Boulder, CO 80301
Outerwear, packs, tents, bags

Vermont Canoe Products
Rural Route 1, P.O. Box 353A, Newport, VT 05855
Canoes

Voyageur Canoe Company Limited
3 King Street, Millbrook, Ontario, L0A 1G0, Canada
Canoes

Voyageur
P.O. Box 207, Waitsfield, VT 05673
Waterproof bags, accessories

W.L. Gore & Associates
100 Airport Road, Building 2, Elkton, MD 21921
Outerwear, accessories

We-no-nah Canoe Inc.
P.O. Box 247, Winona, MN 55987
Canoes

West Side Boat Shop
7661 Tonawanda Creek Road, Lockport, NY 14094
Kayaks

Western Canoeing
P.O. Box 492, Sumas WA 98295
Canoes, paddles, sprayskirts

Western Canoeing Inc.
P.O. Box 115, Abbotsford, British Columbia, V2S 4N8, Canada
Canoes

Western Mountain Sports
130 Lewis Road, Suite 2, San Jose, CA 95111
Sleeping bags

Wheeler USA
5941 North Broadway, Unit 1, Denver, CO 80216
Bicycles

Wigwam Mills
3402 Crocker Avenue, Sheboygan, WI 53081
Socks, hats, gloves

Wild Country U.S.A.
27 Whitelaw Drive, Center Conway, NH 03813
Tents

Wild Things
P.O. Box 400, North Conway, NH 03860
Backpacks, sleeping bags

Wilderness Experience/Wild X
20721 Dearborn, Chatsworth, CA 91311
Backpacks

Wilderness Systems
241 Woodbine Street, High Point, NC 27260
Kayaks

Wilkinson Boat Seaworthy Designs
2520 Westlake Avenue North, Seattle, WA 98109
Kayaks

Winchester Originals/Kool-Stop
P.O. Box 3480, La Habra, CA 90632
Bicycle trailers

Woodstrip Watercraft Company
1818 Swamp Pike, Gilbertsville, PA 19525
Canoes, kayaks

Woolrich
1 Mill Street, Woolrich, PA 17779
Sportswear, outerwear

WTC Industries
14405 21st Avenue North, Suite 120, Plymouth, MN 55447
Water purification

Yakima Products
P.O. Box 4899, Arcata, CA 95521
Roof racks, bike mounts

Yokota Cycles
2016 Martin Avenue, Santa Clara, CA 95050
Bicycles

Learn how you can move your job outdoors...

Careers in the Outdoors
by Tom Stienstra

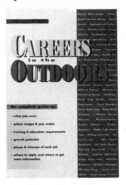

Frustrated by four walls and traffic jams? Does daydreaming about the outdoors make you happy? Well, here's *the* resource to make that outdoor connection, containing detailed descriptions and practical information about more than 50 great outdoor jobs. Provides secrets and suggestions for tracking down your dreams from people who make their living in the outdoors. Whether you're interested in making a hobby pay off or developing a full-time career, award-winning outdoorsman Tom Stienstra provides all the information you need, including pay scales and entry requirements. ISBN 0-935701-56-7

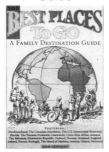